ATOMIC IRAN

COUNTDOWN TO
ARMAGEDDON

HOW THE WEST CAN BE SAVED

Shalom שָׁלוֹם

Dr. Michael David Evans

Psalm 91

MIKE EVANS

ATOMIC IRAN

COUNTDOWN TO ARMAGEDDON

HOW THE WEST CAN BE SAVED

TimeWorthy
BOOKS

P.O. Box 30000 ∘ Phoenix, AZ 85046

Published by Time Worthy Books
P.O. Box 30000
Phoenix, AZ   85046

Jacket Design: Lookout Design, Inc.
Cover Photos: Corbis, iStockphoto

US   ISBN 13: 978-0-935199-40-3
CANADA   ISBN 13: 978-0-935199-41-3

To my beloved grandchildren

Ethan, Owen, Isabelle, Jason, Ashley and Joshua.

TABLE OF CONTENTS

ACKNOWLEDGEMENTS 9

PROLOGUE 11

1. ATOMIC IRAN: AN INTERNATIONAL THREAT 31

2. ATOMIC IRAN: A THREAT TO HUMANITY 45

3. CHAOS, CONFUSION AND INTERNAL INSTABILITY ... 59

4. THE PRESIDENT'S RESPONSE 79

5. A STROLL THROUGH THE PAGES OF PERSIAN HISTORY ... 91

6. A FRIEND FORSAKEN 107

7. A CELEBRATION CREATES CHAOS 119

8. OIL, OPEC AND OPPOSITION 131

9. INDECISION SPAWNS REVOLUTION 143

10. A STAR-CROSSED STATE VISIT 153

11. THE SHAH: AN ALLY ABANDONED 167

12. ISRAEL: AN UNLIKELY ALLY 181

13. THE HANDWRITING ON THE WALL 193

14. THE BALL REPORT: AN INDICTMENT OF THE SHAH ... 209

15. THE SLIPPERY SLOPE TO REVOLUTION 227

16. THE HIGH PRICE OF INDECISION 239

17. SPIRALING OUT OF CONTROL 253

18. THE FRENCH CONNECTION 267

19. ABDICATING TO A RUTHLESS AYATOLLAH 279

20. ENGULFED IN DARKNESS 287

21. THE EVOLUTION OF REVOLUTION 299

22. ABANDONED BY AN ADMINISTRATION 313

23. CANCER: INTERNAL AND EXTERNAL 327

24. AMERICA HELD HOSTAGE 337

25. SLEEPING WITH THE ENEMY 351

26. THE PRICE OF FREEDOM 363

27. UNDER THE MICROSCOPE 373

28. HOW THE WEST CAN BE SAVED 383

29. THE FINAL OPTION 401

APPENDIX A — *Glossary of Names* 409

APPENDIX B — *Bibliography* 431

ENDNOTES 435

INDEX 469

ACKNOWLEDGEMENTS

. . . .

My deepest gratitude goes to the men and women who agreed to interviews: Her Majesty Farah Pahlavi, wife of the former Shah of Iran; Ambassador Ardeshir Zehedi, a special thanks to Iran's last and most powerful ambassador to the U.S.; former President of the French Republic Valerie Giscard d'Estaing; editorial journalist Samuel Segev; journalist and terrorism expert Charles Villeneuve; Dr. Parviz Mina, Director, National Iranian Oil Company under the Shah; Dr. Abol-Majid Majidi, Minister of Planning and Budget under the Shah; Hubert Vedrine, adviser to President Francois Mitterrand and Secretary-General from 1991-1995; Prime Minister of Israel Benjamin Netanyahu; former Israeli Prime Minister Ehud Olmert; former Israeli Prime Minister Yitzhak Rabin; President Shimon Peres of Israel; former Israeli Ambassador to Iran Uri Lubrani; former Israeli Ambassador to the U.S. Dore Gold; Marvin Kalb, award-winning reporter for CBS and NBC; Dr. Alan Dershowitz, professor, Harvard School of Law; Israeli Mossad agent Eliezer Zafrir; General David Ivri, Commander Israeli Air Force and Ambassador to U.S.; General Yitzhak Segev; Dr. Ahmed Tehrani; and Lt. General Shapur Azarbarzin. I especially want to thank Israeli, French, and U.S. intelligence operatives (whose names must remain anonymous.)

This story began with my talks with former Israeli Prime Minister Menachem Begin, and it would not be complete without thanking many of the other key people I interviewed over the years on this subject: Dr. Reuben Hecht, senior advisor to Prime Minister

Begin and my mentor; Yehiel Kadishai, personal aide to Prime Minister Menachem Begin; Prime Minister Yitzhak Shamir; Major General James E. Freeze, Assistant Deputy Director for Plans and Policy, National Security; General Jerry Curry, Department of Defense in the Pentagon; General George Keegan (retired), Chief of Air Force Intelligence from 1972 to 1977; Lt. General Richard F. Schaeffer (retired), Deputy Chairman of NATO Military Committee from January 1974 to June 1975; Isser Harel, former head of Israeli Intelligence and Security; Lieutenant General Moshe Ya'alon, former Chief of Staff, IDF; Mr. James Woolsey, former Director, CIA; General Hugh Shelton, former Chairman of the Joint Chiefs of Staff; General Yossi Peled, Chief of the Northern Command, Israel; General Dani Yatom, head of Mossad, Israeli Intelligence Service; General Ya-akov Amidror, former Chief of IDF Intelligence; Lt. General Tom McInerney; and the late General Robert "Dutch" Huyser, Deputy Commander-in-Chief, United States European Command.

A special word of gratitude must go to Lanelle Shaw-Young, who has invested an enormous amount of time and work from the beginning and throughout this entire project. The book would not have been possible without her contributions. I also wish to thank Arlen Young, who spent hours proofreading the manuscript. My heartfelt thanks to Joe Hilley for his assistance. I am deeply appreciative to research assistant Dan Godzich, Washington, D.C.; Robert Baxter, research associate in Paris; to Ariel University; and especially to Dr. Ronen Cohen, who provided invaluable research information from Israel.

PROLOGUE

. . . .

THE APOCALYPSE

Lebanon

Hamilton Fisk spread his body flat against the tile rooftop and eased closer to the edge. He'd been waiting there all night, staring at the Beirut skyline and Lebanese sky. All the while his ears had been tuned to the street below, listening for the sound of the truck he knew was coming. As the sun broke through the eastern sky, the truck finally arrived and backed up to the loading dock. Fisk adjusted the earphone in his right ear and pressed the button on his radio.

"Someone's here."

"Do they have it?"

Fisk watched the truck for a moment then keyed the microphone once more. "Truck's empty. Looks like they're loading some crates."

"Crates?"

"Wooden crates."

"I thought you said they were making a delivery." Fisk did not respond. The voice on the radio continued. "We need to find out exactly what they have inside."

"Yeah," Fisk replied. He pulled the earphone from his ear and stuffed the radio in his pocket. "That's easier said than done," he grumbled. Moving slowly, he pushed back from the edge of the roof and crept to the far side of the building. Using a downspout as a ladder, he swung his legs off the roof and carefully lowered himself to the ground.

When the truck was gone, Fisk slipped around the corner to a door along the left side of the building. Stealthily he picked the lock and eased open the door. Inside, he found a large room filled with crates and boxes. He closed the door behind him and worked his way across the room. A few minutes later, he reached a workroom near the loading dock at the rear of the building.

In the workroom he found packing material—straw, Bubble Wrap, and clear, shrink-wrap plastic. Along the wall was a workbench. Cubbyholes for tools lined the wall above it. He scanned the spaces looking for something, anything that might give him a clue. On a shelf to the right, he found a radiation exposure badge. He took it out of the cubby and held it up to the light. An LCD panel showed a reading of 95 mrem.

Lying on the bench was a worn diamond-tipped saw blade from a circular saw. Fisk picked it up for a closer look. Beneath the blade was a shipping receipt. Four crates sent to Kornheiser Museum in New York. Fisk stuffed the documents in his pocket, picked up the radiation tag, and started toward the door. Just then, he heard footsteps approaching from behind him. He turned in that direction.

Fisk grinned and nodded toward the pistol. "Tabas, you sure you know which end of that thing to hold?"

Tabas chuckled. "Glad to see you haven't lost your sense of humor, Bill. Or is that your name now?"

"I haven't been Bill in a long time," Fisk shrugged. "Most people call me Hamilton now."

"I liked you better as Bill." Tabas gestured with the pistol. "Move away from the door. I don't want your body to block the entrance."

"What's going on, Tabas? I thought we had a deal."

"Deals change."

"Where's the plutonium?"

"We found a better use for it." Tabas gestured again with the gun. "Move away from the door."

Reluctantly Fisk stepped to one side and moved slowly along the workbench. As he steadied himself, his hand slid across the saw blade. Without taking his eyes off Tabas, he curled his fingers around the blade and flung it across the room toward Tabas' head. Tabas lurched to the side and ducked to avoid the spinning blade. Caught off guard, he stumbled and banged his shoulder against the wall. Fisk lunged for the pistol.

Tabas avoided Fisk's outstretched fingers and brought the pistol around to the side. He pressed the muzzle against Fisk's temple and in the same motion squeezed the trigger. Fisk's skull exploded against the wall.

Late that afternoon Nasir Hamid sat in a café in Beirut, smoking a cigarette. From his table in the corner he had a full view of the dining room. Through the front window he could see all the way to the opposite side of the street.

In a few minutes, the door opened and Fareed Ashwan entered. A slender man about Hamid's height, he had intense dark eyes that constantly darted from side to side. Hamid did not like him but he was the contact Tehran had designated. He caught Ashwan's eye and motioned him over with a nod of the head. Ashwan crossed the room and took a seat at the table.

Hamid stubbed out the cigarette in an ashtray and leaned forward. "You know where it is?"

"Yes."

"And where is it?"

"In a safe place."

"You have it?"

"No. Tabas has it."

"Tabas?"

"Yes," Ashwan nodded. "I told you this would happen."

"So, he didn't trade it like we planned?"

"No."

"Tabas is Hezbollah. Why is Hezbollah interested in this?" Hamid continued.

"Everyone is interested. First Iran has the bomb, then Syria. Now everyone wants the weapon. Even Saudi Arabia has a program, though the Americans are too stupid to see it."

"What does Tabas plan to do with it?"

"Right now he is negotiating with the Syrians. They have access to plutonium, but no bomb. Tabas has both, but he is willing to take...partners. Thinks maybe he can make two bombs."

"So this is how Hezbollah works now? They steal from their friends?"

A smile flickered across Ashwan's face. "Something like that."

"And where did Syria get their plutonium?"

Ashwan shrugged. "Who can say?"

"They can trace it, you know. What Tabas got from us. The Americans can trace it. You realize that, don't you?"

"By then it will be too late. The bomb will be on its way."

"No. I mean after the bomb explodes. The key has never been exploding the bomb; it's always been about avoiding a counterstrike. They will examine the debris and obtain a signature for the plutonium. It has definite characteristics. They will know exactly where it came from."

"You watch too many movies," Ashwan scoffed. "No one can do that. Only in the movies."

"Believe me. They can do it. So whoever supplied the plutonium will get the blame—and the counterstrike."

"The Americans are too stupid to see this coming and too weak to launch a counterstrike."

Hamid leaned away from the table. He took a pack of Gauloises from his pocket and shook a cigarette free. "You cleaned out the warehouse?"

"Yes."

Hamid stuck the cigarette between his lips and lit it. "And you disposed of the body?"

"The American sleeps in peace."

Hamid sighed. "This gets more complicated every moment." He shoved the cigarette package in his pocket and took out a wad of cash. Smoke circled his head as he counted off several bills and tossed them on the table. "Meet me tomorrow." The cigarette hung from his bottom lip as he counted off four more bills, then slid them across the table to Ashwan. "And tell Tabas I want to see him."

Arlington, Virginia

Jim Martin stood in the Operations Control Center and stared at the screen on the wall. A career CIA officer, he had worked through many crises, but none as mystifying as the one he faced this day. Conversation and chatter in the room swirled around his head as analysts and researchers pecked away on their keyboards and worked the phones. Still, Martin's eyes were fixed on the screen and the image of the warehouse in Beirut. Hamilton Fisk was a good man and a capable field officer. They had worked the plan perfectly.

SEAL Team Six was waiting to pounce. Then the whole thing vanished and Fisk was dead.

Martin ran the tips of his fingers over his cheek and whispered to himself. "How did we lose it? Where did it go? What else was in that warehouse besides the package they received from Iran?" Finally he turned to face the others in the room. "Okay, we know for a fact Fisk is dead. Who else can we send into that warehouse?"

Russ Williams glanced up from his desk. "We don't have time for that."

"What do you mean?"

"I mean, we know the plutonium reached the warehouse, and we know it's gone."

Martin frowned, "And?"

"We should assume the worst."

"That they made a bomb."

"Yes. And we should concentrate on where it's going."

"Yeah, well, that's fine. Take you all of five minutes to think that up? There's a big world out there, in case you haven't looked lately. A big scary world. Getting scarier every minute. Everybody from Jordan to Afghanistan has a nuclear program. The ones who don't are scouring the black market for a bomb." He ran his fingers through his hair and continued, talking now to no one in particular. "We never should have believed the Iranians. I tried to tell them eight years ago not to do it. But no, they had to send Neyshabur fuel for his reactor. All on a promise they'd never use it to make bombs. Who in their right mind would believe an Iranian president?"

Someone across the room piped up, "Democrats loved him."

"Ahh," Martin growled. "It's not just the Democrats. Republicans went along with it too. I didn't hear any of them complaining when we made Israel back down. Forced them to do it." He turned to face

Williams once again. "So, Mr. Williams, what do you think they did with it?"

"Plutonium isn't traded out of warehouses just for the fun of it. They made a bomb and shipped it out in the crates Fisk saw them loading on that truck."

"And what did they do with it after that?" Martin chortled. "Where did the truck go?"

"The building is owned by an antiquities dealer named Salaam Katami. Two weeks ago he received a shipment of artifacts from a dig in Sidon, on the Mediterranean coast. The dig was sponsored by Kornheiser Museum in New York."

"Where's Katami?"

Someone else spoke up, "Beirut police found his body this morning."

"So Katami was killed to keep him from talking?"

Williams responded. "Katami was killed to get the warehouse."

"So they could send a bomb in a shipment of artifacts? Come on," Martin grimaced. "How would they get something like that past our scanners?"

"Thousands of containers arrive every day. Not everything gets scanned."

"Still, that's a lot of risk. I mean, it gets caught, we're gonna know who sent it."

Someone else spoke up, "Trigger it with a cell phone. Have someone watching. Inspectors get too interested, press the button on the cell phone. Bomb detonates where it sits."

"That would be one huge suicide bomb."

Martin fell silent for a moment. A frown wrinkled his forehead. "I don't know, Williams. It's a nice idea but it sounds thin."

In frustration, Martin tugged at his hair with both hands. "Feels like we're making this up."

"We've been working this for hours," Williams replied. "You got any better ideas?"

Martin's countenance changed. "All right." His voice took an authoritative tone. "Get up to New York. Find out what Kornheiser Museum knows about those four crates."

"Me?" Williams gave him a blank look. "I'm an analyst."

"It was your idea," Martin replied. "I don't have time to find somebody else. Go see what you can find."

Williams took his jacket from the back of the chair and started toward the door.

Lebanon

That evening Hamid sat on the floor of an apartment just off The Corniche near Beirut's entertainment district. Seated across from him was Yosef Jiroft. He sipped from a cup of tea and glanced over at Hamid.

"Maskutan wants to know where things stand."

"Hezbollah has the item," Hamid replied.

"They made the exchange?"

"No."

"What have they done with it?"

"They have placed it in the bomb, but now they are bargaining with the Syrians."

"And where did they get this bomb?"

Hamid looked Jiroft in the eye. "From you."

"From me?" Jiroft glanced away. "You think that is possible?"

"They have a Mark 4 aerial bomb." Hamid's voice grew tense. "It came from our arsenal in Tehran. How else could they have obtained it if you didn't give it to them?"

"You seem upset."

"I am upset."

"These things will work out." Jiroft folded his hands in his lap and glanced in Hamid's direction. "Didn't we want them to receive the item?"

"Yes. The plutonium, but not—"

Jiroft cut him off with a wave of the hand. He leaned forward and lowered his voice to a whisper. "Do not use that word. People are always listening."

Hamid straightened his shoulders and then continued, "You knew this would happen." Jiroft did not answer. Hamid pressed, "You wanted it to happen."

"You do not need to know everything. Your job is delivery. Not policy. That is why you were chosen." He looked Hamid in the eye. "That is why you have held your job all this time. Working from your offices in Masqat, Dubai, and wherever you were needed. With the cars and planes and women. Privileges others do not have nor seek. No one asked questions of you, because you did not ask questions of us." His eyes bore in on Hamid. "You wish to change all that now? When we are so close? So close to all we have worked for?"

"They will blame us," Hamid replied.

"Who?"

"The Americans."

"How? How will they know it was us?'

"They will measure the fallout, the radiation from the blast, and they will develop a signature."

A frown wrinkled Jiroft's brow. "A signature?"

"The characteristics." Hamid leaned forward and put his lips near Jiroft's ear. "Plutonium can only be made in a reactor. Each reactor creates it with slight differences. They will measure all the radiation from the residue and use that to determine where it came from." Hamid leaned away. "And then they will know it was from us."

Jiroft dismissed him with the wave of a hand. "You worry too much. Even if they do as you suggest, it will take years to locate the reactor."

Hamid wagged his finger. "They built our reactor."

"Yes, but I do not think—"

"And they supplied the fuel. Your friends in Washington arranged it."

"That was the price they had to pay." Jiroft tipped his head back, jutting his chin forward ever so slightly. "They gave us fuel for our reactor and kept Israel pacified, and we did not send our army to crush the Iraqis when the Americans were gone. In this Neyshabur was brilliant." Jiroft's eyes flashed. "The young American president wanted to withdraw his army from Iraq. Neyshabur let them out in exchange for those two favors. Israel and fuel for the reactor." Jiroft took a deep breath. The muscles in his neck relaxed. "Neyshabur was impetuous and stupid in many ways, but in this he was magnificent."

Hamid bristled at the mention of Neyshabur's name. Images flashed through his mind of the short, slender schoolteacher, who somehow convinced the Assembly of Experts that he could run the country. His inept political skills had threatened all their plans and very nearly got Hamid killed. The country had been rescued not by Neyshabur's strategy with the Americans but by Adnan Karroubi's decision to allow a student revolution as a means of wresting control from Neyshabur's allies. With Karroubi's wise leadership, they had developed nuclear weapons, forged an alliance with Al-Qaeda, made peace with the Wahabi, and used their newfound strength to control the region. Hamid took a deep breath, pushed those thoughts aside, and concentrated on the matter at hand.

"The American scientists are smart. They know our reactor and they know our fuel. They will figure out where the plu—...where the item came from."

A cloud spread over Jiroft's face. Then, just as quickly, it disappeared. "It does not matter now. There is no stopping it. Things are in motion. As the Imam has decreed, so it shall be."

Brooklyn, New York

That morning Tommy Jones left his apartment in Brooklyn and headed out Prospect Avenue to Red Dot Trucking Company's dispatch office. He turned in at the main gate, signed the logbook with the guard, and made his way to the office. Fifteen minutes later he climbed in the cab of a White Freightliner truck and drove out the back gate.

As the sun rose over New York, Tommy turned the truck off Columbia Street and entered the main gate at Red Hook Container Port, a facility located across the harbor from Manhattan. A scanner recorded information about the truck from a bar code strip along the side of the cab. A camera perched atop the guardhouse photographed the truck. The guard waved Tommy through without stopping.

In half an hour the Freightliner cab was hooked to a trailer loaded with a standard forty-foot cargo container recently hoisted from the deck of the *Singapore Moon*. An attendant on the ground connected the air hoses from the cab to the brake lines on the trailer. While the attendant worked, Tommy sat behind the steering wheel of the Freightliner sipping coffee from the cap of a thermos. When the lines were in place the attendant called up to him, "Where you going today, Tommy? Pittsburgh?"

"Not today. It's my daughter's birthday." Tommy set the thermos aside and picked up a clipboard from the seat. He gestured with it out the window. "Nothing but local runs today. Gotta get home early. This one's going to a museum on the west side."

"What are you doing with a cushy job like that? You must know someone at the union."

"I know everyone at the union," Tommy grinned. "I'll be back in an hour for another one."

"Okay. We'll be waiting," the attendant chuckled.

Tommy turned away and pressed the accelerator. The truck's engine whined as it started slowly forward.

From Red Hook Tommy took Prospect Expressway to lower Manhattan, then worked his way up the west side. At 11th Avenue he stopped near the corner of 45th Street and got out. A young woman came from the curb and met him as he rounded the front of the truck.

"Hi. I'm Lori Bachman. I work for Kornheiser Museum."

Tommy checked his clipboard. "Is this the place?"

"Yes. This is the place."

Tommy gestured over his shoulder toward the truck. "Where do you want the container?"

She pointed to the right. "There's an alley down by that red car. You can turn in there."

Tommy glanced in that direction and frowned. "Turn in, or back in?"

"Turn in, I guess. Our loading dock is in back. You can go up the alley and then back around to it. You'll see it. There's a sign."

"Yes, Ma'am."

Tommy stepped back to the truck and climbed in behind the steering wheel. He tossed the clipboard on the seat, released the brake, and moved the shifter into gear. The truck started slowly down the street. As he neared the entrance to the alley, he maneuvered the Freightliner to the left into the oncoming lane, and then came back hard to the right. The trailer followed the cab in an arc as it made the turn into the alley. Black smoke poured from the exhaust stacks. The engine lugged and lurched.

Shortly before noon Russ Williams stood in the warehouse at the Kornheiser Museum. Nearby were four wooden crates. Just then a door opened behind him and a voice called out. "Mr. Williams! Sorry to keep you waiting."

Williams turned to see a tall, slender man dressed in a gray business suit coming toward him. The man thrust out his hand. "David Lansing. We spoke on the phone earlier."

"Yes." Williams shook his hand.

Lansing gestured to the crates. "These are the items we discussed. Came in this morning in a cargo container from our dealer in Lebanon."

"Have you looked inside them?"

"No. I mean, we would have but after you called I thought perhaps we should wait."

"Good. I have a team outside. I'd like for them to take a look at the contents."

"Certainly."

Williams pressed a key on his cell phone and brought it to his ear. "They're ready."

The rollup door to the right clattered as it rose. Outside, a four-man nuclear assessment team stepped from a white van and climbed onto the loading dock. The first man pointed to the crates. "This is what we're looking for?"

"Yes," Williams nodded. "These are the crates."

Working carefully and methodically they pried the lid off the nearest crate. Inside they found it packed with statues and urns, each encased in bubble-wrap and padded with straw. One of the men took a handheld dosimeter from his jacket and placed it near the center of the crate. He glanced at the screen and shook his head. "Nothing here." They repeated the process with each of the first three crates. None of them showed the presence of radioactive material.

When they pried the lid from the fourth crate they found it held a large stone container. Over six feet long and three feet wide, it was as deep as the crate and filled it completely. Rectangular in shape, it appeared to be made in two pieces with a base and a lid. One end of the lid was square and smooth. The other end was carved in the shape of a man's head and shoulders. Williams glanced over at Lansing. "What is this?"

"A sarcophagus," Lansing replied.

"A what?"

"Sarcophagus. A coffin." Lansing stepped closer. "This one belonged to Eshmunazar II. King of Sidon."

"What's in it?"

"His remains, I hope."

"His remains?"

"Yes. His well preserved body. At least, we hope it's well preserved."

Just then the man with the dosimeter called out. "Hey, we got something here." He held the dosimeter near the seam where the lid of the sarcophagus joined the base. "Got a little chip missing from the edge of the lid. I'm getting something." Williams leaned in for a look. "Not much," the man continued, "but it's more than background."

24

Williams nodded. "We need to see what's in there. Get an x-ray machine."

"We have one," Lansing spoke up. "Will ours do?"

Williams gestured toward the sarcophagus. "Can it penetrate that stone? It looks pretty dense."

"It is dense," Lansing smiled. "Made of diorite. But our machine will see through it. It's right down here. We were going to x-ray it anyway."

Lebanon

That evening Hamid sat at a corner table in Zawat, a café near the southern edge of Beirut. He sipped from a cup of tea and waited. Ten minutes passed and still there was no sign of Ashwan. After two more sips Hamid took a cell phone from his pocket and scrolled down the contact list. At that moment Ashwan appeared.

"So sorry," he said as he took a seat. "The car."

"You have too much trouble with your car these days." Hamid closed the phone and slipped it in his pocket. "You spoke to Tabas?"

"He is not worried about the Americans."

"No?"

"No." Ashwan shook his head. "He says they do not wish to use it now, anyway. They only want the power it brings. He likes to see the Americans squirm, and he is enjoying his dealings with the Syrians."

"This is no time to play games."

Ashwan leaned forward. "You should not push yourself. Tabas deals directly with Jiroft. He does not have to deal with you."

Hamid peered at Ashwan over the rim of the teacup. "He said that?"

"No." Ashwan tapped the table with his index finger. "I am telling you." He sighed and leaned back from the table. "As your friend."

Hamid took a sip of tea. "You want something to eat?"

"No." Ashwan leaned forward. "I told Tabas you wanted to see him. He will show you the bomb for yourself."

"He will?"

"Yes. You would like to see it?"

"When?"

"Tonight, I think." Ashwan took a cell phone from his pocket. "Let me make a call." He pressed a button on the phone with his finger, then put it to his ear. After a moment he lowered the phone and flipped it closed. "He does not answer. Perhaps we can see it tomorrow."

Hamid did not like the sound of Ashwan's voice. He took another sip of tea and glanced around the café. Something was not right.

Brooklyn, New York

Russ Williams looked up as David Lansing hurried toward him. From the look on his face, Williams knew something was very wrong. In his hand Lansing held an x-ray picture. It flopped at his side with every step. He thrust it toward Williams without a word. Williams took it from him and held it up to the light.

The picture taken with the x-ray machine showed the compartment inside the sarcophagus had been reshaped to fit an aerial bomb. The housing near the top of the bomb was open. Wires and switches protruded from it. Inside the bomb casing was the unmistakable image of a fusion-type nuclear warhead—a pit of plutonium surrounded by a shield of uranium, encased in conventional explosives. But why was the casing open? And what was the object to which the wires were attached? Williams stared at the image in silence and tried to make sense of what he saw. Then, from inside the sarcophagus, came the faint sound of a ringing cell phone.

Lansing looked puzzled. "There's a phone in there?"

Williams' face turned white. Wires from the trigger were connected to a cell phone. He shouted as he turned away, "It's a—"

Before Williams could complete the sentence the room disappeared in a brilliant flash.

In a sudden burst of heat and light, the bomb inside the sarcophagus detonated. Instantly the city block on which the museum sat was consumed by an inferno that stretched a mile in every direction. As hot as the sun, it rose in a giant column straight up into the sky.

Within seconds of the blast, a shockwave equivalent to wind traveling at more than seven hundred miles per hour extended in every direction. Traveling at the speed of sound, it rolled quickly north through Harlem and south through the Financial District. Windows shattered, trees were torn from the ground, and cars and buses were tossed about like toys.

Behind the initial shockwave came a rolling firestorm pushing temperatures well over three thousand degrees Fahrenheit. Within minutes every building on Manhattan Island burst into flames. By the time the thermal column above the museum billowed into a cloud, everything from Central Park South to Canal Street was reduced to a gray, ashen wasteland.

Five minutes after the bomb detonated, the firestorm that swept Manhattan reached Newark to the west and Plainview on Long Island to the east. Brooklyn, Queens, and the Bronx were engulfed in flames. Ships moored at Red Hook Container Port were lifted from the water and shoved across the container yard. Fuel tanks exploded, sending steel shrapnel flying through the air.

At the same time, an electromagnetic pulse generated by the blast rendered non-shielded electronics instantly inoperable. Communications systems throughout the region went dead. Cell phones, telephones, radios, and televisions fell silent. Computers stopped working. Electronic control systems ceased to function. Engines in cars and trucks, regulated by onboard computers, lurched to a halt. Planes plummeted from the sky. Trains jerked to a stop.

Then the electrical system collapsed. New York, New Jersey, and Pennsylvania were plunged into a blackout. Unable to communicate, and without water or other supplies, the few available emergency personnel were rendered helpless. Those who survived the blast were trapped in the smoking ruins of a once-proud city. The stench of death hung in the air.

Automatic switches designed to limit catastrophic failure of the electrical power grid proved no match for the excessive load generated by the blast. By mid-afternoon, the blackout that began in New York reached as far south as Washington, D.C. Richmond, Charlotte, and Atlanta quickly followed. As nightfall descended, every state east of the Mississippi River was without electrical power. Darkness prevailed from Maine to Miami and westward as far as New Orleans, Memphis, and Minneapolis. Confusion, terror, and panic gripped the nation.

*This material is used by permission of Dr. Michael D. Evans. It is an excerpt from his latest fiction book. If you would like to be informed when it is to be released, please write to Dr. Michael D. Evans, P.O. Box 30000, Phoenix, AZ 85046. Dr. Evans' last fiction work, *Jerusalem Scroll*, was released in 1999 and was based on a plot by Osama bin Laden to target New York with a nuclear device.

· ·

You have just read a fictionalized account of events that could happen anywhere around the globe at any moment—in New York, Paris, London, or Jerusalem. This chapter is from a work of fiction to be released in 2010. To receive prior notice upon the release of the book, please contact memi@jpteam.org. Much of the scenario presented is based on the fact that Iran is actively and diligently pursuing the acquisition of nuclear arms. With Iran's history of contempt for the United Nations, the United States, Great Britain, and of course, Israel, such an apocalyptic event could happen at any moment. The clock is ticking...the Countdown to Armageddon has begun.

· ·

CHAPTER 1

. . . .

ATOMIC IRAN:
AN INTERNATIONAL THREAT

"The problem in Iran is much bigger than weapons.
The problem is the terrorist regime that seeks the weapons.
The regime must go." (RICHARD PERLE)

I ran has moved with great determination to become a nuclear
weapons power as fast as possible. The strategy employed to get
to this goal has been both subtle and brilliant.

Iranian physicists decided it was important to study just how
Israel was able to launch a military strike against Iraq's nuclear
reactor at *Osirak*. As Professor Louis Rene Beres noted, because of
the courage of Prime Minister Menachem Begin in approving an
Israeli attack on Iraq's *Osirak* reactor,

> *Israel's citizens, together with Jews and Arabs, American, and*
> *other coalition soldiers who fought in the [Persian] Gulf War may*
> *owe their lives to Israel's courage, skill, and foresight in June 1981.*
> *Had it not been for the brilliant raid at Osirak, Saddam's forces*
> *might have been equipped with atomic warheads in 1991. Ironically,*
> *the Saudis, too, are in Jerusalem's debt. Had it not been for Prime*

Minister Begin's resolve to protect the Israeli people in 1981, Iraq's SCUDs falling on Saudi Arabia might have spawned immense casualties and lethal irradiation.[1]

"Operation Opera" was launched on June 7, 1981. The task force included fourteen F-15s and F-16s, which took off from Etzion Air Force base in the Negev. The pilots' route took them over Jordan and Saudi Arabia and into Iraqi airspace. Their mission was to attack and destroy *Osirak*, the nuclear reactor built for Saddam Hussein by the French.

While on vacation in Aqaba, Jordan's King Hussein is said to have seen the Israeli planes as they flew overhead. He attempted to notify the Iraqis, but it was apparent that his message either did not reach its destination, or the Iraqis chose to ignore it as speculation.[2]

Although the surprise attack shocked the Iraqis and the world, it had not been planned overnight. It was the final resort after all diplomatic efforts had failed and the French could not be persuaded by world opinion to halt the construction of the reactor. Prime Minister Begin consulted closely with his cabinet, and a decision of monumental proportions was reached: The only avenue open to insure that Saddam Hussein did not achieve nuclear arms capabilities and thereby carry out his threats against Israel was to attack *Osirak*. Intelligence sources within Israel determined that within one to two years Iraq would have possessed nuclear weapons. Later resources confirmed that Saddam was, in fact, within one year of his goal.[3]

Prime Minister Begin and his cabinet did not take lightly the choice to attack Saddam Hussein's pet project. Moshe Dayan, Begin's foreign minister, worked zealously through diplomatic channels to forestall such an attack. Casper Weinberger and Alexander Haig, defense secretary and secretary of state under Ronald Reagan, agreed with the Israeli evaluation of the seriousness of the circumstances in Iraq. However, the U.S. refused to take the lead in combating the situation. It might have been that the true danger was not evident, or it might have been simply that Iraq was engaged in a war with Iran, an avowed enemy. Had not the Grand Ayatollah Ruhollah Khomeini abandoned the Shah's nuclear program because it drew from the "satanic" West, it is highly likely that he would have used any available nuclear weapons against Iraq. The same may be said for Hussein against Iran...or both against Israel, an avowed enemy of Islam.

Israeli Minister of Justice Moshe Nissim recorded that Prime Minister Begin was likely swayed to approve the attack because he realized that an unprincipled and irresponsible Arab ruler such as Saddam Hussein would not have thought twice about launching an attack on Israel. Begin realized the exigency to stop Hussein's quest for nuclear arms.

The Israelis explored every option open to them militarily—jets, ground troops, paratroopers, helicopters—before making the final decision to remove a fuel tank on each of their newly-purchased F-16s in order to make them capable of transporting the armament needed to destroy *Osirak*. More importantly, perhaps, was that they could make the foray flying under Iraq's radar without having to refuel. The date of the attack was set after Begin was notified that Iraq was about to take possession of a shipment of enriched uranium fuel rods from France. This was crucial because once the rods were in place the danger of nuclear fallout from the attack would have been a certainty.

Yitzhak Shamir stated the obvious in Israel's decision to act:

Deterrence was not attained by other countries—France and Italy —and even the United States. It was attained by the state of Israel

*and its prime minister, who decided, acted, and created a fact that
no one in the world today—with the exception of our enemies—
regrets.*[4]

The Israeli attack was relatively simple because Iraq had
only one major nuclear facility. Later, Iran resolved not to make
this same mistake. As a defensive move, Iran's leaders decided to
decentralize their nuclear facilities around the country. Many nuclear
facilities could be embedded in population centers. Thus, to attack
successfully Israel or the United States would have to launch a
multi-pronged strike which would be more tactically difficult to
plan and implement successfully. Even worse, with nuclear facilities
inside Iran's cities, a military strike would cause civilian casualties.
Would Israel and America be willing to kill thousands of Iranian
civilians to take out Iran's nuclear facilities in a pre-emptive military
attack? Clearly, this would raise the stakes among Israel's enemies.

Iran's leaders further determined that each separate nuclear
installation would be devoted to a single purpose, a piece that could
be fitted into the puzzle. This way, if a particular facility were
attacked and destroyed, Iran would lose only the functionality
fulfilled at that location. Some operations would be duplicated
in other facilities; others might be replaced by out-sourcing the
fulfillment of the functionality to a friendly country, perhaps to
Russia or Pakistan. No successful attack on any one facility could
knock offline Iran's total nuclear capabilities for long.

Each step of Iran's nuclear technology has been designed to
allow access to the "full fuel cycle," going from uranium ore to
weapons-grade uranium. Since 1988 Iran has opened an estimated
ten different uranium mines. Exploration at these sites estimates that
the uranium resources of Iran are in the range of 20,000 – 30,000

tons throughout the country, more than enough to fuel Iran's civilian nuclear power plants well into the future.[5]

In February 2003, Iran announced that a uranium mine was opened at Saghand (Sagend), near the central Iranian city of Yazd, in the central Iranian desert of Kavir, some three hundred miles south of Tehran.[6] In September 2004, Iran allowed the international press to tour the uranium mine at Saghand for the first time. Ghasem Soleimani, the British-trained director of mining operations at the Energy Organization of Iran, reported on plans to begin extracting uranium ore from the mine in the first half of 2006. He claimed, "More than 77 percent of the work has been accomplished."[7]

The mine was reported to have a capacity of 132,000 tons of uranium ore per year. Uranium ore is processed into uranium ore concentrate, commonly called "yellowcake" at a separate yellowcake production plant located at Ardakan, about sixty kilometers from Yazd. Iran's uranium processing facility is located at yet another site, at Isfahan, a central Iranian city some 250 miles south of Tehran.

The Nuclear Technology and Research Center in Isfahan is said to employ as many as three thousand scientists in a facility constructed about fifteen kilometers southeast of central Isfahan, at a research complex constructed by the French under a 1975 agreement with Iran.[8] Isfahan also houses one of Iran's major universities, with some one thousand graduate students and approximately ten thousand undergraduates in fields that include science, social science, and humanities.

On the eastern outskirts of Isfahan is the Uranium Conversion Facility, a cluster of buildings surrounded by razor wire fencing and protected by anti-aircraft guns and military patrols.[9] In this facility yellowcake ore is processed into uranium hexafluoride gas (UF4), the first step required to convert uranium ore to the enriched state needed to run a nuclear power plant or to provide the weapons-grade uranium needed to make an atom bomb. An alarming report from Isfahan on September 12, 2008, indicated that enriched uranium sufficient to assemble six atom bombs had been removed from the facility:

> *The [International Atomic Energy Agency "IAEA"] inspectors only have limited access at Isfahan, and it looks as though Iranian officials have removed significant quantities of UF6 at a stage in the process that is not being monitored.... If Iran's nuclear intentions are peaceful, then why are they doing this?*[10]

The New York Times quoted several experts as concluding that Iran is already in possession of enough supplies to create an atomic bomb.[11] The French have further predicted that such an event could occur sometime in 2009 or 2010. A study by the foreign affairs department, headed by Jean-Louis Bianco, reported, "Tehran possesses plans for a nuclear bomb." Bianco was certain that the Iranians had definite military objectives in mind for their nuclear program.[12] Coupled with the intelligence information that Iran's military is significantly involved in the so-called "peaceful" nuclear program, this is a sobering situation.

From Isfahan, uranium hexafluoride gas is transported to yet another facility, this one at Natanz, about ninety miles to the northeast of Isfahan. Here the uranium hexafluoride gas is enriched in centrifuges to the higher grade, uranium-235. This completes the "full fuel cycle," ending the range of processes needed to get from uranium ore to highly enriched uranium. At lower grades of enrichment, the uranium can be used to fuel peaceful power plants. Uranium enriched to uranium-235 can be fashioned into the metallic form needed to serve as the fissile core of an atom bomb.

The Fuel Enrichment Plant at Isfahan is located about ten miles to the northeast of the town of Natanz, set off from the surrounding desert by a perimeter security fence and military guards. The Natanz Fuel Enrichment Plant houses two large underground halls built eight meters below ground. The halls are hardened by thick, underground, concrete-reinforced walls built to protect the facility. The construction was designed to house an advanced centrifuge complex of as many as fifty thousand centrifuges.

Experts estimate that the Fuel Enrichment Plant was prepared initially to house some five thousand centrifuges in the initial stage of the project scheduled for completion by the end of 2005 or early in 2006.[13] Operating at full capacity, fifty thousand centrifuges would be capable of producing enough weapons-grade uranium to build over twenty weapons per year. When completed, the underground facilities were planned to have no visible above-ground signature, a move designed to complicate precise targeting of any munitions that could be used in an attack.

Precise satellite imagery of the nuclear facilities at both Isfahan and Natanz show the exact location of the operation. The images document various phases of facility construction and concealment, from the time the facilities were first begun to very recently on a continuously updated basis. Inspection of the satellite images reveals that the complexes were designed to include dormitory/housing facilities for those working at the plant. Also visible are various complexes of administrative and scientific buildings needed to operate the facilities.

Even these publicly available satellite images show the military defense and anti-aircraft installations designed to provide security. Inspection of these images makes clear that Isfahan and Natanz are both sophisticated facilities. The Iranians paid careful attention to design both for the professional operation of nuclear activity and the military preparedness needed to protect the facilities from attack.

In November 2004, Iranian leaders agreed to stop all processing of uranium at both Isfahan and Natanz. Iran made this decision to comply with a condition set by the EU3 (the European Union countries of France, Germany, and the United Kingdom) for negotiations to begin.

The goal of the EU3 was to settle with Iran the IAEA requirements for facility inspection. The IAEA wanted to determine that Iran was compliant with the provisions of the NPT (Nuclear Non-Proliferation Treaty) prohibiting the development of nuclear weapons. The IAEA was obligated to hold Iran to a standard of "transparency," meaning that all Iranian nuclear facilities and operations should be open to IAEA inspection at times and places of the IAEA's choosing.

A transparent nuclear program is one that is open to inspection; a non-transparent program is one where restrictions are placed upon inspections. The argument was that Iran was using inspection restrictions to conceal nuclear weapons activities. If Iran were allowed to limit inspections to certain times and to certain facilities or particular areas within facilities, the advanced warning requirement would give workers the opportunity to sanitize operations prior to inspection.

International skeptics argued that Iran had only agreed to suspend uranium processing because Isfahan and Natanz were not yet complete in November 2004. More time was needed to finish facility construction and resolve technical problems. By agreeing to "stop" operations Iran was truly not ready to begin, it seized the opportunity to appear cooperative. Skeptics argued Iran's primary goal was simply to buy more time.

In September 2004, Iran told the IAEA in a report little noticed at the time that the country planned to process some forty tons of uranium into uranium hexafluoride gas. This notice tended to be forgotten as soon as Iran announced in November 2004 that uranium processing and enrichment was being voluntarily suspended.

Then, in February 2004, an IAEA report was leaked to the Associated Press suggesting that Tehran was planning to process thirty-seven tons of yellowcake uranium oxide into uranium hexafluoride gas, estimated to be enough to make about five small atomic bombs once the UF4 gas was enriched to uranium-235. The report caused a blow-up in the press. Ali Akbar Salehi, a senior advisor to Iran's Foreign Minister Kamal Kharrazi, reacted sharply when questioned about the AP report. "That we want to process thirty-seven metric tons of uranium ore into hexafluoride gas is not a discovery," he told the international press. "The IAEA has been aware of Iran's plan to construct the Uranium Conversion Facility in Isfahan since it was a barren land. We haven't constructed the Isfahan facility to produce biscuits but hexafluoride gas."[14]

This type of forced admission raised concerns in the international community that Iran was deliberately lying about its nuclear intentions. Was Iran going to process uranium or not? The answer to that question was not clear.

Then, in May 2005, international rumors circulated suggesting that Iran had gone ahead with processing the thirty-seven tons of uranium ore, and that work at Isfahan had never been suspended after all. To resolve this conflict, Mohammad Saeedi, the deputy head of the Atomic Energy Organization of Iran (AEOI), came forward. He explained to the international press that thirty-seven tons of uranium ore had been processed but before formally suspending nuclear processing at Isfahan the previous November: "We converted all the thirty-seven tons of uranium concentrate known as yellowcake into UF4 at the Isfahan Uranium Conversion Facility before we suspended work there," Saeedi told the international press.[15]

In a separate statement Hasan Rowhani, Iran's top nuclear negotiator, admitted that Iran had produced both UF4 and UF6 gas. Rowhani also discussed the suspension of uranium processing in a way that suggested Iran's real intent was work on the Isfahan and Natanz facilities. "It is true that we are currently under suspension," Rowhani commented, "but we conducted a lot of activities in 2004. Today, if we want to start enrichment we have sufficient centrifuges at least for the early stages, while we didn't have such a capacity twenty-five months ago."[16]

Rowhani was responding to internal criticism from Iranians who wanted the country to move ahead, hard-liners who had argued that the suspension of uranium processing had harmed Iran's technological advancement. The problem was that Rowhani's statement sounded like Iran was flip-flopping, claiming it had processed uranium before it stopped processing uranium.

Mahmoud Ahmadinejad was elected president on June 25, 2005, and Ayatollah Khamenei had everything needed to take the regime in the ultra-conservative direction he believed would fulfill the late Ayatollah Khomeini's prophecy. Never had the moment been so right for Iran and so wrong for the United States and Israel.

Iran openly resumed processing uranium at Isfahan on August 2005, defiantly breaking the earlier promise to suspend uranium processing while the EU-3 negotiations were proceeding.[17] Iran was beginning to feel it had the upper hand. Its aggressive defiance was being met by confusion and inaction from the United States and the Europeans.

Officials moved to resume uranium processing at Isfahan, knowing that their unilateral decision would throw a monkey wrench into the U.S. plan to corner them. Yet even here, the Iranians were calculating carefully, taking one step at a time. Re-opening Isfahan meant the Iranians were resuming uranium processing, defined as the refinement of uranium ore into uranium hexafluoride. By not opening Natanz, the Iranians technically were not yet engaging in uranium enrichment, defined as the process of converting uranium hexafluoride gas into uranium-235. Stealthily, the Iranians moved their pieces on the chessboard, always with a view to soon declare a surprise "checkmate."

In response, the IAEA fell into a series of crisis meetings. On September 24, 2005, the International Atomic Energy Agency voted at the urging of the United States to hold Iran in non-compliance with the Nuclear Non-Proliferation Treaty. This locked in place a key piece of the U.S. strategy.

When the IAEA vote was taken, Iran was celebrating "Sacred Defense Week," marking the 25th anniversary of the Iran-Iraq War. In Tehran Foreign Minister Manouchehr Mottaki called the IAEA resolution "political, illegal, and illogical." On state-run television, Mottaki portrayed the EU-3 as puppets of the United States, claiming, "the three European countries implemented a planned scenario already determined by the United States."[18]

John Bolton, the U.S. ambassador to the UN, spoke of Iran's nuclear program during an on-the-record briefing:

> *There's not a single permanent member of the Security Council that accepts that Iran should have nuclear weapons...I think foreign ministers and indeed, heads of government going back to the Sea Island Summit in 2004 have made that clear. The issue is how to demonstrate to the Iranians that the course they're pursuing is not acceptable.*[19]

Reuters next reported on November 17, 2005, that Iran was preparing to process a new batch of 250 drums of yellowcake uranium at Isfahan.[20] This left no doubt about Iran's intentions. It evidently did not want to resume negotiations with the EU-3 if that meant forfeiting the right to process uranium. The Iranian decision was particularly defiant, given that the IAEA was expected to meet on November 24 to vote on the September resolution to take Iran to the Security Council.

Immediately, Russia put a proposal of its own on the table. To break the impasse Russia offered to establish a joint venture with Iran to operate a uranium enrichment facility located in Russia.[21] Once again the IAEA postponed a decision to take Iran to the United Nations Security Council for additional sanctions, preferring instead to give Russia time to develop more fully the alternative and to win Iranian acceptance of the idea. And once again, Iran had calculated correctly. By taking the defiant path Iran had thrown the IAEA and the EU-3 into confusion. Rather than confront Iran, the first impulse of the IAEA and the EU-3 was to retreat, hoping they could still work out a diplomatic solution.

Skillfully, the Iranians had gone from enriching uranium to not enriching uranium to *maybe* enriching uranium and finally to enriching uranium again, defiantly. They danced the same dance over negotiations—first the Iranians refused to negotiate, and then they began negotiating, only to defiantly break off negotiations again.

At that point the Iranians said they would negotiate again but would not give up the right to enrich uranium in their own country, not even to Russia. The Iranians would talk, but only as long as the talks were on their terms. With every move Iran bought more time. With every start and stop, confusion set upon the United States and the Europeans, just as Ayatollah Khomeini had foretold decades earlier.

Finally, after more than a quarter century following the 1979 revolution in Iran, Ayatollah Ali Khamenei was gaining confidence that he had mastered the game of international diplomacy. With his team of radical true believers more firmly in command than ever, Khamenei felt increasingly confident he could get to the end game and win. Iran would have the nuclear weapons needed to fulfill the vision to annihilate Israel just as Ahmadinejad had proclaimed.

CHAPTER 2

. . . .

ATOMIC IRAN:
A THREAT TO HUMANITY

*"Humanity is entering a radically new epoch in which,
for the first time in history, it has the power to destroy itself
by deliberate or unintended action."* (YEHEZKEL DROR)[22]

January of 2006 introduced new developments regarding Iran's nuclear pursuits. Israeli Defense Minister Shaul Mofaz indicated that Israel was preparing for a raid on Iran's nuclear infrastructure. He said Israel could not tolerate an Iran with nuclear weapons, especially given Ahmadinejad's threat to "wipe Israel off the map" during the "World without Zionism" seminar in Tehran.

Condemnation from the West only seemed to strengthen the resolve of Iran's leaders. The world was informed that the Natanz nuclear facility was back online and small-scale uranium enrichment—the first step in producing fuel for atomic weapons—had been added to the mix. In another apparently subtle challenge to the United States, a member of the Iranian parliament suggested to Venezuelan dictator Hugo Chavez that Iran might assist him in the development of nuclear technology.

The nuclear facility at Natanz was clandestine until the National Council of Resistance for Iran (NCRI), a political resistance group, revealed the site in a press conference held in Washington, D.C., in mid-August 2002. The NCRI press release was highly detailed, revealing for the first time that the Natanz site was being built to contain two large underground structures designed to house the centrifuges necessary to enrich uranium to weapons grade. Each of the structures was reportedly being buried twenty-five feet underground, sheltered by eight feet of concrete and surrounded by a protective shield to make the structure resistant to explosions.

The NCRI press release even disclosed the names of the construction companies that had been hired to start building the Natanz facilities. The press release made public how the Atomic Energy Organization of Iran (AEIO) had set up a front company through which the AEIO intended to pursue the project's needs for facilities and equipment, including such detail as the street address of the fronting company in Tehran.[23] None of this information was known to the UN International Atomic Energy Agency (IAEA) until the NCRI held the Washington press conference. Afterwards, the IAEA investigated and confirmed the accuracy of the NCRI report.

On November 14, 2004, the NCRI issued a press release disclosing a major nuclear site in Tehran that had been kept secret. According to the document, the Iranian Ministry of Defense (MD) had set up the Modern Defense Readiness and Technology Center (MDRTC) on a sixty-acre site previously occupied by three heavy transport battalions operating under the Ministry of Defense. The NCRI report listed the street addresses of the facility's entrances and described the buildings and installations on the site in detail. The report explained "activities in nuclear and biological warfare" that had previously been performed elsewhere were moved to the

MDRTC. The press release gave the names of commanders and described how the Iranians had deceived IAEA efforts to investigate.

This was an important report. For the first time the NCRI gave a full explanation of how the Iranian government had assigned nuclear work to the military, calculating to keep the military operation secret even to Iran's own atomic energy agency.

> The MD and the AEIO are the two bodies conducting Iran's nuclear activities in a parallel manner. The AEIO is pursuing the nuclear power stations and the fuel cycle, whereas the MD is seeking to achieve nuclear bomb technology and keeps all its activities secret from the AEIO. For this reason, redoing of works is a major problem in Iran's nuclear project and many research and preparations are carried out repeatedly and in a parallel manner at huge expense.[24]

The NCRI information was obviously obtained from its underground agents operating in Iran. Much of what was reported had been previously unknown by the IAEA, or by American intelligence units, including the CIA.

Regardless of the State Department designation of the NCRI as a "terrorist organization," what is clear is that the MEK or PMOI (People's Mujahedin of Iran) and NCRI hate the Iranian regime of the mullahs. One of the key weapons in this unrelenting attack has been information. The NCRI is determined to expose the lies of the mullahs regarding their nuclear weapons ambitions. NCRI reports have repeatedly revealed to the world the exact nature of the clandestine nuclear weapons activities going on in Iran. This does not mean that all aspects of the NCRI's reports are fully accurate. Still, the vast majority of what it exposes is subsequently verified by the IAEA or one of the major intelligence operations run by the United States or other governments around the world. It has provided ammunition for increased calls for Iran to halt its nuclear program.

On September 2, 2005, the IAEA Board of Governors issued yet another report concluding, "Iran had failed in a number of instances over an extended period of time to meet its obligations under its Safeguards Agreement with respect to the reporting of nuclear material, its processing and its use, as well as the declaration of facilities where such material had been processed and stored."[25] The multi-page report listed violations going back to 1991, when Iran had failed to disclose the importing of uranium, through recent violations.

What the diplomatic language takes pains to gloss over is the international embarrassment caused to the IAEA every time someone else reveals Iran's deception. Third-party disclosures and international press reports are information leaked from within Iran by internal dissidents. These disclosures force IAEA inspectors to go back and look for what they had missed. Finally, the IAEA issued new, corrected reports. The embarrassment to the IAEA is immediate as the world realizes that the Iranians have fed the IAEA lies, half-truths, and outright deceptions.

It took the release of the truth by opposition groups such as the NCRI before Iran's clandestine nuclear activities were disclosed publicly. The obvious conclusion is that the IAEA could not be relied upon to do its job.

In a rare move, the U.S. State Department released a set of briefing slides on Iran that were presented to foreign diplomats in Vienna in September 2005.[26] The whole purpose of the slide presentation was to question whether Iran's pursuit of the nuclear fuel cycle was intended for peaceful uses, as Iran maintained, or for the creation of nuclear weapons, as the State Department contended. The slides were meant to make the argument that the way Iran had constructed its nuclear facilities is more consistent with the way a country would build a weapons program and not a peaceful program intended to generate electricity.

In the slides the State Department "confirmed a record of hiding sensitive nuclear fuel activities from the IAEA," charging that "Iran's rationale for a 'peaceful' nuclear fuel cycle does not hold up under scrutiny."[27] With Iran sitting on proven oil reserves of 125.8 million barrels, roughly 10 percent of the world's total, plus 940 trillion cubic feet of proven natural gas reserves, 15.5 percent of the world's total reserves and the world's second largest supply in any country, the State Department doubted that Iran needed nuclear power in order to provide civilian electricity.

Even more damning, the State Department argued that instead of spending $6 billion to develop the seven new nuclear reactors Iran proposed to build, Iran could make the same dollar investments in the country's aging and neglected oil and natural gas infrastructures. This investment would permit Iran to build one or more new refineries designed to reduce Iran's domestic cost of energy and eliminate the need to import refined gasoline. The State Department slides argued that: "If Iran were to invest $5.6 billion in a high gasoline yield, Western-type refinery, it could eliminate its dependence on imported gasoline and increase its annual net oil-related revenue by approximately $982 million."[28]

The State Department slides also showed the diplomats in Vienna satellite photographs of Iran's nuclear facilities. Taken over time, the photos showed how Iran had misrepresented the facilities and constructed them so as to bury and hide key functions. Some facilities Iran had simply failed to disclose at all. With regard to the gas centrifuge uranium enrichment at Natanz, for instance, the State Department identified the site as "a covert facility in a remote location, which could be used to enrich uranium for weapons."[29]

Satellite and ground photographs showed dummy structures designed to prevent detection and identification, as well as facilities that were concealed underground, hardened and well defended.

Significant progress constructing the Arak heavy-water reduction complex was shown for the time period of June 2004 through March 2005. These photos demonstrated that the reactor construction was progressing rapidly despite IAEA Board requests to forgo construction altogether. The State Department dismissed Iran's claim that the Arak reactor was needed for medical and industrial isotopes, a capability that Iran already had inherent in its ten megawatt Tehran research reactor. The slides also documented the development of the uranium mine at Gachin, a facility that was larger and more promising than the one at Saghand, the only mine Iranian reports had bothered to disclose prior to 2004.

The State Department concluded that Iran's nuclear program is "well-scaled for a nuclear weapons capability," especially when compared to the progress being made in the nuclear weapons facilities of another rogue state, North Korea. "When one also considers Iran's concealment and deception activities, it is difficult to escape the conclusion that Iran is pursuing nuclear weapons."[30]

Finally, so as to leave no doubt, one of the last slides drove home the point: "Iran's past history of concealment and deception and the nuclear fuel cycle infrastructure are most consistent with an intent to acquire nuclear weapons."[31] (The last part of the sentence was underlined for emphasis in the original State Department slide.)

Whenever the subject of rogue nations sharing nuclear weapons secrets comes up, the name of A.Q. Khan is not far behind. On February 4, 2004, Abdul Qadeer Khan, the father of Pakistan's nuclear weapons program, went on Pakistani television and apologized to the nation for having sold Pakistan's nuclear secrets to other countries. "It pains me to realize that my lifetime achievement could have been placed in jeopardy," he said with an emotion that looked like regret.[32]

This expression of regret was touching; however, the record shows that Khan profited handsomely by selling nuclear technology. He sold nuclear warhead blueprints and uranium enrichment technology to the "Axis of Evil" states—Iraq under Saddam Hussein, North Korea, and Iran—as well as to Muammar Qaddafi's Libya.

The CIA's "721 Report," released in November 2004, emphasized that Iran's nuclear program "received significant assistance" in the past from "the proliferation network headed by Pakistani scientist A.Q. Khan."[33] This report is named for Section 721 of the 1997 Intelligence Authorization Act, which requires unclassified disclosure to Congress regarding the acquisition of nuclear weapons technology by foreign countries during the preceding six months.[34]

Suspicion regarding Khan's secret nuclear black market was reinforced on November 18, 2005. On that date, the IAEA released a report disclosing a handwritten, one-page document that constituted an offer made by Khan's network to Iran in 1987. The document, which had been voluntarily turned over to the IAEA by Iran, represented an offer to sell the country nuclear components and equipment. Iran admitted that some components of one or two disassembled centrifuges, as well as supporting drawings and specifications, were delivered by Khan's procurement network, and that other items referred to in the document were obtained from other suppliers.

In July 2005, Iran announced that a solid-fuel engine had been successfully tested for the country's mainstay missile, the Shahab-3.[35] The Shahab-3 is a single-stage missile based on the North Korean "Nodong" missile series, with a reliable range of approximately

995 miles (1,600 kilometers), with a maximum range estimated at 1,250 miles, more than enough to hit Tel Aviv or U.S. military troops stationed in Iraq. The Shahab-3 was first successfully tested by Iran in August and September 2004.

On September 21, 2004, a Shahab-3 missile was first paraded in Tehran with banners proclaiming "We will crush America under our feet" and "wipe Israel off the map."[36] The significance of equipping the Shahab-3 with a solid-fuel engine is that less time is required to prepare the missile for firing. Anti-missile systems are most effective when they detect early preparations to fire a missile and hit the missile when it first leaves the launching pad. Missiles in full flight are a more difficult ballistics problem, similar to the difficulty of hitting one bullet in flight with another bullet fired at it. Also, solid fuel technology generally adds greater reliability and accuracy to the missile's performance. The acquisition of more sophisticated rocket delivery systems makes the situation in Iran even more ominous. Today, Iran's missiles can reach Israel and much of Europe. Within a few years, Iran's ICBMs should be able to strike anywhere on the globe.

Despite pressure from the EU to adjourn its nuclear pursuits, Iran has continued to defy the worldwide call to halt uranium enrichment. In April 2006, Ali Larijani, secretary of Iran's Supreme National Security Council, announced, "If sanctions are imposed on Iran, then we will suspend our relations with the IAEA...If the USA attacks Iran's nuclear facilities, we will stop acting transparently in the nuclear field and continue covert nuclear work at other facilities."[37]

Iran's leaders announced intentions to hasten uranium enrichment by mid-year 2006. A spokesman indicated it was hoped cascades of some three thousand centrifuges would be established by the end of the year or early 2007. A cascade contains 164 centrifuges linked together. According to the Congressional Research Service, Iran has eighteen cascades (2,952 centrifuges) of first generation (IR-1) centrifuges installed in the facility. Iran is feeding uranium hexafluoride into five additional 164-centrifuge cascades and is installing and testing thirteen more cascades.[38]

In typical fashion, Russia reacted to its neighbor's nuclear arms program by rushing to sign an agreement that would provide fuel for a new power plant set to open in 2007. In reaction to Russia's largess, a bill was introduced and approved by the U.S. Congress to sanction any country agreeing to provide supplies or assistance with Iran's quest to purchase "chemical, biological, or nuclear weapons."[39]

Ahmadinejad traveled to Arak, host city to the Khondab plant, in August 2006 to preside over the opening of a heavy-water plant. The Atomic Energy Organization of Iran (AEOI) oversaw the construction of the plant at Arak, operated through a fronting company, the Mesbah Energy Company.

The plant was designed to produce plutonium, a major ingredient in the production of nuclear arms. Although Khondab's reactor was set for start-up sometime in 2009, a cloak of invisibility seems to have fallen over the facility. Even though Tehran has indicated that the Khondab reactor is only to be used to produce isotopes for medical use, a major concern centers on the by-product of spent fuel that contains plutonium.

The only reason Iran would need a heavy-water facility is if the country were planning to build a plutonium bomb. The Russian-built reactor at Bushehr does not use heavy-water, which is required to moderate the nuclear chain reaction needed to produce weapons-grade plutonium. Fission bombs requiring plutonium are more sophisticated to design and detonate than bombs using uranium-235, but the explosive magnitude of plutonium bombs is many times greater.

By focusing the discussion on uranium enrichment, the Iranians were telegraphing their decision to build first a simpler, more reliable uranium bomb. Even when the first nuclear bombs were designed by the Manhattan Project of World War II, scientists had known that the mechanics of building a gun-type uranium device were simpler and more reliable. The first atomic bomb ever exploded in combat, the one dropped on Hiroshima, was a simple gun-type design uranium-235 atomic bomb. The *Enola Gay* dropped on Hiroshima a bomb known as "Little Boy." At the time the U.S. did not have a second "Little Boy." Moreover, testing a gun-type nuclear device was considered unnecessary. The gun-type design was so simple and reliable that the scientists were confident it would work.

Building a heavy-water facility at Arak suggested that Iran was on the same path. First, Iran would build a simple, gun-type design uranium bomb. Yet, not far behind Iran evidently plans to be able to build a plutonium device of higher yield and greater destructive power.

In October 2006, Ahmadinejad threw down another gauntlet in his never-ending battle to provoke Israel during the annual Jerusalem Day protest. Not-so-veiled threats erupted as he declared:

> The Zionist regime, thank God, has lost all reason to exist. The efforts to stabilize Israel's fraudulent regime have failed. Believe me; soon this regime will be no longer. The Zionist regime was established in the heart of Islamic territory for one purpose—to pose a threat to the region through constant attacks and killings. This regime has lost its way of existence. Today, there is no reason left for it to remain, and it is about to disappear.[40]

Just days later, Ahmadinejad had another startling announcement for the Western world and for his Arab neighbors:

Today the Iranian nation possesses the full nuclear fuel cycle and time is completely running in our favor in terms of diplomacy.[41]

He later told a cadre of Iranian reporters:

We will commission three thousand centrifuges by the year-end. We are determined to master the nuclear fuel cycle and commission some sixty thousand centrifuges to meet our demands.[42]

Though handed various sanctions and threats of sanctions, Iran has not waivered from its nuclear arms race. During 2007 Ahmadinejad and the International Atomic Energy Commission danced around each other like fencers exchanging parries and thrusts. The National Intelligence Estimate published in 2007 indicated:

We assess with moderate confidence that convincing the Iranian leadership to forgo the eventual development of nuclear weapons will be difficult given the linkage many within the leadership probably see between nuclear weapons development and Iran's key national security and foreign policy objectives, and given Iran's considerable effort from at least the late 1980s to 2003 to develop such weapons. In our judgment, only an Iranian political decision to abandon a nuclear weapons objective would plausibly keep Iran from eventually producing nuclear weapons— and such a decision is inherently reversible.

We assess with moderate confidence that Iran probably would use covert facilities—rather than its declared nuclear sites—for the production of highly enriched uranium for a weapon. A growing amount of intelligence indicates Iran was engaged in covert uranium conversion and uranium enrichment activity, but we judge that these efforts probably were halted in response to the fall 2003 halt, and that these efforts probably had not been restarted through at least mid-2007.[43]

By September 2008, the IAEA still had not been able to make any inroads in its mission to determine the magnitude of Iran's nuclear program. Ahmadinejad's penchant for overstating facts further clouded the issue. In one statement the president revealed that Iran had "five thousand operational centrifuges." When his duplicity was uncovered, another official explained that some three thousand centrifuges were coming online. In fact, November 2008 Gholam Reza Aghazadeh, the chief of Iran's Atomic Energy Organization, confirmed that the five-thousand number was correct with more to come. He audaciously explained, "Suspension has not been defined in our lexicon."[44]

Following the 2009 elections in Iran, Aghazadeh resigned his post in a shocking move that was viewed as a key hindrance to Ahmadinejad. Aghazadeh is an accomplished technical expert whose administrative skills helped quickly develop Iran's nuclear program.

The UN Security Council persists in passing resolutions denouncing Iran's nuclear proliferation, while Ahmadinejad and Khamenei continue to thumb their collective noses at its actions. Uranium enrichment is still the main focus at the Natanz facility. The IAEA indicated in February 2009 that Iran possesses "839 kilograms of low enriched uranium," which can be further enriched to produce weapons-grade uranium.[45] Estimates vary on how long it would take Iran to produce a quantity sufficient to produce weapons.

An announcement from Tehran in early 2009 signified that the much-awaited Bushehr reactor would be capable of producing electricity at half its capacity in March. The reactor was still offline in April.

In July 2009, the G8—a group composed of Great Britain, the United States, Germany, France, Italy, Canada, Japan, and

Russia—met in L'Aquila, Italy. One of the topics discussed was Iran's nuclear program. A communiqué issued by the leaders defined their concerns regarding the rogue country but stopped short of taking a definitive stand:

> We remain deeply concerned over proliferation risks posed by Iran's nuclear program.... We strongly urge Iran to co-operate fully with the International Atomic Energy Agency and to comply with the relevant UN Security Council resolutions without further delay.[46]

The IAEA points out that questions regarding Iran's military utilization of its program have gone unanswered, and Iran continues to defy global demands for it to halt its quest for nuclear capabilities. Could there be something behind Ahmadinejad's rabid defiance other than his megalomaniacal tendencies? It is no mystery that Iran's president is a fanatical Shia Twelver. He is a follower of the twelfth Imam, otherwise known as the Mahdi. Twelvers believe that at the age of five, this last descendant of Muhammad was hidden away in a state often called "occultation." His followers believe that through some apocalyptic event, in the midst of turmoil and warfare, the Mahdi will be revealed and will establish a worldwide caliphate with Shia Islam at its center.

Ahmadinejad is such a rabid follower that he has claimed to have been contacted by the Mahdi—much to the chagrin of some of the clerics in Iran. Why does his belief in the Mahdi make Ahmadinejad so dangerous? According to Shia theology, only Allah has the knowledge of when the Mahdi will return to Qom, a city southwest of Tehran. In the company of Jesus, the Mahdi will travel along the new roads constructed under Ahmadinejad's auspices to the capital, Tehran, where he will assume his rightful role as worldwide caliph.

Iran's Supreme Leader Ali Khamenei is not a follower of the Twelver sect, but he has chosen to elevate the man, not once but twice, who is militant in his faith. Iran's president believes he can create the catastrophic circumstances that will bring the Mahdi forth. His conviction is made even more menacing with each new revelation regarding nuclear advancements. An assault on either Israel or the United States would launch retaliatory measures that would, in Ahmadinejad's book, bring about the chaos necessary to unleash the Mahdi on the world.

If or when Iran acquires a nuclear device, it could well provide the impetus for other Arab countries in the Middle East to follow suit. Even now the race is on to build reactors in Jordan, the UAE, and Abu Dhabi for the production of nuclear power stations. Like Jordan, Egypt has a treaty in place with Israel to build a reactor. Britain has inked an agreement with Jordan; the U.S. with the UAE (a country with strong ties to Iran); and France signed a multi-billion dollar agreement with Abu Dhabi, which will, in the words of British Foreign Secretary David Miliband, "move the world to a low-carbon economy." He added that nuclear power needed to be a strong part of the mix.[47] Russia, not wanting to be left out, is courting Egypt with its nuclear stores.

Currently Israel is the only country in the Middle East with nuclear capabilities. The world is waiting to see if the Israelis will halt the nuclear arms race by attacking Iran's nuclear reactors. If not, the balance of power may shift to its Arab neighbors who fear Iran's global intentions.

. . . .

CHAPTER 3

CHAOS, CONFUSION
AND INTERNAL INSTABILITY

"The internal conditions in Iran are worsening
in all aspects. Poverty and unemployment are becoming
more severe, despite the fact that Iran has turned into
a developed and industrialized country."

(MOSHE KATSAV)

They marched, as did Martin Luther King and his followers, crying out for freedom and democracy against a Holocaust-denying, demented dictator,[48] who wants to wipe Israel off the map. They were beaten and killed while President Obama looked on and then took days to issue a milquetoast statement.

What prompted the people of Iran to take to the streets knowing they could face imminent death? Why did both men and women openly defy the ruling clerics and the tyrant appointed president by them? The younger population has discovered through technology—the Internet, *Facebook*, *YouTube*, *Twitter*, and cell phones—that the world has more to offer than their dictatorial leaders are willing to admit. The spirit of freedom, which cannot be contained when lodged in the human heart, cannot be restrained. It burst forth in the form of outraged protest directed at their leaders. The men and women who had waited in long lines in order to indicate their choice at the ballot box simply wanted their votes to count. Those seeking reform in Iran were stunned to learn that Mahmoud Ahmadinejad's "overwhelming victory" had been announced long before all the votes could possibly have been counted.

Fouad Ajami, an American university professor and writer on Middle East issues, described Ahmadinejad as "a son of the Ayatollah Khomeini's revolutionary order, a man from the brigades of the regime, austere and indifferent to outsiders, an Iranian Everyman with badly fitting clothes and white socks,"[49] who had somehow managed to finagle the office of president of Iran once again. Although he is hated by the upper echelon, Ahmadinejad should never be underestimated. He has helped to fashion a formidable façade of power and piety for the Supreme Leader Ayatollah Ali Khamenei. He has been described as dogged and ruthless, tyrannical and formidable.

Many, if not most, in the free world assumed that the election had been stage-managed by the mullahs who wanted their candidate of choice to remain at the presidential helm. Let's pretend for a moment that Mahmoud Ahmadinejad *had* won the primary election fair and square. With the voter turnout, it is more likely he would have captured less than 50 percent of the vote, forcing a run-off. In an honestly conducted election without the interference of Ali Khamenei, could it be that such an eventuality might have cost Ahmadinejad his job? Apparently the supreme leader could not take a chance on such an outcome.

Presenting himself as a "reform" candidate, Ahmadinejad's most formidable opponent in the election was Mir-Hossein Moussavi. In 1981 UPI reported, "Moussavi heralds a more vigorous propagation of the radical Islamic foreign policy of exporting Iran's revolution."[50] While attending a demonstration in Tehran in 1987, Moussavi said, "Tomorrow will be the day we step on the Great Satan. Tomorrow is the time for America to see our iron fists."[51] And a statement issued from Tehran in 1988 read, "Israel should be annihilated,"[52] and that the only means to "achieve Palestinian rights is to continue the popular struggles against Israel."[53]

Following the death of the Ayatollah Ruhollah Khomeini in 1989, Moussavi was portrayed as "a leading radical who in the past has competed with Khamenei for primacy in setting government policy pledged subservience, along with his entire cabinet, to the new leader." Given his history, it seems the only thing that might have changed under Moussavi, the "reform" candidate, was the name on the presidential stationery.

What many in the Western world really didn't know was just who exactly Mir Hossein Moussavi was. Would he have been able to rally the dissenters for a long-term protest? As Khomeini's protégé, he served as prime minister between 1980 and 1988 during Iran's long and deadly war with Iraq. (Iran's constitution was amended in 1989 to eliminate the post of prime minister.) Moussavi supported Iran's nuclear pursuits, going so far as to purchase centrifuges on the black market. During the election he reiterated that he would stand behind the nuclear program, but he would try to assuage the fears of Iran's detractors and work to convince them that Iran wanted nuclear power for peaceful purposes only. Mr.

Moussavi said, "Weaponization and nuclear technology are two separate issues, and we should not let them get mixed up."[54]

Moussavi also indicated that, if elected, he might accept President Obama's offer to sit down for talks after nearly thirty years of silence between the two countries. He suggested he was in favor of ending the attacks against the liberal media and bloggers.

Described as composed and purposeful, Moussavi has a hypnotic way of speaking, but he has not been overly gifted with magnetism. In spite of these personality traits he has also been depicted as both steadfast and fearless. He challenged Ahmadinejad's penchant for inflammatory speeches regarding the international community. Moussavi chastised him for denying the Holocaust:

In our foreign policy, we have confused fundamental issues...that are in our national interest with sensationalism that is more of domestic use.[55]

Deputy Interior Minister Mohammad Atrianfar, who served under Mr. Moussavi, had this to say of the former prime minister: "He was an artist, a university professor with no experience, but he managed under harsh conditions to run a country of thirty-five million people through trial and error. The biggest result for him was the self-confidence he gained from that."

Moussavi's hopes of becoming Iran's next president were dashed, however, when supreme leader Ayatollah Ali Khamenei declared incumbent Mahmoud Ahmadinejad the victor by a two-to-one margin. The emotional consequences of that announcement rivaled those of Ayatollah Ruhollah Khomeini's triumphant return to Tehran in 1979. Mr. Moussavi's supporters took to the streets in protest but were literally beaten back by the Iranian Revolutionary Guard, whose leader supported Ahmadinejad. A second recount by the Guardian Council, Iran's top legislative body, did not alter the initial proclamation—Ahmadinejad had won. The council proclaimed that there had been no irregularities in the election:

> The secretary of the Guardian Council in a letter to the interior minister announced the final decision of the Council...and declares the approval of the accuracy of the results of...the presidential election.[56]

Reza Pahlavi, son of the late Shah of Iran and Farah Pahlavi, threw his support behind the protesters. He called Khamenei a "dam in front of this movement, sanctioning theft of the ballot box and flagrant fraud, all in the name of Islam. It was an ugly moment of disrespect for God and man. It will not stand."[57]

Ervand Abrahamian, history professor at City University of New York, was not at all shocked when Ayatollah Ali Khamenei moved to rapidly suppress the election protests:

> The authorities have the ability and the experience to suppress. They trained the Revolutionary Guards for that purpose for twenty years. But at the same time, they know that ruling by force will not help their legitimacy. They may be able to stop the protests, but they won't restore their credibility.... When they announced Ahmadinejad's victory, people in the villages were as angry as those in the cities.[58]

What will happen to the unrest boiling beneath the surface in Iran? Will it seethe and ferment and one day explode into the type of revolution that saw the departure of the Shah of Iran and the arrival of *shariah* law as dictated by the wily cleric with the hooded eyes—Ruhollah Khomeini? We forget that the ousting of the Shah didn't happen overnight. Khomeini's students began to circulate his sermons on cassette tape in 1977, but the final blow to the Shah didn't come until 1979. Khomeini's revolution stunned the leaders of other Islamic countries and was the initial challenge by fanatical Muslims to prove that Islam was the solution to all the world's problems. It was a bold experiment placed on trial in Iran. The Shah learned too late just how much Khomeini's experiment would cost him and the country.

As Thomas Friedman wrote about the events of 1979, "The Shah controlled the army, the SAVAK secret police, and a vast network of oil-funded patronage...people taking to the streets and defying his authority, and taking bullets as well, broke the Shah's spell. All the Shah's horses and all the Shah's men couldn't put his regime back together again."[59]

In was during 1978 that the Ayatollah successfully unified the sundry fragments into a cohesive anti-Pahlavi faction, proof that revolution doesn't happen quickly. Therefore, there is still hope for the anti-Ahmadinejad and by association anti-Khamenei faction in Iran to succeed in its attempt to enact democratic freedoms in the country.

Khomeini, who to untrained and uneducated Westerners seemed to appear from out of nowhere, had in fact been fomenting revolution from Najaf, Iraq, for years. After seizing control in Iran, he introduced the very form of law, *velayat-e-faqih*, or rule by a supreme religionist, which has Iran in an iron grip today. Today's supreme jurist, Ali Khamenei, has declared in no uncertain terms that the elections have been sanctioned by Allah—or as he put it "divine assessment."

Following the reelection of Ahmadinejad, the dissent grew strong enough that many were emboldened to take to the streets in protest against Khamenei and his strong-armed tactics. Of course, the protests were attributed to "The Great Satan"—America—to Israel and, surprisingly, to Great Britain. Such far-fetched accusations may sound a bit suspect to many Iranians, but sadly, not to all. Some will continue to believe Ahmadinejad's vitriolic rhetoric. He has to have someone to blame for Iran's ills, and who better than America? If that ploy were removed from his bag of tricks, how would he explain the country's problems to the Iranian people?

With memories of how Khomeini fostered revolution and then benefited from it, Khamenei was compelled to recognize the need for a post-mortem on the election. He knows, of course, that his ham-fisted hold on power is more tenuous than ever before. Millions, and perhaps the majority of Iranians have seen the emperor's imperfections and heard his lies. He will never again be able to recapture the adulation in which he was once held. His rule will now be that of a dictator holding the strings of his hand-picked puppet. His regime has lost its validity—if indeed it ever possessed any.

A courageous young Iranian reporter who covered events in Iran for *The Jerusalem Post* said:

> I think people recognize that the anger and bitterness at the regime is acute among the young Iranians. I'm talking about youngsters who've been watching Western TV for years, on the little satellite dishes everybody hides in their air-conditioning units, and want those freedoms...well-educated youngsters, graduates, who can't find work....They're aware that the Revolutionary Guards, the military face of the regime, are becoming increasingly powerful—that Iran is tending toward military dictatorship...the slogans of thirty years ago [are] now being directed at those who were supposed to be the guardians of the revolution.[60]

The emperor now stands naked before his subjects. All the silks, satins, and brocades hiding the ugliness of his rule have been stripped away. His hand-picked president is no more than a court jester appointed to deceive the Iranian people with his smoke-and-mirrors act. Ahmadinejad has garnered followers of his Twelver sect, which now totals some 80 percent of the population, by promising a soon-return of the Mahdi. This is the twenty-first century, and modern-day Iranians are finding it difficult to live separately but peacefully with those Shia still stuck in centuries past.

> Iran has squandered a huge opportunity to bridge the gulf between the regime and an increasingly sophisticated population thirsting for greater freedom. A vibrant election campaign opened a door. It has been slammed shut.... Over the past week [Iran] has looked more like a flag-bearing police state.... Khamenei...has looked more like a ruthless infighter.[61]

Cracks have become chasms too great to bridge. Tyranny has become sweeping and vicious. The leadership has lost an entire new generation. Iran's global oratory has been uncovered for what it is—meaningless. Ahmadinejad and the emperor, Khamenei, have lost all credibility. They have prevailed—for the moment—but the cost has been enormous.

Events in Iran herald no mere skirmish between oppression and liberty. The government has not been toppled, yet the political scene has been altered, fidelity extinguished, and the supposed infallibility of Iran's supreme leader obliterated. Khamenei has had to resort to diatribes against non-existent interference from outside influences. He has been reduced to backing Ahmadinejad, the man whose term as president has been divisive at best. One Iranian politician who wished to remain anonymous for obvious reasons said, "This man, Ahmadinejad, is destroying the whole system of the Islamic Republic, which includes Mr. Khamenei. But Mr. Khamenei supports him because he sits like a mouse in front of him and kisses his feet."[62] In the past year, and contrary to the counsel of his peers, Khamenei tied his wagon to Ahmadinejad's star. Rather than the court jester basking in the glow of the emperor, the reverse seems to be true.

Perhaps sensing an opportunity to wrest power from the ruling ayatollah, other clerics seized the opportunity to take sides in the struggle. Yes, the mullahs are divided, some siding with Ahmadinejad and puppet-master Khamenei and others with Moussavi and cleric Seyed Mohammad Khatami, a liberal reformer. As a former president of Iran, Khatami's modifications were thwarted by the Guardian Council before he could achieve any real success. It was because of him the ruling clerics apparently determined all elections, while seemingly democratic in nature, had to be manipulated to insure the victory of the chosen and anointed candidate.

Since 2003 the Guardian Council—the entity charged with vetting candidates——has enacted even more stringent guidelines as to who may or may not run for the office of president. As one editorialist pointed out, "What may seem more surprising is that so many prominent first-generation revolutionaries have sided with Mr. Moussavi.... Even among the clergy, the best minds...have distanced themselves from Ayatollah Khamenei."[63] Moussavi was supported by former presidents Ali Akbar Hashemi Rafsanjani and Mohammad Khatami.

On July 17, a month after the election, Rafsanjani addressed the Iranian people during Friday prayers. In his sermon the cleric and former president of Iran was highly disparaging of the government hard-liners, even when he applauded the unity among the people of Iran. He certainly did not toe the line of official propaganda being spouted by Khamenei and Ahmadinejad. The cleric pointed out the inequities between what was happening in Iran and the teachings of Mohammad, especially when it came to treating the populace with kindness and respect taught by the prophet.

Rafsanjani's sermon was summarized by Muhammad Sahimi:

Rafsanjani's sermons demonstrated the glaring fissures in the leadership of the Islamic Republic. The fact that (a) he called the present conditions a crisis; (b) acknowledged that many clerics and ayatollahs are unhappy with what has happened, contrary to the claims by the hard-liners that the clergy are unified behind them; (c) stated that whatever he speaks of are the results of his consultations with two powerful organs of the Islamic Republic, namely the Expediency Council and the Assembly of Experts; (d) he did not mention even once the supreme leader; (e) he acknowledged that people doubt the election, that people's trust in the system had been destroyed, and he blamed the voice and visage of the Islamic Republic and the Guardian Council for it; and (f) always contrasted what the hard-liners do with what the Prophet and Imam Ali did, in order to demonstrate the false-hood of their claims that they are the true followers of the two revered Islamic figures, demonstrated that he has sided with the people in the crisis. That is bound to reinvigorate the democratic movement.[64]

Dr. David Menashri, director at the Center for Iranian Studies, decries the actual process of selecting candidates which eliminates about 50 percent of the population—the women. In a telephone conference arranged by The Israel Project, Dr. Menashri said these shadow citizens of Iran "have been disqualified because they do not fit the criteria.... [Only] four candidates...[were] approved by the council of experts and deemed acceptable by the ruling elite...what the Iranians are electing is a president in a system in which the president in the best of times can be considered as like the vice-president of the United States." He went on to say, "The council of guardians...disqualified seven hundred candidates...but does not even need to explain why a person is being disqualified."[65]

Dr. Menashri believes Ahmadinejad accomplished two major objectives during his first term in office: He challenged the world regarding Iran's nuclear proliferation; and he "painted all other Iranian officials as moderate pragmatists...[and himself as] more extremist, radical, conservative."[66]

One Iranian writer, Azadeh Moaveni, documents the treatment of women since Ahmadinejad assumed office. She writes that without warning the government of Iran changed the dress code. It resulted in the arrest of 150,000 women whose dress had not previously been questioned. Mosveni wrote: "We were all afraid to leave the house, because it was obvious the authorities were out to make a point, arresting even women who were 'sufficiently covered.'" The author was cited for inappropriate dress even though she was wearing the same attire she had worn for years.[67]

Women, the most repressed in the country since the Islamic revolution under Khomeini, took to the streets in celebration of a much-hoped-for Moussavi rout of Ahmadinejad. One of them would pay the ultimate price for her scant participation in the post-election protests. Nada Agha Soltan, a twenty-six-year-old student, paid with her life. She was gunned down during the melee and bled to death on the streets of Tehran. It is significant that her name means "voice." When Ayatollah Khomeini said that "women in the streets double the strength of the men,"[68] I am certain he didn't mean in the case of opposition to his Islamic dictates. Nada—the silenced voice—became the rallying cry for the protesters.

Almost a month after the election the Association of Researchers and Teachers of Qom, a group of influential clerics, issued a statement calling the election "illegitimate" and condemning the treatment of the protesters. It is a rare show of contempt for Khamenei, who had vowed he would not abide any objections to Ahmadinejad's so-called win.

An Iranian analyst called it a "clerical mutiny." Professor Ali Ansari, the head of Iranian Studies at St. Andrews University, observed: "It's highly significant. It shows this is nowhere near resolved."

According to another observer, "The association's statement also shows how deeply the political establishment is divided, and the extent to which the supreme leader now derives his power from military might, not moral authority. It makes it much harder for the regime to arrest Mr. Moussavi and other opposition leaders."[69]

The mullahs who are in power seized that power by revolution in 1979; they have seen what a united Iranian people can do. This is what Khamenei fears and why he has vowed that a "street challenge is not acceptable."

These mullahs have perfected the art of enmity over the past three decades. In spite of the hatred for all things Western spewing from the mouths of these supposed leaders, the youth of Iran are as passionate about freedom as the mullahs are about repression. I support the Iranian people who want to be free from oppression; yet at the same time, I fear for them. The upheaval that will surely come if they wage a successful revolution would change the complexion of the Middle East—just how dramatically, no one really knows. The challenge is great.

The uprising of angry and frustrated Iranians following the election should have been enough to cause despotic Islamic regimes worldwide to listen for the unmistakable sounds of discontent and displeasure among the populace. Iran is outdistanced only by Saudi Arabia when it comes to funding Islamic schools, organizations, Muslim ideology, and military training. It must send a shiver down the backs of those who rely on Iran to sponsor their terrorist organizations and train the next wave of jihadists. After all,

"From Somalia to Lebanon's Hezbollah, from Hamas to the Egyptian Shiite movement, Iranian support—whether through direct funding or military and training—will be jeopardized if the theocrats are unseated."[70] The uprising in Iran, though seemingly brief, may have severely weakened its ability to continue to send abroad its version of Khomeini's Islamic revolution.

Egyptian expert in international affairs, Emad Gad, wrote:

I think Ahmadinejad will concentrate in the economic field to improve living conditions for his population after this crisis. That means less giving money, less meddling, less penetration in the Arab world, less involvement. The Arab leaders are watching and they are very pleased. The Ahmadinejad after this election will be very different than the Ahmadinejad before this election. He will be weaker.[71]

Also affected will be Iran's support for well-known Muslim organizations in Europe, North America, and South America. Oliver Javanpour wrote:

The number of organizations receiving funding and support from Iranians is probably in the hundreds, if not the thousands.... The global Muslim theocracy movement [as inspired by Ayatollah Khomeini] is in danger at the hands of the Iranian people not only financially, but also in terms of the legitimacy of theocracy as a political system.[72]

The psychological impact of recent events in Iran may be more longlasting than the brutal injuries inflicted on the protestors. The results may be an even more vicious crackdown by those who rule by bullet and rifle butt, or it could be the earthquake that levels the playing field and brings an uprising that will literally rock the Islamic world. It is impossible at this juncture to determine the ultimate outcome, but it is safe to say it has the potential to change the theocracy in Iran and send shockwaves from its epicenter to other fanatical Muslim regimes wherever they may cower in concern.

One of the problems with the street protests was that Moussavi, the leader who prompted the demonstrations, was not seen in public for a week following the announced outcome. Mir Hossein Moussavi, the man for whom many were willing to risk life and limb, was nowhere to be found. Thus, the revolution during that time was without an organizer, without someone to carry the banner at the head of the parade.

Meanwhile, Iranians wounded during the protests were reportedly arrested and taken from the hospitals where they were being treated for wounds received during the violent crackdown by the Basij militia. The dissenters seeking reform took to the streets in support of their candidate. One unidentified woman indicated that while injured during one of the rallies, she feared going to the hospital. She said, "The point is, when they [the wounded] are taken to the hospital, they don't actually get there."[73] Sarah Lee Whitson, director for Human Rights Watch in the Middle East reported, "While most of the world's attention is focused on the beatings in the streets of Iran during the day, the Basij are carrying out brutal raids on people's apartments at night.?[74]

According to The New York Times, scores of the Basij involved in the crackdown were what is termed Joojeh Gasiji—or "chicken Basiji." Just as Khomeini used the children of Iran as minesweepers during the Iran/Iraq war, so Ahmadinejad has gathered a group of teens to mindlessly do his bidding. These youngsters have barely reached puberty, yet they are sent out into the streets to wield bat and club against their fellow citizens. It is reminiscent of Nazi Germany's Hitler Jugend—the youth movement under the barbaric German dictator. Ahmadinejad's children soldiers came face-to-face with the Iranian students longing for freedom. Roger Cohen wrote of one young woman who emailed:

> *I wrote [this] for the next generation so that they know we were not just emotional under peer pressure. So that they know we did everything we could to create a better future for them. So they know that our ancestors surrendered to Arabs and Mongols but did not surrender to despotism. This note is dedicated to tomorrow's children.*[75]

The Basij movement was founded by Ayatollah Khomeini in 1979; it was to be his insurmountable twenty-million-man militia. Its assignment was to help usher in Khomeini's infamous Islamic rebellion. The Basij, a supplementary arm of the Revolutionary Guard, was to defend the ideology of the revolution. Initially staffed with underage children and men too old to serve Iran as members of the Revolutionary Guard, little was heard from this group until it was marshaled for "crowd control" following the 2009 presidential elections in Iran. Prior to that time the Basij's major claim to fame had been its service during the Iran-Iraq War.

It was the younger members of the group—the children—who were used as minesweepers for advancing Iranian troops. Michael Eisenstadt, senior fellow and director of The Washington Institute's Military and Security Studies Program, described the citizen army: "Basij members made up with zeal what they lacked in military professionalism......I think cannon fodder is a fair way to characterize them."[76]

Having been whipped into a suicidal frenzy by Khomeini's promise of the perks of martyrdom, these young Basij died by the tens of thousands. Following the end of the war, the citizen militia became the dreaded morality police. They enforce *hijab*, making certain women are covering the head and dressing modestly and arresting women who violate the dictated dress code. They arrest young men and women who dare to attend parties together or appear in public with someone of the opposite sex who is not a family member. The Basij is also charged with confiscating material deemed "indecent." This includes the satellite dish antennae carefully hidden by a vast number of Iranians.

In an interview with Sabina Amidi of the *Jerusalem Post*, one Basij member who requested anonymity revealed how Ahmadinejad moved young recruits into Tehran following the June election. He told of youngsters who had been imported from smaller villages in Iran to help control the protesters:

> *Fourteen and fifteen-year-old boys are given so much power, which I am sorry to say they have abused. These kids do anything they please—forcing people to empty out their wallets, taking whatever they want from stores without paying, and touching young women inappropriately. The girls are so frightened that they remain quiet and let them do what they want.*[77]

Perhaps the most chilling aspect of the interview with this Basiji was his description of how young Iranian girls are prepared for execution and his own role in the process. In Iran it is forbidden to execute a virgin regardless of what she may have done. Not willing to be deterred by the law, the authorities force the young women to "wed" one of the prison guards the night before her appointed execution. The interviewee was one of the temporary husbands:

> *The young girl is forced to have sexual intercourse with a prison guard—essentially raped by her "husband." I could tell that the girls were more afraid of their "wedding" night than of the execution that awaited them in the morning. And they would always fight back, so we would have to put sleeping pills in their food. By morning the girls would have an empty expression; it seemed like they were ready or wanted to die.*[78]

Following their "wedding night" the young women were summarily executed for their "crimes."

Ali Alfoneh, a fellow at the American Enterprise Institute in Washington, D.C., who studies the relationship between the Revolutionary Guard and the people of Iran, answers the question of how the Basij are funded: "Through the mosques, they have funds, ideological and political indoctrination, and military training."[79] The Basij are not untrained rabble patrolling the streets of the cities of Iran; they are a brutal militia at the beck-and-call of Mahmoud Ahmadinejad and Ali Khamenei.

How many times would the protesters be willing to suffer the beatings, the raids on schools and hospitals, the tear gas and gunfire at the hands of the Basij before being disheartened and fading into the alleys and side streets of Tehran? The question may also be asked: How far will the regime go to maintain its grasp on power? Is it willing to authorize massive killings by having the Revolutionary Guard and Basij fire into the midst of the demonstrators?

Protesters who were taken captive reported that they watched as fellow prisoners were beaten to death while being interrogated. Others were forced to lick toilet bowls as punishment, and some were tortured by having their fingernails ripped away. A *New York Times* report indicated:

> *More bruised corpses have been returned to families.... The prison abuses have also galvanized the opposition.... One young man posted an account of his ordeal at the Kahrizak camp, "We were all standing so close to each other that no one could move. The plainclothes guards came into the room and broke all the light bulbs and in the pitch dark started beating us, whoever they could." He added that by morning four detainees were dead.*[80]

For that matter, who is really in charge in Iran? Is it Khamenei, the supreme leader? Is it the Revolutionary Guard? Is it Ahmadinejad and his Basij militia? These are questions political analysts have bandied about for some time. Some believe the Shiite clergy has a stranglehold on the country. Others believe control may lie within the army, the guardian of the arms and ammunition necessary to repress uprisings. Just who holds the authority and how much has yet to be determined...possibly by the Iranians themselves.

Bernard Hourcade, a French expert on Iran, confirmed the situation:

> I don't know who has the power, and that is the problem in Iran. It's anarchy. No one has got the power. It's dangerous for the people of Iran. It's dangerous for everybody.[81]

A fissure in the façade of civility between Ahmadinejad and Khamenei opened up following the election. The supreme leader objected to the president's choice of Esfandiar Rahim Mashai as first vice president in charge of tourism and culture. He is one of twelve vice presidents in the Iranian hierarchy. Khamenei issued an order to Ahmadinejad to dismiss the vice president; Ahmadinejad refused. One of the concerns stems from the fact that Mashai is a son-in-law to the president. The president's refusal of a direct order from the supreme leader is a surprising turn of events.

During his four-year tenure Ahmadinejad has spent his time establishing a network of cronies in the military, law enforcement, and within the media. It is estimated he has infiltrated the government with more than ten thousand men loyal to him alone. One analyst wrote, "There is a whole political establishment that has emerged with Ahmadinejad, which is now determined to hold onto power undemocratically. Their ability to resist the outcome of the election means they have a broad base...[including but certainly not limited to] all thirty of the country's governors, all the city managers, and even third- and fourth-level civil servants."[82]

Iran's president also enjoys a number of writers and bloggers among his elite supporters. One such supporter, Fatemeh Rajabi, "harridan of the hard right," has proposed that "Mr. Moussavi face the death penalty for promoting anti-government demonstrations.[83]

. . . .

CHAPTER 4

THE PRESIDENT'S
RESPONSE

*The Obama administration came into office with a
realpolitik script to goad the mullahs into a "grand bargain"
on its nuclear program. But Team Obama isn't proving
to be good at the improv.*[84]

During the early days of the rallies while Iranian protesters were being beaten and bloodied, where was President Obama? Even after a tepid response to events in Iran, it seems he was determined to remain aloof to the cries of the people of Iran in favor of doing nothing. He seemed focused on trying to preserve the possibility of negotiating with the very cleric who holds the Iranian people under his thumb...Ayatollah Ali Khamenei—the man who ordered the bloody crackdown on those who voted for Mir Hussein Moussavi—a man so paranoid he had the challenger's supporters arrested.

The young men and women of Iran who stood up to Ahmadinejad and then had their votes stolen waited eleven days for President Obama to issue a supportive statement. It came after the deaths and arrests of a multitude of protestors. We may never know the full extent of the sacrifices many Iranians made in an attempt to demand accountability and a fair election from the Supreme leader.

To many observers, it seemed President Obama was reluctant to assume the mantle of leadership, which he so assiduously sought in November 2008. The leader of the free world, a cloak most U.S. presidents have willingly assumed, didn't quite fit the shoulders of President Obama. He appeared more comfortable standing in the shadows than on center stage, a spot in which he excelled during the election.

Unlike John F. Kennedy, who boldly declared his allegiance to the freedom seekers in Berlin with the now famous *"Ich bin ein Berliner,"* Obama failed to take a stand. And unlike Ronald Reagan's extraordinary demand on June 12, 1987, "Mr. Gorbochev, tear down this wall," Mr. Obama's memorable words were the meek and unassertive, "America does not presume to know what is best for everyone." It was more reminiscent of the Carter administration's response to the overthrow of the Shah. Secretary of State Cyrus Vance said halfheartedly that the U.S. "does not intend to interfere in the affairs of another country."[85]

Shmuley Boteach, a writer for *The Jerusalem Post,* has taken exception to President Obama's statement:

> *We don't presume to know that elections are better than dictator-ships? We don't presume to know that women beaten in the streets for showing an elbow is brutal and refusing to let them ride a bicycle is a form of gender apartheid? Rarely before has an American president spoken out in favor of moral relativism [there is no objective right or wrong]. So much for the Declaration of Independence, which was written by Thomas Jefferson as a universal proclamation of human liberty asserting that freedom is an "inalienable" right possessed by each of God's children....*

Real leadership does not involve having the best mouth but rather the most courageous heart.[86]

The vicious treatment of the protesters following the stolen election was said to be "a clenched fist shoved in Obama's face."[87]

In his first lackluster comments, the president lauded Khamenei because of his "initial reaction." What was the reaction? According to Obama, the "supreme leader…understands the Iranian people have deep concerns about the election." The president inexplicably lauded the man for giving a preposterous answer that did nothing to correct the bogus election. Deep concerns, you say? A fanatical cleric supports a tyrannical president whose underlings wade into an unarmed crowd with guns and clubs wielded against people who are protesting fraud and corruption. In his belated statement Obama offered no support of any kind for the hopeful protestors seeking justice and change.

To add insult to injury, an unidentified U.S. State Department employee confirmed that embassies abroad had been encouraged to "invite representatives from the government of Iran" to attend Independence Day 2009 events. With his smoke-and-mirror show, Obama made America an international laughingstock. He later withdrew the directive.

The French government, on the other hand, responded immediately to the brutal retaliation by the Iranian regime. Foreign Ministry spokesman Eric Chevallier delivered a statement that read in part, "France condemns the brutal repression of peaceful protests and the repeated attacks on the liberty of the press and freedom of speech."[88]

Israel's Prime Minister Benjamin Netanyahu was asked in an interview with German newspaper *Bild* if a Moussavi win would have been beneficial to Israel. He replied:

What would be good news for Israel is a regime that stops crushing dissent, stops supporting terror, and stops trying to build nuclear weapons. It would mean a regime that stops denying the Holocaust and stops threatening Israel with destruction. There is no conflict between the Iranian people and the people of Israel, and under a different regime the friendly relations that prevailed in the past could be restored.[89]

The *Financial Times* reported that Franco Frattini, Italy's foreign minister, had advised the G8 to adopt a firm posture with Iran. According to Mr. Frattini, Iran's interaction with the outside world had come to "a turning point."[90] Just what Italy and the G8 were prepared to do was not divulged by the Italian. The first day of the summit in L'Aquila, Italy the group issued a communiqué, which stated:

G8 countries continue to be seriously concerned about recent events in Iran. Interference with the media, unjustified detentions of journalists, and recent arrests of foreign nationals are unacceptable. Embassies in Iran must be permitted to exercise their functions effectively under the Vienna Convention without arbitrary restrictions on or intimidation of their staff.[91]

While Ahmadinejad supporters in Iran were shouting "Death to America" and "Death to Israel," another demonstration some twenty-thousand-strong was taking place just outside Paris. The organizer, Maryam Rajavi, leader of the Mujahedeen-e Khalq, an opposition group, stood before the crowd and censured the Iranian government for its crimes against the protesters and for flagrantly exporting its revolution to countries outside Iran—including Lebanon, the Palestinian Authority, and Afghanistan. Ms. Rajavi did not exempt Obama from criticism for seeking to open discussions with Khamenei's regime.

The question then became: Did President Obama fully comprehend that events in Iran following the 2009 election really had nothing to do with the fraudulent election and everything to do with freedom? Men and women weren't willing to die for a vote recount; they were willing to lay down their lives for the right to be heard. They were not protesting faux ballots; they were protesting the despotic limitations imposed on them by the tyrannical clerics—the likes of Khamenei—who really run the country.

Iran is not a democracy, although the leaders try to give that impression through its fraudulent elections. It is simply a terror state that was born when a terrorist, Ayatollah Khomeini, and tens of thousands of terrorists who followed him took over the country.

How would President Obama have reacted had the Revolutionary Guard and its rabid voluntary paramilitary force, the Basij, decided to open fire on and mow the protestors down by the thousands in an attempt to halt the protests? Would he have remained aloof if cleric Ahmad Khatami, a member of the Assembly of Experts, had persuaded the Iran judiciary to charge those arrested as *mohareb* or warriors against God? According to Khatami, "They should be punished ruthlessly and savagely." According to Muslim law the punishment is execution.

Mr. Obama took office vowing to extend a hand to America's adversaries. Former President Jimmy Carter held a similar worldview of the Soviet Union, promising to "cure our inordinate fear of communism."[92] The Soviets responded to Carter's naïveté by invading Afghanistan.

Carter's initial awe of Khomeini resulted in his being forced to hand over $7.9 billion to the Iranian in an attempt to secure the release of the American Embassy hostages taken captive in Tehran.

If President Obama cannot use diplomacy to support a fledgling cry for democracy, his extended hand to Iran's ruling mullahs had better have a whole lot more money in it than did Carter's.

Will Obama withhold support to those seeking régime change in Tehran? There is a reason the signs carried by the dissenters were in English; they love the freedom for which America stands. Should the U.S. abandon the "green movement" in Iran, we will have the blood of countless men and women on our hands. Do not our basic principles as a nation dictate that we stand with those who oppose a system that is the exact opposite of what we Americans believe?

As president Obama seems more intent on negotiating with the sworn enemies of the United States, i.e., Ayatollah Ali Khamenei and his purveyors of terror, than with those who seek freedom in Iran. Obama has learned all too well Carter's mating dance with terrorists, while ascribing to them altruistic acts and legitimizing terrorism and those who carry out such heinous attacks.

Mr. Obama extended a hand to the Iranian leadership prior to the June 12 elections. He was lauded by the Liberal Left for his moralistic confidence in negotiation as opposed to George W. Bush's cowboy tactics. If—and that's a big "if"—Mr. Obama succeeds in luring Ahmadinejad to grasp his hand, his palm will be forever tainted with the blood of those who died during the protests. Perhaps he will know, firsthand, how difficult it was for Lady Macbeth to try to scrub away the blood of Duncan.[93]

For some reason Obama cannot fully accept his culpability should he pursue talks with Iran's bloody regime. In a press conference more than a week following the fierce street clashes, the president finally condemned the outrages in Iran in terms he should have used a week before, but he also kept alive the idea that the current Iranian regime could be a fruitful negotiation partner, despite what has already happened in that country. "It's not too late," Obama explained, for the regime to negotiate with the international community.

President Obama was given a legitimate chance to support change for the good of the Iranian populace. He had an opportunity to respond vigorously to those whom poet Emma Lazarus described on the Statue of Liberty as "your tired, your poor, your huddled masses yearning to breathe free." Will he stand with the freedom-seekers, or has President Obama truly become another Jimmy Carter? He does seem to be following in Mr. Carter's footsteps; it was Carter who recognized the Islamic Republic of the Ayatollah Ruhollah Khomeini with catastrophic results.

America's forty-fifth president has all but acquiesced to Iran's nuclear course. Even during the election process Mr. Obama signified that he was agreeable to a meeting with the regime without preconditions, an indication taken to be weakness on the part of the American president. Ahmadinejad has declared the issue closed, not worthy of talks with the leader of "The Great Satan." He has rebuffed the advances of a man who apparently wants to dance with Iran. Ahmadinejad feels he is in the driver's seat, and unless a backbone transplant is in the offing, Mr. Obama, like America's thirty-ninth president to whom he has been compared, will find it difficult if not impossible to engage the leaders in Iran from a position of weakness.

Apparently the president believes he can somehow talk Ahmadinejad into aborting his defiant plan to arm Iran with nuclear bombs. He clings to the possibility of diplomacy as a drowning man clings to a jellyfish; it's all goo, no substance. *Foreign Policy* contributor Laura Rozen wrote of Obama's agenda:

> *"Obama is dedicated to diplomacy in a manner that is almost*

ideological," one Iran hand in touch with the administration said. "Obama has a longer-term vision," he continued. "He wants to do some stuff in the Middle East over the next eight years. He may not be able to achieve half of them unless he gets this huge piece of the puzzle [Iran] right."[94]

Mr. Obama seems intent on bringing about some majestic Middle East messianic makeover, where he magically eradicates any threat of nuclear peril from Iran. His next miracle could be to force Israel to the bargaining table to accede to the demands of the Road Map gang. Then he could accept the adulation for doing what other presidents before him failed to do—achieve peace in the Middle East.

As the Iranian people risk their lives to be heard, President Obama refuses to see the country that is "terror central" as an evil empire. How long will it be before he realizes that stopping the Mahmoud Ahmadinejad's and Ali Khamenei's of this world will require more than an unclenched fist, more than a cordial handshake?

Will the events in Iran, as a result of a campaign that called for hope and change, launch a rowboat that will be overtaken and swamped by the waves of repression? Or will they launch a ship of state sufficient in size, strength, and determination to overcome the storm and set sail on a path that will turn the tide of thirty long years of tyranny in Iran?

Ahmadinejad might have provided a clue when he finally addressed the Iranian people on July 7, 2009—nearly a month after his purported "landslide victory." While the reform candidates worked to reawaken the opposition, Ahmadinejad took center stage. With a straight face he declared, "This is a new beginning for Iran...we have entered a new era. It was the most clean and free election in the world...no fault was discovered."[95] It sounds more like "business as usual" for the pint-sized president and his exposed emperor.

Mahmoud Ahmadinejad has been anointed by Supreme Leader Khamenei to continue his quest for nuclear arms. Although not a follower of the Mahdi, the Ayatollah has nevertheless thrown his lot in with his choice of Ahmadinejad. With the full backing of the cleric, the president can now proceed full-speed-ahead with nuclear proliferation. There is nothing to stop his march toward an apocalyptic event that would result in the return of the Mahdi; nothing to prevent an attack on the U.S. or Israel that would ignite World War III—and usher in the rule of the antichrist, who will head a worldwide government.

According to the Bible this son of perdition, as the antichrist is called, will be acclaimed as the savior of the world for three-and-a-half years; then he will show his true colors. His plan will be heralded as the very one needed to rescue the economy, promote political goodwill, ease military hostilities, and insure freedom of worship for all. After three-and-a-half years, he will set himself up as the one to be worshipped and will allow no obeisance to any other. He will create havoc and will bring times upon the world such as have never been seen before. His cruelty will surpass that of Hitler and those before him who were merciless, ruthless, and vicious. The second half of his rule will be marked by plagues such as mankind has never imagined. It will begin the countdown to Armageddon.

To fully understand how the U.S. has reached this point in its relationship with Iran, we must take a look back through time. The Persian people have a rich and varied history filled with both beauty and strife. They have close ties to the Israelites...a fact that Mahmoud Ahmadinejad and his ilk would like to forget. From Esther and Mordecai to Daniel, Shadrach, Meshach, and Abednego; from Ezra and Nehemiah to Cyrus the Great; there are unforgettable stories of God's deliverance of his people from the hands of those whose only wish for them was destruction. Today Israel is faced once again with threats of an impending Armageddon from a leader whose predominant exercise seems to be rattling the sabers of war and spewing threats of an impending apocalypse.

How did the United States reach this lowly state of weakness from the position of strength it enjoyed during the reign of the Shah? Many believe the answer can be found at the knee of another presidential hopeful who touted hope and change like Mr. Obama. The fault of the cataclysmic upheaval in the land of the shahs rests on Jimmy Carter's shifting policies in the Persian Gulf region. We must, therefore, take a look at the past in order to determine how it affects the future.

In an attempt to illustrate the importance of history, a teacher in New York City stood at the blackboard before his class of sixth-grade students. On the new dry-erase board, he wrote "1." Then he asked, "What is that?"

The class responded, "ONE!"

The teacher added a second "1" beside the first. "What is that?"

"ELEVEN," the class shouted even more loudly. He turned back to the board and wrote the number "9" before the two ones. The class didn't wait to be prompted, but shouted, "NINE!"

The teacher smiled. "What is that?"

"9-1-1," called the excited students.

"Why didn't you say nine hundred eleven? Why did you say

9-1-1?" he asked.

"Because, that's the number you call when you need help—9-1-1," answered one student.

Another youngster sat silently. The teacher noticed his downcast eyes and a tear glistening on his cheek. "Tommy, what does 9-1-1 mean to you?"

"It's the day my daddy died in one of the Twin Towers," he answered with a shaky voice. "I was just a tiny baby. My mom cried and cried; she still cries when she talks about it."

The class didn't realize what had just happened. None of them had ever had to dial 9-1-1 for help; none except Tommy had lost a loved one on September 11, 2001.

The other children were responding in the present—based on current events. Tommy's response was firmly linked to the past and the terror that had colored it.

The teacher used the moment to teach his students a valuable lesson. He explained that the children had been taught to think of the numbers 9, 1, and 1 as 911, because they had been taught to dial that number in an emergency. Only Tommy thought of the numbers as 9/11, because that date had great significance for him. He was interpreting the present through events in his past.

If we want to change people's perception of the present, we have to change their perception of the past. We must write history in a way that it will not be forgotten and diluted by those who wish to forget that the United States of America was attacked by terrorists not "freedom fighters" on 9/11. The past affects our future; we must not bury our heads in the sand and pretend it was a lone attack. I have often quoted Edmund Burke, who said, "Those who don't know history are destined to repeat it." If we choose not to learn from the past, we will have no future.

CHAPTER 5

. . . .

A STROLL THROUGH
THE PAGES OF PERSIAN HISTORY

*"No one is fool enough to choose war
instead of peace—in peace sons bury their fathers
but in war fathers bury sons."* (CROESUS)[96]

Persia. The very word evokes images of kings and princes and tales of Arabian nights, of Scheherazade, the teller of 1001 stories of cunning and derring-do in an attempt to save her own life. As the daughter of the grand vizier, she caught the eye of Shahryar, who was known for marrying a new virgin every morning and sending the previous day's wife to be beheaded. He was betrayed by his first wife and felt he had devised a means to insure it would never happen again.

Knowing there had been some three thousand wives before her, Scheherazade was determined not to be number 3001. She studied the books of Persian history and legends in order to prepare for her "night with the king." Having enlisted the help of her sister beforehand, the new queen made a final request of Shahryar before being led away to the chopping block: She asked to say goodbye to her sibling.

Dinazade, her sister, asked Scheherazade to tell her a story before being dragged away. The gifted storyteller spun a tale that so intrigued the king, he spared her night after night until Scheherazade had spun 1001 tales, the next more exciting and spellbinding than the last. The king became so enchanted with his wifely entertainer that he made her Queen Consort. Legend has it she bore the king three sons.

However, Persia was not solely known for the tales of *1001 Arabian Nights*. Among other things, they achieved mind-boggling engineering feats and created the first postal system. While chess was first introduced in India, it is the Persians who are recognized as having perfected and promulgated the brainy game. They were masterful engineers, credited with pioneering an inventive plan for water management, building a paved roadway that stretched fifteen hundred miles across Persia, and digging a waterway to link the Nile to the Red Sea. With design assistance from Greek architects, the Persians helped fashion one of the Seven Wonders of the World, the Mausoleum of Maussollos in modern-day Bodrum, Turkey.

The kingdoms of Persia and Babylonia inhabited the region that played host to the world's earliest civilizations. They are thought by most archaeological scholars to contain the site named in the Old Testament book of Genesis as the Garden of Eden. Ur of the Chaldeans, the home of Abraham, was also a part of the region that was once Babylonia—later controlled by the Persians.

At its zenith the Persian Empire encompassed the landmass from India to Greece, from the Caspian Sea to the Red Sea, and included the Arabian Sea. Its modern-day equivalent would be the countries of Pakistan, a portion of India, Afghanistan, Iran, Iraq, Syria, Turkey, Jordan, Israel, and Egypt—all combined into one vast empire.

For three millennia Iran has maintained its existence as an autonomous territory. It was the first Pahlavi, Reza Shah Pahlavi the Great, who in 1935 asked the world to stop referring to his nation as Persia and to use the name Iran instead. *Iran* means "land of the Aryans" and was the name the natives used in referring to their country.[4]

Unlike its neighbors, Iran is not Arab—it is Persian, or more correctly, Indo-European. While the Iranians use Arabic script to write, the official language of the nation is not Arabic but Farsi. Unlike its neighbors, Iran's history is not rooted in Islam but rather in the time when kings were treated as gods and massive structures were erected in their honor. Even today Iranians celebrate *No Ruz* (meaning "new day" or "New Year"). This is not a tradition of Islam but was established before Islam conquered Persia.

Cyrus the Great, the first Achaemenid emperor—and incidentally, the first king to add "Great" to his title—established the Persian Empire by uniting two of the earliest tribes in Iran, the Medes and the Persians. He ruled the extensive empire from 550–529 BCE.

Within four years of his ascension to the throne, Cyrus subjugated Croesus, the king of Lydia (of "rich as Croesus" fame), and controlled the Aegean coast of Asia Minor, Armenia, and the Greek colonies along the Levant (a large area in the Middle East bordered by the Mediterranean, the Arabian Desert, and Upper Mesopotamia). Turning eastward, Cyrus seized Parthia, Chorasmis, and Bactria. He ruled over one of the largest empires in early-recorded history. Although he conquered people after people, he was known for his unparalleled forbearance and charitable posture toward those whom he subjugated.

Cyrus and his troops marched into Babylon on October 12, 539BCE and without shedding a drop of blood apprehended Nabonidus, king of Babylon. Cyrus took the title of "King of Babylon, King of Sumer and Akkad, King of the Four Corners of the World....The Iranians regarded him as 'The Father'; Babylonians as 'The Liberator'; the Hellenes as 'Law-Giver'; and the Jews as 'The Anointed of the Lord.'"[97]

He was greeted by roars of welcome from the Jews who had been carried captive to Babylon by Nebuchadnezzar. Following his conquest of that great city, Cyrus permitted some forty thousand Jews to return to their homeland in Canaan. With such an unprecedented move Cyrus displayed great deference toward the religious tenets and social mores of other peoples.

Twenty-three times in the Old Testament we find references to Cyrus, many of them in the book of Ezra. He is praised as the king who assisted the Jews in rebuilding the Temple in Jerusalem. He sent Ezra and Nehemiah to oversee reconstruction of the Temple, as well as sending caravans of materials to aid in the building. When Nebuchadnezzar captured Jerusalem in 604BC, every precious vessel was looted from the temple and carried away to Babylonia.

When nations were conquered by the Babylonians, the idols worshiped by that people were placed in a position of subservience to Marduk, the god worshiped by the Babylonians. The Israelites were an exception. They did not worship graven images; therefore, the vessels taken from Solomon's temple were likely placed in close proximity to but not in subservience to Marduk. Cyrus authorized the return of many of the golden vessels used in Temple observances that had been taken by Nebuchadnezzar and carried off to Babylon.

Cyrus is first mentioned in 2 Chronicles 36:22-23 and in Ezra 1:1-3. Both passages record that God "moved the heart of Cyrus king of Persia" in order to fulfill "the word of the Lord spoken by Jeremiah":

> *In the first year of Cyrus king of Persia, in order to fulfill the word of the Lord spoken by Jeremiah, the Lord moved the heart of Cyrus king of Persia to make a proclamation throughout his realm and to put it in writing:*
>
> *"This is what Cyrus king of Persia says:*
>
> *"'The Lord, the God of heaven, has given me all the kingdoms of the earth and he has appointed me to build a temple for him at Jerusalem in Judah. Anyone of his people among you—may his God be with him, and let him go up to Jerusalem in Judah and build the temple of the Lord, the God of Israel, the God who is in Jerusalem.'"*[98]

Cyrus was unique, not only because he allowed the Jews to return to Israel, but also because the prophet Isaiah foretold his birth and his name almost one hundred fifty years before he was born. God also revealed Cyrus' mission to the prophet. Isaiah recorded that Cyrus would accomplish specific tasks under God's direction during his lifetime. King Cyrus was destined to carry out God's plan as it related to His chosen people. It was through Cyrus that the Babylonian Empire and seventy years of Jewish captivity came to an end.

> *Who says of Cyrus, 'He is my shepherd and will accomplish all that I please; he will say of Jerusalem, "Let it be rebuilt," and of the temple, "Let its foundations be laid."'*[99]

In 1878 CE archaeologist Hormuzd Rassam uncovered what has come to be called the Cyrus cylinder at a dig near ancient Babylon. Written in Akkadian cuneiform and now in the British Museum, the cylinder describes Cyrus' invasion of Babylon and the ensuing treatment of the Babylonian people. The cylinder has been touted as the first known pronouncement of human rights.

The Cyrus cylinder seems to confirm his humanity. He is said to have "allowed many of the nations he conquered to practice their various religious beliefs...even actively assisted captive peoples, including the Jews, to return to their lands of origin. This support was not only political but even financial—as he gave grants both from the Imperial treasury and also from his own personal fortune."[100]

The historian Herodotus records that Cyrus fell while in a battle to defend his northeastern borders from Tomyris, Queen of the Massagetae, a warrior tribe of Iranian people. It is also recorded that Tomyris was so devastated at the loss of her son, Spargapises, during the battle that upon finding Cyrus' body, she had his head immersed in a wineskin filled with blood. Cyrus was succeeded by his son Cambyses II, who attacked the Massagetae, recovered his father's body, and buried it in the city of Pasargadae. Cambyses II reigned only one year but was able to do what Cyrus could not— conquer Egypt. The Persians would rule the land of the Pharaohs for 193 years, until Alexander the Great defeated Darius III in 332 BC.

In 522 BCE Darius I wrested the Persian kingdom from the descendants of Cyrus the Great, but the establishment of his rule was fraught by skirmishes with the surrounding provinces. Darius proved to be quite the tactician. His trusted generals used the small army of Medes and Persians to great advantage and were able to solidify Darius' rule over the entire Persian Empire.

Darius was a forward-thinking ruler whose legal expertise produced the "Ordinance of Good Regulations" used to create a uniform code of law throughout the empire. He followed in the steps of Cyrus as a benevolent leader who hailed the rights of all people to co-exist under his leadership. It was Darius who instituted the satrap—or governor—system of rule throughout the empire. He directed the building of roads, seaports, banks, and canals. It was he who oversaw the construction of the canal from the Nile to the Red Sea.

An inscription that was discovered in Egypt reads: "I am a Persian. I commanded to dig this canal from a river by the name of Nile which flows in Egypt.... After this canal was dug, ships went from Egypt through this canal to Persia, thus as was my desire."[101]

Darius was also responsible for the building of a fifteen-hundred-mile long road from Sardis in Turkey to Shustar (the site of the Prophet Daniel's overnight visit to the lions' den). It allowed the postal service to deliver mail in six to nine days—unlike the era's normal three-month timeframe. This was the prototype for the Pony Express. It was from Darius's time that the U.S. Postal Service got its unforgettable motto: "Neither snow nor rain nor heat nor gloom of night stays these couriers from the swift completion of their appointed rounds."[102]

Darius I was succeeded by his son, Xerxes I—also known as Ahasuerus—the king who took the Jewess Hadassah (better known as Esther) as his queen. The story of Esther has all the elements of a modern-day love story: A beautiful, young Jewish girl is torn from her homeland and taken captive to Persia; a tyrannical ruler banishes his queen, Vashti, from the royal throne, and initiates a search for her successor; and of course there is a dastardly villain, Haman, who desires to perpetrate genocide against the Jews.

Then Haman said to King Xerxes, "There is a certain people dispersed and scattered among the peoples in all the provinces of your kingdom whose customs are different from those of all other people and who do not obey the king's laws; it is not in the king's best interest to tolerate them."[103]

Esther's uncle, Mordecai, challenges her to approach the king (a move that could be punishable by death) and ask for the salvation of her people. In encouraging her to do so, Mordecai confronts Esther with these timeless words:

> For if you remain silent at this time, relief and deliverance for the Jews will arise from another place, but you and your father's family will perish. And who knows but that you have come to royal position for such a time as this?

Esther's response to Mordecai is magnificent:

> Go, gather together all the Jews who are in Susa, and fast for me. Do not eat or drink for three days, night or day. I and my maids will fast as you do. When this is done, I will go to the king, even though it is against the law. And if I perish, I perish.[105]

With great trepidation, Esther approaches Ahasuerus and is granted an audience with the king. The plan for the destruction of the Jews by the foul villain, Haman, is thwarted and Esther's people are allowed to live in peace in Shushan.

The Persian Empire met its demise at the hands of Alexander the Great. However, he adopted many Persian customs, married Roxana, a Persian woman, and ordered his troops to take Persian wives in what might have resembled one of Rev. Sun Myung Moon's mass weddings.[106] Despite his legacy of raping the inhabitants, plundering the countryside, and destroying the city of Persepolis by fire, Alexander is credited with having exported the principles of the law formulated under Cyrus and Darius that were later implemented throughout the Roman Empire. The rule of Alexander the Great over Persia was followed by the Parthians and the Sasanians.

In 570 AD an event took place that would forever change not only the remaining once-great Persian Empire but the entire world:

The Prophet Mohammad was born. The rise of Islam—the religion founded by Muhammad ibn Abdullah, regarded by the Muslim world as a messenger and prophet of God—would result in Persians being conquered by nomads armed with a totally different weapon—a new religion. The Persian people would welcome new leadership and embrace Islam's five pillars of faith: 1) "There is no god but Allah, and Mohammad is the Prophet of Allah; 2) Prayer (to always be in touch with God); 3) Pilgrimage to Mecca; 4) Fasting in order to feel the pain of the disadvantaged and to develop self-discipline; and 5) Alms or charitable contributions."[107]

The Persian population would eventually learn that it had exchanged one tyrannical ruler for another. Under Muslim rule the Persians would be forced to forsake the Persian language in favor of Arabic, which would become the sanctioned language of the Muslim world.

Many empires fall prey to the march of time; however, in Persia—or Iran—the Arab onslaught produced a cultural mix that was unique. Persia would be dramatically influenced by the armies of Muhammad, but their conquerors would be influenced by them. Arabic became the new language, Islam became the new religion, mosques were built, and Islamic customs became the norm for the people of Persia.

It may surprise you to know that political correctness is not an invention of modern-day America; it has dictated the actions of people from the beginning of time. For many Iranian nobles conversion to Islam was a politically correct move that enabled them to keep their vast holdings and coveted social position. For others the impetus for conversion was tax evasion. Their Muslim superiors had levied an exorbitant tax against all non-Muslims, which they wished to avoid. Some Jews living in Iran were forced, on forfeiture of their lives, to convert to Islam. Zoroastrian priests simply fled the country.

Although the conquest of Iran by the Arab hordes was relatively violence-free, the ensuing struggle for leadership culminated in a bloody and lopsided battle. Hussein, the grandson of the Prophet Muhammad, and forces loyal to Caliph Yazid met on the plains of Karbala—today one of the holiest cities in Iraq. (It was to be a watershed event in Islam, for it was here that the grandson of the prophet Muhammad was beheaded. Also, it was here that the irreparable division between the Sunnis and the Shiites began.)

From 820 AD until 1220 AD under various rulers the Persians were to see a resurgence of their culture. The Persian language was revived, as were customs and mores. Scholars would discover the medicinal use of alcohol and write tomes dedicated to medicine. There was a rebirth of Persian poetry and writings, the decimal system was perfected and algebra defined, and Omar Khayyam would be born. He would pen the *Rubaiyat*, a definitive work of poetry that has subsequently been translated into numerous languages and has sold millions of copies.

Just as the name Omar Khayyam brings to mind poems of love and life, so the name of the next conqueror of Persia will forever be linked to brutality and heinous crimes against humanity— Genghis Khan. He and his horde of over seven hundred thousand fighting men invaded Persia with unequaled cruelty. His intent was to conquer the known world.

Upon his death his kingdom was divided among his male heirs. His vicious descendant, Hulagu Khan, destroyed nearly all the major cities, decimated libraries and hospitals, and massacred the inhabitants. The carnage was estimated in the range of millions of people. In 1271 Marco Polo traversed Persia on his journey to China.

He wrote: "How sad it is, the destruction, waste and death inflicted on this once mighty, prosperous, and beautiful Persia."[108]

Persia would remain under Mongol influence until the beginning of the Safavid Dynasty in 1501. After nine centuries of a fragmented Persia, Shah Ismail I, a Shia Muslim, would gather the disjointed peoples together under the banner of Shiism. It would separate them from the Sunni Muslims of the Ottoman Empire. He would be succeeded by Shah Abbas who would fashion a fighting force from the rag-tag army of Ismail I. His troops engaged and defeated the Ottomans. He was instrumental in rebuilding the infrastructure of the country and encouraging Persian artisans to ply their trade. The results included fine Persian rugs (still prized today). Persian arts and crafts were in demand worldwide for their beauty.

In 1722 Mahmoud Khan, an Afghan tribal chief, invaded Persia. His rule lasted until he was expelled by Nadir Shah. Nadir's claim to fame was the invasion of India and the capture of two of the world's most coveted diamonds. They were the Sea of Light (housed in Iran), and the Kohinoor Diamond (Mountain of Light) worn by British queens for decades. Today the diamond—all 108.93 karats—embellishes the crown of Queen Elizabeth II, accompanied by 2,800 smaller diamonds.

After Nadir Shah died in 1747, his army collapsed and the country was taken by Karim Khan Zand. His dynasty lasted a mere thirty-two years before the Qajar Dynasty assumed rule of the land. Noted as being weak and ineffectual rulers, the leaders under the Qajar Dynasty signed treaties with Russia, which gave away Georgia, Armenia, and Azerbaijan. Soon after, the Persians were forced to relinquish the area known as Afghanistan to the British.

Corruption within the dynasty ultimately led to the formation of the Majlis—Persia's first parliament-style government. The dream of establishing a constitutional monarchy such as the one in England was never realized. The nation would ultimately be divided between two early twentieth century superpowers—Russia in the north and Britain in the south and east. In 1921, following World War I, the country that would become Iran fell into chaos.

Stepping to the forefront to lead a coup against the Qajar Dynasty and its corrupt rule was Reza Khan, an army officer, who was crowned Reza Shah Pahlavi by the Majlis in April 1926. His rise to a monarchial position in Iran might be equated to the rise of Napoleon in France. The "Little General" of French fame had, at least, military training. Khan was totally a self-made man with no formal education. It is said, however, that he was an intelligent leader:

> *[Reza Shah] created an extensive system of secular primary and secondary schools and, in 1935, established the country's first European-style university in Tehran. These schools and institutions of higher education became training grounds for the new bureaucracy and, along with economic expansion, helped create a new middle class. The Shah also expanded the road network, successfully completed the trans-Iranian railroad, and established a string of state-owned factories to produce such basic consumer goods as textiles, matches, canned goods, sugar, and cigarettes.*

> *Many of the Shah's measures were consciously designed to break the power of the religious hierarchy. His educational reforms ended the clerics' near-monopoly on education. To limit further the power of the clerics, he undertook a codification of the laws that created a body of secular law, applied and interpreted by a secular judiciary outside the control of the religious establishment. He excluded the clerics from judgeships, created a system of secular courts, and transferred the important and lucrative task of notarizing documents from the clerics to state-licensed notaries. The State even encroached on the administration of vaqfs (religious endowments) and on the licensing of graduates of religious seminaries.*[109]

When World War II began, Reza Shah declared Iran to be a neutral nation. Despite the declaration of neutrality, the country was soon invaded by both Britain and the Soviet Union. The two Allies had been frustrated after the Shah rebuffed an ultimatum calling for the expulsion of all Germans from Iran. Fearing that the Shah might side with the Germans and having itself been invaded by Hitler, the Soviet Union desperately required a route by which to move war materiel. The Soviets and British allied to invade Iran in a joint attack on August 26, 1941.

Reza Khan saw the handwriting on the wall. He knew the Allied Forces would quickly remove him from power. In an attempt to preserve Iran he abdicated in favor of his twenty-two-year-old son. Reza Shah was deported to the Island of Mauritius and later to Johannesburg, South Africa. He died there in July 1944. His body was later transported to Egypt where it was embalmed and placed in the Al-Rifa'i Mosque, to be joined years later by his son, also a king in exile, Mohammad Reza Shah Pahlavi.

The young Shah was charged with guiding Iran through the war years and ultimately joined the Allies, thus giving him entry into the United Nations. As we will see in later chapters, the Shah faced his first major challenge when Prime Minister Mohammad Mossadegh took control of the nation's government and forced the Shah into a brief exile.

The Iranian people are followers of Shia Islam, founded in 661 AD by Ali ibn Abi Talib. It was from his name that Shia evolved. It is literally a derivation of *Shiat Ali*—"partisans of Ali." As a descendant of Muhammad, Ali was thought to be the last of the true caliphs. He was wildly popular until he came face-to-face in a battle with the army of the governor of Damascus in 661 AD. It is said that the Damascene soldiers attached verses from the Quran to the tips of their spears. When faced with fighting a force hiding behind the words of Muhammad, Ali's army declined to fight. Ali, left only with the option of negotiating with his enemy, sought appeasement. While he escaped death at the hands of his enemy in open combat, Ali was eventually killed by one of his own rabid followers.

When Ali died, the governor of Damascus, Mu'awiya, anointed himself caliph. Ali's son, Hassan, the rightful heir to the caliphate, died under suspicious circumstances, while the next in the line of succession, Hussein, agreed to do nothing until Mu'awiya died. He was soon disappointed yet again, however, when Mu'awiya's son, Yazid, appropriated the position of caliph and went to battle against Hussein. The bloody battle resulted in the deaths of Hussein and his army. Only Hussein's baby boy survived the carnage, and he became the hope of reestablishing Ali's claim to the caliphate.

With the ascension of Mahmoud Ahmadinejad to the position of power in Iran, we have heard much about the last known descendant of Hussein, Muhammad al-Mahdi, or the *Mahdi*. Al-Mahdi was the Twelfth Imam in the line of Ali, who disappeared down a well at the age of five. Refusing to believe that he was dead, his followers imbued him with timelessness. They declared him to be merely "hidden," and that on some future date he would suddenly appear to reestablish an Islamic caliphate worldwide. Their eschatology, however, proved problematic; it espoused an apocalyptic upheaval in order for the Mahdi, or Hidden Imam, to ascend to his rightful place of leadership. These "Twelvers" championed the belief that every individual, regardless of his religious belief, would one day bow to Islam—or die.

As time passed and the Mahdi failed to make an appearance, authority passed to the *ulema*, a body of mullahs endowed with the power to appoint a supreme leader. Perhaps one of the best-known imams was Grand Ayatollah Ruhollah Khomeini.

It was under the Safavid dynasty (1501-1736) that Shia Islam became Iran's official religion. It was also during this time that Persia was united as a single sovereignty and became the precursor to what we now know as Iran.

During more than twenty-five centuries of history, Persians have maintained their unique sense of identity. Though they converted to Islam, they have not always followed the accepted views of the religion. To an extent, Zoroastrianism, the religion of the early Persians, colors the Iranian variety of Islam.

Iran is now not only one of the largest countries in the Middle East but also in the Islamic world. Because of past experiences, Iran has developed a thorny separatism. Invaded during both World Wars and later set upon by Iraq, Iran has reason to fear foreign influence.

The borders of Iran have remained largely unchanged during the twentieth century, but the desire to recapture the glory of the vast Persian Empire has apparently lain dormant. Perhaps this pragmatism is the driving force behind Iran's seemingly sudden emergence as a budding player in the world's nuclear superpower game.

The Shah began to amass materials to build twenty nuclear reactors during his reign. Only two were started in Bushehr on the Persian Gulf. They were damaged by bombs during the Iran/Iraq war and were left unfinished. After Khomeini assumed power in 1979, the Ayatollah halted all work on the nuclear sites. Work was eventually resumed, though on a much more modest scale.

Iran's current president has, with the blessing of Supreme Leader Ali Khamenei, launched a full-scale nuclear program much to the chagrin of the Western world.

CHAPTER   6

. . . .

A FRIEND
FORSAKEN

"As nightfall does not come all at once; neither does oppression.
In both instances, there is a twilight when everything
remains seemingly unchanged. And it is in such twilight
that we all must be aware of change in the air however slight,
lest we become unwitting victims of the darkness."
(JUSTICE WILLIAM O. DOUGLASS)

During Richard Nixon's White House, the relationship between the Shah of Iran and the U.S. was at its apex. The two men first met while Nixon was vice president under Dwight Eisenhower. As president, Nixon appointed Henry Kissinger as secretary of state, and the two men quickly determined the Shah just might fulfill a major need in the Persian Gulf region—that of staunch political ally. Unable to police the area due to the war in Vietnam, it seemed that the Shah was an answer to a genuine need for a proxy to provide power and influence in the region. Nixon and Kissinger flew to Tehran to meet with the Shah and to ink an agreement outlining a new military pact between the two countries—Iran would become a "regional superpower" under the auspices of the U.S.:

> *The deal's principle feature was an unprecedented directive from the president of the United States ordering his government to sell the Shah virtually any kind of military hardware he wanted, short of nuclear weapons. No foreign government had ever been given such a shopping spree in the history of American military sales.*[110]

How did U.S. foreign relations transition from the glory days of the Richard Nixon administration to the morass reached in 1979? It would turn on the dime of a presidential campaign. The Shah's friend, Richard Nixon, would leave the White House in ignominy. His successor Gerald Ford would serve just over twenty-nine months before being defeated in his bid for election. Many political analysts believe it was his decision to pardon Richard Nixon that angered the electorate and cemented his defeat.

No one knew, least of all the Shah, just how directly Iran would be affected by the political change in the United States in 1976 when Jimmy Carter entered the presidential campaign. Even before the election Carter was courted by a group called the Institute for Policy Studies (IPS), which seemed determined to infect the political arena with a liberal agenda. The Liberal Left wanted a strong plank in the Party platform that supported leftist regimes and virtually ignored right-wing allies. This seemed to appeal to Carter, as it fed his desire to see the world's poor elevated from abject poverty, disease, and war to a state of plenty. It appealed to his crusade for morality, his sense of community, and his ongoing battle against elitism. To reach his goal Carter would have to rid Washington of former Nixon and Ford insiders and replace them with new names and new faces.

Perhaps the Carter team had determined early in his quest for the White House to hide behind the Foreign Assistance Act, Section 502B, in order to further their agenda in the area of human rights. The import of the document was that the U.S. was duty-bound to observe the values worldwide to which it professed to adhere at home. Congress superseded a presidential veto in 1976 to include Section 502B, a human rights statement, in the more wide-ranging *International Security and Arms Export Control Act*. Its detractors maintained that the inclusion of the rider was more representational; such symbolism, however, can be a weighty force in influencing public opinion. The document read, in part:

> *Sec. 502B. Human Rights.—(a) (1) It is the policy of the United States, in accordance with its international obligations as set forth in the Charter of the United Nations and in keeping with the constitutional heritage and traditions of the United States, to promote and encourage increased respect for human rights and fundamental freedoms for all without distinction as to race, sex, language, or religion. To this end, a principal goal of the foreign policy of the United States is to promote the increased observance of internationally recognized human rights by all countries.*
>
> *(2) It is further the policy of the United States that, except under circumstances specified in this section, no security assistance may be provided to any country the government of which engages in a consistent pattern of gross violations of internationally recognized human rights.*[111]

Some Congressional leaders and many Americans felt that U.S. policy abroad should reflect its policy at home, thus the birth of the human rights movement to which Carter would cling like a drowning man to a piece of flotsam. The decision would deeply affect the Shah of Iran and ultimately decimate his regime. Members of the committee determined that human rights issues should be given precedence when determining foreign policy. A law was passed that established an official prerequisite for the limitation or rejection of assistance for a nation or nations that repeatedly denied basic civil liberties for people. The law was an attempt to dissociate the U.S. from the unethical and abusive actions of beneficiaries of foreign assistance. Aid would no longer be dependent on a seeming pro-American stance; it would be given to those nations that valued human rights and self-determination.

The Foreign Assistance Act was made for Jimmy Carter. In her treatise on human rights, Clair Apodaca wrote:

> *There existed a coalition of those concerned with human rights, those that were looking for any reason to cut the foreign aid budget and foreign commitments, and those that simply wished to attack the Republican Party.*[112]

What made the Act even more attractive to Carter's foreign policy team was a congressional amendment to the Act in 1976 that made the president responsible for the determination of which countries were guilty of abusing the human rights of its citizens. The escape clause giving the president more decision-making latitude was in the words "extraordinary circumstances exist, which necessitate a continuation of security assistance for such country." This allowed the sitting president the leeway to determine what aid to which countries was in the national interest of the U.S. Such wording made it possible for Carter to launch his campaign against the Shah of Iran while simply ignoring other abusive regimes such as the one in Indonesia.

Countries that were particular targets for human rights violations were El Salvador, Nicaragua, South Korea, and Iran. It seemed that Iran, more than the others, raised the ire of many of Carter's staff selections. During the early organizational stages of the Carter transition team and even prior to his being sworn into office, an in-depth report on Iran was requested. John Drumbrell wrote in *The Carter Presidency: A Re-evaluation* that Walter Mondale and his aide, David Aaron, had links to the U.S.-based Iranian resistance. They were persuaded that Mohammad Reza Pahlavi, the Shah of Iran, was not entitled to rule Iran and determined that he needed to be restrained. Others in Mondale's fringe group simply wanted the ruler deposed. Once in office, the president's Liberal Left supporters felt justified in redoubling efforts to remove Pahlavi from the Peacock Throne.

Apparently, it did not occur to anyone in the new administration that the U.S. must be prepared for what might happen if the Shah's monarchy were to fail. As a result, no one was prepared for what the end result of such failure might mean to the United States in particular and the world in general. Jimmy Carter, however, was not alone in his inability to comprehend the state of affairs in Iran; other countries with strong ties to the Pahlavi monarchy, i.e., France, Britain, and Israel either did not count the cost of an Iran without the Shah or simply waited too long to act.

In her memoir, *An Enduring Love*, Farah Pahlavi wrote of the Carter campaign:

> During the whole of his campaign, Jimmy Carter had proclaimed the theme of human rights, the freedom of the people, which in reality has to be treated with caution, taking the economic and cultural context of each country into account. The Iranian opposition saw an ally in Carter for future struggles, and the rush of demands (on the Shah) in the spring of 1977 would doubtless not have been so great had another man been elected to the White House.[113]

When Jimmy Carter took office in January 1977, he inherited the established Iran policies of numerous presidents before him, including Richard Nixon and Gerald Ford. In 1953 the U.S. had backed a coup in favor of the Shah and against Prime Minister Dr. Mohammad Mossadegh. As prime minister, Mossadegh made a commitment to establish a constitutional monarchy, promote democracy, and nationalize the Iranian oil industry, then under the control of Britain. When Mossadegh ejected Anglo-Iranian Oil, the British determined that Mossadegh must be removed in any way possible and enlisted the aid of the United States to achieve the goal. Mossadegh believed the United States would back his plan.

Kermit "Kim" Roosevelt Jr., grandson of Theodore Roosevelt and a CIA agent, covertly joined hands with the British and military forces loyal to the Shah in "Operation Ajax" to remove Mossadegh from office and restore the monarchy of Reza Pahlavi. (In a note of fancy, the CIA operatives chose as their theme song, "Luck Be a Lady Tonight" from the Broadway musical *Guys and Dolls*.) The coup attempt initially failed and the Shah fled to Rome. Kim Roosevelt was so determined to overthrow the prime minister that he ignored communiqués sent from CIA headquarters and launched a second successful coup.

Kermit Roosevelt dispatched U.S. Army General Norman Schwarzkopf Sr., who had from 1942-1948 trained and commanded the Iranian Gendarmerie, to Rome to try to persuade the Shah to adopt the "Operation Ajax" plan, but the Shah declined to commit to the CIA plot. Reportedly, the general carried several bags filled with millions in currency with which he paid members of the covert operation and enticed politicos, clerics, the media, and gangsters to support the overthrow of Mossadegh's government. After meeting with the Shah, the general advised President Eisenhower to approach the Shah to secure his cooperation. Pahlavi eventually agreed, but only after he was assured that both Britain and the U.S. were officially part of the plot to overthrow Mossadegh.

Manucher Farmanfarmaian wrote of the Shah's acquiescence to Kermit Roosevelt's plan:

> A man whom I did not recognize appeared from behind the plane trees. He was dressed neatly in a dark suit...presented him [the Shah] with a document... the messenger was sent by Kermit Roosevelt and the document the Shah had signed appointed General [Fazlollah] Zahedi prime minister. Mossadegh's fall was imminent.[114]

On August 19, Zahedi formally claimed the title "Prime Minister." The following day Mossadegh surrendered. The U.S. immediately stepped forward and promised Prime Minister Zahedi the funds necessary to untangle the Iranians from the ongoing oil disagreement with Great Britain, a total of approximately $150 million.

In 1977 Kermit Roosevelt approached the Shah to discuss his plans to write a book on the "Operation Ajax" plot. Assadollah Alam, the Shah's confidant, wrote of that audience:

> I reported that I've now examined the book and found it most undesirable. It portrays HIM [His Imperial Majesty] as a waverer, forced into various crucial decisions, for example the appointment of General Zahedi as Prime Minister, by pressure from Roosevelt. The man is...hoping to present himself as a hero. HIM said he had no idea the book contained so much nonsense.[115]

In an interview by Amir Taheri with the Shah's former son-in-law, Ardeshir Zahedi, he patently denies that the overthrow of Mossadegh was a direct result of CIA plotting:

*They (the U.S.) may have plotted that. But what is important is
to ascertain whether Mossadegh fell because of American plotting
or as a result of other factors. What I can say with confidence is that
the fall of Mossadegh was not a result of any CIA plot. Victory, of
course, has a thousand fathers while defeat is always an orphan.
Had the August 1953 efforts to remove Mossadegh from power
failed, there would have been no CIA "heroes" claiming the credit.
There is a mass of evidence, including U.S., Iranian, British, and
Soviet official documents and testimonies by people who played a
role in the events that give the lie to the CIA operatives' claims.*[116]

Manucher and Roxane Farmanfarmaian wrote of the Mossadegh affair:

*Had Churchill not won the election in England or had Truman
run again in the United States; had Stalin not died or the Korean
War not wound down when it did; had Senator Joseph McCarthy
been silenced just a bit sooner or Congress not been rocked by a
Carter oil scare—history would have been different. Most bizarre
of all, had the CIA not had an operative named Kermit Roosevelt...
Mossadegh might have at last won. There are still many mysteries.
The greatest is the resonant silence of the Soviet Union, which
was fighting the United States and the rest of the UN on its eastern
flank in Korea yet remained mute about Washington's flagrant
activity on its southern border in Iran. History books ignore this
detail, and the British archives on the subject are closed until 2050.
No doubt there is much to hide.*[117]

President Eisenhower remembered the joy with which the Shah
returned to Iran following the coup:

*The Shah is a new man. For the first time, he believes in himself
because he feels that he is the king of his people's choice and not
by arbitrary decision of a foreign power.*[118]

On March 17, 2000, the Clinton administration gave the nod to Secretary of State Madeleine Albright to deliver a cleverly phrased apology to Iran for its role in the Mossadegh affair:

> *The United States played a significant role in orchestrating the overthrow of Iran's popular Prime Minister Mohammed Mossadegh. The Eisenhower administration believed its actions were justified for strategic reasons. But the coup was clearly a set-back for Iran's political development, and it is easy to see why so many Iranians continue to resent this intervention by America in their internal affairs.*[119]

Just weeks later President Clinton went one step (or perhaps two) further than his secretary of state; he spoke to a group assembled for a Millennial Evening in the White House East Room. Clinton all but grovelled at the feet of the mullahs controlling Iran:

> *I think it is important to recognize...that Iran, because of its enormous geopolitical importance over time, has been the subject of quite a lot of abuse from various Western nations. And I think sometimes it's quite important to tell people, look, you have a right to be angry at something my country or my culture or others that are generally allied with us today did to you fifty or sixty or one hundred or one hundred fifty years ago...So we [the U.S.] have to find some way to get dialogue—and going into total denial when you're in a conversation with somebody who's been your adversary, in a country like Iran...is not exactly the way to begin.*[120]

It is quite obvious to all but Albright and Clinton that the two had chosen to ignore the indignities committed against the hostages taken from the American Embassy and held for 444 days, or that the Iranian-sponsored Hezbollah in Lebanon had murdered Dr. Malcolm Kerr, William Buckley, and Lt. Colonel Robert Higgins—Americans all.

Imagine the impact that Clinton's words had on the people in Iran: A U.S. president was, for all practical purposes, apologizing not only for his country but for the actions of other countries. Clinton went a bit overboard in describing Iran as "a true democracy" and "one of the most stable countries" in the Middle East.[121]

Following the coup to unseat Mossadegh, an international consortium was formed to oversee the petroleum industry in Iran. Dr. Parviz Mina, director, National Iranian Oil Company, related to me the breakdown of the members:

> Five major Americans [Mobil, Exxon, Gulf, Chevron, and Standard Oil of California], seven independents, British Petroleum, Shell, and Compagnie Francaise des Petroles formed the group... 40 percent belonged to British Petroleum, 14 percent to Shell, 6 percent to the French company.[122]

Over time Iran exported $5.2 million in oil daily to the world market, the majority to Western Europe and the United States. The country was second only to Saudi Arabia as the largest exporter of crude. In 1971 the Shah hosted an OPEC conference in his country. He became an instant media target when he spoke in favour of OPEC's demanding the right to control production and oil prices. Pahlavi asked why the OPEC members should not get a higher price for their commodity in relation to rising prices for other commodities worldwide. Newspapers dubbed him a monster and began to blame the Shah for economic problems suffered by the West. According to Mina, the press used the fact that the conference was held in Iran to put pressure on the monarch.

By 1973 the Iranian National Oil Company (INOC) would rank 28th worldwide; in 1974 INOC had captured the third spot and would be on its way to an output of six and a half million barrels daily. Iran in 1977 boasted an export figure of two hundred seventy million tons of oil products and had captured second place. The Iran-owned oil terminal on Kharg Island boasted the largest tanker port in the entire world.[123] The land of the Shah was a shining star in OPEC.

CHAPTER 7

. . . .

A CELEBRATION
CREATES CHAOS

"The lavishness and the emphasis on Western taste turned out
to be a major mistake...we reporters didn't know that
the Persepolis indulgences would become a major milestone in
the Shah's eventual downfall....We were there to cover a party."
(BARBARA WALTERS)[124]

A nother event in 1971 would garner intense dislike for Pahlavi. It began with a desire to pay homage to Cyrus, the founder of the Iranian Empire, on its 2500th anniversary; it escalated to what was likely the largest gathering of heads-of-state in modern history. Such was the magnitude of the celebration that a spokesperson for the Iranian government declared, "During these unforgettable days, this august assembly will make Persepolis [the site of the magnificent party] the centre-of-gravity of the world."[125]

Initially the celebration was to have been a national event for the Iranian people. It escalated to the point that multiplied-millions of dollars were spent to create a field of sixty-eight fireproof tents set on concrete slabs, with every possible amenity for the comfort of the guests. Each tent was resplendent with silk and velvet walls, gold-leaf furnishings, and Persian carpets specially woven for the guests. China and crystal came from the French house of *Baccarat*. Male and female escorts were clad in French-designed dress. Guests were given a collection of gift products by *Elizabeth Arden* named after the Empress Farah. Mercedes 280-SEs transported visitors to and from the elaborate setting on the site of ancient Persepolis. The fact that cost was no object ignited the ire of many Iranians, few of whom even saw inside the "city."

The five hundred guests ranged from Vice President Spiro Agnew to Emperor Haile Selassie; from Kings and Queens of Belgium, Denmark, Jordan, Morocco, Norway, Thailand, and Nepal, to Prince Rainier and Princess Grace of Monaco, Prince Philip and his daughter, Princess Anne of Great Britain; from Marshal Tito and Aga Khan to the socialite, Charlotte Ford. Despite a tiff with Georges Pompidou, the president of France, the country was duly represented by its Prime Minister Jacque Chaban-Delmas. Could it have been the French president's childish insistence that he be seated during the banquet higher-up in the pecking order than any other French-speaking head of state that shaped France's future relationship with the Ayatollah Khomeini?

The New York Times journalist Neil Farquhar wrote:

> *Historians tend to point to the estimated $200 million fete as the beginning of the end for the Shah, a breathtaking symbol of just how out of touch he was with ordinary Iranians, none of whom were allowed within miles of the place during the party.*

> *The festivities ignored centuries of Islamic rule in Iran, provoking scorn from Ayatollah Ruhollah Khomeini, patriarch of the revolution that toppled the Shah.*[126]

This was only another nail in what was to become Pahlavi's political coffin. With three groups in Iran swiftly aligning against him, the National Front, the *Mujahedeen*, and the clerics, the Shah would ultimately fall victim to Jimmy Carter's human rights agenda of change. Change for the sake of change is not always the most productive path to take, however. Once in office Carter antagonistically tackled the agenda that had been proposed by Nixon and his National Security Advisor (and later Secretary of State) Henry Kissinger. Nixon's plan covered the next several decades. Kissinger believed:

> *It was dangerous for us to make the domestic policy of countries around the world a direct objective of American foreign policy... The protection of basic human rights is a very sensitive aspect of the domestic jurisdiction of...governments.*[127]

Nixon adopted the purview that his administration would ignore a nation's human rights history if necessary to secure a geographical edge. He had to look no further than the strong U.S. ally, the Shah of Iran. Shah Mohammad Reza Pahlavi was the son of Reza Shah who had gained the Peacock Throne through a coup d'état against the ruling Qajar dynasty in 1921. His son ascended the throne after Reza Shah was ousted at the hands of the British and Russians. Mr. Kissinger, who enjoyed a close, personal relationship with the Shah, labeled Reza Pahlavi of Iran "the rarest of leaders, an unconditional ally."[128]

President Nixon then instituted what became known as the "Twin Pillar Doctrine." His approach was to establish American military substitutes in various regions, especially in Iran and Saudi Arabia, to deter the Soviet Union and provide protection for U.S. interests. Thus, it behooved Nixon to see that the Shah was adequately supplied with military arms. Following the debacle in

Vietnam, Nixon determined to anoint proxies to act on behalf of the United States within their region. Iran received such a designation and was thus guaranteed access to U.S. arms in abundance.

Having Iran in his corner would give Nixon a deterrent against the Soviets in the Persian Gulf and would insure a virtual unending supply of Gulf oil. Pahlavi had no way of knowing that he was creating "a system capable only of defending itself but incapable of satisfying the people [of Iran.] This was its greatest weakness and the true cause of its ultimate defeat."[129]

Prior to a visit to Iran by President Nixon in May 1972, the Shah called on his friend and former son-in-law, Ambassador Ardeshir Zahedi,[130] who had left Iran for Montreaux, Switzerland. The Shah requested that Zahedi make a trip to Pakistan and Afghanistan before the president's arrival in Tehran in order to promote peace between the two neighbors. Zahedi's long-standing friendship with Pakistani Prime Minister Zolfaghar-Ali Bhutto and Afghanistan Prime Minister Mohammad-Musa Shafiq made him the logical choice for the mission. (Shafiq was executed by the Soviets after the Afghan invasion in 1979.) The Shah was most interested that these two countries co-exist peacefully in order to deter Soviet expansion in the region.[131]

Zahedi, who had known Nixon since his days as vice president, provided the background for the president's visit to Iran and for what eventually became known as the "Nixon Doctrine." The ambassador was in New York for UN discussion regarding the Six-Day War. He and Nixon met for dinner at Club 21 in Manhattan. Zahedi remembered:

> In those days nobody believed in a Nixon comeback, not even the Shah. On his return from a Vietnam trip in 1967, he stopped over in Tehran as my personal guest. I arranged an audience with

His Majesty, which was supposed to be short but lasted several hours. I [invited] Mr. Nixon to dinner in my residence at Hesarak with Armin Meyer, then the U.S. ambassador in Tehran, and my deputy, Amir-Khosrow Afshar. When these two men left, we chatted until the early hours of the morning. We discussed the problems of the region, specifically Iraq, Oman, and South Yemen, which was on the verge of gaining independence... I also arranged for Nixon to travel to Romania, especially as he had not been well-received by the Soviet leaders during a recent trip to Moscow. [The trip was arranged] through my friend Corneliu Manescu [who later became the UN Secretary General.]

When Nixon became president in 1969, he was anxious to further develop his ties with Iran. He sent Elliot Richardson and Governor Harold Stassen to Tehran.

[The Shah made a reciprocal visit to Washington, D.C. accompanied by Mr. Zahedi.]

When I look back at that visit, I think probably the most significant point which was made was related to China. At that time, Nixon's policy toward China had not yet been developed. Poland was acting as the go-between with China. I advised Secretary of State William P. Rogers to use Pakistan more as go-between; Rogers took that advice. (When Henry Kissinger went to China in 1971, he pretended to be in Pakistan.)

We raised a second point with Nixon and Rogers about Iraq... over close ties between Iraq and the U.S.S.R., especially when... Saddam Hussein came to power. Looking back, I can say that these events played an important role and were the roots of the policies that President Nixon and His Majesty developed in 1972. They wanted Iran to assure the security of the Persian Gulf and this was what the Nixon Doctrine was about.

American military sales to Iran began much before Nixon; but once Nixon and the Shah agreed on the role Iran should play in

ensuring the security of the Persian Gulf, it was natural that Iran
would receive the best military equipment. Nixon gave the Shah
full assurance and carte blanche in that respect.[132]

Pahlavi was only too eager to ally Iran with the United States, and he was quite vocal about his vision for the Persian Gulf region: "My policy is honest and straightforward, and I have no hidden agenda," he told Nelson Rockefeller. "I say quite openly that I wish Iran to play a role in the Indian Ocean. I have no objection to America being present; indeed, I shall actively defend your interests."[133]

In a memo to Secretary of State William Rogers and to Secretary of Defense Melvin Laird, Henry Kissinger forwarded the president's approval of a conversation Nixon had with the Shah. According to Kissinger, "The president has also reiterated that, in general, decisions on the acquisition of military equipment should be left primarily to the government of Iran. If the government of Iran has decided to buy certain equipment, the purchase of U.S. equipment should be encouraged tactfully where appropriate, and technical advice on the capabilities of the equipment in question should be provided."[134]

In an interview several years ago with Major General George J. Keegan, air force chief of intelligence from 1972 to 1977, he told me of documents secured near the end of World War II. The documents outline exactly what the Shah and Nixon were trying to prevent:

Russia's desire to dominate the Persian Gulf is long-standing and
well-documented. In 1945 our boys managed to capture records of
the German Foreign Office... One of the files deals with the Soviet-
Nazi Non-Aggression Pact signed by Hitler and Stalin in the late
1930s. Right there in black and white is the Soviets' clear statement
of their desire to be the dominant force in the Persian Gulf.[135]

Nixon was the beneficiary of President Lyndon Johnson's attempts to encourage the Shah to continue his efforts to modernize Iran, but at a steady pace. It was Johnson who declared Pahlavi a model monarch. "What is going on in Iran is about the best thing going on anywhere in the world," said Johnson.[136] The Shah was advised, however, not to overwhelm his people with an excessive number of proposed changes. When Carter took office Iran was well-supplied with U.S. military equipment, it was decidedly pro-American, and it would relieve the U.S. of having an overt presence in the Persian Gulf.

During the five years preceding Carter's inauguration, the Shah of Iran had purchased some $10 billion in U.S. military matériel. The U.S. government's presence in the Persian Gulf region and its supply of oil from that area were contingent on the goodwill of the Shah. The United States looked to Pahlavi for the economic survival of Western industry and he, in turn, relied on the United States for the arms and assistance to implement his vision for Iran's future. Failure on the part of either nation could cause unimagined economic and political upheaval.

Carter's Liberal Left leanings would dovetail perfectly with those inhabitants of "Foggy Bottom," the area in Washington where the State Department is located. The organization was composed of decidedly Left-leaning Arabists with views contrary to most Israel-supporting American presidents. Their grasp of foreign policy often tended to favor accommodation rather than confrontation. This was especially true during the late 1970s; the attitude at State was anti-Shah and anti-Iran. This divisive position would haunt American interests abroad for decades to come. It would open the door for the fanatical Ayatollah Khomeini and his Islamic revolution.

By the mid-70s the Shah changed from an insecure young leader to one fully in control of Iran's bureaucracy. Pahlavi was working to drag the country into the twentieth century and was not seeking advice or direction, not even from his mentor, the United States government. How did the Shah make the transition from a retiring young man to the grandiose ruler?

Marvin Zonis writes in *Majestic Failure: The Fall of the Shah* that Pahlavi "relied on four principal sources of...support to maintain his capacity to act as Shah...the admiration he received from others [i.e., the people of Iran]...strength he received through a very small number of close personal associates...a life-long belief in a watchful and protecting God who had decreed his success in carrying out a divine mission...important diplomatic and personal psychological ties with the United States."[137] Perhaps there was one other well of adulation for the Shah that, when it had run dry, contributed to his unpopularity: the support of the mass media. It is likely that the failure of these five sources of support for Pahlavi led to his downfall.

The liberal media in America became obsessed with turning the Shah from the champion of modernization to the monster of human rights violations. One mass market paperback fiction writer of the times wrote a novel entitled, *A Bullet for the Shah: All They Had to Do Was Kill the World's Most Powerful Man.* In an interview with a former U.S. joint chief of staff, I asked the question, "Who determines when wars are won or lost?"

He replied, "If you will commit not to divulge that I told you, I will tell you the truth." I affirmed my commitment to keep his identity secret. His response: "The media. Take Somalia. Why did we go there? We went there because of the media's obsession. Why did we leave? For the same reason! This is why we lost the Vietnam

War and Cambodia." I was stunned at his revelation. However, in looking back over the life of the Shah of Iran it confirmed that he was riding high when Jimmy Carter took office. Three years later he was, as Henry Kissinger asserted, "a flying Dutchman looking for a port."[138] He was a ruler without subjects, a king without a throne, a man without a country, a long-time ally bereft of its partner, the United States.

Newly elected President Jimmy Carter was also the recipient of the years-earlier Richard Nixon–Henry Kissinger arms sale policies. It relegated the security of one of the world's richest regions into the hands of a monarch whose determination to bring social and economic change to Iran did not take into account the smoldering fire of Islamic instability that would soon explode.

The Shah had enjoyed a prolonged political association with the Republican administrations of Presidents Richard Nixon and Gerald Ford. Under Nixon the Shah purchased vast supplies of military equipment, grew his army to the point that it had doubled the size of British forces, and increased his military budget from $293 million in 1963 to $7.3 billion in 1977.[139] The enormous amount the Shah spent on the purchase of arms was a boon to the U.S. economy during the oil crisis of the Nixon presidency.

Pahlavi was understandably wary of Carter, whose campaign platform stressed both human rights issues and a reduction in arms sales. The Shah was concerned that he would be viewed not as a progressive ruler but rather as tyrannical. This was of major concern because the Shah's regime had been criticized for the actions of its secret police, SAVAK, and had a long-standing and lucrative relationship with U.S. arms suppliers.

Asadollah Alam, appointed prime minister by the Shah in July 1962, was Pahlavi's personal confidant. Alam and the Shah had been classmates at the exclusive Swiss boarding school, *Institut Le Rosey*. He remained in office through major industrial and social reforms implemented by the Shah, sometimes referred to as the "White Revolution." Alam wrote of the Shah's concerns over Carter's election in his diary: "Who knows what sort of calamity he [Carter] may unleash on the world?"[140] He also wrote that Carter was "a political lightweight. He's managed to duck out of any clear statement policy issues."[141]

In September of 1976 Alam met with Ambassador Uri Lubrani, Israel's representative in Iran, and asked for his assistance to help improve the Shah's image with the American people. (It was Lubrani who co-authored, along with Reuven Merhav, a Mossad member, one of two reports that predicted the overthrow of the Shah within twelve months. Lubrani's report was so persuasive that Iranian Jews were cautioned to flee the country and seek refuge elsewhere.) Gholam-Reza Afkhami, an advisor to Pahlavi, felt, "No one could match Iran's power, Iran's culture, or Iran's history...It's important to realize this in order to understand why [the Shah] did what he did...And also why everyone else in the world said that he was arrogant."[142]

Dr. Abdol Majid Majidi, minister of planning and budget under the Shah, revealed to me that Pahlavi did, indeed, have a very good reason to be wary of Carter. He said of Carter's bid for the White House:

> At that time, the Democrats wanted to win in the election. What-
> ever could damage the Republicans, they were using; they were not
> thinking of America's interests in long-term or middle-term...Carter
> was winning at any price, by condemning Iran and human rights...
> All the speeches...were mentioning how they established human
> rights in Iran... [Henry] Precht prepared a report describing the

situation in Iran and what we should do in order to create stability and strengthen the Shah's position...Precht said that he sent it to Brzezinski, who put it in the briefcase of Carter...Two months after that day, Carter read that report...when it was too late... [It was] a positive report for the president who was Jimmy Carter...Two months after...Iran has really, literally deteriorated.[143]

Perhaps Carter felt that he could succeed where Mossadegh and others had failed. He would oust the Shah of Iran in favour of the religious cleric, Ayatollah Ruhollah Khomeini.

CHAPTER **8**

. . . .

OIL, OPEC,
AND OPPOSITION

"Power is not a means; it is an end. One does not establish
a dictatorship in order to safeguard a revolution;
one makes the revolution in order to establish the dictatorship."

(GEORGE ORWELL)

Revolution was bubbling beneath the surface in Iran and Carter insiders seemed determined to strip the Shah of power. Little did they know that foreign policy initiatives that directly affected Iran would have lasting and ever-widening repercussions.

Carter's greatest foreign aid/human rights debacle would occur in Iran, and all because, as Clair Apodaca pointed out, "Although foreign aid may have a humanitarian effect, the primary reason for its allocation is self-interest."[144]

In July of 1979, the Organization of Petroleum Exporting Countries (OPEC) announced yet another oil price increase, and gasoline prices in the U.S. went through the roof. That was followed by purported shortages nationwide. The result was long lines and short tempers at the gas pumps. Gasoline that had sold for $14 per barrel rose to $40 per barrel on the spot market. Prior to that time, the price of OPEC oil had fluctuated between $2.50/barrel and $14/barrel.

I asked Dr. Mina, director, National Iranian Oil Company, if it was correct to blame the Shah for the rise in oil prices. "The whole OPEC was looking for that possibility of increasing the...price of oil," said Dr. Mina. "One day OPEC should be able to control prices and not leave it entirely in the hands of the international companies to decide what the price of [oil] should be...naturally Iran was in favor of one day being able to control the prices. Because nowhere in the world was a commodity produced by a country and the price determined by someone else. It was natural for OPEC countries to say that we are producers of crude oil...we have to have a say in the price of the commodity like any other commodity."[145]

U.S. Energy Secretary James R. Schlesinger lit a match to an already volatile situation when he reported to Congress that the energy crisis and the lack of Iranian oil imports were "prospectively more serious" than the oil embargo enforced by the Arabs in 1973.[146] Although covertly maintaining a diplomatic understanding with Israel, Iran had aided Egypt during the 1973 Yom Kippur War by providing crude. The Shah had also furnished transport planes and pilots to Saudi Arabia and evacuated wounded soldiers to Iran for medical care. (Perhaps it was this, as much as anything, that led Sadat to welcome the Shah to Egypt following the Islamic revolution in Iran.)

Pahlavi refused permission to the Soviets to overfly Iran in military transports, but he did permit civilian airliners to deliver parts and supplies to the Arabs. While not engaged in actual warfare, the Shah allowed Iranian transport planes to ferry a Saudi battalion into battle and to evacuate wounded Syrians to Tehran for treatment.

Covertly and at a crucial time during the Yom Kippur War, Pahlavi returned a shipment of artillery shells and electronic equipment sold to him by the Israelis. The Shah, however, was averse to joining the 1973 oil stoppage and refused to use Iran's black gold as a bargaining chip against the U.S. or Israel. Following the 1973 conflict the Shah offered a multi-million dollar loan to Anwar El Sadat that would enable the Egyptian leader to expand the Suez Canal, reconstruct Port Said, and erect a pipeline between Suez and Alexandria. This action negated the need for the Israeli line from Eilat to Ashkelon and would have allowed the Shah to halt or severely restrict the flow of oil. The Israeli government was able to compel the Shah to honor their past agreement and continue the flow of oil as usual.

It was becoming more obvious to political observers that the underlying turmoil in Iran was at the point of near-eruption. The Carter administration had little, if any, reason to suppose that its policies would ultimately result in plunging Iran into the grasp of the Grand Ayatollah Ruhollah Khomeini; or did it?

President Carter had sent mixed signals to the Shah regarding the action Pahlavi was to take to preserve his leadership in Iran. The Shah had no idea whether or not Carter would support him if he took resolute measures to quell the rising tide of revolution. On the one hand, Carter seemed to support the Shah, while on the other hand he was emphasizing the need to avoid violence and promote human rights initiatives. The Shah was left wondering just what actions he should take. This indecision would prove to be the beginning of the end of the Pahlavi dynasty in Iran.

In May 1977 Carter dispatched Cyrus Vance to Iran for a Central Treaty Organization (CENTO) meeting. Vance embarked with a twenty-page classified memo. The document informed the secretary of state that he would be "the first senior civilian official of the Carter administration to talk with the Shah." It assured Vance that Pahlavi was "in a stronger position internally than at any previous time in his long [thirty-six-year] rule," that well-known terror organizations "have not caught the imagination of the populace, and except for the remote possibility of a successful assassination, are not an immediate threat to the Shah." The memo did not mention a possible opposition led by religious figures. It concluded, "We expect this stability to persist for the next several years."[147] After meeting with Vance, Pahlavi's opinion of the secretary of state was that he was "more a bureaucrat than a politician."[148]

The briefing paper also mentioned human rights initiatives and gave Vance specific directions for its inclusion in discussions with the Shah:

> In discussing the priorities of President Carter, you will want to refer to the importance of human rights to the president personally and as an element of our national consensus. You could comment that we have noted steps taken by Iran to improve certain human rights practices and its image abroad and encourage further steps in this direction.[149]

A CIA report delivered in August of 1977 seemed to support the State Department's evaluation of the situation in Iran. This intelligence organization purported: "The Shah will be an active participant in Iranian life well into the 1980s. There will be no radical change in Iranian political behavior in the near future." The CIA was convinced it was "looking at evolution not revolution" in Iran.[150]

Manoucher Ganji, a historian, wrote of the reality of the situation faced by the Shah and his monarchy:

> As it turned out, the United States offered no help. Instead it often spoke with multiple voices to a distraught Shah. From George Ball and Zbigniew Brzezinski to Cyrus Vance to Jimmy Carter and William Sullivan, each offered a different bit of advice.[151]

A January 7, 1978, article in *Etela'at*, an Iranian newspaper under the editorial control of Minister of Information Dariush Homayoun, sparked riots in the religious center of Qom. The article openly denigrated Khomeini: "He [Khomeini] was not truly Iranian; he had British connections; he led a dissolute life; and he wrote Sufic [mystical Persian love] poetry." The purpose of this article was unclear, but its effect was crystal clear. The seminary and bazaar in Qom closed, and four thousand theology students and other Muslims demonstrated, calling for a public apology...the next day a communiqué from Khomeini began orchestrating the opposition's response.[152]

A meeting of what Ambassador Sullivan described as "An Eclectic Group of [Iranian] Oppositionists...Blaming USG [United States Government] via the Shah for Iran's Ills," drew this comment:

> Except for the problem of fighting for the turn to speak, the group had a grand time. They were polite but pitiless in assailing USG policy and our puppet Shah... [We] delivered our semi-official Embassy message that troops will be ready when the Shah leaves. Therefore, crowds should do nothing to provoke them. And meanwhile, we will use whatever influence we have to restrain [the Iranian] army. Moderate religious leaders had previously accepted this message graciously, as did several leading bazaaris. This group, however, reacted sharply.[153]

Homayoun later told a press conference in Tehran that the troubles in Qom were "extremely well planned." Rioters were being moved from city to city by private transport. He said there was evidence that Palestinian extremists were involved. Demands were being made for the rigid enforcement of Islamic law with the closure of cinemas, bars, and nightclubs. The agitators opposed television and the emancipation of women.[154]

Unlike those who attributed the Shah's downfall to his desire to modernize Iran, Eric Rouleau, a Middle East journalist for the French newspaper *Le Monde*, was of a different opinion. Rouleau wrote in an article on the revolt against the Shah:

> *The first signs of revolt passed unnoticed. The explosions of rage in the spring of 1978, first in Tabriz and then in Qom, were attributed to "obscurantist mullahs" hostile to the Shah's agrarian reform. The immense demonstrations by millions of Iranians, as well as the strikes in the administrations, factories, schools, universities, and oil fields, which paralyzed the state and in the last analysis caused the monarch's inglorious departure, were attributed to the fanaticism of the Iranian people.*
>
> *Rare were those who suggested that modernity is not necessarily synonymous with progress or well-being, or that the concepts of economic development current in the West, where quick material gain is often the only valid criterion, do not necessarily correspond to the true needs and interests of developing nations.*[155]

In April Ambassador Sullivan fired off a secret telegram to Secretary Vance. It was marked "NODIS" (No Distribution). He wrote, "I am becoming increasingly concerned by the evidence that Iranian authorities have decided to resort to heavy-handed means to discourage dissident political action." Undersecretary Warren Christopher responded to Sullivan's disquiet: "We share your concern about recent violence in Iran, including evidence of strong-arm tactics by the GOI (Government of Iran.) We believe GOI should itself be concerned over widespread reporting in U.S. media of these indications of unrest in Iran." Christopher's memo advised Sullivan to discuss his fears with the Iranian prime minister.[157]

A telegram from Sullivan to Vance on June 19, 1978, indicated, "Lawyers have been at the forefront of the opposition movement in Tehran, and we can expect a renewed determination of this group to keep pressing for further change. They have told us privately that they will be monitoring court cases closely for evidence of improper procedure on the part of government officials, including prosecutors and judges."[158] Where were these same lawyers when Khomeini's revolutionaries began to execute their fellow countrymen after the Shah's departure, and why were they not present to represent those charged and condemned before kangaroo courts?

Late in 1978 the Shah presented a lengthy shopping list for arms and communications devices to the Carter administration. Sullivan was concerned about the effects such a massive arms build-up would have on the general Iranian population and on the economy. The other side of the coin was the amount of money such sales poured into American coffers. Iran topped the list of buyers at over $4 billion annually.

In my conversation with Her Majesty Farah Pahlavi, I asked about the quantity of arms purchased by the Shah:

> *In those days when my husband was making a strong army much of the equipment was bought from America. We were buying also from Europe...Then all the opposition people said, "The Shah loves these; it's like toys, a game, buying arms. He doesn't need it." But then, the Iraq/Iran War happened.*

If it were not for that army and for the trained military, especially
pilots, we would have lost to Saddam Hussein in the first two days...
The Islamic Republic had assassinated many of our generals and
military; many flew away from Iran, and some were in jail. They
took the pilots out of jail; their families were held hostage so that
they wouldn't fly away, but rather would fight against the invaders.
Those who were against us must remember that.[159]

The Shah's arms list included F-14 and F-16 fighters, 707 tankers, P-3Cs, and other military supplies. Pahlavi was particularly interested in the purchase of the F-18, but his request was denied. Also on the list were crowd-control devices such as tear gas, ammunition, and riot gear. Ambassador Sullivan strongly opposed the sale of riot gear to the Shah. It was his opinion that such an infusion of equipment would only serve to encourage the Iranian military to consider a coup should the Shah be ousted. Both Sullivan and Cyrus Vance further pointed out that the British had already provided the necessary paraphernalia and instruction needed for crowd-control. Some State Department heads, including Patricia Derian (assistant secretary of state for human rights and humanitarian affairs), Anthony Lake (policy planning), and Leslie Gelb (political-military bureau), were fiercely opposed to the request. According to Sullivan, there were some who "were so strongly opposed to the Shah because of the human rights abuses of his regime that they wished to see him collapse no matter what the consequences for the United States or its allies."[160]

Zbigniew Brzezinski was dispatched to Tehran for talks with the Shah.

The Shah was confident in presenting his shopping list; after all, Brzezinski had assured the king of continuing support:

The U.S. supports you without any reservation whatsoever,
completely and fully in this present crisis. You have our complete
support...Secondly, we will support whatever decisions you take
regarding either the form or composition of the government that
you decide upon. And thirdly, we are not, and I repeat, not encour-
aging any particular solution...it seems to me [you] have a problem
of combining some gestures, which would be appealing in a general
sense with a need for some specific actions which would demon-
strate effective authority.[161]

Now, *that* was certainly a clear-cut solution to the Shah's
growing predicament! Pahlavi telephoned Sullivan for clarification
of Brzezinski's vague advice. Sullivan also sidestepped the Shah with
promises to contact Washington. When no answer was forthcoming
either from Washington or Sullivan, the Shah concluded, "The fact
that no one contacted me during the crisis in an official way explains
about the American attitude...the Americans wanted me out."[162]
The Shah's former son-in-law and ambassador to the United States,
Ardeshir Zahedi, told me of the Shah's frustrations with Sullivan.
Pahlavi felt he was a victim of American hypocrisy. He was getting
mixed signals from Sullivan and felt the American ambassador was
not heeding Brzezinski's instructions.[163]

It was also in 1978 that Moscow issued a warning to the
U.S. regarding support of the Shah. Leonid Brezhnev, the Soviet
Premier, cautioned:

It must be clear that any interference, especially military interfer-
ence in the affairs of Iran—a state which directly borders on the
Soviet Union—would be regarded as a matter affecting security
interests...The events taking place in that country constitute purely
internal affairs, and the questions involved in them should be
decided by the Iranians—the Shah has ruled with an iron will.[164]

Although Iran was vitally important in maintaining security in the Persian Gulf area, President Carter, Brzezinski, and Vance were single-minded in their determination to push the human rights agenda and to halt the sale of arms to the Shah. Vance wrote in *Hard Choices* that, "Neither the president nor I wished to use human rights as an ideological weapon but rather as a basic element of our foreign policy. We applauded and supported the measures the Shah was beginning to take to improve human rights; he had already begun to curb SAVAK...in its use of extralegal measures to control subversion."[165]

The debacle that would come in Iran following the Shah's departure would wreak havoc in the oil-rich Persian Gulf. It opened the door not only to the meteoric rise of Islamic fundamentalism but also for the Soviet invasion of Afghanistan. Almost overnight Afghanistan was converted from a neutral nation to a springboard for the Russians to move closer to the Indian Ocean.

Zahedi had also warned of the Soviet Union's intentions to subdue Afghanistan. Reportedly, the Shah wrote a letter to Carter warning him that Russia had definitely set its sites on Afghanistan and was moving on the region even then. Pahlavi asked for additional arms and supplies to meet the threat. By failing to sufficiently back the Shah in Iran and abdicating its position of strength in the region, the U.S. was unable to take overt steps to halt the forward progress of the U.S.S.R. Attempts to enlist needed allies in Egypt, Pakistan, and Saudi Arabia would still find the U.S. unprepared for the Soviet invasion of Afghanistan.

As Brzezinski wrote in his memoir, *Power and Principle*, "The longer-range strategic and political implications of the Iranian crisis came to be appreciated in Washington only gradually...until [the seizure of the hostages]...the U.S. public was not overly aroused by a shift in power from a relatively unpopular Shah to a group of 'reformers.'"[166]

It is incomprehensible to think that the Ayatollah Ruhollah Khomeini could so mesmerize the majority of an entire nation with his persuasive rhetoric that the populace would blindly follow him. Khomeini had promised them what would be in American political terms "a car in every garage, and a chicken in every pot," and they believed him. Khomeini promised nothing in the way of programs to achieve his ends. Even though he emphasized "change," Khomeini offered no plan to implement changes.

. . . .

INDECISION
SPAWNS REVOLUTION

"Khomeini's main attention was devoted to religious groups
associated with the National Front that were based in the
United States, Canada, France, Germany, and Britain,
and it was these groups which insured, until the time of the 1979
revolution, that his pronouncements were properly circulated
among Iranians studying abroad." (BAQER MOIN)[167]

In 1977 Iranian Islamic leader Ali Shari'ati died, thus removing
a huge potential rival to Ayatollah Ruhollah Khomeini and solid-
ifying Khomeini's support against the Shah in Iran. Shari'ati was
a French-trained sociologist of the same period as Khomeini. He
contributed fuel to the fire of the Islamic revolution when he
contended that:

> All Shia's, irrespective of time and place, have the duty to oppose,
> resist, and even rebel against overwhelming odds in order to eradi-
> cate their contemporary ills...world imperialism, international
> Zionism, colonialism, exploitation, oppression, class inequality,
> cartels, multinational operations, racism, cultural imperialism, and

gharbzadegi [loosely translated as being "besotted with anything Western."].[168]

Khomeini had been in exile since 1963, first in Turkey and then in Najaf, Iraq. His exile was the direct result of political protests against the rule of the Shah. He opposed what he referred to as the "Westoxication"[169] of the monarchy. He ranted against giving Iranian women the right to vote and called for the unification of the Muslim world. Khomeini spent a brief time under arrest in March 1963, but was soon back to his old fiery attacks against the Shah. He was arrested again in June of that year and spent two months in prison. In October 1963 he urged an embargo on parliamentary elections; that cost him eight months in prison and then deportation.

Moving from Turkey to Najaf, Khomeini found himself in an important center of Shia piety. It was there he established his reputation as an uncompromising opponent of Reza Pahlavi. Khomeini was to forever change the West's view of Iran and Shia Islam, and he would drastically change the future of one young revolutionary, Osama bin Laden.

A CIA memorandum states, "While in Iraq, Khomeini began working closely with the Islamic Terrorist Group *Mujahedeen-e-Khalq* (the People's Strugglers). In late 1972 Khomeini issued a religious declaration, or *Fatwa,* that enjoined faithful Shia to support the *Mujahedeen* and called for the devout to provide funds for their use. The money was raised from the *ulema* (Muslim scholars trained in Islamic law) and in the bazaars and funneled to Khomeini, who in turn gave it to the terrorists."[170] The Grand Ayatollah did, indeed, hold the strings of the purse filled with blood money from Libya and the PLO.

The CIA memorandum that documents this information, though severely censored with a black marker, also revealed that Khomeini had supplied funds for the *Mujahedeen* to target Americans:

> *The Mujahedeen embarked on a campaign of assassination of Americans to show their opposition to the Shah and to attract world publicity. In June 1973 two American army officers were killed and in August 1976...three American employees of Rockwell International in Tehran.*[171]

It was also in Najaf that Khomeini first made contact with PLO leader Yasser Arafat and enlisted his help to fight against his enemies: the Shah, the "Great Satan" (America), and the "Little Satan" (Israel.) Arafat was more than willing to join forces with the Ayatollah. Although he did not personally meet the Shah until October 1969, Arafat had an axe to grind because the Shah had parted company with the PLO and its then-leader Ahmed Shukeiri in 1965 due to terrorist attacks on Israel and Jordan.

When the Shah finally met the militant Arafat in 1969, he was unimpressed with the diminutive terrorist. Arafat strutted into the room wearing a pistol and spouting lies about supposed PLO victories. The monarch told his aides following the meeting, "Arafat is no different from Shukeiri [the previous PLO leader]." Pahlavi refused any further meetings with Arafat. Thus shunned, Arafat embraced Khomeini's determination to overthrow the Shah. In just months Arafat would take on the role of an active partner in the revolution by allowing young Iranians to train at his camps in Syria, Lebanon, Libya, and Iraq.

Arafat's notoriety would mushroom during the 1972 Olympics in Munich, Germany, when members of Black September, a militant extremist group with ties to Arafat's Fatah organization, took eleven members of Israel's Olympic team hostage. After hours of negotiations between the leaders of the terrorist group and the German police, the eleven Israelis, five terrorists, and one German police officer would die during a bloody gun battle at the NATO airbase in Firstenfeldbruck.

Arafat blithely swore that he was not responsible for the actions of the renegade arm of Fatah. However, Abu Daoud, the man who helped the terrorists scale the walls of the Olympic village on September 5, 1972, refutes that assertion both in his memoir and in an interview with *Sports Illustrated*.

Daoud's book, *Palestine: From Jerusalem to Munich*, confirms "what many terrorism experts and Israeli officials long suspected...that the Black September organization, which Yasser Arafat and the Palestine Liberation Organization (PLO) always claimed was a renegade outfit, was in fact tightly controlled by Arafat. Even more shocking, however, was the allegation that [a top Arafat deputy, Mahmoud] Abbas...the man President George W. Bush has called a "man dedicated to peace"...provided the financing for the massacre."[173] [174]

Arafat and Khomeini were soon joined by the leftist organization headed by George Habash and other Marxist entities in Iran. (Habash was responsible for providing arms and aid to the *Fedayeen* (the more violent group which employed guerilla-style tactics), while Arafat underwrote the *Mujahedeen*. It was Habash who reportedly said of terrorist attacks against the Jews, "Killing one Jew far away from the field of battle is more effective than killing a hundred Jews on the field of battle...it attracts more attention."[175]) Proof of the alliance between Khomeini, Arafat, and Habash would reach SAVAK in July 1976. An agent seized a missive from Habash to Marxist leader Hamid Ashraf outlining the joint aims of the two groups. Letters from Habash to Iranian students in the U.S. also helped fuel the revolutionary fervor.

Another of Khomeini's closest advisors, Mustafa Ali Chamran, left Iran in 1957 to pursue a degree in physics at the University of California at Berkley. After finishing his degree in the U.S. Chamran moved to Lebanon, married a Palestinian woman, was indoctrinated in PLO goals, and later oversaw the training of Iranians in the PLO camps. His specialty was smuggling PLO terrorists and arms into Tehran. Chamran was repaid for his loyalty to Khomeini and his part in the revolution when he was named Khomeini's minister of defense.

Two events took place in Iran, both linked to the Shah and both spurring Khomeini and his followers to revenge. These two events essentially sealed the fate of the monarch. First, Ayatollah Hossein Ghaffari, a vocal critic of the Shah's regime, was allegedly tortured to death by Pahlavi's security forces. The cleric and Khomeini had corresponded during Khomeini's exile in Najaf; his death only added fuel to the Islamic revolutionary fires already burning in the Grand Ayatollah's chest.

Second, in October 1977 Khomeini's son Mustafa died of bulimia with heart complications, but antigovernment forces pointed the finger at the Shah's secret police, SAVAK, and Mustafa was proclaimed a martyr. This only served to further incite Khomeini's followers against the Shah. While there were various groups opposing the Shah's regime, i.e., leftists, the People's *Mujahedin* of Iran (MEK), communists, and other groups, Khomeini had suddenly become the most popular opponent to Pahlavi's rule.

To observe happenings in Tehran, President Carter tapped Assistant Secretary of State for Near Eastern and South Asian Affairs Alfred L. Atherton to further implement the human rights agenda.

By the time the Iranian monarchy fell, Atherton had been appointed ambassador to Egypt. He was in residence in Cairo when the Shah fled his homeland and flew to Egypt.

The Shah was being pressured by Washington to ease his control and allow more political freedom. This prompted the release of more than three hundred political prisoners, relaxed censorship, and overhauled the court system, which had the unforeseen side-effect of allowing greater freedom for opposition groups to meet and organize.

Pahlavi was confident about the American commitment to Iran during an interview with *Kayhan International* in September 1977:

> *Relations between Iran and the United States are good and I do not think they could be otherwise...When a new administration takes over, there are those who imagine everything will be changed. But it is only individuals who change; the long-term interests of a nation cannot change...We will not accept anything less than a first-class position for Iran...Iran must have a first class status.*[176]

Secretary of State Cyrus Vance was the first in Carter's administration to visit Iran, when he attended CENTO (Central Treaty Organization) to discuss security in the region. While traveling with Vance, an "unidentified spokesperson" for the State Department leaked the information that the United States was pleased with the Shah's human rights efforts and was therefore willing to sell him AWACS aircraft.[177] In July, President Carter informed Congress that it was his objective to sell seven AWACS planes to Iran.

After months of congressional wrangling and intense debate, the sale was approved. The final package included an additional $1.1 billion in spare parts and technical instruction. The Shah, however, sorely missed the Nixon administration's willingness to provide an almost unlimited entrée to military equipment.

Shortly after Vance's return to the States Carter signed Presidential Decision Memorandum 13. Although the document did not specifically mention arms sales to Iran, the country was noticeably absent from the list of nations that would receive American arms largesse. The Shah was decidedly disturbed that the new administration seemed not to value a long-standing liaison with his country. The document mentioned only Israel and the NATO allies: Japan, New Zealand, and Australia.[178] The Shah was mortified: "Does he [Carter] suppose that, strategically speaking, Iran is less significant than a country like New Zealand?"[179]

While the Shah's internal changes were making an impression on Carter, young men and women in Iran were swarming to radical Islam. Iran had never seen anything like this in its history. University students gathered at Islamic study centers to debate the imams of Shia Islam. Young women clothed themselves in the *chadors* (long black veils) that had been outlawed by the Shah. This new, radical Islam exploded on the campus of Tehran University in October 1977. A group of students calling for the isolation of women on campus rioted, leaving behind a trail of burned-out buses and broken windows.

On December 7, 1977, President Carter was asked about the rising instability of the Persian Gulf region and whether or not the Shah could survive the upheaval. Carter's response was:

> *I don't know. I hope so. This is something that is in the hands of the people of Iran. We have never had any intention and don't have any intention of trying to intercede in the internal political affairs of Iran. We primarily want an absence of violence and bloodshed, and stability. We personally prefer that the Shah maintain a major role in the government, but that is a decision for the Iranian people to make.*[180]

The president's assessment only served to widen the chasm between him and Pahlavi and added fuel to the already-smoldering revolutionary fires burning in Iran. The Shah would live to see the results of Jimmy Carter's calamitous statement.

Initially, the Shah had impressed Carter with his progressive programs, but disturbed the American leader with reported human rights violations. The true turmoil that boiled just under the surface in Iran, fed by cassette tapes of sermons by Ayatollah Khomeini smuggled into the country, was difficult to access.

Pahlavi's desire to see Iran dragged, sometimes kicking and screaming, into the twentieth century, to see the Iranian people with the advantages offered by westernization, precipitated his downfall. He wanted to create a modern, industrialized nation that was productive, strong militarily and economically, and diverse culturally. Visionaries require a retinue of detail-oriented people around them to implement the vision and reach the goal. Unfortunately for the Shah, many of those with whom he surrounded himself were not averse to using any means to justify the end result. The outcome, of course, was unrestrained human rights violations. The poorer Iranian classes, seeking wealth, flocked into the cities where they encountered abysmal living conditions. Corruption proliferated and inflation skyrocketed. Violence ran rampant, and the SAVAK did not hesitate to implement any method of torture to control it.

In an article published in *New Yorker*, an unnamed Iranian official in Isfahan summed up the situation very succinctly; the summation was appropriate for any city in Iran:

> *Students have grown up under the Shah, and they don't know*
> *what things were like before development started. All they know is*
> *that the Shah promised that Iran was going to be like France*

*or Germany. That isn't happening. The huge surge in population
means that services are spread too thin and are constantly breaking down. There aren't enough telephones. It's impossible to buy
a car. The schools are jammed. Housing is scarce. During the
past three years there has been a recession, especially in building,
and many laborers are out of work. So the students are in a mood
to reject everything that has happened. They are turning back to
the old days and pursuing an idealized version of what things
were like then. They are pushing the mullahs to go back and
re-create the wonderful past. The mullahs see a chance to regain
their prestige and power. The students provide them with a power
base for putting pressure on the government to give them the
consideration and importance they have been seeking for years.
So the mullahs go along. That's the dynamic of trouble in Isfahan.*[181]

It is quite possible that had Jimmy Carter's advisors been more
astute and less determined to see the Shah deposed, a lesson could
have been learned from either of the two encounters that took place
between the Carters and the Pahlavis—one in Washington and
the other in Tehran. Prior to the meeting in D.C., Carter received a
briefing memo from Cyrus Vance. While the document failed to
list "human rights" as a main objective of their meetings, an
entire page was devoted to the topic. Outlined as the president's
objectives were:

> *We should ensure that the Shah understands that your concern over
> human rights has a continued high priority, that we recognize the
> important positive actions he has taken in the last year, and that we
> would like to see programs continue.*[182]

The Shah had, in fact, instructed his military courts to house
political prisoners in better surroundings. He invited an entourage
from the Red Cross to visit the prisons and inspect the facilities and
handling of political detainees. The group reported that one-third of

the prisoners had been tortured in some measure, but that such method had been forsaken. The Shah was convinced that once the findings of the Red Cross team had been published, the pressure on him would ease.

CHAPTER 10

. . . .

A STAR-CROSSED
STATE VISIT

*"During the outdoor welcoming ceremonies at the White House
a surprising number of unruly anti-Shah demonstrators,
almost all of them Iranian students studying in the United States,
massed outside the gates chanting slogans such as 'Death to
the Shah'—slogans that would in a short time become quite
familiar to Americans."*[183]

In November of 1977 the Shah and the Empress Farah made a state
visit to the White House. Using the freedom of speech rights
available to any citizen, or visitor for that matter, Iranian students
in the U.S. had been widely protesting the Shah's rule. As the two
leaders and their wives met on the South Lawn of the White House,
a group of the monarch's supporters were seated in bleachers on the
Ellipse beneath a banner that read, "Welcome Shah!"

In Lafayette Square on the north side of the White House,
some one thousand Iranian dissidents had gathered to protest with
shouts of angry, anti-Shah slogans. As the two leaders greeted each

other, the protesters broke through police lines and charged the Ellipse.

Ardeshir Zahedi remembered the state visit of the Shah and empress quite vividly. He recalled the day before the White House reception:

> *Several busloads of opposition activists were allowed to come to Williamsburg, which is a small place, for the overnight stay of state guests before the official program started the following day. I don't recall anyone carrying the picture of Khomeini in Williamsburg, but what I recall is that standard security rules were not observed by the Secret Service. These rules call for a distance of five hundred feet of separation between the crowd and the person who is the state guest. The Secret Service allowed the opponents to come very close, just a few meters from the Shah's living quarters.*
>
> *[The following day] a pro-Shah rally [was] organized in front of the White House...a large crowd of pro-Shah demonstrators— maybe about fourteen thousand to fifteen thousand Iranians from all over the States—gathered in front of the White House... The security people arranged things in a way that the Shah's supporters and opponents were one in front of the other. The clash between them could not be avoided.*[184]

Mounted police were able to stop the riot but not before having to resort to the use of tear gas to quell the crowd. Standing downwind from the tear gas canisters, both leaders and their wives were victims of the acrid fumes. An account in *Time* magazine relates how the two men responded to the onslaught:

> *Reeling slightly, the Shah sought refuge behind a white pocket handkerchief. The empress, standing behind him, fumbled in her purse for dark glasses. Vice President Walter Mondale and*

*Secretary of State Cyrus Vance, eyes streaming, covered their
faces. Only Carter, still speaking, refused to flinch. Tears rolled
out of the president's eyes, but he made no move to wipe them.
Recovering his composure when it was his turn to speak, the
Shah thanked Carter for "your very warm welcome," and the
official party quickly retreated to the White House.*[185]

Mr. Carter later toasted the Shah with, "There is one thing I can
say about the Shah: he knows how to draw a crowd."[186]

Appalled by the turn of events, Ambassador Zahedi urged the
Shah to return to Tehran, while members of the Carter administration implored him to reconsider. The Shah relented and calmly
resumed his talks with the president.

The New York Times story the next day chose a photograph of
the ceremony that showed the Shah speaking into a microphone
while both President Carter and Mrs. Carter are seen on either side,
tears streaming from their eyes. The headline read: "Clashes and
Tear Gas Mar Shah's Welcome in Capital."[187]

Just in case anyone missed that headline, the *Times* ran an
editorial the next day entitled "Tears and Sympathy for the Shah."
The editorial stated that the tear gas "signaled the somewhat awk-
ward nature of the occasion. A president committed to advancing the
cause of human rights worldwide was offering a full-honors welcome
to a ruler as close to an absolute monarch as exists these days."
While the editorial pointed out that "there has in fact been some
progress on human rights in Iran in recent months," it went on to
say, "the Shah's monopoly on decision-making creates vast inefficien-
cies. It also has created doubt that stability can survive his reign.
Besides urging further attention to human rights, therefore, the
United States has reason to urge institutional reform as well."[188]

The *Washington Post* Style section reported that the next day the Shah tried to smooth over the incident by saying, "It is true that it started out with tears in the morning, but it was the same last night after President Carter's remarks. There were tears of joy in my eyes knowing of the unshakable friendship between our two countries."[189] *Post* reporter Donnie Radcliffe snidely remarked, "On Tuesday at the White House the Shah had handed his hand-kerchief to Queen Farah as tear gas fired by DC police drifted up from the Ellipse. Yesterday, he kept it in his pocket, the same place, apparently, he kept his shopping list for several billion dollars worth of U.S. arms he wants to buy."[190]

The *Post* editorial page carried a story in the same edition. The writer noted:

> *The brief but ugly outbreaks of street fighting here during the visit of the Shah of Iran leave a number of reputations suffering severe bruises. The American authorities lost control of a crowd that was clearly spoiling for a fight...When a foreign visit ends with a flood of casualties to hospital emergency rooms it's obvious that the hosts mismanaged the affair. Apparently the Carter administration was leaning over backwards to avoid any resemblance to the methods of the Nixon years. The result was to leave an inadequate contingent of Park Police, not even wearing helmets, facing the crowd as it prepared to rush them. For reasons still not clear, federal authorities never called in the Metropolitan Police. That was a serious mistake. The present tenant of the White House...would be exceedingly un-wise to let Washington become known as a city where it is cheap and easy to disrupt public events...Freedom of expression does not include the right to beat up the people who disagree...A riot on the Ellipse is not likely to persuade the Shah to relax police controls in Tehran.*[191]

A follow-up report two weeks later revealed that during the fracas on the Ellipse ninety-six demonstrators and twenty-eight police were injured. According to the *Washington Post* story, Park Police were instructed "to leave their riot gear—helmets, face shields, riot sticks, and gas masks—on nearby buses. When the student attack occurred, just as the twenty-one-gun salute for the Shah was sounded, the undermanned police were overrun...The White House has denied recurrent rumors that it ordered the low-key profile...during the Shah's visit."[192] The article further revealed that Attorney General Griffin Bell was asked to have the Justice Department hurriedly coordinate security for the remainder of the Shah's visit.

The event wreaked havoc in Iran when it was broadcast live on Iranian television. Many in Iran, whether favorable or opposed to the Shah, were not accustomed to the liberty accorded the media in the United States and interpreted the use of tear gas during the ceremony as evidence that the U.S. president lacked confidence in Pahlavi. The *Times* editorial only reinforced that perception.

The Shah learned that arms sales from the U.S. would be curtailed; however, he was told the military pact between the two countries was unwavering.[193] His moves to allow more dissent and criticism of his government while, at the same time, seeking his support both of Israel initiatives and in curtailing oil prices was applauded. Overall, it was a successful trip: Pahlavi met Carter, and the AWACS deal that Carter had presented to Congress in July was finalized.

Zahedi explained his role in the final AWACS negotiations:

> Lord Hartley and Lady Shawcross were houseguests in Washington. I discussed with Shawcross whether Britain may be willing to sell Iran their NIMROD air reconnaissance crafts...Shawcross, of course, was not in the British government and could not make a commitment, but I sent to His Majesty a message in Tehran which was not coded... I said to him that the UK may be willing to sell us these crafts.

Shortly after, some influential senators...Chuck Percy, Abraham
Ribicoff, Jacob Javits—Howard Baker called me and said, "Don't
rush it; after the recess the matter will be settled." That is how in
the meeting of November 15...Carter announced he had agreed to
sell Iran seven AWACS and asked Zbig to brief the Senate.[194]

The fact that the anti-Shah events happened at all in Washington, D.C., and especially during the monarch's visit, added fuel to the opposition movement in Iran. The leaders asked themselves, "Could this have happened at the White House without President Carter's express knowledge and approval?" Obviously, the insurgents in Iran concluded that the answer was a resounding no and at the least signaled Carter's lack of support for the Shah. The empress later wrote that an event such as that would not have happened during the Nixon administration; the rioters would have been held at bay. One of the protesters waved a placard with a picture of the Ayatollah Khomeini, and the visage of the fanatical cleric commanded the front page of the *Washington Post*. This gave the empress pause for thought; she wondered how someone could equate Khomeini with liberty and moderation.[195]

In her own mind, the empress questioned the motives of the demonstrators:

My God, if these people want democracy and freedom, why are they
carrying the picture of this religious man? Many Iranians didn't know
who Khomeini was. Then slowly the cassettes of Khomeini started
with his speeches against the Shah and against the reforms. What
happened is that the opposition was very well organized, and we
were not; we were not politically organized to answer them. How
could our people after what they had lived through go after a man
like this and think that he could bring them happiness and a better
life in Paradise?[196]

In December, while on a presidential jaunt that took him to Poland, India, and the Soviet Union, President and Mrs. Carter made a brief stop in Tehran. The stop was in essence a reward for the Shah's assistance in urging the Kings of Morocco and Jordan to persuade President Sadat to make peace with Israel. Again, Carter's Southern charm and hyperbole only exposed the fact that he did not fully grasp the undercurrents of revolution that were even then gripping Iran. During the visit to Tehran, the Shah gave the president a "grocery list" of some $10 billion in arms supplies. The list contained the full gamut from ships to communication devices. Carter, on the other hand, was to alert the Shah of a new U.S. objective:

> To discuss the recent clashes between Iranian security authorities and student/opposition politicians and to express our hope that these clashes do not portend a reversal of the encouraging human rights developments in Iran...We should indicate that the tough actions by Iranian security forces recently have created U.S. press, public, and congressional concern that the Shah has reversed the encouraging trend in the field of human rights. We should encourage him to continue the positive course in the relaxation in restrictions affecting human rights, which he embarked upon in early 1977.[197]

A memo initiated by Secretary of State Warren Christopher indicated that the U.S. was aware the opposition forces in Iran were regrouping:

> Our analysis indicates that the so-called Iran Freedom Seekers Liberation Movement and various other opposition politicians who were prominent in the 1950s during the period of Prime Minister Mossadegh have attempted to form a broad but loose coalition of all opposition elements...from the far left to the far right...and to recruit students into this grouping. A broad-based effort of this nature, uncommon in Iran, may have reflected the new political openness in Iran in the past year.

According to the State Department, the Shah "would prefer that the issue not be raised, and if it is, will take the line that agitation by students and opposition elements is foreign-inspired or has foreign connections."[198]

No mention is made to Carter of possible Libyan or Palestinian connections to the terrorist groups at work in Iran.

According to Zahedi, rather than attend a banquet in the Shah's honor at the Iranian Embassy in Washington, Carter asked if he could pay the Shah a visit in Tehran. Zahedi replied that the Shah would be delighted. "That is how," stated Mr. Zahedi, "that the New Year's banquet came to be; it was not a state visit, only a courtesy call." Carter, however, was almost upstaged by King Hussein of Jordan. The Shah wanted the president and the Jordanian ruler to meet. Carter's advance group insisted that the king be invited to the dinner, which created yet another problem. If King Hussein were to attend the party, he would displace the president as the guest of honor and be accorded the seat at the Shah's right hand. The Jordanian ruler did join the guests that evening, but after dinner had been completed.[199]

During the banquet the president raised his glass and praised Pahlavi: "Iran, whose destiny is so remarkably well guided by the Shah, is an island of stability in one of the more troubled areas of the world. That is a great tribute to you, your Majesty, and to the great task that you are accomplishing in Iran, and to the respect, admiration, and love that your people bear you...There is no other head of state with whom I feel on friendlier terms and to whom I feel more gratitude."[200] The Shah was gratified by Carter's glowing words, but it was apparent that neither the president nor his advisors were fully apprised of the growing unrest.

When I interviewed Her Majesty Farah Pahlavi in March 2008, I was shown her guest book with an inscription: "Thank you for all your wonderful hospitality." It was signed, "President Jimmy Carter" and "Rosalynn Carter." Princess Ashraf, Pahlavi's twin sister, put her impressions of the president on paper. She wrote, "I looked at his pale face. I thought his smile was artificial, his eyes icy—and I hoped I could trust him."[201]

Rather than supporting the Shah because of his country's strategic importance in the region, Jimmy Carter seemed determined to make a human rights example of the Pahlavi regime. Every tool was available to affirmatively sway the Shah's decisions and influence events in Iran. Rather, the situation in Iran was allowed to rapidly disintegrate to the point that any word of praise or any expression of goodwill toward Iran's ruler only fed the flames of revolt and increased the enmity towards the United States. The Shah had the dubious distinction of being as disliked by much of the American public as the Soviet leader, Leonid Brezhnev.

While the ultimate aims of different groups opposing the Shah were widely varied—some wanted a return to constitutional monarchy, others a socialist/communist government, and the imams and clerics an Islamic republic—it was the Ayatollah Khomeini who cunningly united these groups against the Shah by avoiding the specifics of what would happen beyond toppling the famed ruler from the Peacock Throne. As a result, opposition groups that would normally have been contending with one another instead grew more unified.

The dissenters were of the opinion that the Shah was nothing more than a puppet of the United States, one who moved at the bidding of the American leaders. The other side of the coin was that the same opposition felt that the U.S. was simply repeating a long-established pattern...a period of pressure on the Shah to enact reforms, then a time of retreat and acceptance of Pahlavi's resolve to retain absolute power. In a private setting with the president, National Security Advisor Brzezinski worked to convince Carter that to abandon Pahlavi would damage whatever good reputation the U.S. may have had worldwide.[202]

The Shah was bombarded by those in Iran who saw Carter's embrace of human rights as a signal to press the Shah for deeper changes. A group of lawyer-activists urged Pahlavi to enact new and more encompassing legal reforms. The Writer's Guild shouted for freedom of the press. One member of the Guild attributed the willingness to vocalize their demands was because "the government wouldn't dare jail all of us in the present climate of human rights." Some attribute this remarkable feat of internal unity to Khomeini. Regardless of the instigator, it accelerated the revolution in Iran and later proved to be a deadly mistake, not only for the United States but for all Islamists.

Other new tactics were adopted by the dissidents, including a letter published by National Front leaders Karim Sanjabi, Dariush Foruhar, and Shapour Bakhtiar calling for the king to step down. The empress felt that "these people were acting in that way because they had the support of the United States, the new Carter administration." Coinciding with the internal unrest fomenting in Tehran, a group of well-known Iranians dispatched missives to Kurt Waldheim, the UN Secretary General, and President Carter to enlist their aid in promoting the institution of greater human rights in their country. Carter, with his human rights agenda firmly in place, was more than happy to comply.

In a personal interview, Samuel Segev, Middle East editor of *Maariv,* revealed to me that the military attaché in Tehran, General

Yitzhak Segev (no relation), was certain the Shah would be ousted if the Carter administration continued with its policy. General Segev was convinced that U.S. interference was tying the hands of the Shah's military and making it impossible to act against the opposition.

During the interview, General Segev, who was in Iran from 1977 through February 1979, expanded on the causes of the revolution. The general felt that Pahlavi had tried to expand democracy much too quickly; that he had tried to "take across Western ideas, in an area that was not ready for them. You can't form democracy," said Segev, "in an area that lives as if in the Stone Age...Carter pressured the Shah at every possible moment." Segev believed that Ambassador William Sullivan had no comprehension as to how different was the mentality of the Iranian people toward democratic ideals.[205]

According to Dr. Ahmed Tehrani, former ambassador of Iran, the Shah's demeanor changed the year before he was forced off the throne when he was challenged by strikes, riots, and other turmoil:

> Let me say that the Shah had ruled Iran for more than forty years and knew how to take care of incidents like these...but in 1978-1979, he did not take care of it. He was suffering from cancer. He would laugh and cry alternatively...Now he's saying, "I love my people; I don't want to hurt my people," and the next day, he would say, "Shoot!"... suddenly he's sick...Actually, there are so many reasons for the revolution: the financial situation, the social situation...but it's mainly because of pressure...and Carter's foolishness.[206]

Ambassador Zahedi voiced several factors he felt would have made a difference in the Shah's control of the situation in Iran:

:: If His Majesty had not left the country, Khomeini would never have dared come to Iran, and

:: The army would not have disintegrated.

:: In less than two years, we had three changes of prime minister and government...followed by a military government with practically no power, and then to crown it all, came that demagogue, Shapour Bakhtiar, who destroyed all that remained and presented the country to Khomeini and his cronies as a gift on a gold platter.

:: About Sullivan, I refer you to His Majesty's book, *Answer to History*. When he [Pahlavi] asks Sullivan when he should leave the country, Sullivan looks at his watch and says if he left sooner it would be better than later.

:: His Majesty had problems with his family, especially with his wife...she had surrounded herself with people of strong leftist inclinations; but my beloved king was, rightly, against communism.

:: Most important of all was his sickness, which had been kept secret from the Iranian people...[His Majesty] should have told the truth about his own illness...he was so loved by his people; they would have wept blood instead of tears.

:: The most important point is that I told His Majesty point-blank, in the presence of the...queen, that if he left the country, he would never return; it was a huge mistake to think that his wife or son could replace him.

:: I tell you that whatever the Carter administration intended to do at that point would have been too little too late.[207]

When asked if the Crown Prince or Empress Farah could have succeeded his father on the Peacock Throne, Zahedi replied:

His son could not have succeeded to the throne as he was not of age...His wife could not have succeeded as this was against the constitution, as well as the fact that this could have provided

*ammunition for the opposition. Sadly, there were many elements
and people who were against her.*[208]

The Shah, who had placed the future of his monarchy squarely
in the hands of the U.S., was convinced, as he told Nixon's Vice
President Nelson Rockefeller during a visit to Iran in May 1978, that
"the Americans and the Russians have divided the world between
them." It was this that led not only the Shah and his supporters in
Iran but educated Iranians worldwide to determine that Pahlavi's
reign had ended because the U.S. wanted it to end. Khomeini had
overthrown the Shah of Iran because America had switched its
loyalties to the cold and calculating cleric; it is likely that without
some backing from the U.S., Khomeini would not have gained power
in Iran.

CHAPTER 11

. . . .

THE SHAH:
AN ALLY ABANDONED

"Men and women in Iran broke old chains only to forge new ones. They demolished the rule of one man and then submitted to the tyranny of another." (FOUAD AJAMI)[210]

"The seeds of 9/11 were sown a quarter of a century ago when Khomeini came to power. Khomeini's ascent to power was aided by the policies of Jimmy Carter and his allies on the political Left." (DINESH D'SOUZA)[211]

In an attempt to solidify his position in the region, Mohammad Reza Shah Pahlavi sought to align himself with his neighbors as early as 1974. The Shah, who was able to move Iran into a leadership role in OPEC during the Nixon-Ford administration, felt the time had come to move his country into a more central position in the region. (In 1976 in a display of largess, Pahlavi gave away nearly two billion dollars to countries such as Egypt, Jordan,

167

and Syria in order to achieve his goal.) Pahlavi sent his trusted emissary, General Gholam-Reza Afkhami, to Cairo to research the possibility of greater cooperation between Egypt and Iran. As a result of Afkhami's hard work, Egypt garnered a state-of-the-art radar system and an opportunity for Egyptian pilots to see Iran's Phantom jets first-hand. It also paved the way for the first visit of an Iranian monarch to Egypt in twenty-three years. During that visit Sadat asked Pahlavi to intervene with Rabin over the Sinai oil fields.

The Shah's visit in Cairo led the monarch to inform Rabin that the Eilat-Ashkelon pipeline was in danger of being shut down in early 1975. Rabin sent his Foreign Minister Yigal Allon to Tehran for meetings with the Shah. The two men were able to reach an agreement that allowed the flow of oil to continue, albeit with a higher rate for transfer fees but with a lower price for the oil.

In May of that year, however, the Shah surprised Israel by siding with Sadat over Israeli withdrawal from the territories captured during the Six-Day War. This placed an inordinate amount of stress on Israel-Iran relations. Ambassador Uri Lubrani was informed that relations between the two countries would be deferred until Israel decided to acquiesce to calls for withdrawal at least from the Abu-Rudeis oilfields. Secretary of State Henry Kissinger was finally able to exact a commitment from Pahlavi that he would not stop the flow of oil to Israel. Even with this agreement, Rabin felt it necessary to return to Tehran for another secret visit with the Shah. Unfortunately, Rabin was unable to maintain his anonymity among the Jews in the region. Pahlavi, however, was able to assure Rabin that Israel's oil needs would be met.

While the Shah was also reaching out to Egypt and other Arab countries, he was determined to allow neither the Soviets nor

Americans to establish bases in his area of the Persian Gulf. The fact that the Soviets defied an agreement to withdraw from Iran in a timely manner following World War II and created two republics within the territory occupied—Azerbaijan and Iranian Kurdistan—was very distressing to Pahlavi. It was not until UN intervention in 1946 that the Russians abandoned their territory in Iran. Perhaps that is why the Shah considered the U.S.S.R. to be the most important threat to Iran; after all, the two nations shared a 1,240–mile border. For centuries the Russian agenda included securing a warm-water port facility and subverting any nation considered to be pro-Western. Pahlavi felt the Russians had the most to gain should Iran plunge into internal unrest. An April 1974 document from the State Department outlines the Shah's fears regarding Soviet aggression:

> The Shah believes Soviet activity in the Middle East indicates a continuing use of proxies such as Iraq and South Yemen to accomplish Soviet foreign policy goals. The Shah remains concerned by the potential for instability—and Soviet exploit-ation of it—in neighboring countries. He is concerned about radical movements in the Persian Gulf; Iraq's hostility towards Iran...He recognized the need for, and has been seeking, improved relations and cooperation with the more moderate Arab govern-ments...Establishing this cooperation is not easy because of long-standing Arab wariness toward Iran.[212]

What Pahlavi may or may not have known was that the Soviets began courting the PLO shortly after Israel's success during the 1967 war. Soviet support for the terrorists was documented by Russian General Ion M. Pacepa, a defector to the West in 1978. In an article on *National Review Online*, Pacepa wrote:

> Between 1968 and 1978...security forces of Romania sent two cargo planes full of military goodies every week to Palestinian

terrorists in Lebanon... [The shipments did not stop after the fall of the Shah] ...in 1983 alone [the East German Stasi] sent $1,877,600 worth of AK-47 ammunition to Lebanon. According to Vaclav Havel [president of Czechoslovakia], Communist Czechoslovakia shipped 1,000 tons of odorless explosive Semtex-H (which can't be detected by sniffer dogs) to Islamic terrorists—enough for 150 years.[213]

In actuality, the Soviets extended an invitation to Arafat to set up a PLO bureau in Moscow in 1974. General Pacepa wrote in his memoirs that Arafat possessed "an incredible amount of fanaticism...of tangled oriental political maneuvers, of lies, of embezzled PLO funds deposited in Swiss banks, and of homosexual relationships, beginning with his teacher when he was a teenager and ending with his current bodyguards. After reading that report," said Pacepa, "I felt a compulsion to take a shower whenever [I] had just shaken his hand."[214]

Another Soviet counter-espionage defector from Poland, Colonel Michel Goleniewski, took aim at the Grand Ayatollah himself. The Russian exposed a CIA document from the early 1960s. The document reportedly revealed that "Khomeini was one of Moscow's five sources of intelligence at the heart of the Shiite hierarchy."[215]

Although the PLO was a vital ingredient in the overthrow of the Shah and the return of Khomeini to Tehran, it was, however, the signing of a peace treaty with the Kurds in Northern Iraq that may well have signaled the beginning of the end for the monarch. In allowing some ten thousand religious pilgrims the right to freely travel from Iran to Iraq, the Shah opened the door for the smuggling of Ayatollah Khomeini's fanatical and mutinous views across the border. It was through this pipeline that Khomeini's cassette tapes were transported into the hands of the opposition in Iran.

While the Shah was seen to be the principal patron of the Iraqi Kurds' struggle for independence and had supported the Kurds with arms and training, Iran's assistance came to a halt with the signing of the Algiers Accords between Iran and Iraq. During an OPEC meeting the two sides met and hammered out an agreement to end an ongoing dispute over borders, water, and navigation rights. The Shatt-El-Arab waterway was designated the defining border. On June 13, 1975, the two nations signed the treaty. Unfortunately for the Kurds, the Accords also meant the end of the Shah's support of the Kurdish rebels. Without that support the Kurds were powerless to provide any deterrent to Saddam Hussein's invasion of Iran.

Earlier in 1975 Secretary of State Henry Kissinger and Iran's Finance Minister Hushang Ansary had inked an agreement totaling $15 billion in purchases by Iran from the U.S. It was "the largest agreement of its kind ever signed by the two countries."[216] Such a massive sum of money was unfathomable to the vast majority of Iranians. This served to further distance the Shah from his people.

It was also in 1975 that the Shah established principals regarding private ownership of mining and industrial operations. Pahlavi gave the owners a period of three years to offer to the public 49 percent of the industries. This edict created a chaotic situation for the Shah. Wealthy industrialists were furious. They felt they were being forcibly stripped of their assets. Private citizens were equally disturbed at the thought of having to incur unwanted debt in order to purchase shares in the various companies. In his zeal to better the lot of the Iranian people, the Shah played right into the hands of what would become future President Jimmy Carter's human rights witch hunt by placing what appeared to be an unnecessary burden on the Iranian people.

With an agreement in place between Iran and Iraq, the Shah turned his attention to President Carter. In an attempt to mollify Carter's human rights agenda, the Shah ordered a sequence of liberalization policies. He permitted the reorganization of the National Front, an on-again-off-again, loosely organized political faction committed to "establish Iran's unequivocal sovereignty within and without; in other words...rule of law within, and political independence...without."[217]

In a note from Sullivan to the secretary of state, the ambassador commented that:

> *The GOI (Government of Iran) is continuing to feel its way through*
> *the circumstances, which have resulted from its policy of liberalizing*
> *conditions for public airing of dissent. The decision to avoid the use*
> *of massive police action is encouraging...If the dissidents opt for*
> *violent confrontation some nasty street fighting could erupt...and...*
> *turn into goon squads. We will continue to monitor carefully.*[218]

The National Front had been inactive for a number of years. In its absence a generation of students had arisen who were devoted to radicalism and Islamic fanaticism. As an island of stability of what was increasingly becoming a turbulent sea of discontent in Iran, the National Front seemed content to protect the monarchy with the understanding that the "monarch reigned, but did not rule."[219] This seemed to be supported by the protest marches that crippled Tehran on December 10 and 11, 1978. A CIA assessment of Iran indicated:

> *The protest marches in Tehran...which brought out as many as*
> *a million demonstrators into the streets, were masterfully*
> *organized and controlled. The evidence suggests that local*
> *community leaders called dastehoardan, whose traditional*
> *functions include organizing religious processions, mobilized*

*small crowds around local mosques and then moved these groups
to join others from around the city...The ability of these local
community leaders to bring out large numbers of people in
response to directives from members of the Islamic clergy gives
the religious opposition in Iran an organizational strength which
distinguishes it from any other group within the opposition...
The Ayatollah Ruhollah Khomeini has served as the focal point
for the loyalty of the religious opposition...There is no evidence
to substantiate the claim...that behind the pattern of events lies
the guiding hand of "foreign elements," "leftists," or...the Tudeh
party...demonstrations in Tehran on the high holy days of Mohar-
ram...were the most impressive display of organizational ability
thus far seen in the recent incidents of civil unrest in Iran.*[220]

The report went on to indicate that Khomeini had a strong
following, particularly within the lower classes, urban centers,
bazaar merchants and shopkeepers, and students who often chanted
his name during rallies.

In a manifesto apparently drafted specifically for the December
10-11 marches, the Khomeini-inspired revolutionaries laid out their
position. The document stated:

:: Ayatollah Khomeini is our leader. Whatever he asks we will
carry out. This march is a vote of confidence in Khomeini.

:: The apparatus of the governmental dictatorship must be
overthrown and power transferred to the people.

:: The rule of Islamic social and individual justice must be
established on the basis of the votes of the people.

:: This is Human Rights Day. We ask for the human rights,
which our struggle has sought.

:: The imperialism of East and West must be removed. The
Iranian people will continue and extend their relations with
other nations.

:: People should not make money from money. The exploitation of human beings by others should be stopped. The collection of wealth in the hands of some people and the property of others should be redistributed.

:: We salute the martyrs of the Iranian struggle.

:: We demand release of all political prisoners and return of all who have left the country because of lack of freedom.[221]

The Embassy also asked the questions: Will the Shah call for martial law, and if so, how heavy-handed will the government be? And perhaps most importantly, would the opposition be able to unite sufficiently to be able to approach the Shah convincingly?

The State Department telegram concluded:

Situation...offers both danger and hope. Danger in that radicals will instigate violent incidents which will draw moderates' attention away from rather pleasant feeling of success and provoke severe military reaction. Hope in that opposition can get unified proposal ready to move forward to coalition government reasonably soon.[222]

Also in December the Shah approached National Front leaders Shapour Bakhtiar and Gholam Hossein Sadiqi (the Shah's first choice as prime minister) to pursue the idea of instituting a civilian government or a constitutional monarchy. The men also explored the possibility of military rule. Unfortunately, the National Front, unlike the exiled Khomeini, had no accessibility to a network by which to propagate its message across Iran.

Dr. Parviz Mina told me of his last visit to Tehran and his certainty that the Shah's monarchy would not survive:

When the plane took off it circled over Tehran. And I was looking down...on the northwestern side of the city...there was this famous avenue running from east to west...this street right from the beginning

*to the end was packed with people who were demonstrating against
the Shah. I said, "By God, that's the end of it." That was the day
I thought that he was...not going to survive.*[223]

Waiting in the wings was the Ayatollah Ruhollah Khomeini,
whose vendetta against the Shah of Iran began in 1963 when
Pahlavi's forces successfully thwarted a religious movement headed
by Khomeini and deported the fanatical cleric first to Turkey and
then to Iraq. From that time Khomeini became obsessed with the
overthrow of the Pahlavi monarchy.

It was Khomeini's ability to turn local mosques into cauldrons
of revolutionary turmoil that was absolutely remarkable given
the territorial nature of the mullahs and ayatollahs. Former
Israeli Ambassador Uri Lubrani summarized his feeling about
Khomeini's rise:

*The religious establishment was the only organized body in Iran...
in each village. If you ask about Khomeini having a network,
he had the best possible network in Iran. I tried to touch base
with the religious establishment in 1973; they wouldn't talk to me.
The Shah didn't have an agent in each village, neither a police-
man. Nobody was allowed [by the Shah's government] to organize...
only the religious establishment...add to that what Khomeini was
disseminating from his exile first in Iraq and then in France, you'll
see that this big network was being fed with dissent and sedition...
By the beginning of 1978 I began to have forebodings...to feel
uneasy...to look for more urgent signs...of something brewing.
I went to see my foreign minister, Moshe Dayan, and told him of
my concerns. I said, "I have my forebodings...we ought to begin to
phase out." I knew at the end of the day...Israel will have no place
in Iran...the new regime will be an unfriendly regime to Israel.*[224]

In a move that in hindsight was likely one of the most
imprudent decisions by the Shah, Pahlavi freed a number of

pro-Khomeini mullahs from Iran's prisons in 1978. These disgruntled clerics bent on revenge gladly joined Khomeini's underground and were among the many whose mosques were made available to the radicals.

The network of mosques proved to be much more effective than the efforts of the National Front. Khomeini, however, was slow, methodical, and determined to seek revenge against his adversary, the Shah, no matter the time or cost in money or lives. The Grand Ayatollah recruited from the ranks of mid-level mullahs who whipped their followers into rabid, pro-Khomeini militants.

The Shah, of course, had charted his own path simply because he wanted the favor of his subjects, the Iranian people. He professed to be a pious Muslim; he made the required trips to pay homage at the various shrines. The Shah craved the favor of the clerics and submerged himself in prayer. How could he openly declare war on the mullahs whose support he so actively sought?

Khomeini's charisma was especially appealing to the lower classes, the *mostazafin*...the dispossessed. They saw him as their savior, the one who would rescue them from their lives of toil. Ahmad Ashraf wrote of the Ayatollah: "Khomeini gave the masses a sense of personal integrity, of collective identity, of historical rootedness, and feelings of pride and superiority."[225] In their hysterical longing for the coming of the *Mahdi*, the risen one that would free the masses from privation, discrimination, and tyranny, some claimed to have seen the Ayatollah's face in the moon.[226] This would certainly be consistent with the Persian penchant for superstition, numerology, and dependence on "omens, symbols, prophecies, and revelations."[227]

It would be in the name of this *Mahdi* that a rogue Muslim fanatic and his faction in Saudi Arabia would seize the Grand

Mosque in Mecca, seal the doors, and hold hostage the pilgrims inside the holiest of Muslim sites. The two-week siege would end only when French mercenaries and Saudi National Guard troops stormed the mosque. Hundreds were killed in the crossfire. This attack, though unsuccessful, was to be only a foretaste of the tactics Islamic fanatics were willing to use to achieve their goal...world domination through the return of the revered *Mahdi*. Khomeini was reputed by some to be the long-awaited redeemer of Islam.

Author Jahangir Amuzegar wrote of the mesmerizing Khomeini's appeal:

> He [Khomeini] spoke of such misty but universally popular goals as political and religious freedom, independence from pernicious foreign influences, social justice...the obligation to help the poor... the villainy of corruption, a need to conserve precious natural resources...and other goals.[228]

With his smooth rhetoric Khomeini managed to ensnare leaders of *The People's Mujahedeen-e-Khalq* and the Marxist-inspired *Fedayeen-e-Khalq* ("freedom fighters" with strong ties to the PLO) and entice them to join his brand of Islamic revolution. It was the *Mujahedeen* with its thin veneer of Islam that endowed Khomeini with the venerable title of "Imam." The group joined hands with Khomeini, deeming the Shah to be too secular. The *Fedayeen* was more interested in launching a Marxist revolution akin to that of Fidel Castro in Cuba or Che Guevara in Latin America.[229] Both organizations had ties to the PLO. The Ayatollah had asserted he would be a "guide to the people."[230] Few realized that he would, instead, grip the reins of power in Iran and rule with an iron fist, squashing all opposition in his path. Khomeini managed to pull the wool over the eyes of the likes of intellectual James Bill, who described the tyrannical ruler as a man of "impeccable integrity and honesty, who has denied again and again that he will hold office."[231]

To fund his campaign to depose the Shah, Khomeini relied in part on both the PLO and Syria's Hafez Assad. The Soviet defector, former General Ion Pacepa, also revealed that another source of funds to support this direct onslaught against the Shah came from the Soviet Union. Khomeini's fanatical influence on the mullahs in Iran was to be driven home to Pahlavi with powerful potency on October 9, 1977: twenty-plus students with covered faces rampaged through the University of Tehran, vandalizing classrooms, torching buses, and demanding that women be totally segregated from the male student population.

It was, however, during *Ramadan* (the Muslim month set aside for fasting and reflection) in August 1978 that large protest rallies erupted all across Iran. Curfew was imposed in some cities following days of mass rioting. The city of Abadan was the site of a mass murder said to have been staged by Islamic radicals. The doors of the *Rex Cinema*, hosting an Iranian film, were barred while the building was torched; 477 people died in the conflagration, including a number of children and their mothers. The clergy that directly supported Khomeini avowed that the fire was set by SAVAK, the Shah's secret police. Iranian police determined that followers of the Ayatollah were responsible for the murders of so many innocent people. In retrospect, this reeks of the tactics used by radical Islamic terrorists in countries such as Egypt, Algeria, and ultimately in the United States.

In Qom, the center of Islamic education in Iran, police fired into a group of rioters who were protesting a denouncement of Khomeini in the newspaper. Several clerics were killed in the melee.

The Shah's attempts to suppress the rioting were rejected by his enemies and supporters alike. His enemies saw it as a weak attempt at appeasement, and his supporters just saw it as weakness, period. Khomeini saw it as the beginning of a tsunami that would sweep the Shah out of power. It was becoming more obvious that the threat to Iran was not from the communist Soviet Union, but from socio-economic, religious, and political sources.

Under the tutelage of his former son-in-law, Ardeshir Zahedi, the Shah was encouraged to offer up a scapegoat to appease the mobs of demonstrators. Zahedi, who had been appointed ambassador to the United States, suggested such substitutes as Amir Hoveyda, and SAVAK heads Hasan Pakravan and Nematollah Nassiri. Zahedi assured Brzezinski, back in Washington, that he had the situation in Iran firmly in hand; obviously he was badly mistaken. Not even a counter demonstration organized by the ambassador could quell the unrest in his homeland.

In *Answers to History* Pahlavi wrote of the supposed role of the secret police:

> *The Western press…claims that bloodshed and death that marred our cities had nothing to do with terrorists but was the work of SAVAK agents…If SAVAK had only been as effective as our enemies claimed, they would not have been out in the streets shouting vilifications.*[232]

Dr. Mina talked with me about SAVAK and its purpose in Iran as seen by the Shah:

> *One thing the Iranian people did not appreciate was the lack of freedom of political activity. There was absolutely no other problem as far as individual liberty, religious liberty…It was only political activity which was controlled…the reason that was being done was because…the Shah was always afraid of the fact that*

Moscow would woo the intermediaries of their own choosing, which was the Tudeh Party, the communist party in Iran...he was frightened against communism...It was the United States that encouraged him to encourage the SAVAK...But that secret police was only fighting against communism...That was one of the reasons that they [U.S.] helped the Shah to create this secret police and then asked the Israelis to help Iran in training the people in [SAVAK].[233]

CHAPTER 12

. . . .

ISRAEL:
AN UNLIKELY ALLY

*[Khomeini asked,] 'What is this association between the Shah
and Israel? Is the Shah a Jew?'...Khomeini linked Israel and
America so intimately that there was virtually no distinction
between the two...Israel and America are simply two points of evil
along a vast satanic continuum."* (MICHAEL A. LEDEEN)[234]

September of 1978 found Ambassador Ardeshir Zahedi and
the crown prince on a visit to California. The ambassador
thought it good political training for young Reza to become
completely familiar with the United States. While traveling, Zahedi
was contacted by the Shah, who asked him to return to Iran as
quickly as possible.

Zahedi remembers that visit vividly:

*I arrived in Tehran by nightfall, September 4...Foreign Minister
Amir-Khosrow Afshar and a group of military leaders like Generals
Oveissi and Nasser Moghadam...had come to meet me...I was
surprised because my visit was supposed to be confidential. They
were all worried and pleaded with me to talk firmly with His Majesty*

and encourage him to act...Queen Farah, who had been informed
[of my arrival] by the guards, was waiting for me on the top of the
stairs at the main entrance hall. She warned me that His Majesty's
morale was very low and I had better avoid unpleasant topics...
Queen Farah said, "The Shah was suicidal."

His majesty was suffering from depression...When I saw the Shah
late that evening he was not in good shape. He had lost weight and
looked tired and depressed. As it was late, I suggested [it would be
better if I returned the next day...he insisted that I stay.]

I told the Shah about the gravity of the situation and mentioned to
him what I had heard from the generals and others at the airport.
We also spoke about corruption and what people were saying about
the royal family...At that time, I was not aware that the Shah had
cancer...only five people knew he was gravely ill. I blame these
people. If [the Iranian people] had known the truth about the Shah's
state of health, he would have had a great deal of sympathy and
would not have been demonized by the opposition the way he was.[235]

The queen, in fact, had shipped a quantity of personal and
household items to the United States. She was not alone; many
wealthy Iranians had moved to transfer large amounts of money
to Swiss, French, British, American, and Cayman Island banking
institutions.

Zahedi was informed by the Shah that martial law was
about to be declared by his newly-appointed prime minister, Jafar
Sharif-Emami. Mr. Sharif-Emami, who had been prime minister in
1960-1961, was chosen because of his reputation for personal
integrity and because of his close links with religious leaders.[236]
On his appointment he was charged by the Shah to give priority to
Islamic traditions. As a gesture in this direction it was announced
that the new "Imperial" calendar introduced in 1976 had been

abandoned in favor of the traditional Islamic lunar calendar. The new government of twenty-two included only five former ministers; among them were a former head of the Gendarmerie, General Abbas Gharabaghi, who became minister of the interior; and Mr. Amir Khosrow Afshar, a career diplomat who became foreign minister.[237]

Emami and representatives of Ayatollah Shariatmadari agreed to a series of demands by the moderate opposition. Among those demands granted were:

:: The religious meeting place (Hosseiniye) was allowed to reopen.

:: The Bazargan-Minatchi human rights organization was allowed to register.

:: Complete freedom of the press.

:: The prime minister agreed to try to push the following demands:

:: Royal family to stay out of all business and generally be kept in tight rein.

:: Speedy trials for those charged with corruption.

:: Shah to reign not rule, and thus not interfere with daily government business. Shah would remain commander-in-chief of armed forces.[238]

The prime minister had begun his new administration with an attempt at appeasing the clerics, but the opposite effect was achieved. Sharif-Emami's moves only served to further enrage the radical mullahs. Emami, who served in the post of prime minister in the 1960s, was perhaps not the most auspicious choice by the Shah. He was seen by the Iranian people as the embodiment of the very dissolute system they were trying to overthrow. The ambassador strongly suggested to the prime minister that repeated changes in political direction only served to further destabilize the situation in Iran, and that it was a necessity for any actions by the new government to be seen as honest and above-board. He also encouraged the Shah to relinquish the daily governmental tasks to his appointees and focus on maintaining the respect and confidence of the military.

The opposition to the Shah's government organized a series of demonstrations to begin on September 8. The Shah again called for Zahedi and sought his opinion about the course of action: should he declare martial law or should he refrain? Zahedi advised him:

> "Majesty, you have named a government, now let them take their responsibility…These huge crowds may decide to walk all the way up to the palace if they are left on their own." I insisted that the government must combine firmness with dialogue; otherwise His Majesty may face the same fate as Tsar Nicholas. We spoke more at length about the royal family and concluded that they should all leave the country. I called Princess Ashraf (the Shah's twin sister) that same night and told her to pack. Some royal family members were already outside the country…[later] on my way back to Washington I called each one and told them not to return.[239]

All the while the powers-that-be in Washington had failed to recognize the danger of the downward-spiraling events in Iran. Carter, Cyrus Vance, and Brzezinski were all immersed in discussions with Sadat and Begin at Camp David. Zahedi was a bit surprised when Rosalynn was the only Carter who received him at the White House for a debriefing on the situation in Tehran. The president had shoved the simmering pot that was Iran onto a back burner.

On September 8 marshal law was enacted and a curfew set in place. The next day demonstrations erupted in Iran. In an attempt to suppress a protest rally held in Jaleh Square in Tehran, troops fired into the crowd. Estimates placed the number of deaths at approximately one thousand; the Shah's government admitted to killing 122.

That bloody September day came to be known as "Black Friday." Houchang Nahavandi wrote of an interview with a participant in the riots:

> Elements in the crown opened fire against the forces of orders, whose casualties were all due to bullet-wounds...there were among the demonstrators Palestinians, who had entered the country with "genuine" false papers...In July 1980 I received a first-hand account of the events...[by] someone who, in 1978, had been an activist in the revolutionary movement...He was contacted by a group of "Islamic-Marxists," who assigned to him two armed Palestinians...these two fired indiscriminately, not only at the soldiers, but also...into the crowd, simply to shed blood and create irreparable resentment...Other armed men...lay in ambush...and opened fire in similar fashion.[240]

Zahedi requisitioned a helicopter and with Generals Oveissi and Khosrowdad flew over Tehran to observe the situation on the ground. (The ambassador sadly told me that both men were later butchered by Khomeini's henchmen.) He was in constant contact with the Shah in order to keep him informed of events. Zahedi also mentioned his thoughts on Ambassador Sullivan during those difficult days:

> I learned that Ambassador Sullivan had gone to see Foreign Minister Afshar. He told Afshar he was getting negative noises from Washington about the situation in Iran, and "Ardeshir better return there quickly to fix it." I guess he wanted to get rid of me in order to have a free hand in Tehran.[241]

About that same time, State Department Appointee Henry Precht wrote that he had a "revelation":

> *The day after the massacre, I was taking my morning shower and the thought came to me that the Shah was indeed finished. This was a war between him and his people, and he could not prevail in such a war. When he might go, and how, I didn't know. Whether he would be able to make some compromise that would diminish his powers, I didn't know. But it was clear to me that the Iran of the future was not going to be the Iran of the past. The opposition elements would play a much larger role and the Shah a much smaller role, and we needed to adjust to that.[242]*

An interview with the Shah by a *Time* magazine correspondent reveals the toll that the Jaleh Square incident and the imposition of martial law had taken on him:

> *The Shah was plainly an immensely saddened man. It showed in his face, which was grim and gaunt, and in his eyes, which were tired and melancholy. Even his dress, so often elegant, was somber. He wore a dark, formal suit, an unadorned white shirt and a narrow, conservative tie. There was little life and much caution in his voice. He answered questions after long and painful pauses.[243]*

While the Shah was desperately trying to regain control in Iran, Khomeini had been in Iraq inciting revolution. Amir Taheri wrote in his book, *The Spirit of Allah: Khomeini and the Islamic Revolution,* of the ludicrous charges that Khomeini and his subversive network continuously directed at the Shah. Pahlavi was randomly charged with being a womanizer, a homosexual, a Jewish convert, a drug addict, and a Catholic. He was also labeled the "American Shah" and "Israel's Shah." Even the beautiful Empress Farah did not escape Khomeini's twisted defamation; she was maligned as an adulteress and linked romantically to none other than President Jimmy Carter.[244]

The term "Israel's Shah" was likely due to the fact that in 1957 Iran aided the Israelis by funding an oil pipeline from Eilat to the Mediterranean. In the summer of that year an Iranian representative met secretly with Finance Minister Levi Eshkol and Minister of Trade and Industry Pinhas Sapir. At the end of the negotiations the three men signed an agreement that would permit the sale of Iranian oil to Israel for the now-paltry sum of $1.30 per barrel.[245] The Shah was eager to complete this transaction, as it would allow Iranian oil to circumvent the Suez Canal, which was under Egypt's jurisdiction. This was especially important, as some three-quarters of Iran's oil exports flowed through that strategic waterway.[246] The eight-inch pipeline, completed in approximately three months, was upgraded in 1958 to a sixteen-inch line.

It was also in 1957 that the Shah first asked Israel's Mossad to provide training for his secret police, *Sazeman-e Ettela'at va Amniyat-e Keshvar* (SAVAK.) Some sources record that it was Mossad and American CIA agents who taught SAVAK the means of torture as an investigative tool.[247] My good friend, the late Isser Harel, was the head of Mossad when the Shah made his overture for assistance. The Israelis were not above using flattery with Pahlavi and compared him to Cyrus the Great, who was responsible for freeing the Jews from Babylonian captivity. Harel revealed: "The connection was very romantic, and I would say of great importance at that time... [The Shah] wanted to play the part."[248]

In an interview in 1960 the Shah is said to have confirmed a long-standing association with the Israelis when he acknowledged, "Iran has recognized Israel long ago." (The Shah was speaking of the recognition afforded Israel by the Mossadegh regime in 1951.[249] Reportedly, that recognition came at the cost of a $400,000 bribe to Iran's then-Prime Minister Muhammad Saed Maraghei. In March

1950 Israel had offered a consulate to Iran, although it was forced to work through the Swiss Embassy in Tel Aviv. Tehran then became an effective pipeline, not only for Jews wishing to escape Iraq and relocate to Israel, but also for oil sales to Israel.) Pahlavi's response so incensed Egypt's Gamal Abdul Nasser that he halted all political contact with Iran and launched a vitriolic crusade against the Shah and Iran.

Despite Iran's entente with Israel, the Shah believed that the Jews controlled the U.S. media and held enormous sway in Washington, D.C.; therefore, he took great care not to antagonize the Israelis. The Shah's fears provided Israel with a harvest of concessions from Iran.[250]

Because of Iran's large Jewish population, the largest in any other Middle Eastern country,[251] a number of very secretive meetings between Iranian and Israeli officials took place over the years prior to the Shah's ouster. These included Prime Minister David Ben-Gurion in 1961, Prime Minister Levi Eshkol, Prime Minister Yitzhak Rabin, Prime Minister Menachem Begin, and an invitation from the Shah to Prime Minister Golda Meir in 1972. Meir secretly flew into Tehran's Mehrabad airport for a meeting with Pahlavi. In some circles the Shah has been credited with having tried to arrange a peace agreement between Meir and Anwar Sadat.[252]

Apparently Iran viewed Israel as a strong deterrent to Soviet rather than Arab aggression in the Gulf region.[253] The Shah could readily visualize the possibility of a Russian dual flank operation against Iran through Iraq and Afghanistan and hoped that his covert relationship with Israel would serve him well. Gary Sick recounted that just "seven months after Begin's visit to Iran, the Israeli prime minister tried to convince Carter and Sadat at the Camp David talks that the Shah was finished."[254]

In our personal interview Samuel Segev, author of *The Iranian Triangle*, further suggests that Begin and Sadat tried to encourage Carter to issue a statement in support of the Shah. Segev said he found it "very odd that the president of the biggest country in the world...didn't understand...that the priority was to avoid, to prevent the fall of the Shah, and to get some stability in the region."[255] Each man, of course, had separate insight into the woes of the Shah; Begin had access to Lubrani's report on Iran, and Sadat was a close friend to the Iranian monarch.

Though Israel was not openly acknowledged by Pahlavi, the two countries continued to preserve amiable relations. Israel maintained a permanent mission in Tehran that housed, to all intents and purposes, an unofficial embassy.

Israel's then-Chief of Staff Yitzhak Rabin first visited Iran in 1967. His trip was handled amidst great secrecy, and Rabin was whisked from place to place with little fanfare and clad in civilian clothes rather than his army regalia. Rabin, however, broke with tradition and signed his name in Hebrew when he visited the Tehran Mausoleum that housed the tomb of the Shah's father, Reza Shah.

Rabin was granted an audience with Reza Pahlavi and the two discussed such weighty matters as the possible repercussions of King Hussein's break with then-PLO leader Ahmed Shukeiri and Gamal Abdul Nasser's grip on the Arabian Peninsula and his influence in the Persian Gulf. Less than two months after his visit to Tehran Yitzhak Rabin would lead Israel's Defense Forces in a pre-emptive attack against Nasser's Egyptian army, which had amassed hundreds of tanks and tens of thousands of soldiers on the Egyptian-Israeli border. Given his Arab ties and his covert relationship with Israel, the conflict placed the Shah in a very difficult position. Tehran newspapers were openly and blatantly hostile toward Israel, but not the Shah's military leaders. Chief of Staff Bahram Ariana and his deputy General Feridoun Jam openly congratulated the Israelis on their victory over Egypt, Jordan, Syria, Saudi Arabia, Iraq, Kuwait, and Algeria.

The Shah, who was visiting Paris when the war began, stopped in Turkey on his way back to Tehran. During a press conference, he called on Israel to withdraw from the territories captured during the six days of fighting. Expecting congratulations from the Shah for decimating Nassar's forces, Israeli government officials were stunned by the Shah's hard line and the fact that he halted joint endeavors with the Jewish nation. Pahlavi even went so far as to try to pressure President Lyndon Johnson to force Israel to relinquish the territory captured during the war, but Johnson refused.

Realizing that his efforts to snub Israel were futile, the Shah agreed to purchase another six thousand Uzis from Israel and began to encourage King Hussein to establish ties with that country. (In 1965 the Shah sanctioned the purchase of a quantity of Uzi submachine guns to be used by his Royal Guard and the police.) Of course, oil would still flow between Iran and Israel, but now through a new thirty-two-inch pipeline that was completed in December 1969.

According to one source, "In the aftermath of the Six-Day War, Israel transferred large amounts of oil from Iran to European markets via the Eilat-Ashkelon pipeline. In addition, Israel purchased a significant portion of its oil needs from Iran. Apparently, the two nations had numerous business transactions, although the extent of these dealings was never officially quantified."[256] The Shah shrugged off questions about oil sales to Israel by declaring he did not know the final destination of the oil once the tankers left their ports in the Persian Gulf. At the end of the Shah's rule,

Iran's trade with Israel totaled approximately $400 million per year; and the Shah had purchased some $600 million in light weapons from Israel.[257]

CHAPTER 13

. . . .

THE HANDWRITING
ON THE WALL

*"Man is a strange animal. He generally cannot
read the handwriting on the wall until his back
is up against it."* (ADLAI E. STEVENSON)

Having been fueled by the Iranian media following the Six-Day War, hatred toward Israel and the Iranian Jews gained momentum. Something as simple as a soccer match in Tehran in late 1968 opened the pus-laden sore of anti-Semitism. Swastika-painted balloons floated over the stadium while an effigy of Moshe Dayan was kicked and spat upon. The Shah could not believe his people capable of such barbarism.

Iran and Israel still cooperated militarily, although one Iranian navy commander put the cooperation in terms of its covert aspects: "We couldn't have our ships running around the Persian Gulf with Israeli (Gabriel) missiles onboard."[258] Not only did Israel sell arms to Iran; it provided training for Iranian military officers, secret police, and pilots, as well as instruction in intelligence-gathering.

This and more came to light when Khomeini's rogues raided the Israeli Embassy in Tehran and published documents found inside.[259]

In the summer of 1972 Uri Lubrani was sent to Tehran as Israel's ambassador. Lubrani was to be the first Israeli to present his credentials directly to the Shah. After repeated attempts to gain an audience through Foreign Minister Abbas Ali Khalatbari, Lubrani determined he was being politely ignored by the monarch.

With information gained during his tenure, Lubrani repeatedly warned Israel's leaders of the imminent collapse of the monarchy in Iran:

> For years, at every opportunity we warned that there was an Iranian danger. That it was greater and more profound than any other danger facing Israel. Even more than the Palestinian issue. We said that it should be handled first. Not only in Lebanon, but in Tehran as well. Because from Tehran they send out tentacles to Berlin, to Saudi Arabia, to Argentina.[260]

Lubrani told me that it took weeks for him to muster up enough courage to put his thoughts and feelings down on paper. He had no proof that trouble was afoot; simply a gut feeling gained from talking to people in the bazaar, in the oil industry, and within the trade unions. He felt something very ominous but couldn't put his finger on what that might have been. Lubrani was constrained by the knowledge that when an ambassador puts his assessment in writing, it becomes an official, historical document.

Finally, he wrote a memo that was distributed by Dayan to the Knesset. Lubrani suggested that Israel begin immediately to find an alternative source for the 95 percent of oil that was imported from Iran. Dayan had the Lubrani document paraphrased and forwarded to the CIA as being from a "usually reliable source." According to Lubrani, the CIA responded that the source didn't know what he was talking about. Nothing was expected to happen in Iran for ten or fifteen years.[261]

Lubrani chose to visit the bazaars, not because it was the place to shop but because the bazaar was a place to "pray, to meet friends, to do business, to sit in a café. You can go there to catch up on gossip, can take part in an opposition rally. Without having to run all over town...the bazaar ...is indispensable for earthly existence and, through prayer and offerings, also ensures [for the Shiite] his eternal life."[262]

When after five years as ambassador in Iran Lubrani was recalled from Tehran, Yosef Harmelin, former head of Shin Bet, Israel's security service, was appointed to replace him. When Harmelin was visited by General David Ivry, Israel's commander of the air force and the last senior officer to visit the country before the Shah was ousted, Ivry could sense the imminent collapse of the Shah's monarchy and that the protest movement had become a revolution in the making:

The strikes and demonstrations had spread over the country, oil production was barely adequate for local consumption...banks were closed, and there were serious shortages of basic food items. The Revolutionary Guards, trained in PLO camps in Lebanon and Libya, made their first appearance in the cities.[263]

In a personal interview General Ivry recounted the tension that could be felt in the streets of Tehran just weeks before the start of the revolution. The general had to be flown from location to location by helicopter due to the rioting and demonstrations in the streets. "The army," said Ivry, "was on strike."[264]

Israeli Prime Minister Yitzhak Rabin's second secret meeting in Tehran took place in 1974. He met with the Shah to present a proposal to trade land-for-peace. The two men spent two hours together, during which time each shared his personal analysis of the world situation, especially as it related to the Middle East and relations between Israel and Iran. Pahlavi called for Rabin to be more flexible in his dealings with Sadat and Hussein; at the same time, he refused to grant a billion-dollar loan for a number of projects to the Israeli prime minister.

By November 1978 the Israelis could clearly see the proverbial handwriting on the wall and began to evacuate all Israeli citizens who wished to depart the troubled country. November 6 saw the departure of 365 Israelis, the majority women and children. Although terrorists linked to the PLO had launched attacks on the El Al office in Tehran, the airline continued to operate flights in and out of Iran in order to accommodate as many Israelis as possible.

The Shah's major concerns, meanwhile, centered on three issues:

1. *Afghanistan*—that the U.S.S.R. would invade Afghanistan if Iran was weakened;

2. *Iraq*—that Iraq would take advantage of a weakened Iran and invade; and

3. *Khomeini*—that the popular cleric would be successful with his call for an Islamic Revolution in Iran.

James A. Bill wrote "Iran and the Crisis of 1978;" his opinion paralleled that of Pahlavi:

> Outside of Iran, there are three general opinions on the nature of the opposition to the regime. The Shah's opponents are said by some to consist of a small group of trouble-making Marxists supported in their treasonous activities by the Soviet Union and other radical regimes such as today's Libya. Others would maintain that Iranian opposition is dominated by a number of reactionary religious leaders who resent the Shah's modernization

program, which emphasizes land reform and women's rights. A third position summarizes the Shah's problems in terms of an unholy alliance of these two extreme factions, which have joined forces with the sole aim of dismantling the present political system.[265]

Pahlavi felt he could no longer count on the U.S. to remain a staunch ally under President Carter's administration. By 1977 the Shah was convinced that pro-Soviet Arab nations would unite and launch an attack against Iran. This fear prompted Pahlavi to spend billions on defensive weapons in an attempt to forestall an invasion by Soviet-backed Iraq. He knew that his armaments did not include anti-missile weapons that would help defend his country against Iraq's SCUD missiles. The Shah was concerned that Iraq possessed more armaments, including the Soviet-supplied SCUD missiles, than did Iran. The Iranian monarch felt compelled to arm his country against possible aggression from Saddam Hussein despite the signing of the Algiers Accords in 1975, which were intended to settle land disputes between the two countries.

In an interview with *Newsweek* in November 1977, the reporter asked Pahlavi about the accusations that the Shah's arms purchases represented *"la Folie des grandeurs"* (delusions of grandeur.) The Shah answered:

It's not only U.S. unreliability as we witnessed in Vietnam, Cambodia, Laos, and during the India-Pakistan wars. It's also U.N. impotency. We have settled our differences with Iraq, but their military buildup continues...I wonder how many of your editorial writers and congressmen realize that Iraq has more planes, tanks, and guns than we do—(even ground-to-ground SCUD missiles.) Nor are we just in another state. Look at our borders. What would happen if what remains of Pakistan were to disintegrate? If we don't assume [our own] security in the regions, who will do it?[266]

With the safety of Iran in mind the Shah approached President Carter about the purchase of Pershing missiles; the administration declined based on the fact that the Pershing was capable of carrying nuclear warheads.[267] In a move destined to cause enormous controversy, Iran turned to Israel for assistance. It came in the form of technology that partnered the two countries in the production of ballistic missiles.

The cooperation between Israel and Iran had begun when Israel Aircraft Industry founder, Adolf Schwimmer, secured a contract to overhaul Iranian airliners and American-made F-86 fighters. In order to gain entry into Iranian circles, Schwimmer sought the help of his friend and later business partner, Ya'acov Nimrodi. Nimrodi had spent twenty-five years in Tehran in various Israeli governmental roles. (Much of his work during Israel's early years is still classified.) Through Nimrodi's influence Schwimmer was allowed access to Tehran's inner business circles. He was granted audiences with the Shah several times and hosted Iranian government officials and senior military men in Israel.

In my interview with Samuel Segev, the author related how Nimrodi described a trip to Israel for Iran's Chief of Staff General Bahram Ariani and General Hasan Toufanian. Ariani proved to be an advocate for Israel. He encouraged the Shah to collaborate with the Israelis. Ariani also encouraged the Shah to mediate a peace pact between Israel and Jordan's King Hussein. The king thought Israel's only interest was in securing the territory on the West Bank. Nimrodi escorted the two Iranians on tours of various industrial sites in Israel, leading Ariani to wonder if Iran might be allowed to manufacture 81 mm mortars for the Israelis.[268]

In 1976 Schwimmer outlined an elaborate proposal for technological advancement between the two countries. Shimon Peres,

Israel's then-minister of defense under Yitzhak Rabin, presented the plan to the Shah. The two countries agreed to work together in a collaboration labeled *Project Flower* or "Tzur." The proposal included provisions for the production of a mid-range, surface-to-surface missile with the costs divided between the two countries. "The Flower project…involved the production of missiles with warheads weighing 750 kilograms…with a range of up to three hundred miles. They were to be shipped through a Swiss company to central Iran for assembly and testing."[269] Also included in the agreement was the possibility of jointly building a new-and-improved version of France's Mirage 5 aircraft. Both countries agreed on secrecy for the project because each head-of-state feared interference from what was certain to be a Carter administration in the New Year.

During Shimon Peres' visit with the Shah, Pahlavi was perplexed as to exactly what the United States wanted of him, especially in regard to future dealings with the PLO. When I talked with Samuel Segev, he was able to give me insight into the Shah's feelings toward the PLO:

> *I don't know what they want of me in Congress…to surrender to terror? We recently captured one hundred terrorists, and I have no intention of giving in to their blackmail. The Palestinians poison the atmosphere and do their best to subvert pro-Western governments in our region. Iraq still wants Kuwait and the Soviet Union is after Oman. I have no choice but to trust in Iran.*[270]

At the same time Pahlavi touted Sadat's role in the Middle East and his pro-Western leanings. Peres reassured the Shah that the agreement between Egypt and Israel was moving forward smoothly. The two men talked at length about the Shah's reservations over the upcoming U.S. election and the seeming finality of Jimmy Carter's presidential bid. The Shah, of course, again expressed his reservations about the tack that Carter's Middle East policies would take.

The collaboration of *Project Flower* brought Israel's Defense Minister Yitzhak Rabin and Iran's Procurement Chief Toufanian together to provide security for Iran against a Soviet and Iraqi offensive. One of the discussions during their meetings centered on the development of a submarine-launched missile, and concerns about India and Pakistan's nuclear arms race.[271] Toufanian was an old hand at procuring arms from Israel.

The election of Begin called a halt to the project for a time. It was reinstated in 1978, and according to NTI (Nuclear Threat Institute), "The following year Iran made a down-payment for *Project Flower* by providing Israel with $280 million worth of oil. To support this project, a team of Iranian experts began construction of a missile assembly facility near Sirjan, in south central Iran, and a missile test range near Rafsanjan."[272] Both Iran and Israel chose to play their cards close to the vest regarding this issue and failed to inform their joint U.S. ally of the project. Assistant Secretary of State for Near Eastern Affairs Harold Saunders was forthcoming with his opinion about the Israel/Iran connection: "Israel built a lot of things for the Iranians that we [the U.S.] did not know about."[273] Khomeini's rise to power signaled the death of *Project Flower*.

Dr. Mina talked with me about another joint project between Israel and Iran:

> *We even invested in Israel in a special power plant which connected the Port of Eilat, Ashkelon, in the Mediterranean. This power plant took the oil from the Gulf of Aqaba and delivered it to the Mediterranean port of Ashkelon and also fed the refineries in Haifa. So, we were supplying oil for internal consumption, but at the same time*

they were using that pipeline for the export of our crude oil, which was a shortcut instead of paying a very high rate for tankers to go through the Suez Canal.[274]

The Israeli Mossad held another card close: bringing together the Iranian and Chinese governments to discuss an underground war in Afghanistan against Soviet aggression. In September 1978 a high-level Chinese official, Qiao Shi, flew to Iran to meet with the Iranian secret police.[275] Having the Soviets in a quagmire in Afghanistan, similar to the U.S. situation in Vietnam, would siphon billions from the Russian economy. Whatever plans the two countries may have had to influence events in Afghanistan were upended when the Shah fled the country in January 1979.

After Begin assumed the position as Israel's prime minister, the Shah began to pull back from his support of the Jewish state. The Shah sided with the Arabs on the issue of the West Bank, and in a missive to government leaders called for the United States to compel Israel to reach an agreement with its Arab neighbors: "The Shah feels the U.S. should make every effort to bring about an early resolution to the Arab-Israeli situation. He is on record as opposing the Judaization of Jerusalem and supporting Israeli withdrawal from all occupied Arab territories and restoring the legitimate rights of the Palestinians."[276]

The Shah then instructed his procurement officer to hold back on covert Israeli/Iranian arms ventures. In other conciliatory moves toward his Arab brothers, Pahlavi denied Iranian participation in the celebration of Israel's twenty-second anniversary. He also forbade the Israelis an invitation to the festivities marking Persia's 2500 years as an empire. It was this lavish celebration that had incensed the American press. Pahlavi felt the response was because "the U.S. media was controlled by Jewish interests. He attributed any criticism of Iran in the American media as an Israeli effort to under-mine him."[277]

Pahlavi also warned Israeli Foreign Minister Moshe Dayan that Soviet aggression would not bypass Israel and its Arab neighbors. During his meeting with Dayan, the Shah cautioned the tiny Jewish nation: "Israel would do well to take into account that these countries [Iraq and Syria], at the initiative and backing of Soviet Russia, would again make war on Israel."[278] Dayan suggested to the Shah that Iran and Israel normalize relations by changing the designation of the Iranian diplomatic mission in Tehran to an official embassy. Pahlavi declined Dayan's suggestion for fear of inciting Iran's clerics. Pahlavi's generals sought Dayan's assistance to help the monarch understand the enormity of the threat Iran faced due to the Shah's inability to make critical decisions. Dayan was unsuccessful and concluded that Pahlavi was politically paralyzed.

The Shah's fears regarding the Soviets and the Iraqis would prove to be the least of his worries. It was not to be from countries outside Iran that his greatest challenge would come; it was to be the Ayatollah Khomeini who brought down the House of Pahlavi and the monarchy.

Khomeini's oratory was designed to create fear in the lower classes in Iran, those forced to do without while witnessing the overindulgence of the upper classes. He heralded what was seen as the Shah's complicity with Israel and the United States. The intellectuals, the political frontline in Iran, initially took a wait-and-see attitude, but it was not long before they joined forces with the oppressed and poverty-stricken and took to the streets in protest of the Shah's policies. With the help of PLO-supplied weapons, trained terrorists, and the murders of Iranian demonstrators as a means to incite the mobs in the streets, the mayhem spread. Yasser Arafat, head of the PLO, was hailed as a friend by Khomeini after the Ayatollah seized control of Iran. Arafat's reward was the Israeli Embassy in Tehran with a PLO standard flying overhead. Arafat quickly named a member of Fatah, Hani al Hassan, to head the mission.

The PLO leader was ecstatic. He saw the Iranian revolution as a way to reverse "the strategic balance in the Middle East against Israel and the United States." The Camp David Accords would be "merely ink on paper following the basic changes brought by the Iranian revolution, both in the region and our Islamic nation and in world strategy."[279] Arafat ridiculed speculation that Saudi Arabia's King Khalid, the UAE, or Kuwait might be exposed to the aftermath of Khomeini's revolution in Iran.

Henry Kissinger may have summed up what led to the Shah's downfall better than most in his book, *White House Years*. Kissinger wrote of the 1953 coup that restored the Shah to the Peacock Throne:

He [the Shah] never forgot that. It may have been the root of his extraordinary trust in American purposes and American goodwill and of his psychological disintegration when he sensed that friend ship evaporating. On some levels excessively, even morbidly, suspicious of possible attempts to diminish his authority, he never-theless retained an almost naïve faith in the United States.[280]

Ardeshir Zahedi thought Kissinger a "noble man…who understood that letting down an ally of three decades in his hour of need was a disgrace and not in the longer interest of the United States."[281]

It is possible that Kissinger had read the account of the Shah having reportedly told an aide, "As long as the Americans support me, we can do and say whatever we want—and I am immovable."[282]

The Shah had every reason to believe in the efficacy of the United States' commitment to Iran. After all, was it not the U.S. in conjunction with Great Britain that had removed Mossadegh and returned the Shah to power in 1953? Had not Dwight D. Eisenhower funneled $500 million to Iran between 1953 and 1957? Was it not the U.S. that aided Iran in expelling the Soviets following World War II? There was a long history of cooperation between the two nations, an international version of, "You scratch my back; I'll stake you to Iranian oil for companies in the U.S."

Various presidents paid cherished accolades to the Shah during his visits to the U.S.:

> *Dwight Eisenhower:* "*Under the courageous leadership of the Shah, the people of Iran met [the danger of a communist takeover]. In their efforts to restore economic stability, they received indispensable help from us...Iran remains free; and its freedom continues to prove of vital importance to our freedom.*"[283]

> *John F. Kennedy:* "*[The Shah is] a vital force in maintaining the independence of [Iran]...So when we welcome the Shah here we welcome a friend and a very valiant fighter.*"[284]

Despite Kennedy's kind words, he was not so enamored of the Shah. He, like Carter, called for international reforms. So vitriolic was the U.S. position toward the Shah under Kennedy that Edward R. Murrow, Kennedy's appointee to oversee the United States Information Agency, cancelled a film on Iran simply because the Shah had ordered it shown throughout his country. Said Murrow, "Anything that pleases them so much as that can't be completely accurate reporting."[285] The Shah finally called on the head of the IDF Military Intelligence Branch, Chaim Herzog, for information as to why Kennedy seemed determined to ignore Iran's role in CENTO.

Samuel Segev provided insight to the answer during our interview: He said Herzog explained to the Shah that Kennedy favored economic aid rather than arms supplies.

James A. Bill wrote, "Kennedy's doubts about the Shah were so strong that he even considered forcing his abdication in favor of rule by regency until his young son came of age."[286] Is it possible that Kennedy's view of Pahlavi was colored by a conversation he reportedly had had with Nikita Khrushchev in Vienna in 1961? The Russian strongman declared to the president that the Shah was no more than the son of a sergeant in the Iranian army. Khrushchev predicted that Pahlavi would suffer defeat, but not at the hands of the Soviets. The Russian's warnings were so unsettling to Kennedy that he ordered an analysis of the situation. The Intelligence Estimate concluded: "profound political and social change [probably revolutionary in nature] in one form or another is virtually inevitable."[287]

There are those who believe that Teymour Bakhtiar, SAVAK chief in Iran, was the one courted by Kennedy to attempt a coup against Pahlavi. Apparently the Shah was told of the plot and quickly removed Bakhtiar from his post. Perhaps Carter's desire to be compared to John F. Kennedy went deeper than imagined.

The Shah retaliated against Kennedy's rejection by appearing to court the Soviets and by giving hard-line interviews to U.S. newspapers.[288] Julius Holmes, U.S. Ambassador to Iran, outlined why the Shah was so upset by Kennedy's rhetoric:

> What really upset the Shah was what Kennedy had said in his speeches...The U.S. was for "revolution"—that was the word... The Shah interpreted these words to mean just one thing: we are going to support a revolution in Iran.[289]

The Shah's tough stance didn't last long. In mid-1961, in an attempt at appeasement toward Kennedy, Pahlavi named a leader in

ATOMIC IRAN: COUNTDOWN TO ARMAGEDDON

the opposition party and a clear favorite of the U.S., Dr. Ali Amini, as prime minister. It was U.S. support for Amini that caused the Shah to be increasingly suspicious regarding the U.S. Embassy's sympathy for the National Front in Iran. Dr. Ahmad Tehrani was also able to shed some light on the Shah's relationship with Kennedy during our interview:

> The Shah was an extremely pragmatic man when he was talking to the leaders of the world. I was present and taking notes when he came to meet with President Kennedy. He [Pahlavi] had a profound knowledge of general politics of the world. Even before Kennedy won the election, (he was not particularly pro the regime in Iran)...he decided to meet the Shah privately. When the Shah was invited to Washington, I had a very good friend by the name of Jim Nichols. Jim was a speech writer and public relations man. He was extraordinarily impressed with the Shah and decided to help him with his speeches. We knew Kennedy did not see eye-to-eye with the Shah...and that is why we brought in Jim Nichols... As far as I know, Kennedy was kind to the Shah...The Shah's relationship with Nixon and Ford was the same. [With Carter] in the beginning it was not the same, but it became so that Carter decided to spend the New Year in Iran.[290]

Although he had made thirteen trips to the U.S., it may be that in the end Pahlavi had forgotten his earlier reception at the hands of U.S. presidents. He was reportedly ignored by Franklin D. Roosevelt when the commander-in-chief, in the company of Winston Churchill and Joseph Stalin, visited Tehran in November 1943 during World War II. The three men signed a declaration in support of "the independence, sovereignty, and territorial integrity of Iran."[291] However, Roosevelt did take time later to write a letter chastising the Shah for the lack of forestation (the planting of trees) in the country.[292] Harry S. Truman declined appeals for foreign aid; John F. Kennedy referred to Pahlavi as a despot. Jimmy Carter, with visions of grandeur as a reincarnation of John F. Kennedy, adopted his human rights stance against the Shah, greeted him warmly, and then set out to strip Pahlavi of his throne and country.[293] The Shah must have wondered at some point if Carter really was just another Kennedy clone.

In 1977 the American Embassy took steps to better report on opposition groups in Iran. As we discussed in other chapters, the U.S. renewed contacts with moderate (and some not-so-moderate) politicians under the pretext of human rights. During the fall of 1977 both State Department and Embassy officials determined those contacts must be maintained regardless of the Shah's reaction. The contacts were often arranged through the aide of a former Iranian prime minister. The U.S. ambassador was informed that the U.S. government was well-aware of the arrangements. This go-between was able to assist Embassy officials with better access to the more radical elements in both the bazaars and the clergy.[294]

The by-product of Carter's policy against the Shah was that the United States came to be seen as a capricious ally, one that could not be depended upon in times of crisis. Brzezinski, however, saw the necessity of this commitment. He felt that the only path for the U.S. was unconditional support of the Shah.

CHAPTER 14

· · · · · · · · · · · · · · · · · · ·

THE BALL REPORT:
AN INDICTMENT OF THE SHAH

"In a world in the midst of fundamental transformation,
prudent statesmen are especially in demand. Disconnected idealists
and visionaries...fall short of statesmanship...their wisdom is
impractical...The moral component of politics is sacrificed on
the altar of political expediency." (JAMES A. BILL)[295]

The Shah was in dire trouble, and the Carter administration
seemed unable or unwilling to recognize or acknowledge the
situation. In fact, a CIA report from the late 1970s indicated that
only two operatives were active in Iran. In his book, *All Fall Down:
America's Tragic Encounter with Iran,* author Gary Sick wrote:
"U.S. intelligence capability to track the Shah's domestic opposition
had been allowed to deteriorate to the vanishing point."[296] Furthermore, the State Department under Carter's administration was
openly hostile to the Pahlavi regime, opposing not only the sale
of conventional military weapons but also of ordinary riot gear.
Meanwhile, Carter continued to vacillate between the priorities of

demanding human rights concessions from the Shah and supporting a strategic American ally in the region.

In *Nest of Spies*, Amir Taheri wrote: "Khomeini's supporters also began to think of the 'new possibilities' that the expected rift between Tehran and Washington might offer. Ebrahim Yazdi, an Iranian-born American citizen representing the Ayatollah in the United States, wrote to him in Najaf in Iraq that 'the Shah's friends in Washington are out...It is time to act.'"[297]

Liberal Princeton Professor Richard Falk described Khomeini's entourage of advisors as: "moderate, progressive individuals [with] a notable record of concern for human rights." Furthermore, Falk stated that an Iran under Khomeini's governance would "provide us with a desperately-needed model of human government for a third-world country."[298] Could he possibly have been any more wrong in his assessment? Carter's appointees were equally misinformed when making their evaluation of Khomeini.

During November 1978 Michael Blumenthal, Carter's secretary of the treasury, visited the Shah to discuss oil prices. He was deeply troubled by the Shah's appearance and reported back to Washington that the Shah seemed despondent and out-of-sorts. Pahlavi reiterated to the treasury secretary that he simply did not know what the Carter administration wanted him to do. Since the Mossadegh overthrow in 1953 the Shah had been under the protection of the American government. It was Blumenthal who suggested that the president approach George Ball to head an inter-agency task force on Iran. (Ball had been Blumenthal's mentor in the 60s.)[299]

Thus, former diplomat and Johnson administration Undersecretary of State George Ball was engaged to do an independent and classified study on the Shah and make recommendations to the

Carter administration. One political analyst penned, "Ball pops up, like a cork, every election year."[300] Ball was famous for being the prominent high official opposed to military escalation in Vietnam and a strong critic of Nixon's foreign policy. Ball believed the Shah to be "The son of a colonel in a Persian Cossack regiment, play-acting as the emperor of a country."[301] Now the Shah's fate was in the hands of the man who viewed America's ally of thirty-six years in this manner.

Ball and Carter met for the first time in 1975 at a Lehman Brothers luncheon. James A. Bill said of Ball, "[He] came away from the session singularly unimpressed. Carter appeared naïve, over-confident, and absorbed by the minutiae of electoral politics. He seemed to avoid the substantive issues of politics and, in Ball's judgment, he lacked vision."[302] Although Ball and Carter were never able to establish a personal affinity, and his early opinion of Carter was less than positive, Ball agreed to take on the task. His report was given highly limited distribution in the Carter administration.

Ball suggested that the president restrict the Shah's power while State Department Appointee Henry Precht called upon the Shah to gracefully step down. Precht's opinion of the Shah was less than glowing: "Here we were depending on this autocrat to protect American interests in a very key part of the world, and it appears that he was some kind of nut! This job was going to be a lot more complex than I thought it would be."[303] How absurd! The future of the staunchest ally in the Persian Gulf region now lay in the hands of one man who thought the Shah an impostor and another who openly declared him "a nut!" Only Zbigniew Brzezinski persisted in warning the Carter administration that the Shah's overthrow would spell calamity for the United States. Neither Ball nor Precht was overjoyed with Zbig's stance.

ATOMIC IRAN: COUNTDOWN TO ARMAGEDDON

In my interview with Marvin Kalb, the former network correspondent addressed the friction amongst the Carter administration:

> *I can tell you that a lot of people, serious people in the [State]
> department, including Henry [Precht], were certainly aware of
> what was going on and there was a division...the split between
> Brzezinski and Vance...Iran was only one of the splits between
> the two of them, but it definitely was an important one. And that
> represented the views of those people in the department who knew
> a great deal about Iran, who studied it carefully, who understood
> the increasing weakness of the Shah's position and the increasing
> strength of Khomeini's position and were trying to point this out
> to the U.S. government so that an intelligent American response
> could be orchestrated to meet this new set of challenges. The people
> at the White House were for the most part intent on supporting
> the Shah to the degree that they could because in their minds they
> were seeing it from a larger perspective. They were seeing it from
> a U.S.-Soviet perspective. They believed it was very important to
> keep the Shah in office as long as possible because he had always
> been a strong supporter of an anti-Soviet position. And a number
> of presidents...Ford, Nixon before, Kissinger, they all operated
> on an assumption that it was very wise to retain the closest
> possible relations with the Shah.*[304]

Brzezinski strongly suggested that he be sent to Tehran to
try to help the Shah and expressed that desire in a meeting with
President Carter and George Ball. Ball responded: "With all due
respect, [this] is the worst idea I have ever heard."[305] Ball believed
Brzezinski would reject any plan that suggested contacting
Khomeini. Carter apparently agreed with Ball and nixed the
Brzezinski trip. Zbig later admitted that he had made a mistake in
agreeing to work with George Ball. Although initially very high on
the former diplomat, Zbig reported that he "later wished I had

listened to Cy [Cyrus Vance.] Ball's participation in our debates sharpened our disagreements while delaying basic choices...and his subsequent willingness to discuss what transpired within the White House and State Department with members of the press. Moreover...I violated a basic rule...one should never obtain the services of an "impartial" outside consultant.[306]

The Shah shared his confusion about the Carter administration's role in events in Iran:

> The messages I received from the Americans continued to be confusing and contradictory. What was I to make of the administration's sudden decision to call former Undersecretary of State George Ball to the White House as an advisor on Iran? I knew that Ball was no friend, and I understood he was working on a special report concerning Iran. No one ever informed me what areas the report was to cover, let alone its conclusions. I read those months later in exile and found my worst fears confirmed. Ball was among those Americans who wanted to abandon me and ultimately my country.[307]

While formulating his report Ball met with Israeli Ambassador to Iran Lubrani. The two men and National Security Council member Gary Sick met at the Links Club in New York in the fall of 1978. Sick and Ball were most interested in Lubrani's sources for the report he had forwarded to Moshe Dayan. To counter their demands, Lubrani asked, "Do you have somebody in the entourage of Khomeini at Neauphle-le-Chateau? You know, this is where the next regime in Tehran is preparing to take office, in Neauphle-le-Chateau." Lubrani told me that Carter was to blame, not solely, but to some extent, for the current state of affairs in Iran.[308]

Ball's assessment of the Shah's precarious position was underlined by such inclusions in his report as:

:: The most desirable solution...would probably be for the Shah to remain as chief of state, retaining qualified command of the army but entrusting the exercise of political power and decision to a civilian government.

:: Elements of the moderate opposition are proposing that the Shah abdicate in favor of the crown prince...They hope to clear this scheme with Khomeini, since, were he to approve, it might relieve some of the current pressures.

:: We have...ample clout with the [Iranian] air force, which is the apple of the Shah's eye. We provide them with nearly all of their equipment, including $7.5 billion of highly sophisticated hardware now on order.

:: We should not delay in conveying our private views to the Shah that a transfer of power is indispensable and urgent.

:: The Ayatollah Khomeini, by his fanatical opposition to the Shah for more than fifteen years, has come to personify the revolt. The Iranian people view him as a legendary, almost sacred, figure, whose actions are beyond reproach.

:: We urgently need to open a disavowable channel of communication with him [Khomeini] or his entourage. If we are to undertake a more active role in political developments, we will at least need a means of passing messages or seeking private views.

:: We should also consult closely with the French at a very high level in an attempt to make Khomeini's visit to France as brief as possible and to limit the extent to which he and the shadowy group around him are permitted to manage events in Iran.

:: We should not...encourage the overthrow of an existing government until we are reasonably sure that the successor government would offer a better chance of stability.

:: Unless a man on a white horse should come riding on stage...we could hope for nothing better than the French Fourth Republic, without benefit of the French.

:: Never again should we transfer such vast military resources to an antiquated monarchy that rules largely by force without the consent of the people.

:: The Shah must announce unequivocally that he is transferring all civil power to a civilian government coalition.

:: We should use all our leverage with the military to persuade them not to resort to repressive measures to prop up a bankrupt regime detested by the people.[309]

Ball openly challenged former President Nixon's Twin Pillar policy and declared that the monarchy was on the "verge of collapse" because of it. He pontificated, "We have made the Shah what he has become. We nurtured his love for grandiose geopolitical schemes, and we supplied him with the hardware to indulge his fantasies...his only chance to save his dynasty (if, indeed, that is still possible) and retain our support is for him to transfer his power to a government responsive to the people."[310] Ball proposed a Council of Notables and, with help from the State Department, prepared a list of possible members.

Of course, Ball's assessment of the Shah was most vividly expressed by his contemptuous statement regarding the monarch:

What an absurd, pathetic spectacle! The son of a colonel in a Persian Cossack regiment play-acting as the emperor of a country with an average per capita income of $250 per year, proclaiming his achievements in modernizing his nation while accoutered in the raiment and symbols of ancient despotism.[311]

Ball expressed his disdain following the coronation ceremony of the Shah. He likened the affair to an operetta. He said he and his wife "waited expectantly for the empress to burst into an... aria, or the Shah to shuffle smartly into a soft shoe routine."[312] I can't help but wonder if Ball swallowed his contempt long enough to heap his plate with the Shah's caviar and drink his champagne.

A measure Ball's disdain for the monarch, Ambassador Zahedi believes, was due to a refusal on his part to set up an audience with Pahlavi. When Ball, then Undersecretary of State under Lyndon Johnson, arrived in Tehran, Zahedi had arranged for him to meet with the ministers of finance and commerce. Pahlavi's schedule, however, did not permit a personal meeting with the undersecretary.[313] Apparently, Mr. Ball was not accustomed to being rebuffed by anyone for any reason.

Now, Ball filed his report with the Carter administration and returned home in mid-December. He firmly believed that his recommendation to establish contact with Khomeini had been ignored. Precht, however, had taken Ball's suggestion to heart. In a memo marked "Secret-Sensitive" Precht revealed a luncheon conversation with Yazdi, Khomeini's Iranian champion in the U.S. The two men talked of the possibilities of a new regime with the Shah as a figurehead, but Yazdi was uncompromisingly opposed to that. They spoke also about how a Khomeini-backed government might respond to oil sales and other issues. Precht wrote, "On parting, we agreed that neither of us would acknowledge that there had been any official contact between Khomeini and the U.S. government."[314] Precht was laying the groundwork for the "disavowability" defense suggested by George Ball.

President Carter's inaction following the release of the Ball report seemed to indicate his unwillingness to involve himself disproportionately in maintaining the Shah's monarchy. The indications were that he was more than willing to let the Iranians resolve their own internal crises and let the chips fall where they may.

The State Department seemed to be desirous of the Shah's overthrow. The general consensus among the department's hierarchy seemed to be that the religious leaders in Iran could not and would not participate in governing the nation should Pahlavi abdicate the throne. Chief of Staff to the Senate Select Committee on Intelligence William Miller even suggested that the U.S. openly support Khomeini and his Islamic revolution. Miller was convinced that Khomeini would progressively pursue human rights reforms in Iran.

A former naval intelligence officer and CIA operative during the Carter administration related to me that the U.S. government wrote checks to Khomeini in increments of approximately $150 million, essentially funding his French operation, including the flight that returned him to Tehran. My informant fully believes Khomeini left France because Carter stopped giving him money.

In an article for *Townhall.com*, Dinesh d'Souza wrote: "U.S. Ambassador William Sullivan even compared Khomeini to Mahatma Gandhi, and Andrew Young termed the radical cleric a 'twentieth-century saint.'"[315] This begs the questions: Was anyone in the Carter administration reading the memoranda being sent by the CIA? Was the CIA actually studying the information at hand, or were they convinced that Khomeini was truly an old cleric with little chance of instigating a full-blown revolution in Iran?

When asked about Sullivan's lack of support for the Shah's monarchy, Her Majesty Farah Pahlavi replied:

Ambassador Sullivan...disliked the Shah for whatever reason; and he was not giving the proper advice or reports to President Carter. Dr. Brzezinski was saying at that time that the Shah should remain strong, but I think Cyrus Vance and Sullivan and Mr. Precht (the head of the Iranian desk), hated the Shah. I remember when

Sullivan came to Iran, Mrs. [Ferdinand] Marcos sent a message to me...She said in her message, "Marcos told me to tell you that wherever Sullivan goes, he creates a revolution." Now we know he was in touch with many opposition groups [in Iran.][316]

Apparently, Sullivan did meet with such opposition leaders as Mehdi Bazargan, Nasser Minachi, Amir Entezam, and others who proved to be less than helpful to the ambassador. Bazargan, who would play a major role in Khomeini's Islamic revolution, was a member of the Liberation Movement of Iran (LMI), a minor but decidedly scholarly and significant political faction committed to modernizing Shia Islam. Bazargan was deemed to be the guiding light of the organization that boasted such members as Ali Shariati and Sadegh Ghotbzadeh. Bazargan and members of this same group would travel to Paris in October 1978 to meet with Khomeini. Khomeini gave no indication to the leaders that he would cooperate, although John Stempel sent a telegram from the secretary of state in Washington to the U.S. Embassy in Paris that he was hopeful "some form of cooperation between in-country religious leaders and [the government of Iran] could help start the tension-reducing process."[317]

Ambassador Zahedi revealed to me he was totally unaware that the State Department even knew who Bazargan was. When he and Brzezinski met, the ambassador realized how upset the national security advisor was about events in Iran and how unsuitable he thought Bazargan was for consideration in any governmental position. Zahedi was told the Carter administration would back—100 percent—any decision the Shah and Iranian people made, even if it did happen to be Bazargan.[318]

Sullivan's purpose to court Bazargan and position the U.S. interests for the downfall of the Shah was seen by many Pahlavi backers to be no more than a double-cross of the monarch, and ultimately brought the direst of results.

Embassy Political Officer John Stempel was apparently privy to the meetings between Sullivan and opposition leaders. He sent a classified Memorandum of Conversation to the State Department on May 15, 1978.[319] Just who gave the political officer permission to approach the group has never been divulged. Stempel reported that the group was most interested in whether Carter's nosedive in approval ratings was due to his human rights policies. He wrote, "All the Liberation Front leaders insisted that the Shah must have been forced to liberalize, and they attributed this wholly to President Carter's human rights policy."

In September U.S. diplomat Charles Naas wrote to Victor Tomseth, the American Consul in Shiraz, Iran. Naas verified that several high-level Iranian officials had charged the U.S. was involved in demonstrations and were supporting the opposition in Iran.[320]

Stempel obviously was totally unaware of the clout held by Bazargan, and he was even more astounded to learn that his lowly translator, Mohammed Tavakoli, was a highly regarded member of the LMI. During Stempel's second meeting with the leaders on May 30, Tavakoli not only fielded questions but conversed with the other men as an equal. In less than a year Bazargan would be Khomeini's prime minister under the new Islamic revolution. Tavakoli, it would be discovered, was actually Mohammed Tavassoli, a principal go-between of the Revolutionary Government and the U.S. Embassy. He would later become governor of Tehran.[321]

It was Cyrus Vance who proffered Tavakoli/Tavassoli's name to the Embassy in Tehran in a telegram to Sullivan. According to the U.S. ambassador, an "American academic expert recently gave [Department Office] the name of Mohammed Tavassoli, identifying him as person preferred by Khomeini group for contact with Embassy should that ever be desirable or practical." It listed a Tehran telephone number for Tavakoli.[322]

A telegram from John Stempel seemed to chastise Vance for revealing the identity of Tavassoli:

> *Tavassoli of [reference telegram] is individually known to us as Mohammed Tavakoli, with whom [political officer] Stempel has been in contact regularly since May 1978. He is not, [repeat], not a "Khomeini man" except in a limited sense. He is second-echelon LMI leader behind more prominent figures such as Bazargan...with whom we have also had contacts. LMI is, of course, most pro-Khomeini group in oppositionist galaxy. Tavassoli is somewhat disconcerted to have demonstrated to him that the Embassy knew who he really was.*[323]

This information presents any number of scenarios: Had the Embassy been talking to a Khomeini follower for months and was simply unaware? Was the CIA in contact with the Ayatollah through Tavassoli? Was the Carter administration actively seeking an open, yet disavowable, channel of communication with Khomeini?

Perhaps Ambassador Zahedi was absolutely right in being wary of the new U.S. ambassador in Tehran due to his previous postings in Laos and in the Philippines. He shared his reservations about Sullivan at the onset of his appointment to Iran. Zahedi said his intuitions were confirmed during a welcome party for Sullivan given by Ambassador Sidney Sober and former U.S. Ambassador Richard Helms. Zahedi, then, went so far as to advise the Shah to reject Sullivan's credentials but was rebuffed by the monarch.[324]

Apparently Sullivan was not above trying to recruit members of the Shah's ministry in his search for damning information.

Dr. Abdol Majid Majidi, minister of planning and budget, was approached by Sullivan at a party:

Sullivan [tried] from the very beginning to talk to me and get my personal views of the situation...I couldn't give him clues to weaknesses or mistakes or anything...[Sullivan] took me aside...and was trying to entreat me to talk to him as a sort of opponent of the Shah...He was not like [former Ambassador Richard] Helms. Helms was willing to collaborate and work with Iran and support the Shah and the regime. Sullivan was not.[325]

After having read some of the declassified CIA documents, I wonder if key administration personnel were paying attention to information coming in from Iran and Paris. One document dated November 20, 1978, is devoted to "The Politics of Ayatollah Ruhollah Khomeini." Among the points of the intelligence memorandum are these:

:: Ayatollah Khomeini has long been the central figure in the conservative Shia clerical opposition to the Shah. His influence is now so strong that neither other clerics nor civilian opposition leaders will take action he opposes.

:: Khomeini is determined to overthrow the Shah and is unlikely to accept any compromise. He considers the Pahlavi regime to be corrupt, anti-Islamic, and controlled by the U.S.

:: Khomeini's powerbase is composed of the Shia clergy, bazaar merchants, urban lower classes, and students. Senior military officers generally oppose and feel threatened by Khomeini, but junior officers and enlisted men presumably are more responsive to his Shia message.

:: An Iranian regime under Khomeini's influence would be xenophobic [intolerant] and probably prone to instability. It would probably not be aligned with either the U.S. or U.S.S.R.[326]

Former CIA director Stansfield Turner summarized the situation very concisely in his book, *Burn Before Reading*. He wrote:

> *While I think we in the CIA served the president well...we let him down badly with respect to our coverage of the Iranian scene. We had not appreciated how shaky the Shah's political foundation was, did not know that the Shah was terminally ill, did not understand who Khomeini was and the support his movement had...As far as our failure to judge the Shah's position more accurately, we were just plain asleep...It was egregious, though, that I did not insist on a thorough review of where the Shah stood.*[327]

Marvin Kalb had another opinion about the downfall of the Shah:

> *The thing that is important to note here is the State Department experts were not advancing a specific policy option. They were fighting what they took to be an inordinate U.S. reliance upon the Shah at a time when they saw increasing weakness in the Shah's position. They were in effect saying to the conductor of the train about to go off the tracks, "Please be aware the tracks are unsteady, that your policy has a weak foundation, and you better think about a post-Shah Iran." But the White House...up until the end was not thinking in those terms. And that is why, when the Shah finally had to leave, the U.S. was so surprised, struck dumb by the new situation they faced. They had been made aware of the new situation for a long time, but they simply did not buy into it.*[328]

William Sullivan, appointed by Jimmy Carter in 1977, holds the dubious role of having been the last U.S. ambassador to Iran. (He was the first ambassador appointed following the departure of Richard Helms during the Ford administration.)

In Lifting the Veil; Life in Revolutionary Iran, John Simpson and Tira Shubert wrote of Sullivan's introduction to and influence on U.S. policy in Iran:

Sullivan ...had inherited a bureaucratic machine, which was capable only of viewing the situation from one direction. His Embassy had become an office for selling equipment and weapons systems, and its political reporting role had been heavily reduced...He faced hostility from Zbigniew Brzezinski's National Security Council, which tried to undermine his influence and that of the U.S. State Department... Sullivan was reporting to an administration...concentrating on the Camp David negotiations...to the exclusion of almost everything else.[329]

Right or wrong, Sullivan determined early during his stint in Iran that the Shah had become incapable of making responsible decisions. Soon after his arrival in Tehran, Sullivan recorded his first impression of the Shah. He wrote: "The man to whom I presented my credentials certainly did not fit into the category of national leaders. He was not truly cast to be a leader of men or the nation in time of crisis."[330]

Uri Lubrani provided some insight on Sullivan's mindset regarding the Shah:

Sullivan had little experience in Iran. He was very much reliant on Tony Parsons, the British ambassador...who was anti-Israel and whose wife was pro-Palestinian. He told Sullivan that this..."Lubrani doesn't know what he's talking about." Whom should poor Sullivan believe? Here you have Sir Tony Parsons...telling him straight from the horse's mouth...and Count Lubrani with his gut feelings. Obviously, he didn't take me seriously. But at that time the U.S. had thousands of officials in Iran...the foreign ministry, the Pentagon, information collectors...I talked with the American ambassador a number of times...he relied on access to Tony Parsons for information in Iran more than he relied on the ambassador of Israel.[331]

Sullivan saw the Shah at his best and his worst. In an audience with the Shah in mid-1977 the ambassador related the Shah's growing distrust of the CIA. Pahlavi felt the CIA had played a roll in the demonstrations and protests that had gripped Iran. Sullivan said of his conversation with the Shah:

> He could understand the British intrigue to some extent, because there were those in the United Kingdom who had never forgiven him for nationalizing the oil industry...What bothered him the most...was the role of the CIA. Why was the CIA suddenly turning against him? What had he done to deserve this sort of action from the United States?[332]

Sullivan returned to Washington in June of 1978 for meetings with administration heads. Secretary of State Vance was of the opinion that Sullivan felt "the Shah faced a long, rough period ahead, but that he should be able to weather the storm."[333] Vance encouraged Sullivan to meet with opposition leaders to try to gain more information, particularly about those planners and executers of the anti-Shah protests. It was evident that the mullahs, led by the wily Ayatollah Ruhollah Khomeini, were in the forefront. It seemed more obvious that two elements—the economy and religious forces—were leading and fueling the marches in Iran. At the same time, it appeared the Shah was beginning to suspect the U.S. was turning more toward the opposition in an attempt to situate itself in the winning camp.

Contrarily, the Shah wrote of his interaction with Sullivan in less-than-glowing terms:

> He [Sullivan] said that he knew in September 1978 that I could not survive. He has told this [following his retirement] to the International Herald Tribune and anyone else who would listen. But he never told me. For the next four months the only word I ever received from Mr. Sullivan was reiteration of Washington's complete support for my rule. To be more specific, the U.S. backed me 100 percent and hoped I would establish law and order, as well as continue my program of political liberalization. For the balance of

Michael David Evans and
Empress Farah Pahlavi

Michael David Evans and former French
President Valery Giscard d'Estaing

Michael David Evans and former
Prime Minister Menachem Begin

Iranian Ambassador Ardeshir Zahedi with
whom Dr. Evans had extensive interviews.

Michael David Evans and former
New York City Mayor Rudy Giuliani

Michael David Evans and former
Prime Minister Rabin

Ayatollah Ruhollah Khomeini's compound outside Paris - Neauphle-le-Chateau)

Michael David Evans outside gate at Neauphle-le-Chateau

Michael David Evans at Neauphle-le-Chateau

Michael David Evans, Michael Evans II, and Israel President Shimon Peres

Michael David Evans and former Prime Minister Benjamin Netanyahu

Michael David and Carolyn Evans with Benjamin Netanyahu and his father on the anniversary of his brother Jonathan's death during the raid on Entebbe in Uganda

Michael David Evans and former
CIA Director James Woolsey

Michael David Evans and
Prime Minister Ehud Olmert

Michael David Evans celebrating the Feast
of Tabernacles with Chief Rabbi of Israel.

Michael David Evans and Iraqi Kurdistan
Prime Minister Nechirvan Barzani

Michael Evans speaking at the Kennedy
School of Law, Harvard University

Michael Evans on the front lines with Israeli
soldiers during the Lebanese War, July 2006.

Michael David Evans and Iraqi Kurdistan
President Massoud Barzani

Michael David Evans stands at the border
between Iran and Iraq

Michael David Evans with Marines in Beirut
the day before the Marine barracks
were bombed by terrorists at 6:45 AM
October 23, 1983.

Michael David Evans with the Egyptian Army
in Saudi Arabia during Operation
Desert Storm

Michael David Evans at the Royal Palace
for the Madrid Peace Conference

Michael David Evans, former chief of staff
Lt. General Moshe Ya'alon,
Mayor Ron Nachman (Ariel, Israel).

the year I received numerous messages from various people in and
out of the Carter administration pledging U.S. support.[334]

On December 29 Vance sent a telegram to Sullivan instructing
him to tell the Shah about several power-sharing possibilities and
to warn him that "in any case, it is our judgment that it will be
impossible to restore [Pahlavi's] absolute power."[335] According to
author William Shawcross, Sullivan was the messenger bearing the
news that the Shah was to leave his homeland for exile. Sullivan
painted himself in this episode as the savior of the Shah, even
offering to seek asylum for the monarch. Pahlavi's version differed
from Sullivan's.[336]

Did the duplicitous Sullivan think that by insinuating himself
with the Shah and removing him from Khomeini's path he might gain
an upper hand with the Ayatollah and his cronies? That same day
Sullivan dispatched a telegram to the State Department advising
that John Stempel had met with Richard Cottam, a former CIA
officer who had maintained ties with Iran's religious community over
the years. Cottam had met with Khomeini and formulated the
opinion that Yazdi had become the Ayatollah's chief of staff.[337]
How could such a plethora of information lead to such hindsight?

In 1977 Cottam, then a political science professor at the
University of Pittsburg, testified before the House Subcommittee on
International Organizations. (The committee was on record in
calling Iran "one of the major recipients of military cash sales
from the United States" and in declaring its "active interest in
developments that affect the human rights conditions in Iran.")
In his prepared statement Dr. Cottam addressed the human rights
issue in regard to its effect in Iran:

No one should expect that transition to a less repressive admin-
istration in Iran would be a smooth one. The Iranian public is

bitterly polarized, the regime is vulnerable to charges of foreign sponsorship and control, and the opposition is mutually suspicious, divided, and incapable of serious cooperation. A strategy designed to encourage liberalization in this setting would be difficult but not impossible to devise. The regime has demonstrated responsiveness to pressure to move in a direction of controlled and gradualistic relaxation. The formula, easily stated but requiring artistry to execute, calls for the application of sufficient pressure to produce movement on part of the regime, but not so much as to encourage opposition elements to move so rapidly that the regime begins to see its survival as being in question. Administration policy thus far, unfortunately, has opted for the worst of both worlds. Initial statements concerning human rights encouraged a good deal of opposition activity in Iran.[338]

Other nations were not so handicapped in intelligence gathering. While the U.S. was playing ostrich, Israel was openly voicing its reservations about the Shah's ability to maintain control in Iran. In fact, the Israelis were so convinced the Shah's fall was inevitable that Jews in Iran were warned to flee while there was still the opportunity.

CHAPTER 15

. . . .

THE SLIPPERY SLOPE
TO REVOLUTION

"Jihad means the conquest of all non-Muslim territories.
Such a war may well be declared after the formation of an
Islamic government worthy of that name, at the direction
of the Imam or under his orders. It will then be the duty
of every able-bodied adult male to volunteer for this war
of conquest, the final aim of which is to put Qur'anic
law in power from one end of the earth to the other."
(CLIVE IRVING)[339]

As opposition to the Shah grew in Iran and in an attempt to inhibit Khomeini's influence, Reza Pahlavi appealed to the president of Iraq, Saddam Hussein, to clamp down on the Ayatollah's activities. In my talk with Ardeshir Zahedi, he mentioned that Hussein offered to "liquidate" Khomeini should the Shah ask. "Saddam," said Zahedi "was happy to expel Khomeini, who finally landed in Paris...Letting him stay in Paris was a huge mistake. He became the darling of the media world...the

227

media attention helped him become the unique opposition leader. As usually is the case, the more extreme and radical opinion gets the upper hand."[340]

In the late 1970s the worldwide media was controlled by its counterparts in three very powerful countries. In the United States *The New York Times* was the power media of record. In Great Britain the British Broadcasting Corporation (BBC) led the way; and then there were the newspapers and media sources in France.

It's difficult to imagine life as it was then—no Internet, CNN, CNBC, Fox Network, no iPhones, digital cameras, or text messaging. News was delivered via ABC, NBC, or CBS. At that time, what we now refer to as "mainstream" media was extremely powerful. In the 1960s this newly dominant media outlet introduced America to its first "television war." Night after night Americans ate their evening meal to the horrifying scenes of bloody and battered combat troops, body bags, and atrocities in Vietnam. According to the Museum of Broadcast Communications, the Saigon Bureau was the third largest after New York and Washington. It kept five camera crews busy the majority of the time. The result of the nightly bombardment of horror was revulsion and exhaustion. Eventually, Americans began clamoring for the troops to be brought home.[341]

Just as the Ayatollah Khomeini became the darling of the media, so the Shah became the pariah. He and his monarchy bore the full brunt of media revulsion during the Carter years. *The New York Times* influenced decision makers, especially during the crucial months of 1978 and 1979. In France, Khomeini's country of choice during his exile, the press and television created a soft, fuzzy image of the Ayatollah. But perhaps the most damaging entity of all was the *British Broadcasting Corporation* (BBC). Through its Persian language *BBC Persian Service* network, it became a primary voice for the Islamic Revolution. Pahlavi didn't stand a chance in the battle for public opinion with each of these powerful outlets as his foe. It is said that Bazargan expressed his appreciation for both the BBC and the French *Le Monde* following Khomeini's seizure of power.[342]

Iranian military leaders were very concerned with BBC broadcasts that were being aired from the island of Masirah, just off the Omani coast. The Shah had met with British Ambassador Anthony Parsons in an attempt to stop the broadcasts that were announcing to the Iranian people when planned demonstrations against the Shah were scheduled. The ambassador reminded the Shah's chief of protocol, Mr. Afshar, that the BBC was an independently owned and operated entity and not controlled by the British government.

The most curious and mysterious relationship between the media and the Shah was with the British Broadcasting Corporation (BBC). It was the only Western broadcaster to have a service that broadcast in the Persian language. The BBC Persian Service had been established during WWII to counterbalance the Nazi influence in Iran. In the 1950's it was against the nationalization of Iranian oil, which at the time had been held by the Anglo Iranian Oil Company (AIOC).[343]

At the beginning of the Shah's reign in 1953 the BBC Persian Service appeared to be a friend of his. In fact, early in the Iranian revolution the opposition forces still viewed the BBC Persian Service with distrust. It took Abolhassan Bani Sadr, later president of the republic and the same person who connected Paul Balta of *Le Monde* with Khomeini, to get the Ayatollah to trust the BBC. Bani Sadr said later:

I suggested to Khomeini to give an interview to BBC, assuring him that they will broadcast exactly what he says. Khomeini rejected saying, "BBC belongs to the British and it will not benefit us to give them an interview." I convinced him when I said all the other media you give interviews to are also all foreign, so what is the difference? Khomeini then accepted.[344]

Soon the BBC Persian Service was broadcasting the ranting of the Ayatollah and other leaders of the revolution directly into Iran. In Iran this was very confusing to the Shah and his supporters. It was well known that the BBC World Service, under which the BBC Persian Service fell, was funded by the British Foreign Office. The Foreign Office by the 1970's was claiming to have no control over the journalists. Friends of the Shah appealed a number of times to the Foreign Office and the BBC but to no avail.[345] In the meantime, the BBC Persian Service Broadcast had become a national event.

In Ehsan Naraghi's book, *From Palace to Prison, Inside the Iranian Revolution,* he reconstructs a dialogue between himself and the Shah regarding the BBC:

Shah: "*We've stressed...that while respecting the BBC's right to freedom of expression, we considered that it was taking things too far...The information that it was broadcasting about the situation in Iran was tantamount to instructions to the opposition on how they should behave from one day to the next.*"

Naraghi: "*It's true, Your Majesty, that the BBC has a very large audience in Iran. During the time when it broadcasts its evening program, from 7:45 to 8:30, I've noticed that the city looks completely different because so many people go home to listen.*"[346]

Perhaps understandably, the British Foreign Office has yet to open its files regarding this time period and the BBC Persian Service.[347]

The conversation regarding the BBC Persian Service led to another charge of bugging by Lt. General Azarbarzin. He was called into the Shah's suite following the meeting with Parsons and told:

> *"Destroying this station will create a political scandal...You go*
> *ahead and make all preparations, and I'll give you confirmation*
> *in the morning at 9:00 a.m." When I went to see the Shah, Ambas-*
> *sador Sullivan was ahead of me...he had requested an emergency*
> *audience with the Shah at 8:30 a.m....After Sullivan had left, the*
> *Shah told me, "Don't take any action on what we discussed yester-*
> *day...By the way, did you discuss yesterday's subject with anyone?"*
> *I answered, "I do not discuss my missions with anybody." The Shah*
> *said, "I am surprised, because Ambassador Sullivan mentioned the*
> *words political scandal exactly as I told you yesterday."*[348]

General Huyser recorded that his Iranian counterparts were asking, "Why can't the big United States silence Khomeini? Cannot the U.S. silence the British Broadcasting's Farsi broadcasts?" Huyser said that "young and old alike carried transistor radios...The BBC Persian Service was set up during World War II in order to help destabilize the regime of the Shah's father...and the Shah himself probably had this in mind when they protested against the role of the BBC during this crucial period in the late 1970s."[349]

The New York Times in the 1970's was considered the "Gray Lady" of American print media. It claimed to provide, "All the news that's fit to print." With extensive Foreign Affairs coverage that was only rivaled by the *Washington Post*, *The New York Times* was mandatory reading for foreign policy analysts, professionals, and diplomats in the U.S. and abroad. It was also one of the morning papers on the desks of the television news producers at the three major networks of that day.

Many of the news stories on the national nightly news broadcasts came directly from the pages of the *Washington Post*, *The New York Times* and, occasionally, the *Wall Street Journal*. (It was, after all, Woodward and Bernstein who broke the Watergate scandal in the prestigious *Post*.) These three newspapers had nationwide circulation—making them the only "national" daily newspapers. When it came to an overseas story, no paper had more clout than *The New York Times*.

The Shah and his diplomats were not ignorant, uninformed individuals. They were aware of the sway held by the *Times*. Pahlavi's press office in Iran communicated frequently with news reporters stationed in Tehran, including the famous *Times'* correspondent, R. W. Apple. Unfortunately for the Shah, his attempts to generate goodwill yielded strange results.

When in May of 1977 Secretary of State Cyrus Vance visited Tehran for the CENTO meeting, he gave a speech to the assembly. Vance was quoted in the *The New York Times* by reporter Charles Mohr in an article headlined, "Vance, in Iran, Asserts Stability Depends on Rights." While Vance was actually speaking to the other four CENTO members—Britain, Turkey, Iran, and Pakistan—the article made Vance appear to be speaking solely to the Shah of Iran.

Vance was quoted as saying:

Each country's growth, prosperity, and stability sooner or later depends upon its ability to meet the aspirations of its people for human rights. The success of the nations of the world in mastering the economic and social problems of resource limits, population growth, and the environment will inevitably be linked to our success in promoting individual dignity.[350]

In the fourth paragraph of his article, Mohr instructed the reading audience what it should gain from Vance's speech:

Whether intentionally or not [wink, wink], the secretary's remarks seemed to have a special point when they were delivered in an ornate conference hall in the capital of this ancient monarchy. The Shah of Iran and his government have been criticized by some Iranian exiles and by foreigners for firm suppression of political opposition and for police surveillance of political activity...The Shah was not present when Mr. Vance spoke today...American officials indicated... the United States views the trends in Iranian civil liberties as "favorable."...and that any diplomatic or economic sanctions against the Shah were virtually out of the question.[351]

The article informed its readers that the Shah was "one of the largest customers of advanced American military hardware."[352] Reading this article made me pause to wonder if Mr. Mohr was quantifying the "U.S. soft-sell" with the real reason behind it; the U.S. pocketed a lot of money for the "military hardware" sold to the Shah. No, not to Iran, to the Shah. The writer is clearly indicating that the lack of U.S. sanctions is closely tied to the Shah's purchasing power.

It is also interesting to note that the word "sanctions," brought up only by the reporter, was used against Pahlavi. Today, mention of sanctions applies to the country of Iran not its leader, Mahmoud Ahmadinejad.

Iran's press office responded to the article in four days, as quickly as it could at the time. Iran's representative at the U.N. was Fereydoun Hoveyda. Hoveyda argued that it was unfair to immediately apply 1977 U.S. standards of human rights to developing nations. He pointed out, correctly, that "the political rights of women, about the lot of labor and...the situation of minority groups" was different in the U.S. in 1977 than it had been twenty-five or fifty years earlier. Then he enumerated Iran's achievements in land reform and its advancement in the rights of women. The piece was a brilliant public relations effort. It was torpedoed by a photo the editors placed in the very center of the op-ed. It showed Mr. Hoveyda dressed in a flamboyant military uniform bowing and kissing the hand of the Shah. The monarch was clad in a military dress uniform with ceremonial sword in hand.

A Chinese proverb tells us, "One picture is worth ten thousand words." The picture, with no caption, evoked striking imagery. In 1972 Francis Ford Coppola directed "The Godfather." The Academy Award-winning movie portrayed the life of a Sicilian mob boss, the Godfather. One famous scene depicts minor members of the "family" kissing the Godfather's ring. The picture of Mr. Hoveyda published in *The New York Times* evoked memories of this scene in the movie. Hoveyda, who never mentions the Shah in his article of rebuttal, is obviously portrayed as the minion doing the bidding of the scary, egocentric strongman. Why did a newspaper the size of *The Times* not have a headshot of Mr. Hoveyda, a diplomat at the United Nations? Perhaps it did, but perhaps that picture would have more closely conveyed the message intended.[353]

Over the next few months articles and the editorial page of *The New York Times* repeatedly went after the Shah and the proposed U.S. sale of military aircraft.[354] Eventually, the administration weakened in its resolve to supply the planes to Iran. Finally, in a face-saving gesture to both Carter and itself, Iran withdrew its bid to buy planes.[355]

A favorable *New York Times* book review was a feather in the author's cap and indicated to readers that the literary tome was to be taken seriously. Seemingly, *The New York Times* seized every opportunity to castigate the Shah, even in something as innocuous as the newspaper's June 1977 tribute to *The Crowned Cannibals: Writings on Repression in Iran,* penned by Reza Baraheni. Reviewer John Leonard engaged in the "moral equivalence" doctrine so popular at the time. He drew such a comparison between events in the Soviet Union, Nazi Germany, and among America's allies. Leonard wrote:

> *First of all, the writer as witness of the Holocaust, of Stalinism, of the Shah and his thuggish SAVAK, is one of the few honorable callings in a bestial century.*[356]

This review might have been attributed to a seasoned publicist with a penchant for seizing the moment and linking his client's book to President Carter's human rights campaign; however, the *New York Times* piece was not the end. Another article entitled, "Publishing: Human Rights," also featured Reza Baraheni and his *Crowned Cannibals* book. The article tied the publishing of the book to a meeting in Belgrade to examine the effects of the Helsinki Accords: "Including the human rights section calling for freer exchange of people and ideas, several books are published here that cast light in the dark corners of literary freedom." None of the other books were mentioned. It was simply another opportunity to denigrate the Shah in *The New York Times.*

During the crucial months of late 1978 and early 1979 leading up to the departure of the Shah, *The New York Times* ran a series of editorials along with their news stories. On November 6, 1977, the editorial read, "Suddenly, Iran No Longer Stable." It opened with the question, "How much more time for the Shah of Iran?" Previously, it had been only the anti-Shah protestors who demanded the Shah must go. Certainly no one in the U.S. government had been so crass as to utter those words aloud. Yet, here was the most influential foreign policy daily in the U.S. raising the question. The editorial ended by planting the idea: "Pressure on the Shah has mounted and many of his opponents have raised their sights from reducing his power to driving him from the throne."[358] Apparently that included *The New York Times* editorial board.

On November 8, 1978, and for reasons known only to the editorial staff, *The New York Times* took a step back. It noted that the Shah promised "that newly installed military rule will be brief and will be followed by free elections." It questioned, "Has it come in time?" but concluded, "so far, at least, they warrant continued Western support."[359]

Had the *New York Times* staff had a change of heart? Were they now proposing the monarch remain in power? By December 14th, however, the editorial headline read: "On the Ropes in Iran." They gave the Shah a conciliatory nod by observing he "may yet weather the crisis. He has been a good ally; and as long as his rule remains plausible he is entitled to the respect and support that Mr. Carter has extended. But the Shah has gotten as he has given over the years, and the United States cannot be expected to leave all its stakes piled on one throne...All the avenues require American contacts with the opposition."[360] It obviously did not explain how the U.S. could extend "respect and support" to Pahlavi and at the same time meet with the opposition. Iranians knew the Shah had returned to power with the help of the CIA in 1953. The U.S opening contacts with the opposition would have again been interpreted in Iran as a vote of no confidence in the Shah.

By December 29, 1978, while the Shah was trying to work out a government of national reconciliation, the *New York Times* published an editorial entitled, "The Ideal and the Real in Iran."

While it praised the idea of the Shah staying in a figurehead role, it determined that: "The policy, however, has a serious flaw; it appears to be increasingly unrealistic." Oddly, the editorial concluded, "The United States should not, probably could not, encourage the Shah's departure." Apparently the Carter administration was expected to maintain its silence while *The New York Times*, on the other hand, was free to urge Pahlavi's ouster. The *New York Times* believed, "Every day, there seems to be more reason to doubt that present policy can prevent such an outcome."[361]

In September 1978, before fleeing to Paris from Iraq, Khomeini had been placed under house arrest. At that time, the Liberation Movement of Iran (a group which will play a prominent role later in this book) contacted the U.S. Embassy in Tehran and asked for its help in freeing Khomeini. The missive implied Khomeini wished to leave Iraq. The group's leaders also asked for a high-level meeting with U.S. officials and indicated they would unveil their strong religious connections at the meeting. The Embassy staff declined the request.[362]

In an aborted attempt to flee Iraq, Khomeini and his entourage became stranded at the Kuwait border when that country would not grant him entry, and he was then refused reentry into Iraq. Finally, the Ayatollah received permission to return to Baghdad where, on October 6, he was allowed, at the Shah's urging, to fly to France. The DST, the French secret service, urged French President Giscard d'Estaing to turn Khomeini away. In a personal interview with d'Estaing, he seemed not to have realized just who Khomeini was when the cleric arrived in France:

> *No one knew in France exactly the name...and I heard he was here in Paris after the Interior Minister M. Christian Bonair delivered me a note, the day after his arrival. He [Khomeini] received a*

number of favors. He [Bonair] had a personality who disembarked yesterday at the airport and all his documents were in order saying he was coming from Iraq...Yes, Najaf...He was fleeing Iraq...and he was welcomed by a member of a small group who owns a house in Western Paris. He was driven there by his supporters. And then we realized he was active in politics...and that he was very important in the post-Shah regime. Then we appointed a man from (French Intelligence) to check on him...We considered him...a sort of political refugee. And you know in France, we accept political refugees.[363]

Giscard then seemed to jump on the "downfall of the Shah" bandwagon and agreed to provide asylum for the Ayatollah. Far from halting his interference in Iran, Khomeini's exile only fired the passions of the Islamic radicals in that country. His freedom to plan and execute a revolution while under French protection would prove to be the final straw for the Shah's regime.

A telegram from Ambassador Sullivan to the State Department revealed religious leaders close to Khomeini were urging him to exercise caution and restraint because the civil unrest in Iran was becoming unmanageable. The clerics were also alarmed at surfacing rumors indicating that Khomeini was cooperating with the Tudeh Party, the communist opposition, and some Iranians were beginning to believe the gossip.[364]

It was thought by some individuals that, as stated by Barry Rubin in his book, *Paved with Good Intention*, the French allowed Khomeini into the country because he was perceived as the future leader of Iran.[365] Rubin also writes, "The CIA rented a villa near his [Khomeini's] home. American Embassy political officers began to meet occasionally with one of his advisors, Ebrahim Yazdi [leader in 1968 of the U.S. branch of Muslim Students' Association of America]."[366] Others in France went so far as to try to predict when the Shah's end would come.

CHAPTER 16

. . . .

THE HIGH PRICE
OF INDECISION

*"Defeat is always bitter, but losing without
a fight is the bitterest kind of defeat."*

(ARDESHIR ZAHEDI) [367]

Despite their obvious differences in ideology both the French and the Israelis were convinced the Shah would be overthrown and the alternative, the fanatical Ayatollah Khomeini, would spell doom for the Iranian people. Cavalierly, the U.S. intelligence community rejected both reports as exaggerated. To further exacerbate matters, the CIA failed to investigate Khomeini's radically fanatical diatribes. Apparently Khomeini's threats were not taken seriously by the CIA, which had to scramble to even find copies of Khomeini's writings when the volcano of revolution erupted in Iran.

The *Washington Post* addressed the lack of information about the Ayatollah in an editorial printed on January 16, 1979:

*A great power should never be in the position the United States
is in, in Iran, of knowing so little about a figure—Ayatollah Ruhollah*

Khomeini…Until just the other day the CIA could not lay its hands on some of Mr. Khomeini's voluminous—and revealing—writings… His mandate, he claims, arises from street demonstrations that make him the only leader…"Strongman" is a title he finds acceptable… Khomeini has strong anti-American tendencies…it seems inescapable that he sees his political future in terms that directly undercut American interests…All this does not mean that the United States should risk arousing Iranian nationalism or his ire by working against Khomeini…he gives every evidence of being bad news.[368]

In Iraq Khomeini's communication with his counterparts in Iran was restricted, but France proved to be an open pipeline to funnel information and revolutionary rhetoric directly to Khomeini's information distributors. Every word, every hiccup, every move Khomeini made was duly reported back to Iran through the BBC and other international broadcasters. His was a cause all were rushing to recount to the Iranian people.

In our conversation, the empress questioned why Khomeini was allowed so much freedom to wage his revolution from the suburbs of Paris:

Khomeini is in Paris, why give him so much publicity? When we were in the Bahamas, which was a small country and not so important in international politics, we were told, "You are not allowed to make any political comments." The French said the same thing to Prime Minister Bakhtiar when he fled to France. So why give him [Khomeini] so much publicity? Every day he was on television; every day there was an article in the news-papers. Maybe they thought that with the movement in Iran, with the unrest in Iran, they'd better take care of Khomeini. It is normal that each country thinks of its own interests.[369]

Before his exile to Paris Khomeini's brooding countenance had not been seen abroad in Iran and, in fact, it was forbidden to show his visage on Iranian television. This was not the case in France. During an interview on French television in 1978 Khomeini denied that the Islamic Republic he touted would be run by the clergy. His denial would prove to be as false as other assertions made by the glowering Ayatollah while on his journey to an iron-fisted rule in Iran.

David Pryce-Jones talked about "France's disturbing role in bringing about the Iranian Revolution" in a briefing delivered to the Middle East Forum:

> [The Iranian Revolution was] the most important revolution in
> modern times. France received Khomeini in 1978, when it was clear
> he was planning an insurrection against the Shah, and provided
> him lines of communication through which to mobilize demonstra-
> tions. This is the most dramatic example of the French penchant
> for harboring Islamic extremists...they granted a safe haven to
> Haj Amin el-Husseini, the mufti of Jerusalem, returning him to
> the Middle East when he was wanted as a war criminal in 1945...
> twice now the world has been handicapped by French-harbored
> monsters—Haj Amin and Khomeini—who were fascists.[370]

From Paris, the City of Lights, darkness would slowly but surely engulf Iran. It was from Paris that Khomeini would declare himself the genuine leader-in-exile of the Iranian people. He took full advantage of this freedom to use the media for his purposes. The Ayatollah began to urge the workers in Iran—from oil workers to garbage haulers—to go on strike. Students were encouraged to riot in support of the working class. The strikes proved to be very efficient at creating dissention. One chronicler recorded:

> [On September 9] about seven hundred workers at the Tehran oil
> refinery struck not just for higher wages but as a protest against
> the imposition of martial law and the massacre at Jaleh Square.
> Two days later...the strike had spread to the oil refineries of

Isfahan, Abadan, Tabriz, and Shiraz. [Oil production dropped from over five million barrels per week to just under two million barrels per week.] On 12 September, four thousand print workers and other staff at two leading newspapers in Tehran walked out in protest against the renewal of censorship ordered by General Oveissi, the military governor. On 13 September cement workers in Tehran went on strike, demanding higher wages, freedom for all political prisoners, and the ending of martial law... But in October the situation was transformed...40,000 oilworkers, 40,000 steel-workers, and 30,000 rail workers had put down their tools within three weeks.[371]

Of the oil strikes, Dr. Parviz Mina, said:

"I think the strikes in the oil industry were organized by...the Mujahedin with the help of the clergy...That brought the oil industry to a standstill...created a shortage of products, shortage of income...I was given the assignment to go and buy products... I had to go to Saudi Arabia, to Bahrain, to Kuwait to buy petroleum products and ship it to Iran because the refineries were on strike...We were exporting $5.2 million per day to the world market...the majority was going to Western Europe and the United States...I wish I knew why they [U.S. and Europe] didn't do [anything to stop that]. Not only didn't they do anything...they even helped the revolutionaries.[372]

The downside to Khomeini's call for strikes among the workers in Iran was that he failed to recognize "the radicals evidently are most active among the oil workers in southwestern Iran, where Ayatollah's injunctions to restore oil production...have proved difficult to implement because of the division among the striking workers."[373]

On September 10 President Carter wrote in his daily log that he had had an early morning meeting with Zbigniew Brzezinski and Gary Sick, NSC officer responsible for Iran. At the national security adviser's suggestion, Carter phoned the Shah and spent about five minutes talking with him. Sick recorded later that the Shah dominated the conversation and was firm in his pledge to restore order in his country and to continue to pursue democratic ideals. Following the telephone conference the president sent out a press release reiterating his commitment to the long-standing relationship between the U.S. and Iran.[374]

It was at this juncture that the CIA began to prepare a psychological report on Pahlavi. U.S. Embassy staff was asked to help in the preparation of the profile. Rumors that the Shah was suffering from depression abounded.[375] It is entirely possible the Shah was coming to grips with his cancer diagnosis and was overwhelmed with the unrest in his country. He was also wrestling with the fact that his teen-aged son, Reza, was not of sufficient age to assume the responsibilities of the monarchy.

On November 11, 1978, a document from the secretary of state in Washington, D.C., was released to ambassadors and consulates around the world. It's subject? Iran. The assessment of the situation in Iran from Secretary Vance's point of view was that:

1. Relative quiet continues in Iran, broken by continuing sporadic disturbances in several provincial cities...Embassy believes that current calm, with its various encouraging signs, is merely prelude to [unreadable] when opposition will try to mount serious disturbances to achieve aim of toppling Shah before end of December.

2. Current encouraging signs include primary school attendance is virtually back to normal in Tehran, albeit more

disrupted in the provinces; Tehran bazaar has been open for past two days, with Khomeini and mullahs [asking] shops to open up on December 2 to enable people to stock up.

3. Some oppositionists seek our help in [unreadable] orderly evolution of power from the Shah to them. This last attitude can be expected to continue, as there are realistic expectations of a move to a government and elections in the near future. If government were to continue for six months or more, however, we would see a good possibility of great desperation on the part of the opposition, leading to nastier attitude toward the U.S.[376]

Secretary Vance, who had been preoccupied in September and October 1978 with both the Camp David summit and SALT II talks in Moscow, returned to a State Department in conflict over how to handle the situation in Iran. Some underlings were convinced the Shah's monarchy had come to an end. These individuals were persuaded there were only two viable alternatives: a military solution or a British-style monarchy—a figurehead ruler under the control of a secular governing body. According to Vance:

> They [State Department colleagues] made a strong case against U.S. support for a military government, pointing out that Ambassador Sullivan was opposed to increased military involvement in the political arena. The Iranian military...had shown no capacity to govern or to rally public support. Still, they saw the Shah as the only figure capable of leading a transition to a new regime.[377]

Meanwhile, in Iran the Shah's government was pondering four different possibilities to resolve the crisis:

:: The Shah would attempt to moderate his stance.

:: The coming Islamic Revolution would be soundly crushed before it could be fully birthed (which many considered a total impossibility).

:: The Shah would remove himself from Iran for an unspecified time, briefly abdicating in favor of a regent's council under the leadership of the Empress Farah. The empress would head the government until the crown prince reached his majority. (Farah Pahlavi was convinced that this was the last proposal the Carter administration would consider.)

:: A military coup (favored by the CIA).

Pahlavi's naval commander, Admiral Kamilladin Habib Olahi, delivered a thirty-page proposal to the monarch outlining a military government. Olahi felt the revolution had advanced to the point where the king had to make a decision. (Pahlavi was concerned about a military move that would be against Iran's constitution.) Olahi was persuaded "the blame lay with Iran's allies—particularly the Americans and the British, who were giving him differing advice...the Shah had depended on the counsel of foreigners. Now he was not getting it."[378]

The empress felt Pahlavi had begun to make arrangements for her to act as regent as early as 1973. The Shah met with the prime minister and parliament members to deliver what Farah Diba felt was a governmental "last will and testament":

> I could die at any time. If this should happen when the crown prince is not of legal age to succeed me, authority will pass to the queen and the Regency Council. The armed forces should remain loyal to the queen and later to the young king. Orders can come from a woman or a young man; they should be obeyed. Our security and our lives depend on it.[379]

In late November President Carter asked Brzezinski to summon Zahedi to the White House for a meeting that also included Walter Mondale and Stansfield Turner. Zahedi was disturbed when the president insisted he return to Iran with a message for the Shah. The ambassador reminded Carter he served at the discretion of the Shah, to which the president replied that he, Carter, would fill the role of Iran's ambassador in Washington during Zahedi's absence. Carter particularly wanted Zahedi to reassure the Shah that he should not be concerned about the president's human rights push and to stand firm. He, Carter, would support Pahlavi in whatever decision he made regarding the situation in Iran. The ambassador returned to Iran in the days following the meeting and remained there until the Shah departed in January 1979.

Zahedi was appalled to learn that William Sullivan had summarily received copies of the White House confab but had failed to forward the information to the Shah. The Iranian ambassador wondered if, "by withholding that document, Sullivan may have hoped that my oral report to the Shah would carry less weight." Giving Sullivan the benefit of the doubt, he added, "I cannot be sure, of course, if that was his real intention."[380]

In December Carter dispatched a message to Sullivan from Camp David. In the missive Carter asked the ambassador to meet with Pahlavi as quickly as possible. The president instructed Sullivan to convey to the Shah that:

:: The indecision surrounding Iran's governance was detrimental to both the military and politicians.

:: The resolution preferred by the U.S. was a moderate civilian government.

:: The second choice of the Carter administration was a strong military junta to bring an end to the chaos and carnage.

:: The last resort was a Regency Council that would oversee a military government.

:: Lastly, Sullivan was to reconfirm support from the U.S., but with the understanding that Washington foresaw the loss of the Shah's absolute ruling power.

It was also in December that Carter approached Ardeshir Zahedi about lobbying for the post of prime minister of Iran. The ambassador explained he was more interested in being able to move about freely in order to try to help the Shah resolve the dilemma. Zahedi admitted, "What I was interested in was to be in contact with various actors and help find a solution for the crisis; if I accepted such a post, then I could have been accused of a conflict of interest."[381]

On December 23, 1978, a shot was fired that should have alerted the U. State Department, Carter, and Sullivan that the situation in Iran was becoming dangerous for American expatriates: Paul Grimm, "an American employee of Texaco who was on loan to the Oil Services Company of Iran...was ambushed and shot to death in Ahvaz while driving from his home to work...Responsibility for the well-organized killing was claimed by *Mujahedeen* who, at the time of the slaying, were supporting Ayatollah Khomeini."[382] The Iranian press reported that a second American was found in his apartment with his throat slit and the warning, "Please return to your country" written on the wall.[383] The CIA reported:

> *While Khomeini had in the early 1970s urged [his followers] to assassinate Americans, there is no evidence to suggest he was behind the attacks of December 23. In the aftermath of the double assassinations oil production plummeted.*[384]

Zahedi did, however, talk with military commanders in Iran such as General Gholam-Reza Azhari, joint chief of staff; General

Gholam-Ali Oveissi, army chief and martial law administrator; General Abdul-Ali Badrei, commander of the Shah's elite guards corps; and, General Amir-Hussein Badi'ie, air force commander. The men expressed their frustration that the Shah seemed unwilling to allow them to crack down on the demonstrators and revolutionaries. Zahedi outlined a plan he proposed to the leaders during one meeting:

> *His Majesty would leave Tehran for the Persian Gulf naval base in Bandar-Abbas or else go on a pilgrimage to Mecca in order to give the military government a free hand to restore order. I proposed this plan to His Majesty and he first said, "Yes," but he changed his mind.*[385]

Zahedi felt the military was more than ready to go forward with the Shah as their commander. A plan to arrest the fanatical mullahs for agitation and plotting against the Shah and to imprison them at the sports complex near Tehran or in a temporary prison in southern Iran was also suggested, but it too was vetoed by Pahlavi, whom Zahedi had apprised of his conversations with the various military leaders.

John Simpson and Tira Shubart wrote in *Lifting the Veil* of Sullivan's attempt to apprise the Carter administration of issues surrounding the demonstrations in Iran:

> *On 9 November...Sullivan broached the issues that had been raised by the demonstrators on the streets and by many journalists. His telegram entitled, "Thinking the Unthinkable," suggested that the Shah...might actually leave the country and Khomeini might return to Iran...choosing a leader who would be acceptable to the Iranian military...The telegram was used as ammunition between the State Department and National Security Council and further eroded Sullivan's position in the bureaucratic infighting over Iran.*[386]

Zahedi found the telegram to be a misstatement of the facts as he knew them. He commented on Sullivan's tactics:

Let me be clear. I did not trust Sullivan's reporting. The Shah never intended to abdicate. He was prepared to leave the country temporarily. Even there, I strongly advised him against it. I told His Majesty he should not leave, and if he left, he would never come back. [387]

The opposite view, that of a military coup, was espoused by Zbigniew Brzezinski; He fully supported a military solution, the iron fist approach, to the situation in Iran. Wrote Vance: "Zbig appeared to see a military coup, preferably in support of the Shah, as the only hope of protecting American interests. I strongly advocated a political solution...coupled with efforts to preserve the Iranian military as an institution. The iron fist [approach] was wrong on two counts: First, the Iranian army...could not make it work. Second, support for the iron fist would be antithetical to what I believed the Carter administration stood for. The president refused to give American blessing to the iron fist."[388]

In his book, *The Making of Iran's Islamic Revolution*, Mohsen Milani wrote of the Shah's dilemma:

To weather the storm, the Shah had to act decisively. He either had to crush the growing movement or to relinquish some of his power and strike a deal with the moderate factions of the popular movement. He opted to do neither.

Contradictory counsel was offered to the Shah. On the one hand, William Sullivan and British Ambassador Anthony Parsons admonished him that their respective governments would not tolerate an iron-fisted approach and favored a peaceful resolution to the crisis. "Sullivan," Brzezinski wrote, "never explicitly urged the Shah to be tough." Some of his advisors...also urged the Shah to grant more concessions to the opposition. On the extreme other hand, the

hawks, including General Gholam Ali Oveissi and Brzezinski
pressured the Shah to rescind the liberalization and to begin a mass
arrest of the more powerful members of the opposition. Brzezinski
argued that, "the deliberate weakening of the beleaguered monarch
by American pressure for further concessions would simply enhance
his instability and eventually produce complete chaos."[389]

Zahedi felt the Shah did not have a proper crisis management team in place, and therefore allowed himself to be influenced by "his immediate family entourage and an incompetent government...with catastrophic results."[390] The ambassador arranged for the Shah to meet with what were considered to be political heavyweights to try to influence the ruler to relinquish the daily duties of running the government. The list included such names as former Prime Minister Ali Amini, Abdollah Entezam, and Gholam Hossein Sadeghi (minister of the interior under Mossadegh). Zahedi suggested the establishment of a Council of Notables to select a new prime minister. The new government elected by the Council would be responsible for handling the current crisis and for implementing reforms to calm the impending storm.

The "iron fist" resolution was, indeed, counter to everything Carter espoused as commander-in-chief. He was not in favor of a military crackdown that could result in a bloodbath in the streets of Tehran.

In my conversation with Her Majesty Farah Pahlavi, she confirmed the Shah's reluctance to approve military force against the people of Iran:

> *One of the French ministers wrote in his book that he had gone*
> *to see the Shah, and he told the Shah to remain in power. The Shah*
> *told him (which is true) that, "I don't want to keep my throne*
> *over the blood of my people." All of his life was dedicated to the*
> *Iranian people.*[391]

Pahlavi's former son-in-law, Ardeshir Zahedi, also reiterated the queen's observations concerning her husband:

The Shah was a real patriot and loved the Iranian people...The Shah was kind-hearted and soft by nature and was horrified by bloodshed...The Shah had always believed the Iranian masses loved him, and he could not bear seeing people turn against him with such vehemence...His dream was to help Iran become the Japan of the Middle East, and he was in a hurry to make that wish become a reality. Many of the programs of today by the present regime are ideas and projects that the Shah started or foresaw.[392]

Mohamed Heikal wrote of an encounter between the Shah and the empress in a dispute over the demonstrations and riots that were happening throughout the country. The Egyptian journalist wrote that the empress tried to warn the Shah of events occurring outside the palace as reported to her by trusted friends and relatives. The Shah resorted to an old valet to confirm Farah Diba's claims. The valet, apparently in an attempt to placate the king, gave him a less than honest report on the situation. The empress' claims were perfunctorily dismissed by Pahlavi, and she fled his presence in tears. During the ensuing hours the Shah must have had a change of heart; he ordered his pilot to fly him over the city. The king was appalled at the sight below him: the streets of Tehran were over-flowing with people protesting against Pahlavi. He returned to the palace and gave strict orders that no one—not even the empress— was to be allowed inside his private quarters. He later relented and agreed to see Farah Diba in his chambers.[393]

Near the end of his life Pahlavi is said to have regretted acquiescing to the forces that were determined to relinquish Iran to Khomeini:

I think the one mistake was to adopt this policy [of not spilling blood]...because then the opposition saw that now we were surrendering under duress and pressure and they decided they could go all the way.[394]

. . . .

SPIRALING
OUT OF CONTROL

*"Those who can make you believe
absurdities can make you commit atrocities."*

(VOLTAIRE)

Events in Iran had only begun a downward spiral. Without White House authorization, Ambassador William Sullivan determined the reign of the Shah would have to end and began to communicate with leaders of the opposition to achieve that goal. Apparently, Sullivan felt that the Shah was losing his determination to remain in control. Through negotiations with leaders of Pahlavi's opposition, Sullivan amassed a list in excess of one hundred military men who would be certain to depart Iran with the Shah. It would then be up to the revolutionary organizers to choose their replacements. The more moderate elements in the revolution were expected to assure Sullivan that no revenge would be exacted from the military.[395] What an absolute absurdity for a U.S. ambassador to suppose that he had the authority to retire the top brass of a foreign army and ask a fanatical group of Islamic revolutionaries to submit a list of their replacements!

Was Sullivan's ambiguity regarding the Shah's situation in Iran only a reflection of that of the Carter administration? After all, it was Carter who proclaimed rather indecisively, "We have made it clear through my own public statements and those of Secretary Vance that we support the Shah and support the present government, recognizing that we don't have any control over the decisions ultimately of the Iranian people."[396] And while Sullivan was pursuing his agenda, the president had been in Guadeloupe pursuing an agenda of his own—seeking the backing of European leaders for the deposition of the Shah. Perhaps the president had not read Dante Alighieri's famous quote, "The hottest places in hell are reserved for those who in times of great moral crises maintain their neutrality."[397]

In November 1978 Leonid Brezhnev, the Soviet leader of the Communist Party, stepped into the fray with a warning to the U.S.: "I must be clear that any interference, especially military interference, in the affairs of Iran...would be regarded as a matter affecting security interests [of the U.S.S.R.]"[398] (One of the Shah's major concerns was that civil strife in Iran would open the door for the Soviets to gain a foothold.)

The typically milquetoast response from the U.S. State Department indicated that nothing would be done to interfere with Iran's internal affairs. In fact, it was a statement by President Carter at a December 1978 press conference that seemed to seal the Shah's fate. When asked if the Shah would prevail in Iran, Carter answered: "We [the U.S.] personally prefer that the Shah maintain a major role in government, but that's a decision for the Iranian people to make."[399] The press, foreign and domestic, reported the president's words and many interpreted them to mean that the U.S. government was standing ready to abandon Mohammad Reza Shah Pahlavi.

Following a November 1978 fact-finding mission to Iran by State Department insiders Stephen Cohen, George Griffin, and Carl Clement, they and Ambassador William Sullivan warned of the likelihood that the Shah would no longer rule Iran and that his successors might be less than enamored of a U.S. presence in the country. Sullivan wrote that the State Department needed to make contingency plans for a transfer of power to a coalition government consisting of Khomeini followers and the military. Was it possible that Sullivan was hoping to reach an accord with the opposition after the Shah left Iran? Was he simply waiting for the death rattle before stepping into the fray?

The *Washington Post* again took to its editorial page in late October to try to exonerate Jimmy Carter on his Iran policies with a rather one-sided viewpoint: "This administration inherited a deep American commitment to the Shah, and to his heady view of the importance of Iran in the strategic scheme of things...Jimmy Carter's support of Iran...has emphasized political liberalization...[which] involves a great gamble...But the Shah...seems to be taking that gamble. At least for as long as he does, the United States has no good choice but to help see him through."[400]

Scarcely a month later, in early November, the *Post* cataclysmically intoned, "The countdown [for the Shah's fall] has begun."[401] Not willing to place any blame on the Carter administration for its failure to support a strong U.S. ally in the Persian Gulf, the *Post* declared, "The popular tendency to blame it all on Carter's civil rights policy is at best an oversimplification. In hindsight, it was only a question of time before the system the Shah had built collapsed."

In yet another attempt to absolve the president from any failure, the *Post* continued to build its case by declaring that it was not Jimmy Carter's crisis.[402] Apparently, either the *Post* editorialist did not know Mr. Carter as well as he thought he did, or he was unwilling to place blame where blame was due. The Shah, and therefore Iran, was abandoned to the fanatical element that supported the Ayatollah Khomeini.

According to Dr. Abol Majid Majidi, Carter sent Theodore Eliot Jr. to Paris in October 1978 to talk with Khomeini and his entourage. Majidi said Eliot "had tried to create a new relationship, but Khomeini didn't show any sign of willingness... He was trying to facilitate a dialogue between Khomeini and the American government."[403]

The year had produced the Camp David Accords, Strategic Arms Limitation Treaty (SALT) talks, and top-secret advances to the Chinese government, as well as the turmoil in Iran. Unfortunately, the White House was slothful in closely following events in Iran. For instance, it seemed to have escaped the CIA and other agencies that the military was demoralized, defections were the order of the day, and it would be of little use to a coalition government. In an attempt to shore up the flagging Iranian military, Carter dispatched General Robert "Dutch" Huyser, deputy commander-in-chief of the U.S. European Command, to Iran under Alexander Haig despite the misgivings of both Haig and Sullivan. Haig contacted Deputy Secretary of Defense Charles Duncan to express both his anger and concern over Carter's decision:

> *This is bad policy. It is also just plain wrong, and what you have in mind for Dutch Huyser is no job for a military man. You're sending the wrong man for the wrong purpose.*[404]

Haig's unease over sending Huyser to Tehran was overruled by a direct order from Jimmy Carter and the Joint Chiefs of Staff. Huyser was ordered to Tehran post-haste with an admonition from Haig:

Then you have to do what you have to do, Dutch. But watch yourself. You may end up destroying the Iranian military. And that would destroy any hope of a good outcome in Iran.[405]

The Shah recorded that "as soon as Moscow learned of Huyser's arrival, *Pravda* reported, 'General Huyser is in Tehran to foment a military coup.' In Paris, the *International Herald Tribune* wrote that Huyser had not gone to Tehran to 'foment' a coup but to 'prevent' one."[406]

The Iranian generals, who would not attempt a coup while the Shah was on the throne, were awaiting the arrival of Alexander Haig and for some signal or some kind of guarantee from the U.S. that the Soviets would not invade Iran. But rather than send Haig to reassure his Iranian counterparts, his deputy, Dutch Huyser, was tapped for the mission. Huyser, for some unknown reason, did not notify the Shah of his arrival in Tehran as was customary; the Shah discovered he was actually in the country several days after Huyser's arrival.

Huyser's job was to inform the generals that Carter was in favor of democracy in Iran and to act as a morale booster. His orders were to try to persuade the military heads to remain in Iran and work with the U.S. According to former Israeli Ambassador to Iran Uri Lubrani, anyone who thought he could make a deal with the generals and not have made some arrangement with the religious establishment simply didn't understand the situation in Tehran.

General Huyser was soon to discover the truth in Lubrani's assessment: Although a plan was supposed to have been in place for an eventuality such as an attempted overthrow of the Shah's government, these military leaders simply did not have a cohesive strategy to deal with the Shah's almost certain ouster by the Ayatollah's revolutionary forces. According to Lt. General Azarbarzin, former vice-chief of the Iranian air force, Huyser set the generals to work to draw up a contingency plan, although no one in the palace or the Shah's chain of command had authorized the meetings.[407]

Reportedly, Sullivan was less than ecstatic at Huyser's arrival and tried to intervene with Washington. This is not surprising given Sullivan's list of generals he was trying to place on the last plane out of Iran before Khomeini's ultimate power grab. In Dr. Tehrani's estimation, Huyser's mission was totally compromised when shortly after his arrival in Tehran several top military officials defected to the revolution.[408]

Lt. General Azarbarzin told me why the generals were so opposed to a coup:

> The military commanders [were] picked by the Shah and reported to
> him alone, not through the chain of command. They were not picked
> because they were the most competent, but because they were weak
> and loyal to the Shah. So, when the time came that they could have
> staged a coup, they were not capable of doing it; they were used to
> taking orders not action...The air force cadets were neither officers
> nor non-commissioned officers nor enlisted men. They had a special
> contract that provided them pay higher than the colonels, special
> benefits, and paid education through a Ph.D. They were trained in
> the U.S. to run the most sophisticated technology. As part of their
> contract, once their service was over, they were to get a lump sum of
> money they could use to start their own business. For some reason,
> the chief of the air force decided to renege on the deal for six or seven
> cadets...against my advice. The chief went to the Shah and got his

approval. Word got out…and morale sank. The cadets no longer trusted the military or the Shah.[409]

Empress Farah Pahlavi related in our interview that General Haig was concerned about Huyser's trip to Tehran:

I heard that after General Huyser met with President Carter, he went to Brussels when General Haig was there. General Haig told him, "I hope you go there to support the Shah." Huyser told him, "My instructions are otherwise." I wanted to write this in my book [An Enduring Love]; I called General Haig…to see if what I had heard was correct. He told me, "Yes, it is correct; and even more."[410]

Haig was not the only insider to admit the Shah had human rights problems within his country; however, the general felt that as ruler of Iran, Pahlavi was "an essentially benevolent despot,… a good friend of the United States, an implacable enemy of the Left, and an obstacle to the religious Right."[411] By turning a blind eye to the Shah's predicament, Carter allowed the door to swing open and aided Khomeini's takeover of Iran.

General Huyser was chosen as emissary because he had, over the years, built close relationships with a number of top-level Iranian military men. He had been a frequent visitor to the Shah's palace and had established a mutual respect and trust with the monarch. It had been Huyser to whom the Shah voiced his apprehension that he would estrange President Carter by not moving quickly enough to introduce sufficient changes to placate the administration's human rights policies.

Huyser wrote that Carter had charged him:

…to convey [President Carter's] concern and assurances to the senior military leaders at this most critical time. It was of vital importance to both the Iranian people and the U.S. government that Iran have a strong, stable government which would remain

*friendly to the United States. The Iranian military was the key to
the situation.*[412]

In my book *Showdown with Nuclear Iran*, I wrote of the meeting I had with Robert Huyser:

> *Huyser was a man of principle and moral clarity and believed that
> his mission was to support Prime Minister Shapour Bakhtiar and
> Iran's generals. Carter promised that the U.S. would protect and
> provide all assets needed to shore up the government, which was
> increasingly endangered by violent protests against the regime of
> the Shah, Mohammed Reza Pahlavi. Despite a history of support
> going back to World War II, Carter had no desire to see a pro-Shah
> regime in power. He preferred the Ayatollah, whom he seemed to
> regard as a Gandhi-like figure. The comparison made sense to a
> point: the Ayatollah opposed the Shah, who had a terrible record of
> human rights abuses. But that's where the comparison breaks down.
> Gandhi was nonviolent. The Ayatollah was anything but.*[413]

General Huyser was dispatched to Iran to provide encouragement should a military solution be ordered by the Shah or should the
military decide to implement a coup. According to the general,
the Iranian generals might have been persuaded to take up arms in
defense of the monarchy if—and only if—they had full military
support from the U.S. Another of Huyser's aims was to encourage
the more hard-line military men to accept Feridoun Jam, Bakhtiar's
choice for defense minister. What proved to be even more difficult
was to persuade Jam to agree to the appointment; he declined.

Ambassador Zahedi related his meetings to me, first with
the Shah and later with some of the generals—Oveissi, Bad'ie,
Toufanian, and Major-General Manuchehr Khosrowdad—regarding
Huyser's mission. The ambassador initially suggested to the Shah
that Huyser either be arrested upon arrival or put on the same plane

and sent back to the U.S. The Shah was in favor of waiting to see what Huyser had to say. The military men felt Huyser was encouraging them to disobey the Shah's orders. General Khosrawdad was so angry that he threatened to shoot Huyser on sight. Zahedi very delicately suggested they behave rationally, and that they also wait to see what Huyser proposed. Zahedi was saddened that Huyser's visit seemed to totally destroy morale among the army leaders.[414]

The Shah's opinion of Huyser's mission was vastly different than that expressed by the general, according to Pahlavi's memoirs. He felt that Huyser's interference had destroyed the Iranian army and decimated Bakhtiar's government. Pahlavi wrote that one of his generals, Gharabaghi, said of Huyser, "General Huyser threw the Shah out of the country like a dead mouse."[415]

Huyser's departure from Iran left General Philip C. Gast, chief of the U.S. Military Assistance and Advisory Group, in a leadership role. It was he who then maintained daily communication with both the Iranian military and Secretary of Defense Harold Brown.

Within just two short weeks Pahlavi had flown from Iran, Khomeini had strutted into Tehran a triumphant ayatollah, the Shah's army had crumbled in humiliation and disarray, and the Peacock Throne was barren. Haig tendered his resignation: "I felt I could not continue to serve the Carter administration."[416]

Huyser later recorded one of the ultimate ironies of his mission to Tehran. According to the general, he had the Iranian armed forces at his very command, yet was unable to complete the simplest goal: unloading an oil tanker.[417]

In the midst of the turmoil in Iran, or perhaps because of it, President Carter asked for a meeting on the French Republic island of Guadeloupe in the Caribbean. Although Carter prompted the meeting, ostensibly for him "and the leaders of Britain, France, and West Germany to talk informally about strategic and economic problems,"[418] the invitations were issued by French President Valery Giscard d'Estaing to West German Chancellor Helmut Schmidt and British Prime Minister James Callaghan. Carter was concerned that a meeting called by the U.S. would upset other NATO leaders, i.e., Canada, Japan, and Italy.

In a briefing by Zbigniew Brzezinski prior to his departure for Guadeloupe, the president was to have told the assembled world leaders, "President Carter will reiterate his support of the Shah."[419] In his book, *Le Pouvoir et la Vie*, d'Estaing recalls the meeting:

> The President Jimmy Carter told us suddenly that the United States had decided not to support the régime of the Shah anymore. Without that support, that régime is now lost. I have kept in my mind the summary of the mission that Michel Poniatowski [French minister of the interior] had with the Shah on December 27 [1979]. He had found him with a clear mind but "sad, tired, and disillusioned." He thought the Americans would support him to the end. But in a week, the tide changed...Jimmy Carter tells us what he sees coming. The military will take power and will bring order to the country. Its leaders are pro-West, and most of them have been trained in the United States. The Shah sees more clearly: speaking to Michel Poniatowski, he says, "It is all about a powerful religious renewal, which has allowed a long fifty-years-old struggle between the Shiite clergy and our dynasty to turn into a test of forces." And it is the way things happen.[420]

Although not considered a "formal" meeting that required documentation, National Security Advisor Zbigniew Brzezinski did keep a journal of the Guadeloupe meeting. He recorded his impressions of one session on security issues in his memoirs, *Power and Principle:*

I must say that I was quite impressed by the discussion. It was a thoroughly stimulating and comprehensive review of the security situation, with Carter very effectively taking the lead and pressing the others to define their response to the perceived threat...Giscard was clear, to the point, and quite decisive. Callaghan displayed good political sense, was quite vigorous, and spoke very sensibly... [Schmidt] was the one who was most concerned about the Soviet nuclear threat in Europe and the least inclined to agree to any firm response.[421]

While Carter, Brzezinski, his deputy David Aaron, Vance, and other administration bigwigs were busily plotting the Shah's future, Pahlavi was seemingly adrift in a sea of indecision. Should he form a military government? Should he, as Brzezinski suggested, act decisively toward his opponents? Bombarded on every side to either step up to the plate or step down from the throne, the Shah addressed his Iranian subjects in tones that could only be described as conciliatory and apologetic. He acknowledged that he had digested the calls for revolution and was ready to make amends. Pahlavi's remarks exposed his inner turmoil and struggles with what had become the proverbial handwriting on the wall: the monarchy was in its death throes and the Shah was in complete denial. Unable to make a clear-cut decision, the embattled ruler declared:

I commit myself to make up for past mistakes, to fight corruption and injustices, and to form a national government to carry out free elections...I guarantee that after the military government, freedom and the constitution will be re-implemented...Your revolutionary message has been heard.[422]

During the meeting in Guadeloupe, the president also wrestled with the issue of the Shah and the Ayatollah: Should the U.S. make contact with Khomeini? Would it be beneficial to support a military coup? How long should the U.S. support Bakhtiar's interim government? Brzezinski detailed a telephone conference/meeting to which he was called the afternoon he arrived on the French island. The president was in deep conversation with Secretary of State Cyrus Vance. Vance was concerned that the Iranian military leaders would refuse to allow the Shah to depart Tehran and that massive bloodshed would follow that decision.

At the Guadeloupe summit Secretary Vance approached the president and asked that he "be authorized to open a direct channel to Khomeini in Paris." Vance's plan was to "do this through Ambassador Theodore Eliot, a very able, retired senior Foreign Service officer...I wished Eliot to urge the Ayatollah to give Bakhtiar time to restore order before he returned to Iran...The president rejected my recommendation...After a long discussion on January 10...Carter decided to telephone French President Valery Giscard d'Estaing to ask that the French government urge Khomeini to give Bakhtiar an opportunity to restore order, although he [Carter] agreed that the French should say this also represented American views."[423] The French leader agreed to contact the Ayatollah.

Brzezinski, who along with Secretary of Energy James Schlesinger and Deputy Secretary of Defense Charles Duncan favored military intervention, was appalled that Vance seemed determined to moderate the instructions that had been given to General Robert Huyser. Carter refused to allow that to happen. Wrote Brzezinski: "I was gratified by his [Carter's] firmness and dismayed that anyone at this late stage would actually wish to prevent what was clearly in the collective interest of the West."[424]

Another item on the agenda in Guadeloupe was whether or not the U.S. should reach out to Ruhollah Khomeini. While Ambassador to Iran William Sullivan seemed eager for that to happen, other members of the administration were reluctant to do so without the prior approval of the Shah. Various reports on the four-leader summit indicate that no conclusion regarding Khomeini was reached while on the island.

Giscard d'Estaing expressed his shock at Carter's lack of regard for a country that had been a close ally for decades:

> *We were humanly shocked by the way Carter spoke because we knew at the end it would lead to the torture or the killing of the Shah. And he [Carter] was not embarrassed at all; no, no, he spoke very lightly of a man that we supported very strongly...He [Carter] was a bastard of conscience, a moralist, who treats with total lightness the fact of abandoning a man that we had supported together. At least you need to have some emotion. And we didn't have any discussion...No. No. It was, "We have decided." [We were shocked] by the lack of human consideration of the fate of the Shah. Because it was a man that we knew well. We worked with him, we had met with him and all that; so we could accept or understand that probably politically he cannot survive in Iran, or it would be very difficult; but it was some sort of anguish for us. Not someone who should be disgraced with one public gesture.*[425]

Mir Ali Asghar Montazam wrote of the Guadeloupe meeting in his book, *The Life and Times of Ayatollah Khomeini*:

> *The Guadeloupe summit...was the convenient opportunity he [Carter] found to agree with the three European leaders that the Shah was doomed...all the allies needed was Iranian oil and stability in the region....So, when General Robert Huyser, Carter's special emissary, arrived unannounced in Tehran about the time of Shapour Bakhtiar's becoming prime minister, he represented the entire Western alliance, not the United States only. The Iranian army commanders assented to the Shah's exile only after Huyser showed them the minutes of the allies' summit meeting in Guadeloupe.*[426]

The Shah was more astute than his so-called allies, however. In his memoir, *Answer to History*, the Shah wrote: "Giscard said they hoped to 'evaluate the situation of the world,' with special emphasis on events in the eastern Mediterranean and the Persian Gulf. I believe that during those meetings the French and West Germans agreed with the British and the American proposals for my ouster."[427]

The Shah continued: "About the same time French President Valery Giscard D'Estaing sent a personal envoy to Tehran, a man very close to him [Comte Alexandre de Marenches]. He too advocated a 'political' solution to the crisis, a euphemism for accommodation and abstention from the use of force."[428]

Perhaps it was because, as Amir Taheri wrote in *The Spirit of Allah*, "The French were the first to be persuaded that a government under Khomeini would offer them a golden opportunity in Iran, Valery Giscard d'Estaing...also began advising his Western allies not to try to prolong the Shah's regime."[429]

. . . .

CHAPTER 18

THE FRENCH
CONNECTION

*"The DST, the French secret service, opposed his entry
[to France] but Giscard overruled them and granted Khomeini
political asylum in France. He stayed in Neauphle le Chateau
near Paris. From there, he distributed cassettes to Iran
inciting against democracy, peace in the Middle East, the Jews
and Israelis. He also called for jihad, a violent holy war."*

(F J O R D M A N)[430]

I t was while in France that Khomeini's speeches and writings
were the most prolific and where the planning for his Islamic
revolution gained momentum. Khomeini, the usurper, gave over
one hundred media interviews during his short, four-month stay in
Neauphle-le-Chateau. His pronouncements were quickly translated,
printed, and sent to Tehran. According to Dr. Parviz Mina, the
French gave Khomeini every media advantage and constantly
covered his activities. "On the French news," said Dr. Mina,
"normally there are two special news programs, one at 1:00 in the

afternoon and another at 8:00 p.m. And normally international news takes up ten minutes or fifteen minutes...During the time of Khomeini, every day, fifteen minutes they were talking about Iran and Khomeini, every day...the media was given the free hand...[the French government] provided him security. I think all the facilities he needed is at his disposal."[431] The dour Ayatollah had been transformed overnight into a VIP, the darling of the liberal Western media, and France had become command central for the launch of his Islamic Republic.

France in 1979 boasted three major television outlets: *TeleFrance1 (TF1)*, *Antennae 2 (A2)*, and *France 3 (FR3)*; the latter two were owned by the government. *A2* was similar in style and content to America's Public Broadcasting System. The station set the tone for stories on "Journal 20h" (the 8:00 PM news), the equivalent of the NBC or CBS Nightly News. On October 10, 1978, mere days after Khomeini's arrival, he was pictured in a story on *A2*. The images showed Khomeini dressed in dark clothing and sitting tailor-fashion on Persian carpets. He was posed in a lush green garden surrounded by children. He was described as being a deeply religious man who abstained from worldly things.[432] The images were reminiscent of the beloved Indian leader Mahatma Gandhi, the champion of non-violence. Khomeini was clearly being modeled as a modest man compared to the extravagant Shah.

The most influential daily newspaper in France at that time was *Le Monde* or "The World." Though *Le Monde* was left-of-center, it was not as far left as the communist *Libération*. On the other side of the coin was just slightly-right-of-center, *Le Figaro*. While French President Giscard D'Estaing was purported to be "Centrist," his views more nearly matched those of *Le Monde*.

Many in France thought journalist Paul Balta had been assigned *by Le Monde* to cover Khomeini; it was more apropos to say that Khomeini assigned him. Balta would tell the story years later of how he landed in Paris just after Khomeini arrived in exile at Neauphle-le-Château, a suburb of Paris:

> *While I was covering the Iranian revolution for Le Monde, I came to Paris in November 1978. Abu Hassan Bani Sadr, principal adviser to Khomeini and president of the Republic, told me that the Ayatollah, also called Imam, wanted to meet me. To my surprise, he explained to me that he had had my articles translated from the French press and that Khomeini had said about me, "Who is he? He writes like no other; he knows Islam and Iran. I want to see him." I went to Neauphle-le-Chateau, where he lived in exile since October 5. He shared his frugal meal with me: a large bowl of soup, bread, fruit, and some cakes just for me. He said that first he would ask me questions before answering mine. Once done, he granted me an official interview, which it was not customary.*[433]

Had the Shah established the same conditions for an interview, would Balta have been as kind to Pahlavi in his writings as he was to Khomeini? For example, in a Khomeini biography/profile by Balta for *Le Monde* on February 1, 1979, he wrote:

> *A believer in jihad (in the original sense of the term, generally translated as "holy war," it is the battle against oneself), he (Khomeini) disciplines himself down to the smallest details in daily activities and to an intense spiritual life. "He is an example to all, and even his worst enemies can never contest that," they say in Iran.*[434]

Did Balta later realize just how clever the Ayatollah had been with him? He posed a question to Khomeini in January 1979: "When you win [not "if you win," but "when"], what will be the status of the Iranian women?" Khomeini's answer: "Our women fight like lions. They deserve our admiration. In the Islamic state, they will have the status that they deserve."[435]

Just weeks later Balta joined Khomeini's entourage on the Air France plane that flew the triumphant Ayatollah to Tehran. Delivering a significant speech to his adoring followers in Qom, Khomeini returned the women of Iran to the Dark Ages. Balta explained:

> *He outlined the main orientations of the future Islamic Republic and proclaimed compulsory wearing of the chador—"veil"—which had been abolished by the Shah. At the conclusion of the ceremony, I expressed my surprise about the chador, but he replied to me: "I told you they deserve our admiration. It is always the case, but I added as in the Islamic state, they will have the status that they deserve."*

It was also in France, that most cosmopolitan of countries, that Khomeini received the makeover of all times. This son of an Indian fortune-teller was stripped of his past. His father became the leader of the Khomeini clan who, supposedly, was murdered by Pahlavi's father. Khomeini graduated from second-rate mullah to academic and renowned holy man. If he was the Eliza Doolittle, who was the Henry Higgins? What country (or countries) was so determined to unseat the Shah that it was willing to undertake the transformation?

Dominique Lorenz, a journalist for the French *Libération*, wrote that "having picked Khomeini to overthrow the Shah, [the Americans] had to get him out of Iraq, clothe him with respectability, and set him up in Paris; a succession of events which could not have occurred if the leadership in France had been against it."[436] In France, Khomeini's Iranian visitors totaled more than one thousand per day, all of which the French blessed or, at the very least, turned a blind eye. The Ayatollah became the "Guru of Hate" as he shared his vitriolic dislike for the Shah with all who would listen and learn. These disciples, including a number from various American universities, were not coming just to sit at the feet of the "Teacher" and learn; their pockets, lined with money collected through the Bazaar, the commercial system in Iran, were empty when they left Khomeini's presence. Some estimates place the contributions at approximately twenty million British pounds.

The Ayatollah's compound was reportedly surrounded by representatives of covert agencies from the major powers: the CIA, Britain's MI-6, Russia's KGB, and the French intelligence organization, SDECE. One has to wonder why an unknown, uncultured, old cleric was the focus of such attention.

One visitor to Khomeini's chateau described the mesmerizing effect the Ayatollah had on his visitors:

> *He started to speak in his deep, bass voice, and I never heard a voice as serene and moving. It was said that he caressed the ears of his listeners, in soft waves to put them in a trance state...Here we had an Imam, with his long, grey beard and black turban of the Shiites...and here, all of these men representing the social and intellectual elite of Iran, listened in absolute silence, hanging on every word that fell from his lips with an attentive fascination... Khomeini was always sure that the driving force of the revolution would be religious, and he was therefore destined to take the leadership role.*[437]

French journalist André Fontaine "compared Khomeini to John Paul II, heaping praise upon the [Ayatollah] without reserve. The philosopher Jacques Madaule, referring to Khomeini's role, asked if his movement did not 'open the gates of the future of humanity.'"[438]

Aiding Khomeini during his French exile was Abolhassan Bani Sadr. Journalist Charles Villeneuve related to me that Bani Sadr was responsible for supplying the cassette tapes filled with anti-Shah propaganda and dispatching them through the network that would insure their arrival in the mosques in Tehran. The Iranian had resisted attempts by CIA operative Vernon Cassin (under the alias Guy Rutherford) to enlist him as a mole. Cassin's documents would eventually wind up in the hands of the militants who seized the American Embassy and would signal the downfall of Bani Sadr.

In my interview with him, Giscard d'Estaing shed more light on the messages sent into Iran by the Ayatollah:

> *During his stay, the Imam was active. He sent messages to Iran to Tehran...he used tapes...carried by followers to Iran...to Chayet, the man in charge...we knew the Interior Ministry was still watching closely the activities of the Ayatollah. He seems to deliver violent messages...we have political refugees, but they must abstain from violence. So we warned him...that we would not accept that [he] would go on sending messages...But he went on...we had the tapes. The second time I was warned by our ambassador in Tehran that Khomeini had sent a message asking to kill the Shah...five days later, we had confirmation that he sent another violent tape to Tehran saying the same thing, which was, "Kill the Shah."*[440]

CIA memoranda regarding Khomeini and the Shah seem to have either been deliberately ignored by the Carter administration or lost in the great governmental paperwork shuffle. One such memorandum flatly stated, "Khomeini is determined to overthrow the Shah and is unlikely to accept compromise...Khomeini is anticommunist, but his followers may be susceptible to communist and radical penetration. He has cooperated in the past with Islamic terrorist groups."[441]

A CIA intelligence memorandum dated January 19, 1979, and released three days after the Shah's departure, contained detailed information on Bani Sadr and Sadegh Ghotbzadeh (a Syrian-born leader of the opposition movement), including the fact that both men had ties to Palestinian commandos. Questions arise: Why was the memo released after the Shah's departure from Tehran? Did President Carter and administration officials have access to this information in the months prior to abandoning the Shah and permitting Khomeini to return to Tehran?

Early in 1977 Khomeini had begun to woo the military in Iran through his taped messages. The wily Ayatollah knew that to win the revolution he must first charm and disarm the military. He began to indoctrinate the troops with the message of the Shah's corruption and their own place as soldiers of Allah; as such, they were prohibited from shooting at their own brethren. He exhorted them to return to their homes, to the faith, and to service to Allah. Surprisingly, it was not SAVAK or the Shah's inner circle that stumbled onto Khomeini's tactics; it was the Israeli mission to Tehran that had become apprehensive as evidenced by the fact that it began to evacuate mission personnel from Tehran.

By fall 1977 the Ayatollah was giving the soldiers specific instructions as to how to achieve his goal. He encouraged them to desert their posts in numbers, reminding them it was their God-given right to take their arms with them. Ironically, the very day Jimmy Carter praised Iran as "an ocean of stability in a stormy sea," a battalion of five hundred soldiers abandoned their post in the Meshed region. Said one journalist, "The Ayatollah effectively disarmed the Shah's military before engaging it in final battle."[442]

In another ironic twist, the Shah found himself an unwitting accomplice of Khomeini's revolution. In his efforts to modernize

Iran, the Shah had installed a costly direct-dial telephone system. It allowed Khomeini to pick up the phone in Neauphle-le-Chateau and have direct talks with his cohorts in Tehran.

It was this telephone system that Azarbarzin was certain the CIA had bugged. He cited one incident to support his theory:

The Shah asked me to bring General Nissiri back into the country; it seemed the Shah was considering putting him in as prime minister. Nassiri was then stationed as the Shah's ambassador to Pakistan. I ordered an aircraft at the airport, only told the crew where they were going once onboard. We flew to Pakistan at night and returned with Nassiri to a non-descript gate at the airport, and drove back to the palace. I had made arrangements and alerted the Imperial Guard that we would sneak Nassiri in through an unused entrance after midnight.

Usually Ambassador Sullivan arrived at the palace at 10:00 a.m.... That morning...Sullivan arrived at 8:30 a.m. and asked to see the Shah. When they met Sullivan immediately began to explain that it was a mistake to name Nassiri...because the people demonstrating on the street were there because of Nassiri's actions as head of SAVAK. Instead of making Nassiri the PM as planned, he was placed in jail to please the Iranian masses.

On November 3, 1978, the Shah decided to create a military cabinet. His nominee was General Oveissi...The Shah ordered General Oveissi to start selecting his cabinet members. On November 4 both British Ambassador Anthony Parsons and U.S. Ambassador William Sullivan had audiences with the Shah. They convinced him that people called Oveissi a butcher for the way he had put down protests in 1963.[443]

The ambassadors suggested that the Shah appoint General Gholam-Reza Azhari as prime minister. Was this just another attempt on the part of the U.S. and British governments to manipulate Pahlavi?

It seemed the Shah's government could do nothing to prevent Khomeini from attracting like-minded revolutionaries to his chateau outside Paris. In my interview with Samuel Segev, he confirmed that two of Khomeini's visitors in France were Farouk Kaddoumi, PLO department head, and a Libyan representative of Muammar al-Qaddafi. Khomeini was tendered arms and money in support of the revolution. Soon after, Radio Tripoli broadcast messages in Persian to Khomeini backers in Iran, and PLO terrorists were dispatched to Tehran.[444]

As the turmoil fueled by Khomeini's subversive methods in his country increased, the Shah tried appeasement measures to placate the rioters and strikers. He eased curfews, allowed processions to mark holy days, and ultimately succumbed to the pressure to put a new government in place. He chose Shahpour Bakhtiar, a forthright critic of the monarchy, as the new leader. Ardeshir Zahedi urged General Oveissi to secure Bakhtiar's agreement that he would work with the army to restore order not undermine it, and Bakhtiar agreed.

At Bakhtiar's urging the Shah agreed to leave Iran for what was labeled "rest and recuperation." Empress Farah Pahlavi writes that even though Bakhtiar urged the Shah to leave, the Chief of Staff General Abbas Gharabaghi was opposed to the move and warned the empress that if the Shah left Iran, the army would collapse.

This evaluation was supported by Ambassador Lubrani. He dressed himself as a middle-class Iranian and went out among the rioters and demonstrators. He related that the soldiers simply stood by while women in the crowd placed carnations in the muzzles of their rifles. The army was effectively neutralized by the massive crowds of Iranians. The question then became: Had the Shah given the order to shoot into the crowd, would the army have complied?[445]

The Shah assumed that upon his return, he would become a constitutional monarch much like Queen Elizabeth II in England. Little did he know that once airborne, he would have caught his last glimpse of his beloved country, and that Iran would plunge back into the Dark Ages from which he had tried so hard to lead his people. Pahlavi was convinced the French government was ignoring Khomeini's clever plot to incite revolution in Iran.

From Paris, Khomeini had called upon the Iranian military to forestall any attempt by the Shah to promote a military coup. He had also urged the Iranian people to overthrow the Bakhtiar government, calling it illegal and illegitimate. The Ayatollah wrote:

> There is a possibility that the treacherous Shah, now about to depart, will commit a further crime, a military coup d'état. I have frequently warned that this is probable...The courageous people of Iran know that there are only a few slavish and bloodthirsty individuals in the army, who apparently occupy important positions and whose identities are known to me, and that the honorable elements in the army will never permit these slaves of the Shah to commit such a crime against their nation and religion. In accordance with my God-given and national duty, I alert the Iranian army to this danger, and I demand that all commanders and officers resolutely prevent the enactment of any such conspiracy and not permit a few bloodthirsty individuals to plunge the noble people of Iran into a bloodbath. Iranian army, this is your God-given duty. If you obey these congenital traitors, you will be accountable to God, Exalted and Almighty, condemned by all humanitarians, and cursed by future generations...The Iranian people...must recognize that a few treacherous members of the army cannot sully the army as a whole. The record and responsibility of a few bloodthirsty

individuals is something separate from the army as a whole. The army belongs to the people, and the people belong to the army. The army will not suffer any harm as a result of the departure of the Shah.[446]

According to President Carter's memoir, *Keeping Faith*, President d'Estaing offered to deport Khomeini to halt the discord and stop Khomeini's rabble-rousing from French shores. Carter wrote, "The Shah had thought it would be better to keep Khomeini there [France], instead of letting him go to Iraq or Libya or some place where he might orchestrate even more trouble."[447] A poll taken among the French people found that half [of those] questioned were "sorry that their government granted political asylum to the Ayatollah."[448]

. . . .

CHAPTER 19

ABDICATING TO
A RUTHLESS AYATOLLAH

*"Khomeini...insisted that, since his version of Islam was
the only true version, all Muslims should follow it... Khomeini
blithely allied himself with anyone who could advance his
cause...[His] version of Islam was unquestionably bloodthirsty."*
(MICHAEL A. LEDEEN)[449]

Prior to Khomeini's arrival in France, Giscard had dispatched his
personal representative, Michel Poniatowski, to Iran to meet
with the Shah. Poniatowski reported back to Giscard that, "[The
Shah] understands nothing of what's going on; he thinks Khomeini
is without importance and he asks us to welcome him...I don't want
to; he should not be welcomed."[450]

Former Ambassador Zahedi agreed with Poniatowski:

*Every time His Majesty asked, I advised him to get Khomeini
out [of Paris]. Nothing changed. The prime minister [Jafar Sharif-
Emami] had influenced the Shah and none of us managed to
change his mind.*[451]

Giscard then sent his chief of secret services, Alexandre de Marenches (who referred to Jimmy Carter as a "national and international disaster"[452]) to interview the Shah and to confirm Poniatowski's impression. Marenches reported back to Giscard that the Shah appeared almost beaten and that the best thing to do would be to prepare in France for the aftermath of Khomeini's revolution.[453] According to Marenches, the Shah declined to use armed force against his people. Marenches replied, "Sir, in that case you are lost."[454] Uri Lubrani is of the opinion that France courted Khomeini as a way of "buying political influence...resting on their reputation of being a liberal country [that gave] political asylum to all sorts of renegades...'France is a whore,'" said Lubrani.[455]

General Huyser also pointed out that the United States should have learned how important it was not to abandon a friend. He assessed the Carter administration's lack of understanding:

> *The administration obviously did not understand the Iranian culture nor the conditions that prevailed in the last few months of the Shah's reign. I believe that Washington should have recognized the seriousness of the situation early in 1978. If the real intent was to support the existing government, much could have been done to bolster the Shah's lagging confidence and resolve...The president could have publicly condemned Khomeini for his interference. He could have solicited the support of our allies, and in conjunction with them he could have given material support to the Bakhtiar government.*[456]

Unfortunately, the Carter administration did none of the things General Huyser suggested they might have done to ameliorate the situation. In fact, on January 4 Sullivan met with the Shah. His instructions from Vance were to "listen and report, but not encourage any line of action."[457]

On January 7th a *New York Times* editorial labeled the Shah as, "The Friend That Failed," an interesting title given that reading the previous two years of the *Times* would have made Pahlavi seem more a burden to the U.S. than a close friend and ally. The editorial condemned the American penchant for sticking with its friends abroad as a "suicidal devotion" and that "such theories blind their devotees to all objective diplomatic reckonings."[458] The *New York Times'* strange reversal of standing up for human rights was considered noble, but at the same time the "real politick" of the Kissinger years was denounced. While devotion to principle was considered a weakness, the *New York Times* did not need to worry about such contradictions. In the end, "It was the Shah who failed in Iran, not the United States."[459]

One vastly important decision was reached by Carter on January 14, two days prior to the Shah's departure from Tehran. A meeting between Warren Zimmerman, the U.S. Embassy political advisor in Paris, and Ebrahim Yazdi, Khomeini's U.S. mouthpiece, was approved by the president. Meanwhile, Huyser was equally busy trying to persuade the military heads in Iran to open a line of communication with the Ayatollah. On that same evening Khomeini stunned many in the Carter administration by telling a CBS reporter that a large number of the Iranian armed forces were loyal to his cause, and he would be the "strongman" in Iran.[460]

After the Shah's departure from Tehran on January, 17, 1979, a *New York Times* editorial sighed theatrically, "The Shah Departs, Finally." The question was posed: "Is there something to regret in this turn of events?" The editorialist felt compelled to answer the question for the readers: "Chiefly, that the Shah dallied too long before going."[461]

Zimmerman and Yazdi reportedly held several secret meetings in Paris during which they discussed topics related to possible Iranian military interference with Khomeini's plan to return to Tehran. Yazdi outlined three basic questions to which the revolutionaries wanted an answer. They were:

:: Would Khomeini's return trigger a military reaction or create such an uproar among the Iranian people that the military was forced to respond to the chaos?

:: Would the upper echelon of the military insist on backing the Shah or would it acquiesce to Khomeini's leadership and transfer allegiance to the cleric?

:: Did Americans working in Iran have the right to destroy what was described as "sophisticated military equipment" before departing the country? It was Khomeini's contention that the equipment fell under the auspices of the Iranian military.

On a bitterly cold day, January 16, 1979, the Shah, who had ruled Iran for thirty-seven years, and his empress, Farah Pahlavi, boarded one of two planes destined for Egypt. Ironically, the two passenger jets were parked in front of the lavish and luxurious Imperial Pavilion where the Shah had often greeted kings and politicians who visited Tehran. The *Gulf News* reported his departure:

> Two officers of the Shah's royal guard fell to their knees and tried
> to kiss the monarch's feet at Tehran's airport, but he motioned for
> them to rise, court sources said. Two other officers, standing face
> to face, held aloft a copy of Holy Quran and the royal couple passed
> beneath the impromptu arch to board the "Shah's Falcon," a royal
> Boeing 727...

With tears in his eyes, Shah Mohammad Reza Pahlavi and Empress Farah Diba left Iran for Egypt and the United States, piloting his own jet on a journey many believe will end in permanent exile. His departure touched off jubilant celebrations throughout Tehran.

"The Shah is gone forever," people chanted as millions poured into the streets of Tehran, showering each other with sweets and rose water, cheering and shouting with joy at what they saw as victory in a year-long, bloody uprising to topple the 59-year-old Shah.[462]

During January 1979 meetings among the Carter White House operatives gained momentum, and it was reported that the Shah, while unenthusiastic that Bakhtiar would succeed, was ready to relinquish the reins of government to his hand-picked successor. As a result, administration insiders communicated to the Shah that he and his family were welcome to visit the United States home of Walter Annenberg in California or travel to Egypt at the invitation of Anwar Sadat. (Sadat had no regard for the fanatical Khomeini and felt he would only drastically harm Islam.) The Shah chose to spend a week in Cairo with Sadat and then travel on to Morocco for a two-week visit with King Hassan. It was in Marrakesh on February 11, 1979, that the Pahlavi family heard of the collapse of Bakhtiar's government. The next day, news of the slaughter of military officials reached the king.

Unfortunately, the Shah's stay in Morocco as a guest of King Hassan soon came to an end. Alexandre de Marenches contacted the Shah to inform him that King Hassan was in danger due to the presence of the Pahlavi family in Morocco. Khomeini's far-reaching hand was stirring the pot of unrest among students on the university campuses in that country, and the Shah was asked to leave.

The Shah requested that he be allowed to stay in Morocco, where he was able to maintain constant contact with his most loyal military contingent, the Royal Guard. He felt he could be called upon at any moment to return to Iran and resume the throne. King Hassan was forced to respond negatively to Pahlavi, and the Shah and his royal entourage departed Morocco. He was denied entry into France, which had clasped Khomeini to its bosom. Both Monaco and Switzerland, bastions of neutrality, also rejected a request to host the deposed monarch. Even the "Iron Lady" of Great Britain, Margaret Thatcher, declined to welcome the Shah and his family to England.

Two of Pahlavi's prominent acquaintances, Henry Kissinger and David Rockefeller, attempted to intervene on the Shah's behalf for asylum in Mexico. It seems that Khomeini's new government had withdrawn the royal family's passports. The Mexican bureaucrats were denying the Shah's entourage entrance into Mexico without some official documentation. Morocco had declined aid to the Pahlavi family because King Hassan did not want the Shah to be able to return to Morocco uninvited. Queen Farah was reduced to calling Prince Aga Khan, the UN High Commissioner for Refugees, and literally begging to be granted refugee status in order to secure proper passports for the king and his traveling companions.[463]

At that point the Shah informed the Carter White House that he was ready to take it up on the offer of asylum at the Annenberg estate. William J. Daugherty, one of the U.S. Embassy employees who was later held hostage by the Iranians, wrote of the rescinding of the invitation:

> At a meeting of the Special Coordinating Committee (SCC—the highest level policy and crisis management group in the Carter White House) on 23 February the decision was made to inform the Shah that, while the invitation was still officially open, there were now serious complications. Specifically, the short-lived take over of the American Embassy the previous St. Valentine's Day

*had some senior officials in Washington reconsidering the wisdom
of hosting the Shah. The Shah's entry into the United States was
potentially an inflammatory act and, with a deteriorating security
situation in Tehran, there was still a very real threat to American
interests and the remaining American officials and citizens. The
risk to American lives at that time was serious, apparent, and
exigent: U.S. intelligence personnel at one of the CIA's TACKSMAN
intelligence collection sites had been taken captive days before, a
nd American Ambassador William Sullivan was at that moment
in negotiations over their release (the TACKSMAN sites were a
cooperative effort with the Shah's regime for monitoring the
Soviet missile test ranges). Manifestly, the entry of the Shah would
no doubt unleash severe and potentially uncontrollable repercussions against these and other Americans in Iran.*[464]

In abandoning the Shah and Iran to the Grand Ayatollah
Ruhollah Khomeini, the Carter State Department had completely
overlooked Khomeini's tendency to refer to the United States as the
"Great Satan"—a superpower to be brought to its knees. Under
Khomeini's regime, blood would flow again through the streets of
Tehran and repression would reach new heights in the coming years
simply because multiplied tens of thousands of Iranians viewed the
Shah as a tool of the "Great Satan."

General Huyser had been of the opinion that "the greatest
potential for disaster would be the early return of Khomeini. While
a large segment of the armed forces would remain loyal to the Shah,
there were quite a number who were pro-Khomeini, and even a few
communists. The armed forces were convinced that the return of
Khomeini meant the absolute finish of the Shah."[465]

Huyser's account differs from that of Cyrus Vance. Vance
wrote that Huyser found the generals confused and discussing
the advantages of contacting Khomeini. According to Vance's
recollections, the generals felt that the "anti-communism of the

military and the religious leaders could give them common ground...[and that] Khomeini would surely prefer to have a cohesive, effective army...during the political transition to an Islamic republic."[466]

On February 6, 1979, General Huyser had shared with Ambassador Sullivan his fears of what a Khomeini government would mean for Iran. It was Huyser's considered estimation, "If Khomeini took control and formed an Islamic Republic, the country would drift from right to left...if he took over completely and practiced what he had been preaching, the country would disintegrate."[467]

Huyser's predictions, while true, didn't begin to paint the picture of the bloodshed that occurred in the ranks of the military in Iran. Stunned by the loss of the generals and hierarchy under the Shah, the rank and file of the Iranian security forces were cast adrift. The army was in total confusion. Khomeini was swift to deactivate the Shah's military and substitute his own, drawn from the revolutionaries that now surrounded him.

Khomeini instructed his followers in the ways of martyrdom as a means to disengage the Shah's troops:

> You must appeal to the soldiers' hearts even if they fire on you and kill you. Let them kill five thousand, ten thousand, twenty thousand— they are our brothers and we will welcome them. We will prove that blood is more powerful than the sword.[468]

General Alexander Haig, Supreme Allied Commander of NATO during the Carter administration, said of the ouster of the Shah:

> It didn't take long for the world to realize that the Shah was an enlightened liberal next to the bloody reactionary regime that followed, and which executed more people in three months than the Shah had done in thirty years.[469]

. . . .

CHAPTER 20

ENGULFED
IN DARKNESS

"A man will come out from Qom [Iranian holy city] and he will summon people to the right path. There will rally to him people resembling pieces of iron, not to be shaken by violent winds, unsparing and relying on God."[470]

(AN ANCIENT ISLAMIC PROPHECY)

Mohammad Reza Shah Pahlavi's jet was hardly airborne on January 16, 1979, before Iranian newspapers screamed, *"Shah Raft!"* or "The Shah is Gone." He had ruled over Iran from the age of twenty-one; now, he was leaving in ignominious defeat, not knowing he would never return. Former Iranian Ambassador Dr. Ahmed Tehrani summed up the Shah's feelings, perhaps better than anyone, when he said, "The Shah never, ever believed the United States would let him down. He believed Russia would do it, he believed the British would do it, but not the United States or France."[471]

In an interview with Houchang Nahavandi during a trip to Poland and Czechoslovakia in early 1978, the Shah was certain he was "irremovable." When asked what would happen to him should the U.S. change its policy and forsake the monarch, Pahlavi answered, "The Americans will never abandon me."[472] That assumption would prove to be false, as Jimmy Carter was about to demonstrate.

Mohammad Heikal wrote of the Shah's stay at Aswan in Egypt:

> The Shah comported himself as though he were still a head of state. He took advantage of a summit meeting between President Sadat and former President Ford to give voice to his grievances against the Americans. "Carter," he said, "had decided it [the Shah's ouster]. While he declared in public that he would support you to the end, at the same time, he was negotiating with the opposition behind your back." [The Shah] added that it was curious that the King of Morocco...offered to send troops to help him; the Americans, who were supposed to be allies, did not do so.[473]

Perhaps it was as Ardeshir Zahedi suggested: The Shah didn't think the radical cleric Khomeini could command change in Iran. He was certainly not the most influential ayatollah at the time; that honor belonged to the leader of the Shiite world, Ayatollah Shairatmadari. Though not altogether pleased with the Shah, Shariatmadari was not clamoring for a regime change. Neither he nor the leading cleric in Najaf, Ayatollah Kho'ei, were pushing for the Shah's ouster.[474]

This was not the case with the ultra-radical Khomeini. A declassified document from the secretary of state to the U.S. Embassy in Iran detailed the situation:

> There are...all strains of religious leadership...Those religious elements presently dominating the Iranian scene both organizationally and ideologically are committed to violence and obstruction as tools for attaining power. Ayatollah Khomeini has specifically

*called for the Shah's violent removal, and some of his followers in
Isfahan and Shiraz have openly called for the death of the Shah...
Moderates such as Ayatollah Shariatmadari do not at this time feel
capable of opposing Khomeini openly, though they reportedly still
work for moderation within the religious movement...Whatever
the Shah wishes to do next, he must meet head-on the violent
challenges to both his government and Iran's social fabric...Many
Iranians believe the Shah is not acting forcefully enough...Some
believe the Americans forced him to be restrained.*[475]

Khomeini, as the world would soon see, boasted an underground network of fanatical mullahs, i.e., Ayatollah Mahmoud
Taleghani and Mohammad Behesti, who favored regime change.
Khomeini's calls for an end to the Shah's reign were taken up by
bands of radical hooligans who were only too happy to carry out the
Ayatollah's wishes. Did Khomeini and his followers feel they had the
backing of the Carter administration in their determination to
destroy the monarchy?

I asked Lt. General Shapur Azarbarzin, former vice-chief of the
Iranian air force during the early days of the revolution, what Jimmy
Carter could have done to prevent a revolution in Iran. He replied:

*Carter could have called the Shah personally and told him it was
okay to use strength to take control of the situation. Then, once
order was restored, the Shah could have addressed the people
from a position of strength. [I would have said] don't go through
Sullivan, and Vance, and Huyser, and Brzezinski; this all just
created confusion and signaled weakness.*[476]

Shapour Bakhtiar, who was at the helm of the provisional
government left by the Shah, pled with Ayatollah Ruhollah
Khomeini to delay his arrival in Tehran for several months so that
civil order might be restored. The determined Ayatollah adamantly
refused. Gary Sick's description of the Ayatollah fit him perfectly:

*Khomeini was the arch-type of the medieval prophet emerging
from the desert with a fiery vision...His God was a harsh and
vengeful deity...demanding an eye and tooth of retribution...
Khomeini's philosophy had great tolerance for pain, human
suffering, and political chaos, but no tolerance for opposition.
His opponents were satanic, and the remedy was to "cut off
their arms."*[477]

Given its association with Israel, it would not have been beyond
the realm of possibility for Iran to seek the help of the Mossad to
stop Khomeini. However, Uri Lubrani, who was stationed in Iran in
the 1970s, has suggested that Israel might have considered backing
a military takeover in Iran, but the U.S. was slow to support such a
move. Perhaps, like the United States, Israel had chosen to take
a "wait and see" attitude regarding the situation in Tehran.

Meanwhile, both Ambassador William Sullivan and General
Dutch Huyser requested that the Carter administration reassess its
Iran policy. Sullivan also warned Carter that Khomeini's arrival in
Tehran would certainly mark the end of Bakhtiar and crush the
military. The ambassador was convinced the Iranian military was
"'a paper tiger' [and] the United States had been dealing with
'evaporating institutions,'"[478] prior to Khomeini's arrival in Tehran.
The men could see the strong possibility of a clash between the
military and the clerics. Huyser felt it incumbent to alert the
generals that the U.S. would not back a military junta should
Bakhtiar fail. Carter refused to allow Huyser and Sullivan to divulge
that information.

With the Shah's departure Khomeini's Paris entourage made
hurried preparations to get the Imam back to Tehran. Having
decided against the use of an Iranian airliner for fear of being
attacked by the Shah's air force, a jumbo jet was chartered from Air

France for a mere pittance of $3 million dollars plus an undisclosed sum to cover the insurance premium for the aircraft. The crew that manned the jumbo jet was comprised totally of volunteers.[479]

In his autobiography, *Keeping Faith*, Jimmy Carter purports that on January 14, 1979, he contacted the French president to ask that he not allow Khomeini's departure to Tehran:

> *I called Giscard d'Estaing quite early in the morning, asking him to contact Khomeini and to do everything he could to delay Khomeini's departure from France. Giscard was willing to cooperate. Said...he had no way to prevent Khomeini's leaving France, but could delay it somewhat. His government's only policy was to support the Bakhtiar government. Valery said he has no relationship with the Iranian military, and that he believes a visit by the Shah to the United States would be a mistake. It would be much better if he would go to a neutral country for a while before winding up here in our country. Later in the day, he called back. Giscard reported that Khomeini has no plans to leave Paris for the moment. He didn't know what "for the moment" means, but that Khomeini is afraid he might lose his life if he goes to Iran. Khomeini's final aim is to overthrow the Bakhtiar government.[480]*

One of Khomeini's closest advisors, and coincidentally a naturalized U.S. citizen, Ebrahim Yazdi, was aboard the jet that carried the triumphant Khomeini back to Iran. According to Yazdi:

> *The civil airline in Iran arranged independently a flight from Tehran to Paris to bring Khomeini back. They called it the Revolutionary Flight. But we didn't trust them, because we knew that there was a possibility that the army might attack, or the army might force the aeroplane to land in some remote area. So, we didn't accept that. Instead, we chartered an Air France plane. In addition to that, we took with us more than a hundred and twenty journalists—reporters from all over the world. I have to*

confess that we took them as a human shield, so to speak. We knew
that nobody would dare to shoot at such a plane, with so many
reporters from so many nationalities.[481]

Fear of an attack on the Air France jet prompted Khomeini to leave behind his wife, daughter, and grandchildren, as well as the wives and children of his inner circle. Before departing Paris the Ayatollah thanked the French government for allowing him to remain in France. Perhaps subtly, he was thanking the French for allowing him to wage an unhindered war against the Shah of Iran and to topple his government. Were the truth known, it is more likely that the government of France was happy to see the backside of his turban.

On the plane with Khomeini was a young ABC reporter, Peter Jennings. During the flight Jennings is said to have asked the Imam, "What do you feel [about returning to Iran]?" Khomeini replied, "Nothing." That was a strange answer from a man whose life had been consumed in recent years with the overthrow of the Shah and a triumphant return to Iran.

Bakhtiar, in an attempt to discredit Khomeini and persuade the air force cadets to support his government, sent a copy of the tape of the Ayatollah's response to the interview question. Unfortunately for the future of Bakhtiar and Iran, his plan backfired. The cadets remained faithful to Khomeini.

The Air France jet that bore the Grand Ayatollah Ruhollah Khomeini touched down in Tehran at precisely 9:33 AM on February 1, 1979, following a brief discussion on whether or not the airport should be reopened. It had been closed for five days due to demonstrations and riots. Lt. General Azarbarzin received a phone call from the air force chief instructing him to open the facility. Azarbarzin asked on whose authority he was to proceed, and he was told it was at the direction of Prime Minister Bakhtiar. When the lieutenant general questioned the order, Bakhtiar personally ordered him to reopen the airport.[482]

The Imam, who had slept for much of the five-and-a-half-hour flight, was ending an exile that had lasted more than fourteen years. There exists a photograph of Khomeini while on that historic Air France flight. While traveling through the night, Khomeini sat off by himself in a comfortable, first-class seat. The surviving photograph shows the Imam in a moment of self-satisfied meditation. A deep inner joy appears to emanate from his face. At this moment, Ayatollah Khomeini was savoring the approaching moment when his life-long aspirations were finally to be realized.

In the photograph his eyes have a distant look, as if he is peering into the past or maybe into the future. He is 78-years-old. He appears venerable, but by no means vulnerable. His trademark black turban sits atop his head, his visage is distinguished by a flowing white beard, and his dark eyes highlighted by thick eyebrows are fierce and piercing. The Imam's lips are pursed in a private smile, and his hands lie quietly in his lap, gracing the folds of his long robe. Perhaps he realized that, at last, his deal with the devil was about to produce his date with destiny.

The photographer captured a moment of calm before the storm of frenzied public adulation broke upon him. Khomeini was now ready to receive his triumphant welcome and lead an Islamic revolution that would shake the entire world. He stepped off the plane surrounded by his entourage and knelt to kiss the soil of Iran. Some say that his welcoming committee boasted several American officials.

There is a certain irony in the fact that Khomeini, despiser of all things American, the man who had referred to Jimmy Carter as "the vilest man on earth,"[483] was hustled into a Chevrolet Blazer for the trip to his first destination—the Behesht-e-Zahra Cemetery, the burial place of ten to twelve thousand who died during the revolution. According to a BBC report,[484] some five million Iranians lined the streets from the airport to the cemetery. Not even fifty thousand Iranian police could control the massive crowd. They were so overjoyed at the sight of their returning Imam that, again, Khomeini had to be rescued by an American-made air force helicopter in order to complete his pilgrimage to the cemetery. Occupying the helicopter with Khomeini was the Shah's Commander-in-Chief of the Air Force General Amir Hussein Rabii.

In the days that followed Khomeini's progress was hampered by the disarray in the Iranian military following the Shah's departure. General David Ivry explained the confusion in the ranks:

> Some of them were not secure and they sent their families abroad...
> with money...deep inside they were afraid...[After Khomeini's
> arrival.] They were called to a meeting and told, "You are fine.
> Stay in your positions." Everyone went home calmly, and then they
> were caught in their homes.[485]

The first act of the Ayatollah was to declare in no uncertain terms that the caretaker government of Bakhtiar was illegal. "If they continue," said Khomeini, "we will arrest them. I will shut their mouths. And I will appoint a government with the support of the Iranian people."[486]

Ambassador William Sullivan, on the front line in Tehran, could see signs of increasing instability. He felt the Carter administration was not heeding his information until long after it was presented. Sullivan was not surprised, therefore, when Khomeini seized control of the government on February 11, 1979. When Sullivan received a call from the White House on February 12, giving him the go-ahead to encourage the Iranian military to keep the revolution in check with the use of deadly force, if necessary, it is said, "Sullivan declined, using colorful language."[487]

Ayatollah Khomeini had returned to bring his radical Islamic rebellion to Iran. He believed this was the first step of his revolution sweeping across the world. Khomeini's one, fervent desire was to see the West, led by the United States, submit to the grip of radical Islam. Soon, he felt the "illegitimate" state of Israel would be decimated. He was certain all other religions would yield to his version of Islam. Then a Muslim theocracy would be established in every corner of the world. This was the Grand Ayatollah Khomeini's vision of destiny. He informed the Iranian people, "This is not the final victory, but only a prelude to victory." He called upon the army to destroy its new, sophisticated American weapons, and for the people to strike and demonstrate against the Bakhtiar regime. As to Carter's suggestion that he cooperate with Bakhtiar, he simply declared that this had nothing to do with Carter."[488]

The day following Khomeini's arrival in Tehran, the Israeli Embassy was ransacked and set afire. Several dozen Palestinians were among the rioters, who breached the walls of the building, tore the Israeli flag from its mooring on the top floor, and burned it. Cries of "Death to Israel! Long live Arafat! Israel get out!" could be heard from the mob. The Palestinian standard was then raised from the roof of the mission.[489] Israel's friends in the Shah's government turned a blind eye. General Yitzak Segev, military attaché in Iran, called on a friend in the Iranian air force to afford them a military cargo plane to fly to safety. The contact, General Rabii, responded:

The Revolutionary Guards control the airport and I cannot help you. But if you find a plane, please evacuate me as well.[490]

What influence Rabii may have had with Khomeini was short-lived. He was tried for "corruption on earth; war on God and the people of God; actions designed to weaken the country's independence and security; shaking the foundations of the country's system of government; defiling all that is sacred, whether religious or national, to the Muslim people of Iran and the world." Rabii was executed by firing squad on April 8, 1979. During the first year under Khomeini's rule, the Iranian armed forces saw their ranks dwindle by one hundred thousand troops. Even as Iran's military might faded, Saddam Hussein was building his Iraqi army and was stockpiling military supplies at an alarming rate.

It was left up to Israeli Mossad agents in Tehran to try to protect those Israeli attachés that remained in the city. Eliezer Tsafrir, a Mossad agent stationed in Iran recalled: "Israel was now the infidel enemy ("the Little Satan") and [I] had to evacuate thirteen hundred Israeli engineers, agronomists, and businessmen from Iran before they fell into the hands of the mullahs...[The Iranians] intended to shoot first and ask questions later."[491]

Samuel Segev wrote of the harrowing escape from Iran of the thirty-three last remaining Israelis, including General Yitzhak Segev, Ambassador Harmelin, former Knesset member Mordechai Ben-Porat, and El Al employees:

> *The Israelis left the Hilton Hotel for the airport in a bus plastered with pictures of Khomeini. Two sixteen-year-olds, armed with Kalashnikov rifles and trained in Palestinian camps in Syria, served as bodyguards. Other armed youngsters...members of "the Imam Khomeini's Guards," subjected the Israeli passports to minute examination. They arrested the El Al and Kour Corporation representatives and one Israeli security man, charging that they were ...Iranian Jews who were forbidden to leave the country. Harmelin...would not leave Tehran without the three men. After*

five hours...and at the personal intervention of...a leading
member of the religious establishment, the three prisoners were
freed and allowed to leave Iran. The Israelis took off on a Pan Am
Flight to Frankfurt, arriving in Israel in a special El Al plane...
bringing an end to twenty-five years of Israeli cooperation with
the [Shah].[492]

CHAPTER 21

. . . .

THE EVOLUTION
OF REVOLUTION

*"We do not worship Iran, we worship Allah. For patriotism
is another name for paganism. I say let this land [Iran] burn.
I say let this land go up in smoke, provided Islam emerges
triumphant in the rest of the world."*

(AYATOLLAH RUHOLLAH KHOMEINI)

Soon after his arrival in Tehran Khomeini, contrary to his in-exile
rhetoric about retiring to Qom, commandeered the Refah girls'
school as his nerve center and appointed Mehdi Bazargan to
head a new "Provisional Government." Bazargan, who had been
incarcerated several times by the Shah, had met in late 1978 with a
contingent from the U.S. Human Rights Committee. The Iranian
proffered five points that both he and the Ayatollah felt essential to
the future of Iran:

:: The Shah must leave the country.

:: The Shah must be replaced by a Regency Council.

:: A liberal government acceptable to all must be established.

:: Iran's current parliament must be disbanded.

:: Iran must be allowed to have national elections.

The U.S. committee agreed to Bazargan's stipulations but balked when a mention was made of removing all references to the Shah from the country's constitution. In a later meeting the group also insisted upon the restoration of law and order within Iran. What no one was willing to admit was that only Khomeini could stop the run-away train of Islamic revolutionary fervor that gripped the country. In the end, the Ayatollah flatly rejected the proposals by the U.S., calling them a "joke, a compromise destined to abort the revolution."[493]

What would later come to light was the fact that Bazargan and members of his government, including Ebrahim Yazdi and Amir Entezam, had met secretly on two occasions with American officials Robert Clayton Ames and George Cave (CIA), Bruce Laingen (Chargé d'Affaires), and Ron Smith (an energy specialist). Minutes of meetings taken from the American Embassy would be used to damage the reputation of Bazargan, Yazdi, and Amir Entezam, and would ultimately end in their being targeted by Khomeini's extremists.

Carter was so eager to establish relations with Khomeini's hand-picked prime minister that he gushed:

> *He and his predominantly Western-educated cabinet members cooperated with us. They protected our Embassy, provided safe travel for General Philip C. Gast, who had replaced Huyser, and sent us a series of friendly messages. Bazargan announced publicly his eagerness to have good relations with the U.S. and said that Iran would soon resume normal oil shipments to all its customers.*[494]

Clark Clifford, former Secretary of State under Lyndon Johnson, had somehow managed to establish communications with Khomeini insiders and confirmed that initially Khomeini planned to leave the determination of Iran's future up to the people. Bazargan's appointment was a shrewd political move by Khomeini, as it gave a false sense of security to the moderates in Iran whose vision of an "Islamic republic" may not quite have meshed with that of the Imam. Lt. General Shapur Azarbarzin, former vice-chief of the Iranian air force during the early days of the revolution, related to me that the United States was committed to supporting Bazargan rather than the Shah's choice for prime minister, Shapour Bakhtiar.[495]

The moderate Bazargan's government would be used to quietly pacify the military and create a rapport with Khomeini. Ambassador Sullivan was dispatched to assure Bazargan that the Carter administration looked with favor on Khomeini's moves in Iran and would continue to furnish arms. Meanwhile, defections from the military were occurring at an alarming rate, and ultimately Chief of Staff General Gharabaghi declared that the armed forces had become a neutral factor. Bazargan's Provisional Government (PG) was ecstatic with the general's announcement.

As might have been expected, one of Bazargan's early moves as the new leader was to sever all ties with Israel, although the Israeli government attempted to establish a working relationship with Khomeini's regime. Though both countries espouse different ideologies and outlooks, it was a move designed to sooth the leftist revolutionaries, who felt Israel was a protégé of "The Great Satan," and the mullahs, who felt that Israel's very existence was offensive to Islam.

Khomeini was shrewd enough to couch his aversion to Israel in religious terms. He simply declared Israel a "cancer" that had to be removed, a usurper in the Middle East that despised the Koran and would destroy the Muslim holy book.[496] The fanatical new regime occupying Tehran saw Israel as "an illegitimate state and a usurper of Muslim land,"[497] and was "by its very nature against Islam and the Koran."[498] Khomeini's ultra-fanatical mullahs and clerics lectured that it was the responsibility of every Muslim to challenge Israel. By August of 1980 Iran's foreign ministry office demanded an end to the export of oil to nations that supported the Jewish state.

The truth is, both Israel and Iran are countries with vastly differing ideologies that will never mesh. Only one vision and one value system will survive. For Jews and Christians, there is only one answer: the long-awaited coming of the Messianic Age. For Muslims too there is only one solution to this age-old problem: a worldwide caliphate with all inhabitants bowing a knee to Allah. Because these Islamic extremists believe this caliph will return due to a cataclysmic war, it is critical, therefore, for Israel to call attention to the probability that as soon as Iran's mad mullahs have full access to nuclear weapons, not only Israel but the world as a whole will face an imminent attack.

In spite of the Ayatollah's rabid pronouncements against Israel, just months later the Israelis returned a number of tanks the Shah had sent to be repaired. Soon thereafter Ahmed Kashani visited Israel. Kashani, whose father, the Grand Ayatollah Abol Qassem Kashani, had a vital part to play in the nationalization of the Iranian oil industry in 1951, flew to Tel Aviv to discuss arms purchases and military teamwork between Iran and Israel. It seems that clandestine meetings between Israel and her Arab neighbors in the Middle East were acceptable, as long as it was kept under the radar. At one point Khomeini accepted a large shipment of arms from Israel. (Being supposedly unaware of the origin of the weapons, the Ayatollah could adopt a "laissez-faire" attitude.)

Menachem Begin's decision to accommodate the Iranians was in direct opposition to U.S. wishes to segregate Iran during the hostage crisis. Carter retaliated by withholding needed spare parts shipments to Israel.[499] (After Ronald Reagan was elected to the White House, Israel and Iran continued to communicate regarding Iraq's nuclear threat. Both countries felt that each would be targeted if Saddam Hussein were to develop a nuclear warhead. In *October Surprise* Gary Sick wrote of meetings between officials of the two countries prior to Israel's attack on Iraq's *Osirak* reactor. According to Sick, "The officials reportedly agreed that in the event of an emergency, Israeli aircraft would be permitted to land at the Iranian airfield in Tabriz."[500]) General David Ivry recalled in a personal interview that the Iranians had attacked *Osirak* twice with Phantom jets during the Iran-Iraq War. It accomplished little other than to encourage the Iraqis to reinforce the thirty- to forty-meter thick walls around the facility.[501]

Various news reports stated that an Argentine "cargo plane crashed on the Soviet-Turkish border on July 18, 1981, revealing an arms deal between Israel and Iran—in direct defiance of the U.S. embargo on arms supplies to Khomeini's regime. The cargo was 360 tons of American-made tank spares and ammunition."[502] Sick also suggested that Israel sent "spares for F-4 aircraft, M-48 tanks, and M-113 armored personnel carriers, a total of $246 million" to Iran.[503] It is thought that Israel sent over $500 million in arms to Iran following the freeing of the U.S. hostages taken captive at the

U.S. Embassy in Tehran.[504] It seems that Khomeini had few, if any, qualms about doing business with his arch foe, "The Little Satan."

Khomeini felt it was his divine duty to advance the cause of Islam. "Islam," he said, "is not peculiar to a country...Islam has come for humanity."[505] For Khomeini, Iran was a launching pad for an Islamic revolution that would engulf the entire world. His calling was to secure Iran for Islam and then spread the revolution. His ideology was one of world dominance, and his fanaticism strained ties with his Arab neighbors.

Even as Khomeini reassured the Shah's military leaders that they had nothing to fear from his newly-established regime, the slaughter began. General Dutch Huyser had already departed Iran at this point, but he would tell me later that he was grief-stricken because he felt he had betrayed the Iranian generals. According to one observer:

> Of the eighty top generals, more than seventy were tortured and executed, along with hundreds of lower-ranking officers. By one estimate almost 75 percent of the Shah's senior officers were killed by the end of summer. The Bakhtiar government protested these often-grisly executions...The executions, coupled with the appointment of mullahs as military prosecutors, totally demoralized the military and sent a signal that the real power lay with Khomeini and his Revolutionary Guards. The PG was equally powerless to stop the purge and arrest of some 15,000 to 30,000 civilian members of the Shah's regime.[506]

General Yitzhak Segev sadly recalled the mass executions of army generals following Khomeini's arrival in Tehran:

> Some succeeded in running away and reaching America...most of them were executed...The executions were merciless. They were brutal, not only for revenge purposes, but because...they were

*preventing the option of revolution against themselves [Khomeini's
regime.] The first four were executed while I was still there...[the
executions] were broadcast live on television. Then, one at a time
they killed hundreds of generals...each general had a carpet placed
beneath him...before he was shot in the head...They executed the
generals because they were connected to the old regime, and because
they were a threat to the new regime...There was total purification.*[507]

One of those executed by Khomeini's kangaroo court was
former Prime Minister Amir-Abbas Hoveyda. Under Hoveyda's
leadership in the mid-1960s Iran had filled the vacuum left by
departing British troops from Persian Gulf bases by establishing
two armored divisions that were outfitted with U.S.-made Patton
M-60 tanks. He was also responsible for major expansions of the
Iranian air force and navy. Hoveyda, who had been placed under
house arrest by Pahlavi, was a sitting target for Khomeini's
revolutionary forces. Having been the Shah's prime minister for
thirteen years, Hoveyda was a senior official in the monarch's
government and, therefore, a prized catch. He was dragged out
and tried in short order.

In his book detailing his tenure as president of France, Giscard
d'Estaing wrote of his attempt to persuade Khomeini not to execute
Hoveyda:

*I decided to intervene personally with the Ayatollah Khomeini...
I asked someone to bring him a message. Some Iranian sources
told me that after he received my letter...Khomeini wrote a letter
to the prime minister. In his note he says: "His Excellency the
President V. Giscard d'Estaing...has asked me to prevent the
execution of Mr. Hoveyda. To the request of the French president,
I would ask you to delay any action in this way." Unfortunately,
the revolutionary court prepared its work very quickly, and Mr.
Hoveyda was executed three days later, on April 7,...after he was
interviewed by a journalist from the French television...Two days*

later the Tehran revolutionary court met during the night and allowed the execution of eleven persons from the old regime only half an hour after the verdict.[508]

Senators Jacob Javits and Henry Jackson, staunch supporters of Pahlavi, endorsed a resolution criticizing Khomeini's new government for its violent executions of those associated with the Shah's rule. James Bill wrote:

> *The resolution was triggered by the execution of a Jewish businessman named Habib Elghanian...Javits and others immediately moved to condemn Iran in the strongest possible terms...Elghanian had been one of twenty-nine executed May 7 to May 11, 1979,... all had been targeted because of their close associations with the Shah's regime. Elghanian, who for years had been identified in U.S. Embassy reports as one of the three wealthiest individuals in Iran, was charged with corruption, capitalist exploitation, and treason for close political and economic associations with Israel. The Javits resolution...resolved that the Senate "expresses its abhorrence of summary executions without due process."...Senator Robert C. Byrd was especially supportive of the resolution, which he termed "very timely. For as we speak, the killing continues in Iran."...Senator Laughton Chiles added that "too many of us have stood by too long and have been silent too long.."[Senator Abraham] Ribicoff added that "the Shah was a proven and true friend of the United States. The entire world should condemn the excesses now taking place in Iran."*[509]

One can only wonder why a nation of radical Islamists with no thought of "human rights" was preferable to the regime of the insecure and ailing Shah. Although the leaders of the Islamic revolution boasted that between 60,000 and 100,000 had perished as martyrs for their cause, the more realistic number of deaths in Iran, as reported by Said Arjomand in *The Turban for the Crown:*

The Islamic Revolution in Iran, was "approximately three thousand in the whole of Iran." Arjomand calculated the number from September 1978 until the fall of the monarchy in February 1979.[510]

Shortly after assuming the role of leader in Iran, Khomeini approved the erection of a training center on the site of what was to have been Empress Farah University for Girls. Manzarieh Park was to become the training ground for Iran's elite Revolutionary Guards and for Shiite Muslim fundamentalist terrorists. Although Khomeini later banned the training of Yasser Arafat's terrorists in Iranian facilities, he apparently had no such qualms about using North Koreans and Syrians as trainers. The camp was also the site where the fifteen- to eighteen-year-olds that would become the first line of attack against Saddam Hussein's troops were instructed. Especially singled out were those students who had flooded back into Iran from the U.S. to serve as volunteers under the revered Ayatollah Khomeini. They were often required to recount the decadence found in America, the decadence that would be its downfall by the sword of Islam.

The Ayatollah espoused and quoted the tenet of Islam that declared, "Islam says: Whatever good there is exists thanks to the sword and in the shadow of the sword! People cannot be made obedient except with the sword! The sword is the key to Paradise, which can be opened only for the Holy Warriors! There are hundreds of other [Qur'anic] psalms and Hadiths [sayings of the Prophet] urging Muslims to value war and to fight. Does all this mean that Islam is a religion that prevents men from waging war? I spit upon those foolish souls who make such a claim."[511] In Khomeini's Iran, training "with the sword" began at an early age.

On February 18, 1979, soon after Khomeini's arrival in Tehran, Arafat and a delegation of PLO bigwigs, sixty strong, jumped on the revolutionary bandwagon. Unannounced and uninvited, Arafat and his rag-tag band flew into the not-yet-reopened Tehran airport. Upon entering Iranian airspace, Arafat's plane was met by a team of Phantom jet fighters. Arafat, whose experience with Phantoms had been limited to Israeli incursions over Palestinian territory, responded, "This is the first time Phantoms have been on my side."[512]

The group was met at the airport, welcomed to the city, and afforded posh housing commensurate with their long-standing opposition against the monarchy. Arafat went so far as to offer to send a contingent of PLO commandos to track down and eliminate the Shah.[513] Within days, Arafat had been presented the keys to the Israeli compound in Tehran, and the street on which the mission was located had been renamed Palestine Street. Arafat, who claimed responsibility for training and equipping thousands of Iranians, equated flying into Tehran with marching triumphantly through the gates into Jerusalem. He was lauded by Khomeini:

> The Iranian Revolution will repay the Palestinians for the help they gave us in overthrowing the Shah, and Iranian volunteers will take part in the struggle to end the Zionist conquest and to liberate Jerusalem.[514]

The PLO was allowed to establish bureaus in Iranian cities, but relations between Arafat and Khomeini were not cordial. Although Khomeini had rewarded the PLO with the Israeli Embassy in Tehran, by 1980 the Ayatollah was said to both dislike and distrust the PLO chairman based on Arafat's tendencies toward worldly pursuits. Arafat's "religious" tendencies would not surface until the end of the Islamic revolution. Khomeini felt that the PLO representatives in Iran were trying to incite an uprising between factions.

By 1985 Khomeini had overseen the establishment of fifteen terrorist training facilities in the country, including commandeering the ritzy resort hotel near Qom. The Afghans, Arabs, Southeast Asians, Irish, Americans, and Lebanese, as well as women terrorists trained in these facilities were slated to become "the spearhead of the Islamic conquest of the world."[515]

While Khomeini was wary of Arafat, he declared his support for the Palestinian cause by naming August 17 Qods (Jerusalem) Day and calling on Muslims around the globe to march in support of their Palestinian brothers.[516] Arafat's favored-terrorist status was jeopardized when he began to align himself with the *Mujahedin*. Khomeini saw that as a personal affront and refused to meet with Arafat during the Iran/Iraq War. The PLO terrorist departed Tehran with empty hands. Khomeini was quick to erase all references to the PLO from the Iranian media outlets.

Meanwhile, back in Washington and just after Khomeini's return to Iran President Carter's straddle-the-fence diplomacy had permeated the administration. Far from having studied the writings of Khomeini for any indication of his political leanings, the president's advisors were now playing catch-up and were trying to deduce what the events in Iran might mean for the region. Secretary of State Cyrus Vance urged Carter to reach out to the Ayatollah. This suggestion was supported by Ambassador William Sullivan and by Vice President Walter Mondale.

Egyptian journalist Mohamed Heikal wrote of Vance's attempts to contact Khomeini's Revolutionary Government to reassure them of four critical directives:

The Shah's reign was at an end.

The U.S. and Iran must remain allied against the Soviets.

The Iranian Revolution and Khomeini's seizure of power were recognized by the American people.

The U.S. wished to open a door of dialogue with Iran.

Upon hearing Vance's proposal, Khomeini, with Hafiz's communiqués regarding the Shah's arrival in the U.S. in hand, asked: "You mean he didn't talk about the Shah's arrival in the United States?"[517]

Vance would later write that the Carter administration was erroneously charged with the downfall of the Shah because of the president's human rights agenda.[518]

Dr. Majidi talked to me of his disappointment in the Carter administration's stance in Iran:

> *Even if someone would have told me that Americans are willing to help Khomeini and his group, I would have said, "Certainly, it's impossible." American long-term and short-term interests both require that America stand behind the Shah, behind Iran...That was my idea, my philosophy, and my thinking; and I think was the same as the Shah's...You never forget the [New Year's] speech of Carter...he talked of stability in the area of turmoil of the region. I think he was believing that; but he didn't have the guts to implement it and present it...It's only how brave and how courageous to make the hard decision. Carter to my mind was not that person, and he didn't have the confidence in what he's doing and what he must do.*[519]

Italian journalist Oriana Fallaci interviewed Khomeini shortly after the end of the Islamic revolution in Iran. It was she who wrote: "[The] art of invading and conquering and subjugating [is] the only art at which the sons of Allah have always excelled... Islamism is the new Nazi-Fascism. With Nazi-Fascism, *no compromise* is possible. No hypocritical tolerance. And those who do not understand this simple reality are feeding the suicide of the West."[520] Excerpts from her interview with Khomeini ran in the *New York Times* in October 1979. Fallaci, who came to believe "the Western world is in danger of being engulfed by radical Islam," wrote of her encounter with the Imam:

It did not take long to realize that in spite of his quiet appearance he represented the Robespierre or the Lenin of something which would go very far and would poison the world. People loved him too much. They saw in him another Prophet. Worse: a God...Do believe me: everything started with Khomeini. Without Khomeini, we would not be where we are. What a pity that when pregnant with him, his mother did not choose to have an abortion.[521]

CHAPTER   2 2

. . . .

ABANDONED
BY AN ADMINISTRATION

*"There seemed to have been at least four different U.S. centers
of decision-making during Iran's revolutionary movement:
the White House, the State Department, the National Security
Council, and the U.S. Embassy in Tehran...All four centers made
flawed judgments about the Shah's regime and its opponents."*
(MOHSEN MILANI)[522]

The toppling of the Shah's monarchy would prove to be a
tactical catastrophe for the United States. Maybe the calamity
could not have been prevented under any circumstances; perhaps the
rise of Islamic fanaticism was preordained. In the final analysis,
however, it is just possible that the U.S. could have done more to
maintain stability in the region.

The failure of the U.S. to support the Shah's faltering
monarchy was of great concern to other allies in the region. Surely
the Saudis, responsible for an infusion of billions of dollars
annually into the American treasury market, must have questioned
how a staunch American ally like the Shah could have been allowed

to fall. The House of Saud must have wondered if its kingdom would be the next domino in the Middle East to topple. Added to those questions was one of much larger import: What would U.S. leaders do to prevent a recurrence of the ouster of the Shah from happening in the kingdom? The concern stemmed from the fact that the Saudis, with the fall of Pahlavi, would take on the role of protectors of the shipping lanes in the Persian Gulf region.

Several countries were named by the U.S. Foreign Relations Committee as possible deterrents to attacks in the Persian Gulf; among them were Israel, Oman, Egypt, Kenya, and Somalia. Egypt was dismissed because of its weakness militarily and its instability. While Israel with its stable government and strong military would have been an excellent choice, Israel as a protector was dismissed out-of-hand because of the animosity of the Arabs toward the Jewish nation. The Carter administration felt it would be a direct affront to the Arabs and would potentially cause those nations to acquiesce to Soviet aggression in order to protect themselves from what they saw as an Israeli threat.

Is it more likely that the members of the inner circle in Washington each had his own agenda and not the needs of U.S. allies in the Middle East in mind? There were those who wished to promote democracy in the region, while others were persuaded only a military coup was the answer to restoring stability.

The State Department was focused almost solely on the extraction of U.S. citizens from Iran. Some felt only a constitutional monarchy with a figurehead king akin to those of Sweden and Great Britain would resolve the disastrous situation. The priorities were as many and varied as the departments involved in the crisis. Of course, the administration's priorities had changed over the months. In November 1978 Carter declared his undying support of the Shah and his regime. By January 1980 the president was seeking advice on whether or not to approach the extremist Ayatollah Khomeini.

Zbigniew Brzezinski, one of the more hawkish of Carter's appointees, clearly favored top Iranian generals staging a military coup following the Shah's departure. However, with the lower ranks of the military in open rebellion and Iran poised to fall prey to fanatical Islam, what was Brzezinski to do? Should he woo Bakhtiar? The generals? Bazargan? Amir Taheri writes that Zbig ultimately reached a decision: "Just weeks after the mullahs' regime was formed, Brzezinski traveled to Morocco to meet with Bazargan… At the meeting, Brzezinski invited the new Iranian regime to enter into a strategic partnership with the United States."[523]

Brzezinski, most vocal in urging the president to withdraw support of the Shah, suggested a "wait-and-see" attitude toward Khomeini. It was all part of Brzezinski's so-called "Green Belt" strategy. This concept would see the establishment of a series of Islamic regimes designed to insure the destruction of the Soviet Union—a Godzilla versus King Kong scenario, with the most vicious monster surviving the clash. Brzezinski's vision and Russia's nightmare was played out in Iran with the brutal regime of Khomeini and in Afghanistan with the rise of the cruel and repressive Taliban.

In an attempt to assuage Khomeini and invoke Brzezinski's Green Belt philosophy, a long-forgotten memo from Dwight Eisenhower was produced. His communication was a reaffirmation of Washington's commitment to defend Iran against Soviet aggression. It was all that was needed to lift a ban on arms sales to Iran and supply the new revolutionary government with arms and materials. Going one step further, Carter declined to issue a visa to the deposed Shah that would have allowed him entry into the U.S. to obtain much-needed medical treatment.

Meanwhile Henry Precht, a foreign service officer and the State Department's "golden boy," was hard at work trying to enhance Khomeini's reputation within the administration. Precht had served as a liaison between the Embassy and U.S. military personnel in Iran from 1972 to 1976. Precht claims that one of his first visitors at the Iran Desk was an Israeli who warned him that the Shah was in big trouble. He was told that Henry Kissinger had just returned from a visit to Tehran. According to the story told Precht, the Shah believed the current unrest in Iran was too well-organized to be run by internal forces. Pahlavi felt that the CIA (which had helped him regain power in 1953) was behind it all. Precht's reaction: "I was dumbfounded. This was the man [Pahlavi] we were relying on to save our terribly important interests in Iran. He was a nut. This was the person I was going to have to deal with."[524]

Precht was adamant about forging ties with what he felt would be a liberal democracy under Khomeini. Precht's advisors suggested a number of ways to normalize relations, including a radio program and student and scholar exchanges. Although Embassy dispatches and CIA reports to the contrary were funneling into Precht's in-box, he failed to give credence to the fact that anti-American sentiment was growing.

Precht went so far as to make an appearance on a television show with Ebrahim Yazdi, the American-educated Khomeini advisor and representative in America, to discuss events in Iran. Yazdi's description of an Iran under Khomeini was akin to biblical descriptions of the Millennium...freedom for all, repression and torture for none, open elections, uncensored press, and cordial relations between countries. It was reminiscent of the old campaign promises of "a car in every garage and a chicken in every pot." Either Yazdi was a master at the game of smoke-and-mirrors, or he was totally mesmerized by the dark, hooded eyes of the Ayatollah.

Precht, in fact, circulated a memo that came to be known as the "Precht Doctrine." In essence, it said the Iranian people were tired of the resulting mayhem caused by the revolutionary process and were ready for a more sanguine leader like Bazargan. Precht was in favor of normalizing relations with Khomeini's hand-picked puppet as quickly as possible and defended the Ayatollah against his detractors. Ignoring admonitions to the opposite from American Embassy workers, Precht was adamant in his opinion that Khomeini was simply a figurehead for the more moderate forces that were actually in control in Tehran. He was convinced that Khomeini, a religious man, had no knowledge of how to run a country or a desire to do so. He felt the military would fall in line with the new, more moderate, Shah-less government. Precht was sure Iran would become a model country under Khomeini's auspices. UN Ambassador Andrew Young piped-up with a comparison of Khomeini to those Blacks struggling in the American Civil Rights Movement.

Just as Precht assumed his new duties as Iran desk officer, both Stempel and Sullivan left on vacation. Sullivan detoured through Washington to assure everyone at the State Department that things were copacetic in Tehran; the Shah's people had identified the key religious leaders and had paid them to keep quiet.[525] It had been rumored that the CIA was involved in paying hush money to the clerics, but Zahedi debunked that tale:

> This was an entirely internal affair and did not concern the CIA. Due to the rivalry between Hoveyda, Amouzegar,[526] and Alam, the money paid to the clergy was stopped, so I can tell you very strongly that the CIA had no role to play and no money to pay. They want to have credit for something they did not do.[527]

Following his stopover in D.C., Sullivan departed to Mexico for two months. His lengthy absence seemed to indicate that if the administration were truly concerned about unrest in Iran, Sullivan's leave would have been shortened.

Sullivan returned to Tehran to find a memo from John Stempel on his desk. It was titled, "While You Were Away." It was subtitled, "...the place really didn't turn to crap, but it might have looked like it." The memo reflected the administration's fervor to monitor human rights issues above that of the growing unrest that was roiling through Iran.[528] Sullivan indicated to the State Department that the Shah seemed determined to move Iran toward a more democratic government. The ambassador believed that "the United States policy on human rights has had only a peripheral bearing on the decision, and [should] refrain from claiming this as a 'victory' for the policy." He also warned that partisans of the Shah were "mindful of rumors that the U.S. wished to 'dump' the Shah or destabilize the country."[529]

Cyrus Vance saw the situation in Iran for what it was, chaotic and confused. However, his aversion to such violent instability set the course for cooperation with the Khomeini regime. His policies were dubbed by one observer as the "let's placate Khomeini policy."[530] Vance, the idealist, simply could not grasp the possibility that the new regime might refute American standards of justice.

It was to the credit of Cyrus Vance, however, that all non-essential American employees, dependents, and all Americans not attached to a U.S. government agency were ordered to evacuate Iran in late January 1979. The successful flight from Iran of some forty-five thousand Americans was accomplished without a single incident.

The walls of the American Embassy compound in Tehran were a testament to the long-time relations between the Shah and the

American presidents who held office during his reign as monarch. Lining the stairway were photographs of Pahlavi and U.S. presidents from FDR to Jimmy Carter. The photos represented decades of U.S./Iranian cooperation. So lengthy had been the relationship between the two countries that no one was prepared for the first attack on the U.S. Embassy in Tehran on February 14, 1979.

Shortly after 10:00 a.m. and under the cover of sniper fire, armed men breached the outer walls of the Embassy compound. Armed with everything from rifles to machine guns, the intruders opened fire inside the grounds. The Marines on duty tried to repel the attack with simple bird-shot in order to give Embassy staff sufficient time to destroy sensitive documents and coding devices. Ultimately, Ambassador Sullivan ordered the Marines to stand down.

Sullivan's staff assembled in the first-floor communications room while the Marine Guards flooded the lower floor with tear gas. It had little effect on the determined invaders, who eventually forced their way into the Embassy proper. The gunmen ransacked the east wing, smashing communications equipment and cutting off electricity and water. Sullivan's appeal to Khomeini's lieutenants went unanswered for over an hour. The siege was finally ended and Khomeini placed a group of "guards" outside the Embassy to provide protection for the staff. In order to safeguard classified documents housed at the Embassy, Sullivan had hundreds of boxes sent to the U.S. Within weeks the documents were returned to the Embassy in Tehran. (U.S. Ambassador to Afghanistan Adolph "Spike" Dubs was kidnapped the same day the Embassy was attacked. He was murdered in Kabul.)

Perhaps it was being held at gunpoint by members of the *Fedayeen* that prompted Sullivan to write a memo to the State

Department titled, "A Comment on Terrorism in a Revolutionary Situation." The ambassador's memo outlined disquieting facts about the funding of various terrorist organizations:

> The [Fedayeen] is very well-trained. Instruction is received from the Popular Front for the Liberation of Palestine...the Popular Front for the Liberation of Oman...and the People's Democratic Republic of Yemen. SAVAK accusations of Cuban training were never confirmed. Early funds were obtained by robberies, stealing from parents, and salaries. In 1976 and 1977 large sums of U.S. currency were found on members and in [Fedayeen] safe houses. The money was allegedly provided by Palestinians and Libya.[531]

Sullivan also outlined *Mujahedeen* involvement:

> In 1975 the Mujahedeen infiltrated the U.S. Embassy...by using Iranian national employees. It collected information on various segments of the official U.S. community, especially those affiliated in some way with the Embassy. The [Mujahedeen] believed attacks on U.S. targets had greater impact than on Iranian ones. They attracted media attention, discredited the Shah, and contributed toward forcing the exodus of U.S. technicians...Instruction is received in Lebanon, Libya, and Syria from the Palestinian Liberation Organization, al-Fatah...and other rejectionist groups...SAVAK claims of Mujahedeen training in Cuba were never confirmed.[532]

Unconfirmed SAVAK claims of terrorists being trained in Cuba was particularly revealing. It implied that the information regarding the PLO, Libya, and Yemen had been confirmed. The memo also revealed that Libya sent funds in excess of one hundred thousand dollars to the *Mujahedeen* every three months.

Renowned scholar Walter Laqueur wrote, "U.S. foreign policy has written off not only Iran but a far wider area...the countries concerned would be therefore well-advised to come to terms with the Soviet Union as best they can...It may also encourage the Russians to engage in a forward policy elsewhere, as the risks involved must now appear small or non-existent."[533] Before year's end Laqueur's prophetic words were proven to be true. Russia invaded Afghanistan. The Carter administration would have yet another concern: How would the invasion and America's subsequent reaction affect neighboring countries?

Prior to the overthrow of the Shah, Laqueur had warned of the mentality of the ruling party that would assume power following the Shah's expulsion. "No gifts of prophecy are needed to understand the next Iranian government," he said. "The next will rule the country more harshly than the Shah."[534] Again, time would prove Mr. Laqueur correct.

By April 1979 Shapour Bakhtiar could see the proverbial handwriting on the wall and fled Iran for Paris. Much like the Ayatollah whom he now battled for the soul of Iran, Bakhtiar released cassette tapes and pamphlets in an attempt to form a cohesive opposition to Khomeini. He became a target of one of Khomeini's fanatical lieutenants, Ayatollah Sadegh Khalkhali, for "making a campaign against Imam Khomeini."[535] The first attempt by assassin Anis Nakash to murder Bakhtiar failed. Not so the second; Bakhtiar paid with his life on August 6, 1991: "It was almost a perfect crime. Three well-dressed men walked into the suburban compound of Iranian exile Shapour Bakhtiar in broad daylight, passed through X-rays and metal detectors manned by 24-hour police guards, slit his throat, [murdered his secretary, Soroosh Katibeh] and disappeared."[536]

According to journalist and terror expert Charles Villeneuve, the plot to assassinate Bakhtiar came directly from the PLO:

It's not at all the Iranians in SAVAK; that has to be known...in the beginning all of the officers [or framework] of the Iranian

> *revolution [was] developed in Beirut...Khomeini asked the*
> *Palestinians...Arafat, Abu Jihad, Abu Mussa...the entire major*
> *Palestinian State, to supply them men to come and kill...it is them*
> *who will come to try to kill Bakhtiar...I was born in Beirut; I was*
> *raised there, so I talk with them and I become aware of all this*
> *business that is happening...all the anti-Westerners helped at the*
> *destabilization of the Shah. The Soviet Union also helped, if only*
> *in allowing the Palestinians to form the [framework]...of the*
> *Iranian revolution...because the Shah did not give money to*
> *Arafat. Arafat was a great racketeer. The entire Arafat system*
> *[was] based on a great deal of money.*[537]

Slowly but surely Khomeini began to move his hand-picked mullahs into place in the moderate transition government. Fundamentalists soon began to seize power more openly. Dr. Parviz Mina related how shocked the National Front, the Tudeh (Communist) Party, and the Marxists were in Iran when they realized the mullahs had used them as a way to achieve their aims. They were even more shocked to realize they had been bested by a cleric. Khomeini's radical revolutionary forces exiled or murdered the members of these groups and completely seized the reins of the country.[538]

Had the Tudeh Party leaders had access to a declassified State Department document, it would have shown what Khomeini's intentions were. The Ayatollah "expressed his conviction that the young malcontents who today claim communism will tomorrow rally to the Islamic government. 'Even supposing those who demonstrate with communist slogans are Marxists, they do not constitute a force in the face of thirty million Persians who are in revolt in the name of Islam.'"[539] A March referendum gave the Iranian people only two basic choices for which to vote: Yes, they wished an Islamic Republic; or no, they did not wish an Islamic Republic. Overwhelmingly, the people voted yes, although few Iranians knew what Khomeini meant by "Islamic Republic." According to the Shah's assessment of the referendum:

> It was a grotesque farce. People over the age of fifteen voted. A green ballot meant one vote for the "Islamic Republic" and a red indicated a no-vote. Since this public election was held under the surveillance of the Guards of the Revolution, is it surprising that 98 percent of the voters cast green ballots? The Iranian media announced that the "Islamic Republic" had been voted on by approximately 23 million Iranians...nearly 18 million people were less than fifteen years of age...that would make at least five million votes too many...and Iran...returned to the Middle Ages.[540]

Many political organizations inside Iran protested this election on the grounds that "it did not provide any opportunity for the people to express their ideas about the government's reform."[541] The new constitution drawn up by Khomeini's emerging Islamic Republican Party was vastly different from that proposed by the moderates. The core of the resulting document endowed Khomeini as the ruler of Iran for life, or *velayat-e-faqih* (guardianship of the jurisprudent.) The rule of law, of course, was Islam. Everything was permitted except when it was contrary to Islamic law; and almost everything, presumably, was contrary.

In a confidential memo from Bruce Laingen in Tehran to the State Department, he reported a meeting with Tehran lawyer, A. E. Lahidji. Laingen related some interesting observations regarding Khomeini:

> Khomeini currently controls the masses in Iran, and there is little moderate intellectuals...can do to check Khomeini's creation of a totally Islamic state. Khomeini...is becoming increasingly isolated and surrounded by "yes" men. Most of his advisors are weak...or opportunists...Khomeini has changed since [Lahidji] visited him in Paris. At that time Khomeini told the moderates that the clergy should stay out of politics. Lahidji said he and several other lawyers...

had written the original draft constitution along Western lines...the religious leaders [in Qom] objected to the secular draft...and when Khomeini returned the draft to the lawyers several weeks later, it had been changed to give it a more Islamic flavor...Lahidji felt that Khomeini was behind the much more Islamic constitution...and, in particular, behind the idea of velayat-e-faqih. Absolute power corrupts absolutely, and Khomeini has apparently decided he must run the country himself...Khomeini has alienated all the moderate groups...Few clergymen are willing to make an open break with Khomeini and face charges of weakening revolutionary unity.[542]

By summer's end in 1979 Khomeini's true vision began to be revealed. Far from establishing the enlightened, democratic government anticipated by some U.S. State Department employees, Khomeini, now the supreme leader of Iran, created a medieval Islamic totalitarian state controlled by the mullahs and ayatollahs. It was defined by intolerance, censorship, revenge, tyranny, vile torture, and executions. Khomeini's murderous attacks against the Shah's former officials had spread to include ethnic and religious cleansing. Compared to Khomeini's regime, the Shah had been a benevolent ruler!

Her Majesty Farah Pahlavi talked with me about the human rights issue:

What happened to those who cared so much for human rights? How come when the Shah left, the Iranian people didn't have any rights anymore? What happened to the women?...Flogging, stoning, amputations, insults, all the killing of not only women, children, workers, intellectuals, and whoever even comes outside to demonstrate peacefully for their salaries...the head of the bus drivers, they took him and they cut his palms...They took his family to jail, his wife and his children of three or four in the jail. There is oppression, which exists in the name of religion in Iran.

What happened to those who cared?[543]

Rule by "scapegoat" seemed to be the order of the day under Khomeini. When his government or authority was challenged, he looked for a scapegoat. His first were the Kurds in Northern Iran. They were declared enemies of the Ayatollah and his Islamic Republic, and open season was declared against the Kurdish population.

Although Khomeini was initially ambivalent about ties with the U.S., the fear of U.S. intervention and the return of the Shah plagued the Iranian people. That fear was, of course, fueled by the clerics. It was within the context of this domestic chaos that the death knell for the Carter administration sounded.

CHAPTER 23

. . . .

CANCER:
INTERNAL AND EXTERNAL

"I think we should take Iraq and Iran and combine
them into one country and call it Irate."

(DENIS LEARY)[544]

In 1974 Dr. Jean A. Bernard, a French physician, had been summoned to Tehran to treat an unidentified patient. He was stunned to discover that his anonymous client was Mohammad Reza Shah Pahlavi. The Shah's enlarged spleen and resulting bone marrow tests revealed the presence of lymphocytic leukemia and *Waldenstrom's macroglobulinemia*, a condition of the blood.[545] Pahlavi, who declined further tests because he wanted to keep his condition a secret, opted instead for a medication to control the cancer.

The cancer that ravaged Pahlavi's body may have been the catalyst for rumors of an assassination attempt in the summer of 1978. After a trip to a Caspian Sea retreat, the Shah was reportedly sickly. While the illness was attributed to influenza, it is likely that even then he was feeling the affects of the medications and the disease that would ultimately claim his life.

While even the Empress Farah Pahlavi was kept in the dark about her husband's cancer diagnosis, it is highly likely that the closely guarded secret was known by the French government; after all, Pahlavi was being treated by French doctors. The empress learned of the diagnosis on a trip to Paris in 1977. She writes:

> *I can still feel the icy fear that filled me at that meeting [with the Shah's doctor.] Time has not erased it...the first symptoms had appeared in autumn of 1973! This...added confusion to the pain: these doctors had been treating my husband for four years, but I had been kept out of the secret at his request...I knew my husband's courage and willpower. He had wanted and still wanted to protect me from this ordeal.*[546]

In an interview with *Le Figaro* Magazine, Empress Farah talked further about the Shah's cancer and his mission to modernize Iran:

> *It was because of the news of the illness that he wanted to build up a modern Iran so rapidly. It is a haunting fear: to disappear before completing one's work.*[547]

The Shah and Empress Farah fled to Egypt in January 1979, and then traveled from Cairo to Morocco, the Bahamas, and Mexico. He was literally a man without a country, dependent on the good graces of former friends in high places. The Shah's physical condition soon worsened to the point that his physician believed he should be treated in New York City. The Shah was reluctant to travel to the U.S. When family members pressed him to follow the doctor's suggestion, the Shah replied that he'd "never gone where I'm not welcome."[548]

The Shah's twin sister, Princess Ashraf, not only urged her brother to seek treatment in the U.S., she privately petitioned the president to allow the Shah into the country despite her poor opinion of Carter. The princess believed her brother's monarchy had been abandoned by the United States and by Jimmy Carter particularly. In her missive to the White House, she wrote:

> One of the best-known traditions of the United States throughout the world has been its record of hospitality and refuge to those who are forced to leave their own countries for political reasons...I believe at one time that your government was concerned over the possible harm to American citizens in Iran which might result from him being given refuge...I cannot believe that means could not be taken by your country to assume the essential safety of the United States citizens in Iran, rather than to submit to any such blackmail.[549]

Unfortunately for the princess and her royal brother, that was exactly the case. The rabblerousers in Iran were dictating the terms of the relationship with the U.S. At the same time Khomeini's vile henchman, Ayatollah Sadegh Khalkhali, had ordered the execution of the Shah's family wherever they could be found. Princess Ashraf's son, Shahriar Shafigh, was found in Paris on December 7, 1979. He was gunned down by a sniper wearing a motorcycle helmet.

The president called on Secretary of State Warren Christopher, Cyrus Vance's replacement, to respond to Princess Ashraf. His answer was that the U.S. was thinking about her request. The Shah interpreted Christopher's ambivalent answer as a "thanks-but-no-thanks," which only reinforced his determination not to go to New York for medical attention. Finally, friends and family persuaded him to reconsider.

In the meantime National Security Advisor Brzezinski, contacted Mehdi Bazargan in Iran to seek his advice on admitting the Shah for treatment. Bazargan and Ebrahim Yazdi agreed, "If it is a humanitarian matter, then we agree. We still have time to settle our accounts with [the Shah.]"[550]

On Friday, October 19, 1979, at a weekly foreign policy breakfast, the decision was made to admit Pahlavi to the United States for hospitalization. It seems some in the Carter administration felt they owed the Shah some consideration, given the treatment he had received at the hands of American officials. Those present at the meeting, Vice President Mondale, Cyrus Vance, Zbigniew Brzezinski, Secretary of Defense Brown, and Carter's Chief of Staff Hamilton Jordan voted to admit the Shah. Carter asked the assembled group, "What are you guys going to recommend that we do when they take our Embassy and hold our people hostage?"[551] Others on the staff relayed their concerns: If Pahlavi were allowed to enter the United States, many in Iran would see that as a move to return the Shah to the Peacock Throne in Tehran. It was suggested that Americans might even be taken hostage in retaliation.

Henry Precht, head of the Iran desk, sent a communiqué to the American Embassy marked "Secret/Sensitive." The document posed three queries:

> What new circumstances justify a change of policy by the American government? What conditions do we need to find for the Shah to enter the United States? What precautions have been taken to defend the Embassy personnel? [Based on the possibility of a new government in Tehran, Precht answered his own questions:] We can alert this new government of our wish to answer certain outstanding questions, notably the status of the Shah; the intense pressures to welcome the Shah into the United States, pressure that we resist despite our traditional open door policy. In either of these scenarios, we propose changing our attitude towards the Shah in a positive direction around January 1980. Nevertheless, the risk of hostage-taking persists. Nothing should be done to admit the Shah without first substantially reinforcing the guard at the Embassy.[552]

The Carter administration bandied about many solutions for the situation in Iran. They discussed everything from positioning a platoon of Marines and helicopters in the Azores for rapid deployment to putting the 92nd Airborne on alert. A plan was also approved to gain access to air and naval facilities on Diego Garcia, a British-controlled island. Evacuation of Americans was suggested but was nixed by Warren Christopher. It seems Ambassador Sullivan had not yet deemed the situation drastic enough to warrant such action. Another was to send the Iranian military leaders to Khomeini with hats in hand to pledge their conditional support. None of the suggestions were implemented.

As Brzezinski wrote later: "The Shah did not act; the military did not move; Washington never ordered a coup. Could Iran have been saved by a timely coalition?...did Washington have sufficient warning?...Should Washington...have triggered a military coup...without the Shah?" Brzezinski's summation was that effective remedies had not been proffered in Iran during the 1970s. One immediate result of that oversight was the darkness that became the Ayatollah Ruhollah Khomeini's regime [and ultimately, the takeover of the Embassy with the ensuing hostage crisis]; another was the blow to the American economy. Oil prices tripled because of the stoppage of Iranian oil production and an OPEC increase in the price of crude oil.

Another by-product of Khomeini's seizure of power in Iran was an income of some $76 billion from oil. Dr. Mina reported to me that most of the money was used to finance the terror groups that are now fighting against the U.S., i.e., Hezbollah, Hamas, and the Taliban. This included money, arms, and ammunition.

In September 1980, another of the Shah's concerns was realized. Saddam Hussein acted upon the Shah's fear of a spreading

Islamic revolution and seized the opportunity to attack Iran. Uri Lubrani related a meeting he had had with Pahlavi. He asked the Shah why he spent so much on armaments rather than on education and economic development. His reply to the question surprised Mr. Lubrani. "I have to have a strong army in order to defend my country...I'm going to be attacked by Arabs....I know the United States will protect me if I'm attacked by the Soviet Union; that's why they have their [listening] posts north of Iran...But they will not protect me when Iraq attacks me...they were saying this is a regional conflict in which the United States is not going to take sides. When that happens, I have to have a strong army to deal with it."[553]

No matter his fear of the Shah's past military, Hussein was not at all intimidated by the brooding countenance of Iran's ruling Ayatollah. He called Khomeini a "maniac playing prophet, when in truth he is nothing but a heretic working in the service of the U.S. and Israel." Not to be outdone in the slur department, Khomeini retaliated by referring to Hussein as "a criminal and enemy of Islam whose hand pokes out of an American sleeve and grasps the hand of Israel."[554]

In 1984 Khomeini entertained a delegation from the Islamic Conference Organization. The group traveled to Iran in an attempt to persuade Khomeini to call a halt to the Iran-Iraq War. Khomeini refused to entertain the suggestion of a cease-fire; instead, he wanted to know what punishment would ultimately be meted out to Hussein for starting the war. Another four years of death and destruction would pass before Khomeini was forced, due to a lack of ammunition, to "drink the poisoned chalice" and call a halt to the conflict.[555]

Empowered by his assault on the Shah and the success of his Islamic Revolution in Iran, Khomeini had set forth to spread his particular brand of Arab nationalism throughout the Middle East. Next on his list was Saddam Hussein's Ba'athist regime. His tactic of engaging the people had worked in Iran; why would it not work again in Iraq? The Ayatollah had begun to exhort the Iraqi people to rebel against Hussein's government. Iranian terrorists had attacked principal Iraqi leaders. Then Hussein invaded Iran.

Khomeini saw the Iraq invasion as the perfect vehicle to bring the Ba'athist regime to its knees. The Ayatollah was forced to repair relations with other Persian Gulf states, reach out to the Europeans, and even contemplate talks with the dreaded "Great Satan." It was a setback to his hopes of uniting the Arab world under the banner of his Islamic revolution. His only real success was the export of Hezbollah to Lebanon, and even that was tied more to the destruction of Israel than to a globe-encircling Arab state. Khomeini firmly believed Israel was simply a diversion instituted by the West to keep Muslims from uniting as one.

Lured by the turmoil in Iran, seduced by visions of power, and backed by other Persian Gulf regimes, Hussein was determined to conquer his equally oil-rich neighbor. Like so many others, Hussein may have thought the chaotic take-over in Iran, the execution of so many of the military hierarchy, and Khomeini's lack of experience in conducting warfare, would open the door to a swift and decisive victory for the Iraqis. He was as wrong as those who thought Khomeini was only interested in spiritual matters. Khomeini rallied the troops in Iran and somehow produced an effective war machine to repel the Iraqis.

It seemed the entire world sided with Saddam Hussein against Iran. In Iraq's corner were Saudi Arabia and Kuwait, which infused Iraq's coffers with billions in loans and grants. Support came primarily from the Gulf States that viewed Iran as the greater danger. Also involved in furnishing arms and other war materials to Hussein were Egypt, Jordan, the United States, France, the U.S.S.R., and the PLO. Iran's backing came from Syria, North Korea, Libya, and China…mostly in the form of missiles.

It took two long years of death and destruction before the UN Security Council felt it incumbent to seek troop withdrawals. It would be another five years before questions of chemical warfare used by Hussein against Iran's troops and civilian population would arise.

Khomeini's newly-instituted "Government of God" in Iran failed to draw the majority of the Arab world to his side; in reality, the opposite was true: Iran became abhorrent, friendless especially in the Gulf region, and squandered its most productive resource—oil revenues—by slowing oil production. At the same time, Saddam Hussein was taking advantage of the chaotic situation in Iran to bolster his relationship with the U.S. There are those who believe the U.S. may have subtly encouraged the Iran-Iraq conflict because of what it surmised to be the benefits of such an encounter. Khomeini, who had outwardly shunned both Washington and Tel Aviv, was suddenly faced with the dilemma of how to hold off an invasion by Saddam Hussein without much-needed spare parts and arms from both the U.S. and Israel.

After eight long and bloody years, on August 20, 1988, an embittered Khomeini agreed to the UN Security Council Resolution for an immediate ceasefire. In the aftermath, nothing was resolved between the two nations. Besides the horrific loss of human life, the toll to achieve this impasse was a cost of hundreds of billions of dollars and the disruption and wreckage of the oil fields in both countries. One major outcome of the war, however, was to produce a growing alliance between Iran and Syria and a slackening of the relationship between Khomeini and Arafat's PLO.

During those eight years of warfare between Iran and Iraq, statisticians place the death toll on both sides at seven hundred thousand to one million people, most of them Iranians. Baghdad resorted to the use of chemical weapons against the Kurds and Iranian troops, while Tehran conscripted children to act as human minesweepers in advance of Iranian troops.

Just as it had been in Afghanistan, Egypt was drawn into the conflagration as a U.S. surrogate by supplying technical assistance and arms for Saddam Hussein's battle against Khomeini. Sadat would pay the price for helping the Iraqi dictator by permitting the revival of the Muslim Brotherhood. The group had been banned by Gamal Abdul Nasser in 1954 when Sayyid Qutb, its leader, proclaimed Nasser's rule was a deviation from Islam and should be opposed. This was a contradiction of Sunni traditions to support the state and its leader. Fueling Qutb's passion was an ardent hatred of all things Western, especially of all things American. He viewed the United States as a spiritual vacuum, profligate, and antagonistic to Islam. Qutb felt Christianity was no match for Islam; Islam was a total system of laws, social codes, economic rules, and with its own form of government. He believed ultimately Islam would triumph. Although Qutb was put to death in 1966 for treason, his was the forerunner of terrorist organizations such as Al-Qaeda, which continue to call for the violent overthrow of governments that oppose Islam and call for jihad.

The Muslim Brotherhood found an ally in Anwar El Sadat. He used it as a tool against the communists and socialists who opposed his leadership. The Brotherhood would find a recruiting ground at the al-Azhar University in Cairo. Students from Muslim countries worldwide filled the halls of the famed learning center.

Sadat lost their support when he signed the peace accords at Camp David. He was beset with calls for the return of control of Jerusalem to the Muslims and for Israel to be punished for the attack on the *Osirak* reactor in Iraq.

The Muslim Brotherhood saw the agreement between the two neighboring countries as an affront to Islam. Sadat was also castigated for backing his wife, Jehan, in a push to grant more privileges to Egyptian women, i.e., the right of divorce and the freedom to doff traditional Islamic dress. When Sadat withdrew his support of the Brotherhood, he would eventually pay with his life for what the extremists saw as his "treasonable acts or sins" against Islam. These were some of the same civil rights accorded women under the "Family Protection Act" passed under the Shah in Iran. According to Princess Ashraf, Pahlavi's sister, it, like the one passed later in Egypt, gave Iranian women "the most sweeping civil rights in the Islamic Middle East."[556]

Not having learned his lesson from the disastrous war with Iran, it took only two years for Saddam Hussein to again accost a neighbor—Kuwait. On August 2, 1990, Hussein's army invaded its neighbor and quickly seized Kuwait's rich oilfields. Tehran took advantage of Iraq's invasion of Kuwait to remind Washington and the Arab world that Iraq, not Iran, was the enemy in the region.

. . . .

AMERICA
HELD HOSTAGE

*"Our youth should be confident that America cannot
do a damn thing...America is far too impotent to interfere
in a military way here. If they could have interfered,
they would have saved the Shah."*

(GRAND AYATOLLAH RUHOLLAH KHOMEINI)[557]

I ran was free of the Shah but in the grip of diabolic revolutionary
cleric Ruhollah Khomeini and his Islamic Republican Party. For
the moment, Khomeini's dissenters had been silenced—or executed.
However, unrest lay just beneath the surface. University students
were forming demonstrations to protest the tack his revolution had
taken. A far-from-happy middle class had become dejected and
disheartened by the economic upheaval and the strict Islamic code
that was being enforced. The political vanguard was crestfallen by
the new constitution and the curtailing of civil liberties, and the more
traditional religionists were appalled that Khomeini had been
granted *velayat-e faqih* or rule-for-life status. Thrown into that mix

was Mehdi Bazargan, hand-picked by the Ayatollah and in open rebellion against the constitution that would guide the new Islamic social order.

It is safe to say that Jimmy Carter faced his worst foreign policy disaster in November 1979, and it was one of nightmare proportions. Not even the CIA was prepared for the events that unfolded.

A report on Iran to the House of Representatives stated:

> CIA intelligence reporting on the Iranian international situation was minimal before late 1977. No reports based on contacts with the religious opposition had appeared during the previous two years, and there was absolutely no reporting on the internal situation based on sources within the opposition during the first quarter of 1978.

> In sum, intelligence field reporting from Iran provided a narrow and cloudy window through which to observe the sweeping social and political changes underway...During 1978 intelligence community analysts struggled to produce a National Intelligence Estimate (NIE) on Iran...Clearly, policymakers were not served as well as they needed to be. Weaknesses in the intelligence community's performance in this case are serious.[558]

Perhaps sensing that his control was slipping, on October 28 Khomeini declared the beginning of a new purge of those who would defy him. Calling them traitors, he announced his opponents must be eradicated. Bazargan's control was almost non-existent by this time; however, he was able to intercept the call for a massive protest march on the American Embassy on November 1 and divert the demonstrators.

Upon the Shah's arrival in New York City, the Ayatollah launched his fanatical diatribe against the U.S. He demanded the

Shah be returned to Tehran to face criminal charges. Khomeini called for university and theology students to increase attacks against U.S. interests in Iran, especially what he called the "nest of spies" that inhabited the Embassy. He played on the fears of the Iranian people that the U.S. would forcibly return the Shah to the Peacock Throne. His fictional scenario of the return of the Shah reached his desired end, and on November 4, 1979, a group of PLO-trained students and rabblerousers from Qom, calling themselves "Students Following the Line of Imam" or SFLI, again attacked the American Embassy in Tehran. Their thirty-two-year-old leader, nicknamed "Ayatollah Dollar" because of his reputation for dealing on the black market, led the assault.

The first line of attack on the Embassy was the most unexpected...a group of women engulfed in black chadors began to march around its boundary with shouts of "Death to America." This diversionary tactic allowed another group of armed students to enter into the main offices through a basement window. Protected by a contingent of only thirteen U.S. Marines and a few Iranian policemen, the Embassy quickly fell to the SFLI. Soon, every American in the building had been bound, blindfolded, and paraded outside the Embassy. (Six Embassy officials eluded capture by taking cover in the Canadian and Swedish Embassies. They were later smuggled out of Iran using Canadian passports.)

In his book, *All Fall Down*, Gary Sick writes, "According to one of the students who participated in the attack, the revolutionary guards had been alerted in advance and had cooperated by withdrawing their forces assigned to protect the Embassy."[559]

A *History News Network* article reported the frustration of at least one of the Marines on duty at the Embassy:

Years later one of the Embassy guards, former Marine Sgt. Rodney Sickmann, regretted that he'd been ordered not to fire so much as a tear gas canister at the Embassy invaders. "Had we opened fire on them maybe we would only have lasted an hour," he told The New York Times in 2002. But "we could have changed history" by showing that Americans could not be attacked with impunity. Instead the Embassy surrender showed that Americans were easy targets. "If you look back, it started in 1979; it's just escalated," Sickmann says.[560]

Secretary of State Cyrus Vance recalled the heroism of Kathryn Koob and Political Officer Elizabeth Ann Swift. Ms. Swift locked herself inside the operations center at the Embassy in Tehran and for over two hours reported on the actions of the rioters attacking the compound. Vance wrote: "Swift said the remaining staff...was going to surrender before the mob began to harm the captives...At 4:57 a.m., phone contact with the Embassy ceased. [Kathryn] Koob, who was working in another building away from the compound, was still able to get through to the operations center by phone...At 5:30 a.m....communications with Koob stopped. That was the final contact with the compound."[561] (Elizabeth Ann Swift and Kathryn Koob were the only two women held for the entire 444 days of captivity.)

In a separate building other Embassy employees began to quickly shred documents, but they too were soon captured and driven outside to join the frenzied parade. The rampage of hatred that followed the taking of the Embassy mesmerized the American public. The SFLI conducted "press conferences" that were simply a means to parade its American captives before the world while enraged Iranians roared in the background. Anti-American slogans covered the walls of the Embassy compound. The world awaited the fate of the sixty-six individuals taken hostage.

One writer noted:

U.S. intelligence activities inside Iran during the previous twenty years had been directed primarily at the Soviet Union and entailed mostly the monitoring of missile tests from bases along Iran's northern border. The warehouse basement where the [hostage takers] initially stashed most of the hostages...had been built to house data processing and communications equipment for those listening posts. Iran, as a staunch American ally, was not even a minor target for intelligence gathering. There is no better proof of this than the way the CIA was blindsided by the revolution. No one in Washington saw it coming.[562]

Even CIA Director Stansfield Turner admitted the oversight in *Burn Before Reading*. Turner wrote that the news of the first so-called student incursion into the American Embassy in Tehran in February 1979 was "startling and totally unexpected."[563] Rather than learning from that brief debacle, the CIA snoozed and was once again caught off-guard on November 4, 1979.

Thomas L. Ahern, the CIA station chief in Tehran, was inside the Embassy when the walls were breached and captives taken. Ahern had been working to develop a relationship with Bazargan and the Revolutionary Council prior to the attack on the American compound. The bureau chief was taken captive along with the other hostages and held for the 444 days of infamy.

When CIA Director Turner received the second call about an Embassy incursion in the middle of the night, it was to summon him to an emergency session of national security advisors in the White House situation room. Why was everyone so stunned by the turn of events? Turner attributes it to the fact that the Shah had been a trusted friend of the U.S., and there was no reason to be caught "spying on friends."[564]

Faced with domestic challenges, Khomeini desperately needed a diversion for the Iranian people. The opportunity fell into his hands when the Shah was granted permission to travel to New York City for the removal of a gallstone. The news of the Shah's arrival on U.S. soil initially made little impact on the Ayatollah, other than his demand that Pahlavi's vast assets be uncovered and returned to Iran. In fact, Khomeini only urged student demonstrations at the hospital in New York and demanded that political asylum not be granted to the deposed and ailing king. Instead of Iranian students picketing outside the hospital, in the beginning only a group of American students arrived bearing placards that read, "Take Carter; we'll keep the Shah."[565] Empress Farah penned in her diary, "Will this start the Third World War?"[566]

Former Ambassador Zahedi lamented the other demonstrations outside the hospital: "The authorities allowed hostile anti-Shah crowds to come close to the hospital. They were yelling all day long. This was such an unbelievable move, and so un-American."[567]

Two visitors to the Shah during his hospital stay were former Ambassador to Iran Richard Helms and his wife Cynthia. An ailing Pahlavi told Helms:

> *The real difficulty was caused by too precipitate liberalization... The Americans and the British kept pushing me to be more liberal with my opponents. The changes were genuine on my part. But Iran is not ready for Western-style democracy.*[568]

As soon as the Shah was declared well enough to leave the hospital, he and the empress were hustled to Lackland Air Force base in San Antonio, Texas. There they were virtual prisoners of the U.S. government. The empress requested and received permission to telephone a trusted friend, Kambiz Atabai, to ask if the Shah had been remanded to prison. After two weeks' confinement at Lackland, she and the Shah were allowed to fly to Panama at the invitation of General Omar Torrijos.

After a short stay in Panama, it was determined that the Shah would again require surgery for the removal of his spleen. There were lengthy discussions between Carter's legal advisor, Lloyd Cutler, and the Panamanian government before Torrijos denied permission for U.S. surgeons to perform the operation in Panama. At her wits end, the empress telephoned her friend, Jehan Sadat in Egypt. Farah Pahlavi recounted the stress and frustration of those events during our interview:

> When we were supposed to go, after all the turmoil, from Panama to Egypt, President Carter had evidently talked to President Sadat and said to him, "Don't permit the Shah to come back." President Sadat told him, "Jimmy, I want the Shah here." When all this trouble started in Panama and we were very worried, Mrs. Sadat called me and said, "Come to Egypt. We will send you an airplane." We decided it was best to go to Egypt because in those days there were some murmurs from the Iranian Islamic Republic to try the Shah for war crimes. At the last moment, the Americans sent some messages that they would give us an airplane. We had to rent an airplane for a lot of money. It was not an Egyptian plane; it was an American plane.

> We stopped in Azores, and I am wondering why we are stopping in Azores. They told us that they wanted to ask permission for a route. An American plane asks before for the way to travel; they don't have to stop somewhere. The foreign minister of Portugal told me that when [the Portuguese] asked them, "Why are you staying here for such a long time?" they said, "We cannot tell you." It was Portuguese land! They had sent an ambassador to Washington asking, "Why did you keep the plane so many hours in Azores without telling us?" They were told, "This is something that is almost none of your business."

*Later on, we found out that it was written, I think, by Mr. Salinger
(ABC news bureau chief in Paris), or some other person, that the
Carter administration was discussing with the Iranian Islamic
Republic that if the Shah was taken back to Panama, they would
release the hostages. The Iranian foreign minister could not gather
the revolutionary committee because it was our New Year's holiday.
So, we went to Egypt.*

*I felt very bad for the hostages and their families, and it was
ridiculous for the Islamic government to say that America was
supporting the Shah. The Shah could have been anybody; and for
America to support him, it could have been anywhere. It didn't
have to be in America. It was just an excuse.*[569]

The empress, who had been appointed regent by her husband
and forced by his illness to take charge of both the family and the
large population of exiled Iranians, was also in actuality the caretaker of her son's future as Shah of Iran. She related the quandary
surrounding her son, Crown Prince Reza Pahlavi, and his ascension
to the Peacock Throne:

*I remember when my husband passed away and according to our
[Iranian] constitution, the crown prince would have to come after
his father at the age of twenty. It was in July and he was becoming
twenty in October. I thought that in these three months something must be said; otherwise, the Iranian people in favor of us
would think, "What's happened?" So, we decided that he would
just give the message to the Iranian people that he would accept
his duties according to our constitution. Then, Mr. Sadat called
me and said that President Carter had called him and told him
not to [let the crown prince make his statement]. Mr. Sadat told
me it had put him in a very difficult situation. I said to Mr. Sadat,
"I'm sorry, but we have sent some press releases that he is going
to make a speech on the 31st of October 1980. So all the press*

knows. I cannot stop it now." Thank God, because if he had not done this press release, what could I have done? We were their guests. Thank God, I had sent the press release. When Mr. Sadat told President Carter what I said, I fancy President Carter smiled and said, "Farah did what she wanted."[570]

After the outbreak of the war between Iran and Iraq, the heir-apparent, Reza Pahlavi, had informed the government in Tehran that he was willing to return to Iran as a fighter pilot. (The crown prince had trained at Reese Air Force Base in Lubbock, Texas, and was an accomplished pilot.) The young Pahlavi wrote to the chief commander of the armed forces in Iran, "I would like to offer my blood to save the inviolability of our dear native land." There was no response to his offer.

The Shah would succumb to the ravages of cancer just months after his return to Egypt. Zahedi talked of the almost circus-like atmosphere that surrounded the Shah during his final days... quarreling doctors, an Iranian general trying to persuade the Shah to return to Iran to roust Khomeini, among other things. He also talked of the Shah's realization that he was dying. Zahedi made arrangements for the Pahlavi children to be brought to Cairo shortly before their father's death. It was Zahedi who performed the Muslim tradition of washing the Shah's body before it was transported to Kobbeh Palace Mosque prior to his burial.

The ambassador paid tribute to President Anwar El Sadat, who would accord the Shah dignity in death and a funeral worthy of a head of state. It was also because of Sadat's intervention that the empress, the Shah's sister Ashraf, and Mrs. Sadat were permitted to attend the Shah's funeral.[571]

Richard M. Nixon, who also knew the agony of exile, attended the funeral and was less than pleased with the U.S. response to the Shah's death:

Nixon was furious with the State Department, with other govern-
ments who declined to send delegations, but particularly with
Carter, whose behavior during the Shah's wandering exile he had
yet to forgive. To a crowd of waiting reporters, he pronounced
Carter's handling of the Shah "one of the black pages of American
foreign policy history." It was "shameful" said Nixon, that the
administration didn't even have the grace to point out that he had
been an ally and a friend of the United States for thirty years."
He paused to glare at the journalists. Then he added, "I think
President Sadat's guts in providing a home for the Shah in his last
days at a time when the U.S. turned its back one of its friends is
an inspiration to us all."[572]

Just fourteen months later, the empress would again join mourners behind another casket. This time it would be to comfort her friend Jehan Sadat following the assassination of her husband at the hands of Islamic militants.

The question remains: Did the wily cleric plant the seed that grew into the attack on the Embassy, or did he just take advantage of the situation? Whatever the circumstances surrounding the planned take-over, when it came to the cunning Khomeini's attention, he was not above using the Embassy seizure to his advantage.

The timing could not have been more perfect for him to unite all of the divided elements—Nationalists, Marxists, and Islamics—behind his banner of anti-American outrage. He could now launch the final stage of his planned Islamic Republic by purging pro-Westerners from Iran. With the new witch hunt in full force, it is little wonder the majority of Iranians remained silent regarding the assault on the U.S. Embassy.

Alhough the Ayatollah himself did not deign to visit the captured Embassy, he sent his son, Ahmad, to praise the students for their actions. Khomeini's callousness proved to be the straw that broke the backs of both Mehdi Bazargan and Ebrahim Yazdi. Bazargan resigned his post and Foreign Minister Yazdi was relieved of his duties. Khomeini and his own particular brand of Shia fundamentalism had Iran firmly in a stranglehold.

Dr. Ebrahim Yazdi, a product of American medical schools and a member of the faculty of Baylor College of Medicine in Houston following his last flight from Iran, later became a member of the Iran Freedom Party and a zealous adversary of the ruling clergy system. He now believes the clerics tainted Islam through their political activities, and religion was no longer truly the predominant force in Iran. Yazdi thinks a growing xenophobia (dislike of all things foreign) had been exacerbated by the nuclear proliferation in Iran, and that Ayatollah Ali Khamenehi (Khomeini's successor as supreme leader of Iran) and the mullahs used this issue to enrage the general population.

In an effort to gain the release of the captives immediately, President Carter approved sending an envoy to meet with Khomeini. Former Attorney General Ramsey Clark and William Miller, a former member of the foreign services, were dispatched to Tehran to attempt to negotiate with the hostage-takers. During a stopover in Turkey, the two were informed that Khomeini had taken a hard line and refused to allow any official in Iran to negotiate with the U.S. government. Clark and Miller were forced to abort their mission and return home.

The American people were stunned at the barbaric behavior aimed at their fellow citizens by the Iranians. What followed the takeover of the Embassy was described by George Lenczowski as "a saga of Iranian cruelty, duplicity, violation of diplomatic rules, and utter disregard of elementary human rights on the one hand,"

and he outlined the American response as one of "indecision, confusion, vacillation between the use of diplomacy and force to rescue the hostages, and of serious humiliation suffered by the U.S. government and military establishment."[573]

For six long months the hostages had endured treatment of which few Americans could even conceive. April 6, 1980, Easter Sunday, was a day of hope and prayers; prayers for the American hostages in Iran and their families, and hope that a negotiated release might soon be achieved. In fact, the hostages had been granted authorization to attend Easter services, and a group of American clergy flew from JFK in New York City to Tehran with what was purported to be a statement of understanding between the two nations.

Unfortunately, neither the messengers nor the message produced a favorable response from the Iranian captors. Negotiations came to a halt Easter weekend, and the Americans and Iranians were as divided as they ever had been.

Efforts to free the hostages included attempts to find an interlocutor to mediate a release. U.S. intermediaries contacted an Argentine negotiator, Hector Villalon, and a French attorney, Christian Bourguet. Both Bourguet and Villalon had originally been hired by Iran to attempt to secure the extradition of the Shah. Taking a hint from Israeli Ambassador Abba Eban, who disguised himself for a secret mission to Tehran in 1966, White House Chief of Staff Hamilton Jordan, thirty-five, donned a grey wig, mustache, and dark glasses to portray a middle-aged man. In this disguise he flew to Europe for several clandestine meetings with these two mediators. In an attempt to spur on negotiations, President Carter wrote two letters to Iran's interim leader, Abolhassan Bani Sadr.

The Carter team was amazed to learn from the Iranian news source, *Pars*, that the letters were said to have been addressed to Ayatollah Khomeini. In the letters Carter had purportedly admitted to U.S. errors in judgment and had called the capture of the hostages a "reasonable reaction of the youth of Iran."[574] While Carter denied having written to Khomeini, a Swiss intermediary confirmed that he, Carter, had corresponded with Bani Sadr. Whether the letters were addressed to Bani Sadr or to Khomeini, neither was swayed by the president's appeal.

U.S. foreign policy advisors also contacted Mr. Bazargan and Prime Minister Yazdi to seek their assistance in obtaining the release of the hostages. Neither man held sufficient clout in Khomeini's new Islamic Republic to be of any help to U.S. negotiators. Bazargan likened the Embassy crisis to a simple student sit-in that would end in a few days. Unfortunately, that proved not to be the case. The American captives were not released. With the sudden and unexpected departure of Bazargan and Yazdi, the U.S. had no friends in high places in Iran. America had plunged into the boiling cauldron that was Islamic fanaticism—Khomeini-style.

Despite having agreed to furnish replacement parts for U.S.-made military equipment previously purchased by the Shah and providing intelligence to Bazargan's government, the U.S. was now deprived of level heads that would provide access to Persian Gulf oil. A relationship that for decades had been friendly was now adversarial—and not just in the exchange of words. A deviously clever, manipulative fanatic was now in control of all decision-making in Iran, an old man who had labeled America "the Great Satan" and had no desire to negotiate with his sworn enemy.

What prompted Khomeini to dub the U.S. with that label? He "reached far back into Shia tradition for the symbol he needed for his revolution...In Shiism, it is believed that Satan exerts his influence by acting within a person...Khomeini applied the concept to the United States: Satan dwelled within the global superpower, directing its power toward Iran."[575] Thus America was "the Great Satan" and America's ally, Israel, was tagged "the Little Satan."

CHAPTER 25

. . . .

SLEEPING
WITH THE ENEMY

*"The Iran-Iraq War would never have occurred
had Jimmy Carter not toppled the Shah."*

(LOWELL PONTE)[576]

The response to the hostage crisis in Iran was to resort to diplomatic channels to attempt to end it. Later President Carter would write that the government "asked the Algerians, Syrians, Turks, Pakistanis, Libyans, PLO, and others to intercede on behalf of the release of our hostages."[577] Arafat reportedly dispatched a top lieutenant, Abu Walid, to meet with Khomeini, but the Ayatollah refused an audience. The students holding the hostages ridiculed the delegation sent by Arafat with, "We told them we knew how to make a revolution and succeed. We knew how to defeat American imperialism. The Imam showed us the way. We did not need their advice how to conduct our revolutionary struggle."[578]

The PLO, of course, tried to take advantage of the hostage situation to improve its standing in the international community.

Arafat demanded the United States grant recognition to the PLO, welcome an official PLO delegation to the nation's capital, and defer recognition of the Camp David Peace Accords between Sadat and Begin. That would have put in deadly peril Carter's hopes of achieving a Middle East Peace in his time, so he declined Arafat's demands.

In the middle of November the jailers holding the hostages decided to show their commonality with what they saw as the oppressed minorities worldwide and released thirteen African-Americans and women. Khomeini was infuriated by Arafat's claims that the PLO had been instrumental in obtaining the release of the hostages and angrily condemned the terrorist organization for its attempts to insinuate itself into the good graces of the U.S. In July of 1980 hostage Richard Queen was released after being diagnosed with multiple sclerosis. The hostage-takers were left with fifty-two Americans, fifty male and two female prisoners.

By mid-November U.S. oil imports from Iran had halted. Treasury Secretary G. William Miller had frozen $12 billion worth of Iranian funds in U.S. banks, and all shipments of military supplies to Iran were halted. This was followed by other, lesser sanctions against Khomeini's Islamic Republic. Mining the harbors in Iran, halting the import of Iranian oil, petitioning the UN to impose sanctions on Iran, striking selective targets inside the country, and seeking the assistance of U.S. allies in bargaining with Khomeini were all avenues which had been explored.

The Iranians retaliated by threatening to withdraw all funds from U.S. banks. The president was now in the uncomfortable position of trying to decide what to do to secure the release of fifty-two Americans whose lives were now filled with daily humiliation, threats of execution, being blindfolded and paraded before cameras, and chained to the walls or bound and stretched out on cold, bare floors for hours at a time.

One of Khomeini's repeated demands, that the Shah be returned to Tehran and his wealth deposited in banks outside Iran be returned to the revolutionary government in Iran, were dashed by the Shah's death on July 27, 1980. Khomeini, the behind-the-scenes instigator, appeared to remain aloof from any negotiations with the U.S. for the release of the hostages; that is, until it seemed that a resolution might be near. Whenever that occurred Khomeini would support the outlandish demands of the radicals and ruin any possible deal.

Within his own cabinet, President Carter was caught between a dove/hawk duo. Secretary of State Cyrus Vance weighed in as the dove who wanted to make whatever concessions deemed necessary to the Iranian fanatics in order to secure the release of the detainees. The hawk in the administration, Brzezinski, was ready and willing to mount a military operation in order to free the hostages. Carter, who stalwartly opposed any military intervention early on, sided with Vance. Although administration officials were able to inveigle both the U.N. Security Council and the International Court of Justice to issue calls for the release of the captives, neither had any impact on Khomeini's government.

In December 1979, while U.S. leaders were focused on Iran, the Soviets marched into Afghanistan. Although the U.S.S.R. had been clearing roads to the Afghan border, the Carter administration appeared to be shocked by the invasion. The U.S. ambassador from Moscow was recalled and a grain embargo instituted, but only on grain meant for animal consumption.

Speculation by some has indicated that perhaps the Russian invasion was in direct response to Khomeini's Islamic revolution in Iran. The Soviets may have been concerned that the fanaticism would spread into Afghanistan and from there into other mostly Arab countries on the southern border of the U.S.S.R.

Before the Soviet incursion began in 1979, the minority Shiites in Afghanistan (approximately 20 percent of the population) had relied on Iran under the rule of the Shah for encouragement and assistance. Once Khomeini seized power, Iranian revolutionaries tried to force the Afghan Shia to submit to the Ayatollah's oversight by eliminating the more moderate Shiites. The Afghan Shia population (mostly Hazara from the central region of Afghanistan and among the most economically deprived) refused to be dominated by Khomeini. In 1988 Iran successfully integrated eight of the Shia factions into the Unity Party (*Hizb-i-Wahdat.*) Khomeini's Revolutionary Guards tried to force Shia clerics to submit to the oversight of the Ayatollah, but the clerics rebelled and joined with the Afghan Unity Party—*Hizb-i-Wahdat.*[579]

Khomeini's anti-communist Foreign Minister Sadegh Ghotbzadeh, a product of Georgetown University, was not impressed with U.S. support for the Afghan guerillas and was quick to condemn the Russians for their hostility. He suggested the Soviets and Americans had inked a secret agreement to conquer and divide the world between the two superpowers. Not to be outdone, Moscow accused Ghotbzadeh of being an undercover CIA agent. Amir Taheri notes: "It is significant that anti-Americanism was first propagated as a major theme of Muslim fundamentalism by young men and women from Islamic countries who had spent time in the United States as students or workers."[580]

The United States petitioned the U.N. Security Council to pass Resolution 461, which was built on the earlier resolution 457, demanding the Islamic Republic of Iran release the hostages seized from the American Embassy. The Soviet Union, as expected, abstained. Vance was of the opinion the incursion into Afghanistan was simply one symptom of a much more complex problem.

In January 1980 aid to the Afghan underground was approved. This move prompted Anatoly Dobrynin, Soviet ambassador to the U.S., to liken Carter to a "bull in a china shop." One prominent member of the resistance was none other than Osama bin Laden, the same man who spearheaded the attack on the World Trade Center in 2001. The CIA applauded bin Laden's presence. As one writer related: "Delighted with his impeccable credentials, the CIA gave Osama free rein in Afghanistan, as did Pakistan's intelligence generals."[582]

What the CIA apparently didn't know or chose to overlook was that young bin Laden was also influenced by Palestinian academic and spiritualist Abdullah Azzam. "Azzam's trademark slogan was, 'Jihad and the rifle alone: no negotiations, no conferences, and no dialogues.' This intoxicating message, breathtaking in its expansiveness, played an important role in the ideological formation of bin Laden, Ayman al-Zawahiri...and many other Islamic radicals."[583]

Azzam's teachings on jihadists and martyrs would influence the likes of Al-Qaeda and its global following, and they would help found Hamas to balance Arafat's terrorist organization, the PLO. A local hero to Hamas, Azzam's likeness appears on posters dedicated to his prowess. He would, however, run afoul of al-Zawahiri, who decried a jihad that pitted Muslim brother against Muslim brother. Although a fanatical foe of the U.S., the radical Azzam also saw nothing wrong with plundering U.S. mosques to fund his own brand of jihad.

The Soviet invasion of Afghanistan gave some members of the Khomeini regime pause for thought and brought a request that the U.S. give some indication it was willing to acquiesce to some of

Khomeini's demands in order to precipitate a resolution to the hostage situation.

In his role as *faqih*, in early January 1980 Khomeini banned Muslim clerics from running as candidates in the upcoming presidential election. On January 25, 1980, Abolhassan Bani Sadr was elected president of Iran. This Western version of an Iranian leader was exactly what Khomeini needed to bridge the gap between Bazargan and the soon-to-emerge, iron-fisted rule of Khomeini and his Revolutionary Guard. Bani Sadr was destined for failure,[584] caught in the middle between the militant clergy and the more moderate elements. Bani Sadr called for the hostages to be placed under legitimate government jurisdiction, while the mullahs demanded they remain under the control of the so-called students.

It seems ironic that the pilot who flew the Shah and his entourage from Tehran to Cairo later transported two Khomeini insiders, Abolhassan Bani Sadr and Masoud Rajavi, to Europe when they fell out of favor with the Ayatollah. (The pilot later became a member of the *Mujahedeen*.)

Meanwhile, the U.S. enlisted the aide of U.N. Secretary-General Kurt Waldheim. Waldheim was given a checklist to present to Bani Sadr on behalf of the State Department. The points included:

The acceptance of the government in Iran under Khomeini.

The acceptance of a U.N. resolution of any issues between the two countries.

Like a chess master contemplating his final checkmate, Khomeini sat back and watched the machinations. He only had to wait until April 24, 1980, when the U.S. launched an attempt to rescue the American captives under his control.

Obviously, sanctions were not effective against Khomeini. Negotiations had stalled. Only coercion in a threat to mine Iran's harbors elicited even a lukewarm response from the international community. Out of frustration, the U.S. opted for a military solution—*Operation Eagle Claw*. The logistics of such a rescue were astronomical, and in the final analysis it was probably doomed to failure from the outset.

Although Director of the CIA, Stansfield Turner had been excluded from the planning meetings for the rescue operation. He challenged national security head Brzezinski and was essentially told the CIA's help was not needed for a military operation. Turner advised Zbig of the foolishness of that assumption and was finally admitted to the inner planning circle.[585]

As the preparations for an attempted hostage rescue escalated, the U.S. called on Israeli General Dan Shomron, who had commanded *Operation Entebbe*. General Yitzhak Segev recounted his thoughts on the plan to free the captives:

> *Every Friday Khomeini leaves the city...bring in aerial resources, [grab Khomeini] and tell the Iranians if they want Khomeini back, they better release the hostages...Everyone said I wasn't fair. [Segev warned about the dangers of using helicopters in the attempt:] When six helicopters were needed, we would take ten. A helicopter is a very delicate animal. Take it there, bring it around, every moment something breaks down. They needed six helicopters... by the time they got there two had already broke down. They had no reserves. It was bound for failure...a huge mistake.*[586]

Regardless of reservations, the rescue plan was launched. Completely shrouded in darkness, the aircraft carrier *Nimitz* plowed through the waters of the Arabian Sea just southeast of Iran. Sitting on the deck of the huge nuclear-powered craft were eight Sea Stallion RH-53D helicopters. The rescue attempt would prove to be one of the most difficult operations of the newly-launched U.S.

Army Delta Force, members of which were aboard the Sea Stallions. The plan was dangerous and complex. Six helicopters were the bare minimum to accomplish the mission. The fuel range of each chopper necessitated a rendezvous for refueling in the middle of the desert, about 200 miles north of Tehran, a site codenamed *Desert One*. Already en route to the location from a base in Oman were several C-130 transports loaded with fuel for the helicopters.

The plan was simple, but the execution was complex: Fly the Delta Force to a location near Tehran (*Desert Two*), storm the Embassy, free the hostages, and fly them out on C-141 transports under cover of navy fighters. What the plan did not allow for was the fickleness of desert dust storms. Unfortunately, a serious error in judgment resulted in the removal from the helicopters of the very sand filters that might have meant the difference between success and failure. The filters, each weighing approximately 200 pounds, were discarded in an effort to give the machines greater lift capacity. It may be too that the Israelis, who closely monitor all Middle East events, including the weather, could have given the U.S. a heads-up regarding the approaching storm.

While the U.S. did not seek their assistance in planning and execution, the Israelis were totally aware through their monitoring posts of the operation taking place in the Iranian desert. The U.S. had failed to take the basic precaution of scrambling their transmissions between the USS *Nimitz* and the Delta Force. As the RH-53Ds were traversing the desert for their appointed refueling, the rogue sandstorm enveloped the aircraft. The resulting unrelenting sand, heat, and ensuing equipment malfunctions caused one helicopter to be abandoned in the desert. Another returned to the *Nimitz*, and a third reached the rendezvous point but was unable to continue to Tehran because of a hydraulic leak. With only five helicopters instead of the six needed, Colonel Charles Beckwith, who was in command, called a halt to the mission.

As the choppers refueled for the return trip to the *Nimitz,* one of the helicopters collided with a C-130 fuel transport and both burst into flames. Eight Americans, five Air Force crewmen in the C-130 and three Marine crewmen in the RH-53D, died in the horrific explosion. The survivors of the crash were quickly evacuated aboard the C-130s to an airfield on the island of Masirah off the coast of Oman. The injured men were then transferred to a C-141 Medevac and transported to Ramstein Air Base in Germany.

Although the mission itself failed, the actions and dedication of these men who attempted the rescue were heroic nonetheless: Sergeant John D. Harvey, Corporal George N. Holmes Jr., Staff Sergeant Dewey Johnson, Major Richard L. Bakke, Major Harold Lewis Jr., Technical Sergeant Joel C. Mayo, Captain Lyn D. McIntosh, and Captain Charles T. McMillian. Three of those who died share a common grave at Arlington National Cemetery, and all the men are honored on a remembrance panel inside that hallowed burial ground.

Marine Gunnery Sergeant John McClain offered his take on the rescue attempt:

> *Marine helicopters were designed to fly over ocean or desert and have a system known as EAPS, or "electro-static air-particle separators," which use high voltage and the static generated to separate dust and dirt from the air entering the engines. They "cost" eight or ten percent in power, but they allow "knap of the land flying" in combat conditions.*[587]

The air force helicopters are set up to land in permanent landing areas with concrete landing pads and runways. They have almost no "air cleaner" apparatus at all because it is not an issue if one does not fly close to the ground. They also didn't have the capacity for aerial refueling, so they were tied to a specific straight-line mission due to fuel restrictions. The entire reason the mission failed was due to the destruction of an engine on one of the choppers, caused by ingestion of sand and dust from the desert.

This failed attempt to rescue the Embassy hostages was not, in fact, the first hostage rescue as a result of Khomeini's Islamic revolution. The first was that of twenty-two American employees from one of two top-secret listening posts in Kapkan, Iran (Tracksman1 and Tracksman2). The technicians at the outpost were being held hostage by unfriendly local employees, who were demanding back wages be paid. In a clandestine plot, two American military men, Captain H.F. Johnson and Colonel T. E. Shaefer, commandeered an Iranian C-130, flew into the town, exchanged thirty million rials for the captives, and transported them to safety. Unfortunately, sensitive information-gathering equipment was left behind in the hands of hostile Iranians.[588]

The botched and deadly rescue mission to free the Americans held in Iran was a blow to American prestige worldwide. Coupled with the hostage crisis and exacerbated by domestic issues such as energy and inflation, this was perhaps the final straw for Jimmy Carter. It would cost him a second term in office. Secretary of State Cyrus Vance suddenly resigned on April 28, 1980, in protest of the botched mission. According to Vance's personal papers, "he was opposed to the ill-fated hostage rescue attempt in Iran, and he sensed that the extensive use of force would make the U.S. dangerously vulnerable to further acts of hostility."[589] Vance was eerily prescient.

Andre Fontaine, editor-in-chief of the Paris newspaper, *Le Monde,* summed up the situation very succinctly from the European point of view:

That Uncle Sam was powerless to prevent the collapse of the imperial Iranian regime, in which he had invested so many dollars and hopes, struck Europeans the harder for the fact that at the beginning of 1979, at the Guadeloupe summit conference, the president [Carter] had still expressed great confidence about how the situation would evolve. Who would have supposed that, as we have learned he did, he would have gone so far as to push the Shah out himself—the same man on whom, during his visit to Tehran, [Carter] had heaped the most extravagant praise, even hailing him by the title (a deeply debatable one at that) of champion of human rights?

The hostage affair ended by discrediting [Carter], even if European leaders were secretly relieved that "the Great Satan"...abstained from using force in so inflammable a region. That the richest and most powerful country on earth was unable to force a gang of frenzied revolutionaries to yield seemed a chilling illustration of America's decline.[590]

The revolution in Iran produced more than a change in leadership from that of the Shah to the inscrutable Khomeini. With the taking of the Embassy and the hostage crisis in Tehran following decades of favorable decisions toward Iran by U.S. presidents, both Democrat and Republican, America was faced with a massive failure in foreign policy. It would mark an immediate change in the balance of power in the Persian Gulf region and ultimately a change worldwide for Islam. The Shah, who had once held all of the power in Iran, had lost it all—his throne, power, acclaim from foreign entities—and had become a pariah, a man without a country, dependent on the hospitality of the few who would welcome him.

The horror for which no one in America seemed to be prepared engulfed Iran. The Shah was not the only Iranian to flee the country; he was joined by multitudes of his fellow countrymen.

Europe and the United States were the recipients of many of these well-educated and technically skilled émigrés. They fled from what would become a massacre of vicious proportions and a reign of terror the likes of which the Iranian people had never seen nor imagined under the Shah. Not only was Iran gripped in the iron fist of murder and mayhem, it was stripped of an entire generation of highly trained and competent young men and women—all at the whim of a fanatical old man bent on revenge.

. . . .

CHAPTER 26

THE PRICE
OF FREEDOM

*On January 20, 1981, the day of President Reagan's
inauguration, the United States released almost $8 billion
in Iranian assets and the hostages were freed after 444 days
in Iranian detention; the agreement gave Iran immunity
from lawsuits arising from the incident.*[591]

During October 1980 circumstances were such in Iran that it was
thought Ayatollah Khomeini might be willing to barter for
the release of the hostages. Economic hardship brought about by the
sanctions imposed after the Embassy takeover, a slowdown in oil
production, isolationism, and the threat of war with Iraq gave hope
that the powers-that-be in Tehran (Khomeini) might be willing to sit
down at the bargaining table.

Just days before the election the Carter administration heard
from the Iranians holding the American hostages. The Iranian
government had dictated the terms on which they would free the
captives: 1) return of the late Shah's wealth, 2) cancellation of all

U.S. claims against Iran, 3) release of Iranian assets frozen in the U.S., and 4) an American guarantee of noninterference in Iranian affairs.[592]

Advisor Hamilton Jordan suggested the president release a statement to the American people regarding a possible hostage release. A nation already leery of a last-minute deal for a hostage release was advised that: "We are within two days of an important national election. Let me assure you that my decisions on this crucial matter will not be affected by the calendar...I wish that I could predict when the hostages will return. I cannot."[593] The announcement had the diametrical opposite effect. Many undecided voters jumped ship to the Republican Party. Ronald Reagan carried forty-four of the states and won a decisive victory over the incumbent. From that moment President Carter's most ardent pursuit was a renewed effort to secure the release of the hostages before Ronald Reagan took office. Warren Christopher and a small contingent of State and Treasury Department officials were sent to Algiers for face-to-face negotiations with an Algerian team representing the Khomeini government.[594]

The Iranians were relentless in the pursuit of the Shah's assets, purported to be stashed in American banks. In a move seemingly designed to further insult the United States, Khomeini's negotiators demanded a total of $24 billion dollars be transferred to a bank in Algeria. On the heels of this ridiculous stipulation, the Iranians distributed a synopsis of their demands.

The U.S. retaliated by printing a summation of its own correspondence with the rogue nation. The deadlock between the two countries seemed insurmountable until January 15, 1981. Just days before he was to leave office, Iran capitulated and agreed to Carter's demands to pay off loans owed to U.S. banks. In marathon sessions new drafts were produced, new documents drawn, and the

Bank of England was approved as the repository of escrow funds. Shortly after 4:00 a.m. on Inauguration Day, January 20, 1981, the Carter administration relinquished $7.977 billion to the Iranians. According to one source, the transfer required fourteen banks and the participation of five nations acting concurrently.[595]

Could it have been Ronald Reagan's unwavering challenge to the Iranian regime that tipped the scales? Reagan openly referred to those holding the Americans as "criminals." Was it his no-nonsense tone that moved the Khomeini crowd to action? Reagan's message to the Iranians, delivered by Edwin Meese, leader of the transition team, was: "'The Iranians should be prepared that this country will take whatever action is appropriate' and they 'ought to think over very carefully the fact that it would certainly be to their advantage to get the hostages back now.'"[596] Perhaps, the Iranians finally understood Newton's Third Law as applied by Ronald Reagan: for every action there is an equal and opposite reaction.

As a final insult to President Jimmy Carter, the Iranians refused to release the hostages until after President-elect Ronald Reagan was sworn in as 40th President of the United States. Headlines around the world screamed, "Tehran Releases U.S. Hostages after 444 Days of Captivity."

The release of the hostages proved to be Ronald Reagan's first triumph over a fanatical regime, and no shots were fired. A member of the outgoing administration resentfully admitted, "We probably would not be getting the hostages out now if Carter had been re-elected."[597]

Ronald Reagan wrote of the treatment of the Shah in his autobiography, *An American Life:*

> *Our government's decision to stand by piously while he [the Shah]*
> *was forced from office led to the establishment of a despotic regime*

in Tehran that was far more evil and far more tyrannical than the
one it replaced. And as I was to learn through personal experience,
it left a legacy of problems that would haunt our country for years
to come.[598]

George Bush's (41) Secretary of Defense Robert Gates participated in a meeting with National Security Advisor Zbigniew
Brzezinski during the Khomeini takeover in Iran. Gates later
divulged details of the meeting, indicating that Brzezinski outlined
the U.S. stance regarding the ouster of the Shah and Khomeini's new
Islamic Revolution very succinctly: Acceptance of the revolution;
recognition of Khomeini's government; supplies of arms contracted
by the Shah delivered to Khomeini; and a future working relationship. The American Embassy in Tehran was overrun by terrorists,
and Americans were taken and held hostage for 444 days. Rather
than take a stand against Khomeini's radicalism and defend
America's long-time ally Reza Pahlavi, Carter remained aloof; his
inaction proved deadly.

One must ascertain that the U.S. government had done
some horrible injustice to the Iranian people or to Khomeini in
particular. Not so! Negotiators in our national capital had gone
above and beyond the call of duty to negotiate, conciliate, and
establish trust. Carter and Brzezinski bent over backwards, exposed
this country's vulnerable underbelly, and groveled like wounded
animals to Khomeini's representatives, only to be challenged
with further demands of, "Give us the Shah, and then just maybe
we'll consider talking with you." Even Carter could not stomach
such a move.

Iran, on the other hand, has never been punished for its
capture and incarceration of fifty-two American citizens for
444 days. Other than being labeled a terrorist state, the Iranian

government has had absolute freedom to fund and fuel terrorism on many fronts. It has had the liberty to import the materials to build centrifuges in order to acquire the materials needed to construct nuclear weapons, and it has been free to kill Americans in countries around the world. Why? The U.S. begged, pleaded, cajoled, and ultimately paid off the Ayatollah and his gang of thugs. In so doing, we presented a face to the world that said, "We're weak and ineffective. Come and get us."

The U.S. was soon to come face- to- face with the blowback from the revolution in Iran. The term "blowback" was apparently coined by the CIA to describe "the unintended consequences of covert operations."[599] Ironically, its first usage has been traced back to the 1953 *coup d'état* in Iran. It aptly describes the events that have transpired since the Carter administration first conspired to oust the Shah of Iran. This "liberation" of Iran from the Shah set in motion events that have resulted in untold death and destruction for the past twenty-eight years.

Mohammad Reza Pahlavi and Ruhollah Khomeini, despite their disparities, had similar visions for Iran: a primary leadership role in the Gulf region. The two men had vastly different ideas on how to achieve that dominance. Khomeini espoused the theory that only a theocracy with not only the Iranian people but the Muslim world as a whole, firmly under the iron fist of Islamic radicalism, would suffice. The Shah's vision was the diametrical opposite; he felt that a modernized and democratic Iran backed by strategic alliances with the West would afford his country the respect and admiration he sought from the nations in the region.

Khomeini, though outwardly advocating a coalition with other Arab countries in the vicinity, in reality wanted only to dominate through his own brand of radicalism. In order to begin his march beyond the boundaries of Iran, however, Khomeini had to first subdue the Persian influence and replace it with a maniacal devotion to fundamentalist Islam. The Ayatollah knew too that he would have to eradicate all traces of the Western influence from Iran.

For the West, the loss of a major ally in the Gulf region was a devastating blow. Perhaps Khomeini never intended to completely sever ties with the United States; only the Ayatollah knew with certainty. Whatever his plan, it was thwarted by a few purported "Iranian students" who made the determination to attack the U.S. Embassy on November 4, 1979. When the dust settled and Khomeini assessed the situation, he was left with little choice but to back the students and forever lose any hope of an ongoing alliance with America. Rather than a future ally, Washington had become a menace. The Iranian revolutionaries now saw the U.S. through Khomeini's eyes—"The Great Satan" that must be defeated.

For future U.S. relationships in the Persian Gulf region, "Iran's location at the perimeter of the Arab world, its economic and military ties to Israel, its oil and its traditional enmity with Iraq and the Soviet Union, made it next to irreplaceable."[600] With the Shah's departure, Israel lost a strategic, though understandably covert, ally as well. The Israelis had a difficult time following Khomeini's power play, but they did make several attempts at restoring relations between the two countries. Then-General Ariel Sharon had been in favor of sending Israeli troops into Iran to preserve the Shah's monarchy.[601] Sharon would later warn American leaders not to allow Khomeini's rabid rhetoric to invalidate Iran's strategic importance in the Persian Gulf.

Many in Israel's upper echelon had clung to Prime Minister David Ben-Gurion's periphery doctrine. This doctrine, as defined by Ben-Gurion, "held that the improbability of achieving peace with the surrounding Arab states forced Israel to build alliances with the non-Arab states of the periphery—primarily Iran, Turkey, and Ethiopia—as well as with non-Arab minorities such as the Kurds and the Lebanese Christians." A note in Ben-Gurion's diary reveals his mindset about this attempt at an alliance: "We are in historic times, and this opportunity for action will not repeat itself. Elias has notified me of Turkey's agreement in principle to a meeting of the two prime ministers. If the Arabs find out about this, the whole thing will explode, and then the Americans will interfere as well."[603]

Having already lost the support of Haile Selassie in Ethiopia, Israel was anxiously searching for ways to shore up the Shah's regime. Prime Minister Menachem Begin, under whom Sharon served, was as hawkish as his general. He believed that the fanatical arm of Islam responded only to a show of force and strength greater than its own. Begin feared that with the loss of Iran as an ally, Iraq would become a major player in the Middle East and pose a deadly danger to Israel. The prime minister was right on target.

This periphery doctrine, coupled with the treaty signed by Israel and Egypt, would continue to skew Israel's view of Iran and Iraq into the 1980s. The Israeli government continued to view Iran favorably. Samuel Segev, the author of *Khomeini and Israel* wrote of Defense Minister Yitzhak Rabin's unchanged opinion that Iran was "Israel's best friend and we do not intend to change our position in relation to Tehran, because Khomeini's regime will not last forever."[604] In that assumption Israel was wrong; in many cases dead wrong, as Yasser Arafat began to court Saddam Hussein, who then funded PLO suicide bombers and encouraged attacks on Israel.

From the moment Ayatollah Ruhollah Khomeini stepped from the plane onto Iranian soil in 1978 and on April 1, 1979, (April

Fools day) declared his Islamic Republic, he had given little thought to Israel. Instead, he was emboldened and determined to begin the spread of fanatical Islam using a network of terrorist organizations. According to the Council for Foreign Relations, today Iran supports such proxy groups as Hamas and Palestinian Islamic Jihad[605]; and Brookings Institution reports that another sub-contractor, Hezbollah in Lebanon, has been responsible for killing more Americans than any other single global terrorist group.[606] While the PLO was not a religious organization, groups such as Al-Qaeda, Hamas, Hezbollah, and Islamic Jihad combine radical Islam religious tenets with an extremism that is difficult for Western cultures to comprehend. These fanatical Muslims are, thanks in large part to Iran, parked on the borders of Israel—Hamas in Gaza, Hezbollah in southern Lebanon, and the Muslim Brotherhood in Egypt.

I could fill page after page with terror attacks that have implicated Iran or Iranian proxies since the taking of the American hostages in 1979. Below are just a few instances:

:: Iran's proxies have attempted to infiltrate and/or smuggle arms and explosives into France, Germany, Saudi Arabia, Tunisia, and Turkey, to name a few.

:: Kidnappings and murders:
William Buckley, American, kidnapped and murdered by Iran's Revolutionary Guards; Peter Kilburn, librarian, American University, Beirut, kidnapped and murdered; Michel Seurat, French writer, kidnapped and murdered by hostage-takers; Colonel William Higgins, American officer assigned to the U.N. in Lebanon, kidnapped and executed by Iranian agents; Professor Hitoshi Igarashi, Japanese translator of Salman Rushdie's *Satanic Verses,* stabbed to death; Ettore Capriolo, Italian translator, survived being stabbed; William Nygaard, the Norwegian publisher of Rushdie's book, barely

survived an assassination attempt in Oslo in 1993; Hikmet Cettin, a Turkish journalist, murdered.

:: Iran has been linked to bombings worldwide:

:: 1983 U.S. Embassy in Beirut (sixty-one killed, 120 injured); U.S. Marine headquarters in Beirut (241 killed, 80 seriously injured); series of Paris bombings in 1986; 1989 bombings in Mecca (scores injured); Amia Jewish Center, Buenos Aires (95 killed, 230 injured); 1996 bombing outside the Khobar Towers in Saudi Arabia (20 murdered, nearly 400 wounded).

:: Hijackings and airline explosions:

1983 Air France 747 plane destroyed at Tehran's Mehrabad Airport.

1985 TWA Boeing 727 U.S. Navy diver, Robert Dean Stethem, severely beaten and later executed by hijackers.

1987 Air Afrique DC-10 French passenger murdered.

1988 Kuwaiti 747 landed at Mashhad, Iran; two passengers murdered.

1988 Pan Am Flight 103 exploded in midair over Lockerbie, Scotland, 270 passengers from 21 countries perished.[607]

:: Iran and 9/11:

The 9/11 Commission report linked Iran to at least facilitating the travel plans of the 9/11 terrorist/murderers by not stamping their passports.[608] There is also evidence that Iran assisted Al-Qaeda when that organization was forced to withdraw from Afghanistan in 2001 and has, in fact, allowed that rogue group to continue to operate from within Iran's borders.

In a *Jerusalem Post* article, Barry Rubin wrote of Iran's collaboration on the attack of the U.S. Marine barracks in Beirut, Lebanon in October 1983:

> *Former US Marine Col. Timothy Geraghty was Marine commander in October 1983 when suicide bombers attacked the barracks of US peacekeeping forces in Beirut, killing 242 Americans. He now reveals that a September 26, 1983, U.S. intelligence intercept showed Iran's government ordering the attack through its embassy in Lebanon. The timid response to that operation set a pattern leading directly to the September 11 attack.*[609]

Iranian officials deny, of course, that they support terrorist groups; but that is a matter of semantics. What the Western world calls "terrorists," such as Hamas and Hezbollah, the Iranian hierarchy simply calls liberation movements. Iranian political analyst Hassan Abbasi addressed Iran's ties with Hezbollah. Referring to the group's agenda as "sacred," he said:

> *If something can be done to terrorize and scare the camp of infidelity and the enemies of God and the people, such terror is sacred. This terrorism is sacred. Lebanon's Hezbollah was trained by these very hands. Pay attention! Do you see these hands? Hezbollah, Hamas, and Islamic Jihad were trained by these very hands.*[610]

It seems that Mr. Abbasi was readily boasting of training the very terrorists who continue to threaten the security of Israel and the United States.

C H A P T E R   2 7

. . . .

UNDER THE
MICROSCOPE

"When [Pandora] opened [the box],
all of the evils, ills, diseases, and burdensome labor
that mankind had not known previously escaped
from the jar."[611]

O nce the Shah, America's staunchest ally in the Persian Gulf
region, had been abandoned, Pandora's Box was opened and
the demon of terrorism was allowed to escape. As the biblical
prophet Hosea predicted, the whirlwind had been unleashed. Islamic
fanaticism has inarguably become the most important issue with
which the West has to contend. Once democracy had been sought
by the multitudes as the panacea for all ills; now Islam appeals
to the masses with its seemingly unlimited resources due to
oil money, its global spread, and its message of world domination
through intimidation. Khomeini's success against the Shah and
the resulting Islamic revolution have become a model for other
terrorists worldwide.

In 1982 Iran scored a logistical victory when Revolutionary Guard troops were moved into Lebanon. When both Israeli and American troops were forced to withdraw, as were the Italians and French, Lebanon was destined to become a hotbed of terrorist activities. Israel and America became the main targets of Syrian-backed and Iranian-funded Hezbollah. The plan: to wage war against Israel, America's staunchest ally in the Middle East. Iranian Major General Ataollah Saleh, declared, "The Americans will run away, leaving their illegitimate child [Israel] behind, and then Muslims will know what to do."[612] Khomeini then set his sites on Iraq's holy city of Karbala, and from there marching on to liberate Jerusalem.

Riding the wave of Khomeini and his predecessors, a new president in Iran, Mahmoud Ahmadinejad, is utilizing every opportunity. Following the death of the Grand Ayatollah in June of 1989, Ali Akbar Hashemi-Rafsanjani, a former student of Khomeini's and dedicated to his cause of establishing an Islamic Republic, became president of Iran and successfully served two terms. His successor, Ali Mohammad Khatami-Ardakani, won a landslide victory in 1997 and served until replaced in 2005 by Tehran mayor Ahmadinejad.

It appears that under Ahmadinejad's regime Iran is returning to the tactics of Khomeini. Ahmadinejad seems to have embraced the Ayatollah's dream of Iran as the primary leader in the Persian Gulf region. Khomeini had foreseen a time when Islamic revolutionaries would embrace his ideology, unseat American-backed leaders, and form Islamic republics based on Khomeini's interpretation of the Koran. Unlike the Shah, who based his monarchy on the belief in a strong armed forces and a U.S. ally, the Ayatollah believed his version of fanatical Islam and his fervor would be sufficient to defeat any adversaries, inside or outside Iran. It is also possible that the formidable Ayatollah had visions of routing Saddam Hussein in Iraq and joining the two countries into one dominant Islamic power.

Perhaps Ahmadinejad was "channeling" the late Ayatollah Khomeini when he passionately declared the UN Security Council had little, if any, control over Iran's nuclear pursuits. Ahmadinejad has asserted that the resolutions passed by the Security Council are worthless and, in his words, "illegitimate." That could be due in part to the fact that the United States is responsible for having given Iran the technology and equipment to implement the nuclear cycle and ultimately produce a nuclear bomb.

Yes, Washington is responsible. During the reign of the Shah, Richard Nixon's Secretary of State Henry Kissinger negotiated the sale of nuclear equipment to Iran. Why should Ahmadinejad not mock warnings of sanctions against Iran, just as Khomeini did? Why? The country threatening the sanctions is the U.S., the very country that, along with its allies, was responsible for bolstering Iran's nuclear program as early as the late 1960s.[613]

With Ahmadinejad's threats falling on their ears, our European "allies" are breaking all speed records to assist the U.S. in confronting Iran and halting its nuclear ambitions, aren't they? Of course not! As it did during the hostage crisis in 1980, NATO has turned a blind eye and a deaf ear to America's pleas for help despite the diminutive dictator in Iran threatening to "wipe Israel from the map," sponsoring global terrorism, and continuing to thumb his proverbial nose at the Nuclear Non-Proliferation Treaty. I wonder just what our NATO allies *will* do, and when?

Ahmadinejad's utter contempt for the UN Security Council in particular and the world in general was never more apparent than in March and April 2006. In March the Security Council insisted

Iran halt the enrichment of uranium; in April Ahmadinejad proclaimed a major advancement in his country's enrichment program. Did his actions anger the Europeans? No! It only encouraged them to offer Iran's president a list of incentives, one of which was the possibility of talks with the United States.

The proffered enticements included wording closely resembling those of Jimmy Carter when, in his 1981 State of the Union address, he made an offer to Khomeini, the mad mullah of Tehran: "We are prepared to work with the government of Iran to develop a new and mutually beneficial relationship."[614] The latest, almost identical offer to Iran's government came from international envoy Javier Solana. In typical fashion Ahmadinejad responded not by decreasing but by increasing the enrichment of uranium.

In an article for *The Wall Street Journal*, Bret Stephens offered this observation:

> For three years, the administration has deferred to European and U.N. diplomacy while seeking to build consensus around the idea that a nuclear-armed Iran poses unacceptable risks to global security...Today, the international community is less intent on stopping Tehran from getting the bomb than it is on stopping Washington from stopping Tehran.[615] (Emphasis is mine.)

Of course, none of this has fazed the superegotistical Mr. Ahmadinejad. He was not deterred from sending an eighteen-page letter to President George W. Bush (43) in which he urged the president to convert to Islam.

Amir Taheri suggests the letter not be dismissed out-of-hand. According to Taheri, Ahmadinejad is simply following the lead of the Prophet Mohammad:

> To some in Washington, Ahmadinejad's epistolary exercise may look like another of his quirks. But it is based on a long historic tradition

and fits into a framework of religious practice developed by Muslims over the past fourteen centuries.

Prophet Muhammad himself initiated the practice of writing letters to "the rulers of the world." In 625 AD, having consolidated his position in Medina and established a secure power base for his rule, the prophet decided it was time to call on "the infidels" to abandon their faith and submit to Islam. Accordingly, he dictated three letters: to Khosrow Parviz, the Persian King of Kings, a Zoroastrian; and to Emperor Heraclius of Byzantium and the Ethiopian monarch Negus, who were Christians.

The prophet's offer to the three recipients of his letters was simple: convert to Islam and secure a place in paradise or cling to your beliefs and face the sword of Islam.[616]

In his epistle to the president, Ahmadinejad issues a veiled warning, nay threat: "Those with insights can already hear the sounds of the shattering and fall of the ideology and thoughts of the liberal democratic systems."[617] Rather than give proper credence to the Iranian president's letter, the Bush administration chose to ignore the threats contained therein. Having done so, at some point the president of the United States, whether Democrat or Republican and regardless of ethnicity, will be confronted by the question: Do the non-Muslims of the world prefer freedom of choice or living under the dictates of a mullah-controlled society?

Ahmadinejad seems to have adopted the motto of his hero, Ruhollah Khomeini, who said: "America cannot do a damn thing."[618] The Iranian leader has succeeded in thwarting any efforts made by the U.S. to sanction Iran because of its nuclear program. It seems, all too often, that the Liberal Left is determined to assist Mr. Ahmadinejad in his attempts to discredit the sinister United States by giving him the benefit of the doubt. Iran, the liberals believe, has justifiable complaints against the "Great Satan." After all, in some minds 9/11 was caused, not by a fanatical hatred for all things American, but by the failure of the U.S. to empathize with the privation and hopelessness in Third World countries. "Along these lines," wrote David Limbaugh, "is it any surprise that Obama... thinks we are at fault for not trying hard enough to meet Iranian tyrant Mahmoud Ahmadinejad halfway?"[619]

As a side note to Ahmadinejad's flaunting of world opinion, four former American Embassy hostages identified the Iranian president as one of the prison guards during the 444 days of captivity under Carter. In a *New York Times* article published in 2005, intelligence officer William J. Daugherty was quoted first:

> *"I recognized him right off. When you're in a situation where your life is in jeopardy, where you know your family is going through hell because of what you're in, and your country is being humiliated, you don't forget the people who cause it."...Another former hostage, Kevin Hermening...a Marine guard at the Embassy, remembered Mr. Ahmadinejad as an interrogator and "higher-ranking security official."*[620]

These identifications were categorically denied by Iranian officials.

A precedent was set with Iran, which still proves true today. The U.S. cowers behind a group of allies that are as toothless a tiger as can be found on the planet. Also, the world is again being challenged by what may be the best student to emerge from Khomeini's *madrasas* (Islamic schools), Mahmoud Ahmadinejad.

The global reach of Khomeini is not restricted to Iran. In a treatise by Gen. (Ret.) Moshe Yaalon, he writes, "According to Iranian Supreme Leader Ali Khamenehi and Iran's Syrian partners, the Second Lebanon War [August 2006] was launched by

Hezbollah—Iran's proxy—as a hostile probe of U.S. reflexes via the engagement of Israel, which for Iran and Syria is a direct extension of Washington in the Middle East."[621] It is apparent that Tehran wishes to neutralize America's influence in the Middle East as a major step in the plan to defeat Western civilization. Foremost in that effort is the funding, training, and arming of Hezbollah in Lebanon, and not just with pistols and ammunition.

Not only does Iran directly support Hezbollah, but also it supplies Hamas with funds, arms, and training. For years Lebanon has played host to about 250 members of the Islamic Revolutionary Guard Corps, the elite of the Iranian military, and is best at training other terror units. It is obvious to me that Iran has a long-term plan to take control of the Middle East region by using proxies: Hamas, Hezbollah, and Palestinian Islamic Jihad, not to mention Muktada al-Sadr's Shiite Mahdi Army in Iraq. Would the spread of such terrorist entities have been assured had President Jimmy Carter worked with rather than against the Shah to correct human rights issues?

Ahmadinejad is equally determined to destroy Israel. Recalling Khomeini's earlier rhetoric, in October 2005 he declared, "This regime that is occupying Qods [Jerusalem] must be eliminated from the pages of history."[622] Despite Ahmadinejad's hateful proclamation, Persian Jews continue to live in Iran. The Iranian Jews were content to remain there following the establishment of the State of Israel (only about eight thousand emigrated), but the safety of the Jewish population is no longer guaranteed under the radical regime of Mahmoud Ahmadinejad. According to available research:

> The Islamization of the country has brought about strict control over Jewish educational institutions. Before the revolution, there were some twenty Jewish schools functioning throughout the

*country. In recent years, most of these have been closed down.
In the remaining schools, Jewish principals have been replaced
by Muslims. In Teheran there are still three schools in which
Jewish pupils constitute a majority. The curriculum is Islamic,
and Persian is forbidden as the language of instruction for Jewish
studies. Special Hebrew lessons are conducted on Fridays by the
Orthodox Otzar ha-Torah organization, which is responsible
for Jewish religious education. Saturday is no longer officially
recognized as the Jewish Sabbath, and Jewish pupils are compelled
to attend school on that day. There are three synagogues in Teheran,
but since 1994 there has been no rabbi in Iran, and the bet din
[rabbinical court of Judaism] does not function.*[623]

Rather than being the savior of Iran and the champion of human rights, the Ayatollah Khomeini instead became the personification of Islamic terrorism, a man whose cruelty and hatred knew no bounds. It was Khomeini who, during the Iran/Iraq conflict, is said to have ordered hundreds of thousands of plastic keys from Taiwan. According to an article by Marcos Aguinis in the Argentine newspaper, *La Nacion,* these cheap bits of plastic were presented to some 450,000 children as the keys to the gates of paradise. These unsuspecting youngsters between the ages of twelve and seventeen were then dispatched to the front lines to be used as minesweepers. One Iranian soldier described the scene: "The kids destroyed the mines with their bodies. It was an almost enthusiastic race...each and every child wanted to be the first to explode."[624] Of course, not all died; sadly, some were maimed beyond belief. I cannot begin to fathom the unspeakable horror of using children in such an inhumane way in an attempt to achieve military superiority.

Would the Iran/Iraq conflict that elicited this heinous murder of children even have occurred had it not been for the ouster of the Shah? Would Saddam Hussein have attained such power in Iraq?

Would Kuwait have been invaded by the determined Saddam, triggering *Desert Storm*? Lastly, will the power vacuum left by Saddam Hussein be filled with another of the likes of the Grand Ayatollah Ruhollah Khomeini or his apt pupil, Mahmoud Ahmadinejad?

CHAPTER   2 8

. . . .

HOW THE WEST
CAN BE SAVED

*"September 11th was a wake-up call from hell that
has opened our eyes to the horrors that await us
tomorrow if we fail to act today."*
(BENJAMIN NETANYAHU)[625]

The world is almost a decade into the twenty-first century.
At the end of the twentieth century Americans could look back
on the halting of the Cold War, the collapse of the Berlin Wall, the
end of the first Persian Gulf War, and a time of prosperity. As the
clock struck midnight on New Year's Eve, December 31, 1999, we
discovered we had averted catastrophe. The world had not come to
a standstill either technologically or mechanically. Folks did not
need to hole up in their homes with shelves of canned goods,
bottled water, and weapons to protect their property from the
midnight marauders of a new millennium. It was, surprisingly to
many, business as usual.

However, the eyes of our enemies never strayed from their
focus upon us; they simply waited to determine our next move.

383

Despite the tragic warning of 9/11 and the certainty that there are those out there who only want to see us dead, we have too quickly and easily returned to the monotony of everyday life and the belief that we are somehow immune to another devastating terrorist attack.

When I see such apathy, I am reminded of an encounter I had with Isser Harel, the head of Mossad (Israeli Intelligence from 1947-1963) at a dinner in his home on September 23, 1980. It was just a few months before the presidential election. That night I asked Harel, "Who do you think will be America's next president?"

Harel responded, "The word on the streets is that terrorists might have a say about that. They are going to attempt to influence your elections by releasing the hostages precisely when Reagan is sworn into office."

Completely stunned, I responded, "What? Why?"

Harel said, "They want Carter out because of his challenges to Islam." The former intelligence officer was referring to the Camp David accords and Carter's insistence that Sadat give a speech in Egypt stating that religion and politics must be separate. This speech was heard by a blind cleric named al-Rahman who issued the *Fatwa* to assassinate Sadat; the same cleric was later indicted for his part in the first bombing of the World Trade Center in 1993.

We talked about America's foreign policy and the tensions in the Middle East, Saddam Hussein's power play in Iraq, and how Carter manipulated the overthrow of the Shah of Iran through the American Embassy in Tehran—contrary to the advice of Israeli intelligence. Mossad asserted that instead of improving the country it would give impetus to Islamic fundamentalists and provoke the Soviets to invade Afghanistan.

"They want to kill Sadat," Harel said. "And now, they want to kill Carter's chances of re-election. They feel that if the hostages are released early, it would put Carter back in office."

Later on that same evening, I asked Harel another question: "Will terrorism ever come to America?"

"Will terrorism come to America?" He repeated my question back to me. "America is developing a tolerance for terrorism. America has the power to fight terrorism but not the will; the terrorists have the will, but not the power. But all of that could change in time. Oil buys more than tents. You in the West kill a fly and rejoice. In the Middle East, we kill one, and one hundred flies come to the funeral. "Yes, I fear America will experience terrorism in time."

"Where will it come?" I asked him.

He thought for a moment. "New York is the symbol of your freedom and capitalism. It's likely they will strike there first. At your tallest building, which is a symbol of your power."

That conversation took place in September 1980. Little did I know that both of Harel's predictions—the release of the hostages at the exact hour of President Reagan's inauguration and the terrorist strikes against the tallest building in New York—would come to pass within a dozen years. A little more than a decade after the hostages were released, the United States would plunge headfirst into an apocalyptic tornado on September 11, 2001.

There are many who think the West cannot survive the onslaught of fanatical Islam of which Iran is only one, but the primary, example. In spite of the tremendous upheaval we are witnessing with the rise of terrorism worldwide, we fail to recognize the danger. Surrounded by those who wish to see both America and Israel wiped off the map, one must ask: How can the West be saved?

Just as the world in Hitler's day did not recognize the process by which that cruel dictator began to dehumanize the Jews in

Europe, so it does not recognize that Iran has, for decades, been using those same guidelines to question the legality of the State of Israel and the proprietary claim of the Jewish people in that small spot in the Middle East. The Supreme leader Ayatollah Ali Khamenei has questioned:

> Who are the Israelis? They are responsible for usurping houses, territory, farmlands, and businesses. They are combatants at the disposal of Zionist operatives. A Muslim nation cannot remain indifferent vis-à-vis such people who are stooges at the service of the arch-foes of the Muslim world.[626]

Khamenei's intent toward Israel cannot be more obvious than in his following statement printed in the Daily Telegraph:

> There is only one solution to the Middle East problem, namely the annihilation and destruction of the Jewish state.[627]

One of the most powerful things that can save the West is a zero-tolerance for terror policy. After Harel's warning, it became clear that America did, indeed, have a tolerance for terror. Today, it is still operating by that policy. Iran is responsible for more deaths through IEDs and the injuring of more American soldiers than anyone in Iraq. Through its proxies, Hezbollah and Hamas, it is responsible for killing more Jews in the State of Israel than any other supporter of organized terror, and still U.S. presidents have sidestepped that issue when trying to coerce Israel to the bargaining table.

Syria, too, is in the business of terror. It allows Iran to fly its planes into Syrian air space in order to arm Hezbollah and Hamas. The U.S. must immediately establish a policy by which it will not, under any circumstances, negotiate with any regime that supports, aids or funds terror. That includes the PLO, Syria, Iran, and virtually any nation aligned with radical Islam. A zero-tolerance policy will shut down the engine of terror. All diplomatic relations with terror-supporting states need to cease. The diplomatic missions for those countries in the U.S. need to be closed, and the harshest penalties imposed for sustaining terrorist factions. They should be isolated from the world.

In addition, the U.S. government must stop the hypocrisy of Jew-baiting. It's appalling for the U.S. to continually promise Muslim, Jew-hating bigots an Islamic state with its capital in Jerusalem. An ironclad bond needs to be established between Israel and the U.S., with Jerusalem recognized as Israel's undivided capital and Judea and Samaria acknowledged as Israel's land.

A secure and strong Israel is in America's self-interest. She is a major strategic ally to America. Israel is not a client state, but it is a very reliable friend. To weaken Israel is to destabilize the region and risk the peace of the world, for the road to world peace runs through the Middle East.

God deals with nations in accordance with how those nations deal with Israel. Israel does not have to offer an excuse for its existence; Israel lives today as a right that has been hallowed by the Bible, by history, by sacrifice, by prayer, by the yearnings of the Jewish people for peace.

It seems the tyrants of this world must always have a scapegoat, someone or some ethnic people to blame for their own inequities. All too often those people have been the Jews. Iran President Mahmoud Ahmadinejad has joined his supreme leader in castigating Israel as a puppet regime planted in the Middle East by Western Zionists simply to usurp Muslim claims to the land. Khamenei once again threw down the gauntlet when he asked:

What are you? A forged government and a false nation. They gather wicked people from all over the world and made something called

*the Israeli nation. Is that a nation? Those [Jews] who went to Israel
were malevolent, evil, greedy thieves, and murderers.*[628]

Both of Iran's most visible leaders have further characterized
Israel, at varying times, as a "filthy germ," a "cancerous tumor," a
"stinking corpse," and a "stain of disgrace [on the] garment of
Islam." The intent is to demonize the Jewish people and mark them
a tool of the devil, a "manifestation of Satan"[629] to be used against
the poor, unsuspecting Muslim people. They are dedicated to make
the Jewish people seem subhuman—thus the moniker "monkeys
and apes" is often ascribed to Jews.

In my interview with Prime Minister Benjamin Netanyahu, he
alluded to Iran's determination to destroy Israel:

*Israel could be in great jeopardy; so will everybody else. In short
order, the Western-oriented regimes of the Middle East would fall
by the wayside. That is why you see the Arab countries siding
against Iran, against Hezbollah; they understand what I am saying.
The Middle East could be taken over, and that means the oil fields
—the oil spigot of the world—would be in Iranian hands.*[630]

He further stated:

*Imagine what would happen later if Iran were to have missiles that
would reach into every European capital. Within a decade into
the Eastern coast of the US, and would be armed not with explosives, but with nuclear weapons.*

*Iran could inspire the 200 million...300 million Shiites...That's
what it intends to do—inspire them into a religious war, first against
other Muslims, then against Israel and the West. The reason they
despise us so much, the reason they want to eradicate us is that they
don't hate you because of us, they hate us because of you. They say
we are the "Small Satan" and that America is the "Great Satan."*[631]

Iran is obviously the greatest immediate threat to the State of Israel, as it is Iranian currency that funds many of the major terrorist movements determined to decimate the Jewish people and wrest their homeland from them. When the fundamentalism that fuels the likes of Mahmoud Ahmadinejad is married to the proliferation of its nuclear program, the threat to Israel grows exponentially.

What Ahmadinejad and the clerics who rule Iran seem to overlook is that Israel possesses the capacity to retaliate on a large scale. It boasts an advanced anti-missile system in collaboration with the U.S. and has the capability of crippling Iran's growing nuclear program. "Israel has a whole arsenal of capabilities to make sure the Iranians don't achieve their result," said Efraim Halevy, former head of Mossad.[632]

Following the death of the Ayatollah Ruhollah Khomeini, it seemed that the mullahs and ayatollahs in Iran were simply waiting for the likes of a Mahmoud Ahmadinejad to burst upon the scene and verbalize their hateful rhetoric. Today it doesn't take much insight to determine the identity of the one out to destroy Israel, or in his own words to "wipe Israel off the map."

What, I wonder, does the world really think of him? Are most people aware of his devotion to the Mahdi? Do most understand that he is an ardent Twelver, a dedicated disciple of the Twelfth Imam, who will do anything to insure that the world is made ready for the second coming of a false messiah—even if it requires manufacturing his own apocalyptic event to insure a rush to Armageddon? When I met Mahmoud Ahmadinejad's spiritual advisor in New York City in 2007, he declared to me that his leader would usher in the Mahdi—the twelfth descendant of Mohammad—through an apocalyptic event within three years.

Unfortunately, one need look no further than Ahmadinejad's speech at the United Nations on September 17, 2005, when he closed with the words: "O mighty Lord, I pray to you to hasten the emergence of your last repository, the promised one, that perfect and pure human being, the one that will fill this world with justice and peace."[633] No, he was not speaking of the return of Jesus Christ. He was speaking of the coming of the Mahdi. Ahmadinejad went home to Tehran and regaled his compatriots with a story about how mesmerized his listeners were when he spoke:

> On the last day when I was speaking, one person in our group told me that when I started to say "bismullah Muhammad"' he saw a green light come from around me, and I was placed inside this aura...I felt it myself. I felt that the atmosphere suddenly changed and for those twenty-seven to twenty-eight minutes, all the leaders of the world did not blink. When I say they didn't move an eyelid, I am not exaggerating. They were looking as if a hand were holding them there, and had just opened their eyes.[634]

The miniature martinet that leads Iran had the audacity to write a letter to President George W. Bush and one to the American people. If I were to put the message of each into a nutshell, they were both basically saying, "Become Muslim and we shall all live at peace."

The intentions of its leaders are deadly serious; they can neither be taken for granted nor underestimated. They seek converts to their fanatical lifestyle from every nation, not just among the Arabs. Remember, after all, Iranians are not Arabs but Persians. Theirs is not a racial war but a religious one. Ahmadinejad reveres terrorists, whom he defines as "martyrs": "Is there an art that is more beautiful, more divine, more eternal than the art of the martyr's death?"[635] He wants nothing more than that every knee on earth should bow to the Mahdi, and that there will be no real peace in the world until the whole world is Muslim.

It is belief in the Mahdi that drives Ahmadinejad and his fellow Twelvers in Iran. They are by far the largest group of Shias, making up approximately 80 percent of the total Shias. Twelvers represent the majority of Muslims in Iran, Iraq, and Bahrain. They also make up large communities in Lebanon, Syria, and Saudi Arabia.[636] Ahmadinejad believes the return of this descendant of Mohammad will come in a mushroom cloud suspended over Israel and America. His regime is a suicidal one, and reminiscent of the statement made by Ayatollah Ruhollah Khomeini: "I say let Iran go up in smoke, provided Islam emerges triumphant in the rest of the world."

Given his determination to usher in the Mahdi, it is likely that Iran's fiery president will, with Ayatollah Ali Khamenei's blessing, continue his defiance against the Western world and forge ahead with Iran's nuclear program. According to Israel's Prime Minister Benjamin Netanyahu, Iran is the greatest threat to Israel since that nation was founded in 1948. This is true not only regarding the Islamic Republic's atomic aspirations, but because Iran fully undergirds the fanatical groups that surround Israel—Hezbollah in Lebanon and Hamas in Gaza. Both groups have drawn Israel into wars to defend her citizens. Netanyahu has not ruled out a military strike against Iran's nuclear sites, and after a meeting with President Obama in May 2009, the prime minister reiterated that Israel reserves the right to defend itself.

Iran seems intent on standing aloof from the world community. Its leaders thumb their noses at calls from the UN Security Council to halt the enrichment of uranium in the quest of nuclear arms. And yet, this same entity entrusted with peacekeeping has failed to recognize the link between Iran's pursuit of weapons of mass destruction and its persistent threats to Israel and the United States. The Security Council has become the proverbial ostrich that buries its head in the sand in order not to see the approaching threat to global safety. Its refusal to recognize the danger has made the United Nations an even more ineffective body. The leaders in Iran flaunt their violation of international law, and thus far, no one has been courageous enough to challenge them. No one has made a move to hold them accountable—either for their infractions in the nuclear arena or for their terrorist activities.

The pursuit of nuclear arms has placed the Sunni states in the Gulf region on alert. Leaders are concerned about the vulnerability of their countries should Iran complete the fuel cycle and actually manufacture nuclear weapons. Iran, a Shia majority, would then possess the means to intimidate its moderate Sunni Arab neighbors and create a climate of fear throughout the Middle East. The ghost of a nuclear arms race between the more radical Shia and the moderate Sunnis hovers over the area and fuels anxieties. During a visit to Israel in late 2009, I was told that should Iran achieve its nuclear ambitions, it would then have a nuclear umbrella which would allow it to accelerate terrorism throughout the Sunni Gulf oil states. An ensuing nuclear arms race between the Sunni and Shia states in the region would drive the price of oil to never-before-seen levels for decades to come. The estimate given me was that oil prices could go as high as $200 per barrel. This would further decimate the world economy. This is another obvious reason why an atomic Iran is unacceptable; it will precipitate a trillion-dollar arms race in the Gulf region and provide a nuclear umbrella for a terrorist state.

Given the hatred for Israel and the West demonstrated by the radical Muslim world and Iran's fanatical pursuit of nuclear weapons, the question must again be asked: How can the West be saved? What will checkmate Iran's endgame in the nuclear arena? Will sanctions drive the country into bankruptcy? Will it be pressure from the U.S., the EU, Russia, or China? Will globalization be the straw that breaks Ahmadinejad and Khamenei's backs? Will an embargo on refined oil be the answer? Will it be a direct strike on their nuclear facilities by Israel? Let's examine these possibilities to see how each might act as a deterrent to Iran's pursuits of nuclear arms.

Will sanctions be a strong deterrent? It has long been thought by politicos that sanctions are not effective. That idea can be supported by gauging their effectiveness against Fidel Castro who quickly established a dictatorship on that island nation despite sanctions imposed. However, in recent years, the perception that sanctions don't work has been disproven by their effectiveness against North Korea.

Why have these newest attempts been more effective? The USA Patriot Act, Section 311, allows the U.S. Treasury to label foreign banks as being of "primary money laundering concern."[637] This prevents the institution from being a clearinghouse for U.S. dollars, disallows any transactions with banks, and halts any affiliation with American financial institutions. This proverbial shot-in-the-arm in applying monetary sanctions effectively quarantines the targeted country and keeps it from infecting other banks worldwide. This is due in large part to globalization, another tool that could be effective in isolating Iran.

In September 2006, the U.S. Treasury department targeted one of Iran's largest government banks—Bank Saderat. The bank was charged with channeling approximately $50 million in payments to terrorist organizations Hezbollah and Hamas. All contact with the

U.S. banking system was shut off. Similar actions were taken in January 2007 against Bank Sepah in order to slow Iran's purchases of ballistic missiles.

Washington Post reporter David Ignatius summed up these moves by the U.S. Treasury:

> The new sanctions are toxic because they effectively limit a country's access to the global ATM. In that sense, they impose—at last—a real price on countries such as North Korea and Iran that have blithely defied UN resolutions on proliferation. "What's the goal?" asks [Treasury spokesperson, Stuart] Levey. "To create an internal debate about whether these policies [of defiance] make sense. And that's happening in Iran. People with business sense realize that this conduct makes it hard to continue normal business relationships."[638]

Although sanctions imposed by the UN have generated little response, that organization has gathered some support from China and Russia, as well as the EU and U.S, which have all released statements supporting the determination that Iran should be banned from possessing nuclear weapons. Furthermore, U.S. financial sanctions, "creatively administered by the Treasury Department, are working to discourage European and Japanese banks from financing important projects in Iran and are having an adverse impact on Iran's economy."[639]

Stronger action needs to be taken to educate the global community as to the threat Iran poses to civilization—to worldwide stability and wellbeing. Iran has long been described as simply a threat to the Jewish state of Israel and to the United States; that is a complete fallacy. The possession of nuclear arms by a fanatical entity, whether Iran, North Korea, Al-Qaeda, or any of the myriad other radical countries or groups, is a menace of great magnitude and must be addressed with equal alacrity.

One of the avenues which must be explored is what the Western allies might be willing to discuss with Russia and China in order to gain their backing on the Iran question. The U.S. has negotiated with China on separate issues involving currency and Iran; what would be the end result should those become joint discussions? China and Russia have formed what might be loosely described as a protectorate for Iran. This tripartite, back-burner agreement has proven to be reciprocally advantageous for all. Steve Schippert, co-founder of the Center for Threat Awareness, says:

No nation at the UN Security Council has been more steadfast or consistent in resistance to US and Western sanctions efforts there than either the bear or the dragon. The reasons for this are quite simple: synergistic strategic advancement against a common enemy, oil and money. Iran is rightly portrayed as one of the most pressing threats to the United States and her interests. But Iran remains in many respects a piece on the chessboard of a greater Russian and Chinese game. Iran seeks greater power and regional dominance and enjoys the support of both Russia and China in its pursuits. Both afford Iran the protection of cover and interference at the UN Security Council and other diplomatic endeavors, allowing Iran to continue its nuclear efforts under a fairly comfortable security blanket.

For Russia...the gains are monetary and psychological, with Iran as a major arms client...China...signed a massive long-term energy deal with Iran worth billions. The United States in particular had made...public calls for other nations to specifically stop making energy agreements until Iran complies [with UN calls for halting the nuclear program]. Signing the energy deal...[afforded] the oil-starved dragon energy relief...All seek to weaken the United States to the point where each is enabled to act on their respective interests.[640]

Each of the three nations has a different agenda in seeking relationship with the others in the group: Iran wishes to gain superiority in the Persian Gulf and continue its support for the terrorist groups that act as its proxies; Russia, the once proud bear, desires to regain a dominant role on the world stage; and China, the Johnny-come-lately to the international political scene, wants to wrest the "superpower" title from the United States and desperately needs the oil flowing in from Iran. So long as America remains strong politically, economically, and militarily, those wishes will be thwarted. The United States needs to delineate ways to put increased pressure on both Russia and China to bring Iran to heel and force the leaders of the rogue nation to the bargaining table.

Having taken a snake into one's bosom, it is imperative not to think all is well and relax one's vigil. It might behoove both China and Russia to take notice of an event that took place following the botched elections in Tehran in June 2009. According to a *Miami Herald* report:

> In Tehran University's huge prayer hall, the Islamic regime's most powerful clerics deliver heated Friday sermons to thousands. These diatribes are normally accompanied by the chant, "Death to America!"

> But at the last Friday prayers [July 17, 2009]—an electrifying event that will affect the core of President Obama's foreign policy— the loudest chants were, "Death to Russia!" and "Death to China!" Also, "Azadeh!" which means "freedom" in Farsi... Consider the impact of this new list of enemies. Ahmadinejad has been trying to distract attention from rigged elections by blaming the West for stirring up demonstrations.[641]

The next issue to be addressed when contemplating the question of how the West can be saved from an apocalyptic event orchestrated by Iran is that of globalization. What is it and what effect might it have on saving the West from Iran's nuclear pursuits and apocalyptic mission? Globalization is defined as:

> A process of interaction and integration among the people, companies, and governments of different nations, a process driven by international trade and investment and aided by information technology. This process has effects on the environment, on culture, on political systems, on economic development and prosperity, and on human physical well-being in societies around the world.[642]

Globalization knows no borders and crosses international boundaries. That is why the fight against terrorism in any form must first be global. No one is exempt from the hatred and fanaticism that grips radical Islamic countries such as Iran. Having explored the dangers of nuclear weapons in the hands of leaders such as those in power in Tehran, we must define ways in which the world community can halt the forward progress of an atomic Iran.

A unified world marketplace would have a major impact on the economy of Iran. Such global tools as the Internet, Twitter, Facebook, and others are used by terrorist groups to plot and plan strikes, to fundraise, and to engage new members; those same tools could be used to discourage trade with Iran. Globalization could be a vital tool in halting the forward march toward an apocalypse, but only if world leaders are engaged. It directly affects markets, economies, communications, transportation, trade, service industries, and capital. It clearly could be a determining factor in whether or not sanctions against Iran were effective. It could be used to leverage Iran's oil-based economy.

In a speech delivered at the National Defense College graduation ceremony in July 2009, Benjamin Netanyahu addressed the effectiveness of globalization:

> *Eventually radical Islam will be defeated by the global information*
> *revolution, by the freedom of ideas which are breaking out, through*
> *technology and through ideas of freedom. This won't happen*
> *immediately, but it will happen...The only thing that can postpone*
> *and disrupt the rate of the extinguishing of radical Islam is the*
> *possibility that it will be armed with a nuclear weapon.*[643]

Another action that would require a global response centers on the credit card industry. The director of the Israel Atomic Energy Commission told me one of the greatest weapons the world has against Iran's nuclear program is the credit card. If the credit cards and bank accounts used by mullahs and members of the Revolutionary Guard were frozen, it would have an enormous and immediate impact on their nuclear ambitions. This would amount to tens of billions of dollars.

While there are those who feel that "globalization" is a word not to be used in polite company or in political circles, it might well be a most effective weapon against Khamenei and Ahmadinejad if wielded unilaterally. It would require a united front, which would of necessity include China and Russia, not to mention a decline in the purchase of crude from Iranian oil wells.

Is oil a possible key to halting an atomic Iran? In 2008, an analysis of the Iranian oil industry began:

> *The Iranian oil and gas industry approaches its 100th anniversary*
> *bloated, corrupt, and nearly bankrupt, managing four times the*
> *employees but two thirds of the oil production it had before the*
> *Islamic Revolution of 1978-79.*[644]

Even with that gloomy report, Iran continues to export 2.1 million barrels of oil per day. The majority of its exports go to Asia, with Europe taking the leftovers. Japan is the largest consumer of Iranian oil, with China a close second. While it is able to export crude oil, Iran is forced to import 40 percent of its refined petroleum because of increased demands, which its refineries are unable to meet. Iran is, however, spending its oil and gas revenues to fund terrorism. Some estimates indicate that Hezbollah receives as much as $200 million annually from Tehran.

It is conceivable that Iran could be persuaded to halt its nuclear program if stronger sanctions against imported refined gasoline were implemented. This is one proposal being investigated by American lawmakers. The 111th Congress introduced H.R. 2194: Iran Refined Petroleum Sanctions Act of 2009. In Section 3, Amendments to the Iran Sanctions Act of 1996, the following is found:

PRODUCTION OF REFINED
PETROLEUM RESOURCES:
Except as provided in subsection (f), the President shall impose
the sanctions described in section 6(b) (in addition to any sanctions
imposed under subparagraph (A)) if the President determines
that a person has, with actual knowledge, on or after the date of
the enactment of the Iran Refined Petroleum Sanctions Act of 2009,
sold, leased, or provided to Iran any goods, services, technology,
information, or support that would allow Iran to maintain or expand
its domestic production of refined petroleum resources, including
any assistance in refinery construction, modernization, or repair.

A similar tactic was considered and then rejected by the Bush administration. It was decided that trying to enforce a refined petroleum embargo would present a dangerous and complex challenge. Both Russia and China would have to be induced to join such an effort. Iran could retaliate by halting exports and bringing traffic in the Strait of Hormuz to a standstill. That could prove to be a fiscal nightmare for an already susceptible world economy.

With H.R. 2194 on the table, Iran retaliated by announcing that it would end refined petrol imports. Seifollah Jashnsaz, managing director of National Iranian Oil Company, announced that Iran has planned the erection of nine refineries. He added that the country is currently constructing seven refineries. He indicated that the star in the refinery crown was "the biggest and most outstanding of all refineries being constructed in Iran and makes use of state-of-the-art technology...The said refinery, once fully operational, can produce 35 million liters of petrol on a daily basis. The production will not only satisfy Iran's demand for petrol but will also be sold at export markets."[645]

If Iran continues on the course of nuclear proliferation the U.S. government must quickly take the extreme measure of a complete oil embargo, not allowing fuel to be sold by Iran or refined petroleum to be delivered to the country. This would collapse the economy of the Islamic terror state.

These are all things that could work against Iran: sanctions, engaging Russia and China, globalization techniques, and a refined oil embargo. They are tools that could be instrumental in intercepting the countdown to Armageddon and saving the West from an Iranian-induced apocalypse.

CHAPTER 29

. . . .

THE FINAL
OPTION

"It would only take three nuclear weapons in the hands
of terrorist groups or a government to destroy Israel.
The United States has a compelling interest in preventing
nuclear proliferation and nuclear terrorism."

(BENJAMIN NETANYAHU)[646]

The most formidable option I have saved for last: an attack by
Israel on Iran's reactors. Israeli officials have indicated it would
do whatever was expedient to halt Iran's pursuit of nuclear weapons.
A pre-emptive strike by Israel has always been a possibility as a
deterrent to Iran's open defiance of the IAEA and the UN. Israeli
Defense Minister Ehud Barak indicates that Israel would consider
all options:

We clearly believe that no option should be removed from the
table. This is our policy. We mean it. We recommend to others
to take the same position, but we cannot dictate it to anyone.[647]

Israel has been placed in the uncomfortable position of having to decipher whether the administration of Barak Obama is more interested in courting the mullahs in Iran than in supporting America's long-time Middle East ally. President Obama, taking a much sterner approach toward Israel than did President Bush, rejects that interpretation of his foreign policy towards Iran, while at the same time taking covert steps to discourage an Israeli attack.

In a statement issued by Prime Minister Netanyahu's office, the prime minister "reiterated the seriousness (with) which Israel views Iran's nuclear ambitions and the need to utilize all available means to prevent Iran from achieving a nuclear weapons capability."[648]

While some believe Iran is as much as three years from nuclear arms capabilities, unnamed intelligence sources have predicted that it would only require approval from Supreme Leader Ayatollah Ali Khamenei to begin production on its first nuclear arms device. The technology, say the sources, has been in place since 2003:

> A US National Intelligence Estimate two years ago concluded that Iran had ended its nuclear arms research program in 2003 because of the threat from the American invasion of Iraq. But intelligence sources have told The Times that Tehran had halted the research because it had achieved its aim—to find a way of detonating a warhead that could be launched on its long-range Shehab-3 missiles...The Iranian Defense Ministry has been running a covert nuclear research department for years, employing hundreds of scientists, researchers, and metallurgists in a multibillion-dollar program to develop nuclear technology alongside the civilian nuclear program... "If the Supreme Leader takes the decision [to build a bomb], we assess they have to enrich low-enriched uranium to highly-enriched uranium at the Natanz plant, which could take six months, depending on how many centrifuges are operating. We don't know if the

*decision was made yet," said the intelligence sources, adding that
Iran could have created smaller, secret facilities, other than those
at the heavily guarded bunker at Natanz to develop materials
for a first bomb.*[649]

In my book, *Showdown with Nuclear Iran*, I outlined in detail
how Israel might launch a strike against Iran. That book was
written in 2006. In the ensuing three years, Iran has made enormous
progress on its nuclear program and in its air defense systems, which
has not escaped the attention of the Israeli government. Time is not
on Israel's side; a decision will have to be made soon. Will Israel
attack, or will it accept the inevitable—a nuclear-armed Iran?
It would surprise few people should Israel decide to strike before Iran
reaches the critical point in developing a nuclear bomb.

Former UN ambassador John Bolton summarized the situation:

*Clearly, negotiations with the White House are not exactly topping
the Iranian agenda. Beyond that, Mr. Obama's negotiation
strategy faces insuperable time pressure. French President Nicolas
Sarkozy proclaimed that Iran must re-start negotiations with the
West by September's G-20 summit. But this means little when,
with each passing day, Iran's nuclear and ballistic missile laborato-
ries, production facilities, and military bases are all churning. Israel
is focused on these facts not the illusion of "tough" diplomacy.*

*Israel rejects another feature of Mr. Obama's diplomatic stance:
the Israelis do not believe progress with the Palestinians will
facilitate a deal on Iran's nuclear weapons program. Though
[Secretary of Defense Robert] Gates and others have pressed
this fanciful analysis, Israel will not be moved.*[650]

The refugee crisis faced by the Palestinians should be dealt
with as such by the Arab world. The terror camps in Lebanon must
be shut down, and refugees absorbed by Arab countries. All arms

being sent to terrorists must be halted. The majority of the Palestinians living within the Palestinian Territory are Jordanian citizens, and should become part of the Hashemite Kingdom of Jordan. An economic summit on the Palestinian refugee issue would provide funds donated from the nations of the world, especially the Arab nations, in order to assist Jordan in building an army, police force, schools, hospitals, housing, and other needs. The suffering of the Palestinian people could be resolved once and for all.

Unable to focus world opinion on Iran and its proxy, Hamas, Israel is becoming more isolated in its determination to stop Iran's march toward the means to decimate the Jewish state. World opinion seems to focus more on the saccharine explanation that Hamas, Hezbollah, and other terrorist groups are "freedom fighters" even while they target innocent civilians, not just in Israel but in countries around the world. Iran, one of the largest suppliers of arms, funding, and training to would-be terrorist states, is allowed to escape almost unscathed from consequences for the choices its leaders make. In fact, many Arab heads of state would secretly applaud an Israeli solution to the Iran threat.

While the U.S. continues to support sanctions as the most viable alternative to halting Iran's nuclear program, Israeli leaders believe their country's very existence is being threatened—and with good reason. Infighting among Iran's radical conservatives could produce an even more rogue regime determined to use any means necessary to regain total control in the nation—even its outright attack on Israel or through one of its proxies.

Israel's leaders believe the window of opportunity to eliminate the menace posed by Iran is closing sooner than expected. While the Obama administration is working overtime to restrict available options, Israeli leaders will not allow themselves to be boxed in by President Obama, Robert Gates, Hillary Clinton or anyone else. Speculators have given Netanyahu until October to make a move concerning Iran. Israel doesn't have the alternative of waiting for negotiations and sanctions to be effective; her very existence is at stake. Benjamin Netanyahu has said, "The Obama presidency has two great missions: fixing the economy and preventing Iran from gaining nuclear weapons."[651]

It seems obvious that the world is threatened by Iran's resolve to complete the nuclear cycle on its mission to possess an atomic bomb. It would seem equally evident that global measures could and should be initiated to stop the radical Islamic Republic from achieving its purpose. Czechoslovakian psychologist Stanislav Grof said, "At a time when unbridled greed, malignant aggression, and existence of weapons of mass destruction threaten the survival of humanity, we should seriously consider any avenue that offers some hope."[652]

We have explored a number of options, but perhaps the most vital ingredient in the survival of the West is best described by E. M. Bounds who wrote:

> God shapes the world by prayer. The more praying there is in the world the better the world will be...the mightier the forces against evil.[653]

The West can be saved, but only if it has the courage to respond to this crisis swiftly and with moral clarity.

The alternatives outlined here can work and save the West, but their success is dependant upon the cooperation of world leaders. No one is immune from an attack by Iran or its proxies. No country is exempt from the wrath of the radical Islamists who govern the country... not its Arab neighbors, not Europe, not Russia, not China, not the U.S., and especially not Israel.

Twenty-three years ago Benjamin Netanyahu warned of the threat posed by Iran:

The spread of lawlessness and the blatant disregard of any constraints by governments are, as in the thirties, gradually becoming accepted norms again, and the consequences could be intolerable. By far the most disconcerting prospect would be acquisition of weapons of mass destruction by the principal terrorist states in the Middle East— Iran, Libya, and Syria. These regimes pose a much greater threat to their neighbors, and to the democratic world generally, than has yet been acknowledged.[654]

Mr. Netanyahu was correct in 1986; let us hope and pray that his assessment of Iran's nuclear threat in 2009 is wrong. The security of the global community depends upon it.

The Wisdom of Solomon resonates:

For everything there is a season,
And a time for every matter under heaven...
A time for war, and a time for peace.[655]

What time is it? It is time to take a stand against the apocalyptic threat posed by Iran. The father of our country, George Washington, said, "There is nothing so likely to produce peace as to be well prepared to meet the enemy." Are we prepared? In the words of President Ronald Reagan:

We must make it clear to any country that is tempted to use violence to undermine democratic governments, destabilize our friends, thwart efforts to promote democratic governments, or disrupt our lives that it has nothing to gain and much to lose.[656]

The Western World has not yet made that clear to Iran.

APPENDIX A:
GLOSSARY OF NAMES

. . . .

A

Abbas, Shah (king) of Iran, and the greatest ruler of the Safavid dynasty. He was the third son of Shah Mohammad. In his later years he became suspicious of his own sons and had them killed or blinded.

Abdullah, King. Current king, Kingdom of Saudi Arabia, head of the House of Saud. He also serves as prime minister of Saudi Arabia and commander of the Saudi National Guard.

Afkhami, Gholam Reza. Senior scholar and director of Social Science Research and International Studies at the Foundation for Iranian Studies, a Washington-based research institution dedicated to the study of Iranian history, culture, economy, and politics; created with the financial support from the twin sister of the Shah of Iran, Princess Ashraf Pahlavi.

Afshar, Amir Khosrow. Iran's minister of foreign affairs, appointed in the last days of the Shah's rule.

Aghazadeh, Gholam Reza. Vice president for Atomic Energy of the Islamic Republic of Iran and the president of the Atomic Energy Organization of Iran. On July 16, 2009, the semi-offical Iranian Students News Agency reported that he had resigned as Iran's nuclear chief for unspecified reasons.

Agnew, Spiro. Thiry-ninth vice president of the United States, serving under President Richard Nixon, and the 55th governor of Maryland. He was formally charged with having accepted bribes totaling more than $100,000, while holding office as Baltimore County executive, governor of Maryland, and vice president of the United States. On October 10, 1973, Agnew was allowed to plead no contest to a single charge in 1967, with the condition that he resign the office of vice president. He is the only vice president in U.S. history to resign because of criminal charges, and he was the second U.S. vice president to resign. Deceased.

Ahasuerus. Ahasuerus is given as the name of the king of Persia in the book of Esther. Nineteenth-century Bible commentaries generally identify him with Xerxes I of Persia.

Ahern, Thomas L. CIA station chief, and later author on counter-insurgency books. One of the sixty-six American hostages captured in Iran.

Ahmadinejad, Mahmoud. Sixth and current president of the Islamic Republic of Iran. He became president after winning the 2005 presidential election and was re-elected in 2009 after a disputed election. Many Iranians were involved in mass protests claiming election fraud and other abuses.

Al-Assad, Hafiz. President of Syria for three decades. Assad's rule stabilized and consolidated the power of the country's central government after decades of coups and counter-coups. He was succeeded by his son and current president Bashar al-Assad in 2000.

Al-Deek, Khalil (aka Joseph Adams). Held dual US-Jordanian citizenship. Came to USA to study computer science and became a naturalized U.S. citizen living in Los Angeles, California, where he worked as computer engineer and Charity Without Borders staffer. The Charity was discovered to be an Al-Qaeda organization used to funnel money overseas but wasn't shut down until after September 11, 2001. He was reportedly killed in Pakistan in April 2005. It is unclear how his death occurred. It has been rumored he was killed by Al-Qaeda for cooperating with Jordanian authorities, but it is also likely he was killed by Pakistani forces in a raid.

Al-Sadr, Muktada. Iraqi theologian and political leader. Al-Sadr is one of the most influential religious and political figures in the country not holding any official title in the Iraqi government.

Al-Zawahiri, Ayman. Prominent leader of Al-Qaeda and the second and last "emir" of Egyptian Islamic Jihad. He is a qualified surgeon and an author of works including numerous Al-Qaeda statements. He is under worldwide embargo by the UN 1267 Committee as a member or affiliate of Al-Qaeda. He is often described as a "lieutenant" to Osama bin Laden, although bin Laden's chosen biographer has referred to him as the "real brains" of Al-Qaeda.

Alam, Asadollah. Longest serving minister of the Pahlavi era. As the minister of the royal court he was the closest man to the Shah Mohammad Reza Pahlavi, who at that time ran the country autocratically. Deceased.

Albright, Madeline. First woman to become United States secretary of state. She was appointed by President Bill Clinton on December 5, 1996, and was unanimously confirmed by the United States Senate 99-0.

Alexander the Great. An Ancient Greek king of Macedon, Alexander succeeded his father Philip II of Macedon to the throne in 336 BC and died in Babylon in 323 BC at the age of 32. Alexander was one of the most successful military commanders of all time, and it is presumed he was undefeated in battle.

Ali Bhutto, Zolfaghar. Pakistani politician who served as the president of Pakistan from 1971 to 1973 and as prime minister from 1973 to 1977. Deceased.

Ali, Hussein ibn. (see Mahdi)

Allon, Yigal. Israeli politician, a commander of the Palmach, and a general in the IDF. He served as one of the leaders of the Ahdut HaAvoda Party and the Israeli Labor Party, acting prime minister of Israel, as well as being a member of the Knesset and government minister from the tenth through the seventeenth Knessets. Deceased.

Ames, Robert Clayton. Near-East CIA station chief. Deceased.

Amin, Mohammad Haj. Member of the al-Husayni clan of Jerusalem, he was a Palestinian Arab nationalist and Muslim leader in the British Mandate of Palestine. From 1921 to 1948 he was the Grand Mufti of Jerusalem and played a key role in opposition to Zionism. In 1937, wanted by the British, he fled Palestine and took refuge successively in Lebanon, Iraq, Italy, and finally Nazi Germany, where he met Adolf Hitler in 1941. He asked Germany to oppose, as part of the Arab struggle for independ-

ence, the establishment of a Jewish national home in Palestine. Deceased.

Amini, Ali Dr. Prime minister of Iran from May 6, 1961, to July 19, 1962. During the 1950s the Shah came under increasing pressure from the United States to appoint Amini as prime minister. He was finally declared prime minister in 1961. In 1962, however, he was replaced by the Shah's close friend and a major Birjand landowner, Asadollah Alam. In the late 1970s Amini attempted a comeback into Iranian politics at the age of seventy. He served as advisor to the Shah during the final days of the Pahlavi Dynasty. Deceased.

Amouzegar, Jamshid. Prime minister of Iran in August 1977, he rapidly became unpopular as he attempted to slow the overheated economy with measures that triggered a downturn in employment and private sector profits that would later compound the government's problems. In the wake of Khomeini's revolution he soon resigned.

Anne, Princess. Only daughter of Queen Elizabeth II and Prince Philip, Duke of Edinburgh.

Annenberg, Walter. American billionaire publisher, philanthropist, and diplomat. During his lifetime, it is estimated that Annenberg donated over US $2 billion to various causes. "Education,"," he once said, "holds civilization together." Many school buildings, libraries, theaters, hospitals, and museums across the United States now bear his name. Deceased.

Ansary, Hushang. Minister of finance and economic affairs under Prime Minister Hoyveda of Iran, he also served as ambassador to the United States before Ardeshir Zahedi and was the last president of National Iranian Oil Company.

Arafat, Yasser. Palestinian leader and chairman of the Palestine Liberation Organization, president of the Palestinian National Authority, and leader of the Fatah political party, which he founded in 1959. Arafat spent much of his life fighting against Israel in the name of Palestinian self-determination. Deceased.

Ariana, Bahram. Commandant of Iran's Military Academy, he was professor of infantry training at the military academy and taught general tactics at the war university. Deceased.

Asad, Hafez. President of Syria for three

decades, his rule stabilized and consolidated the power of the country's central government after decades of coups and counter-coups. He was succeeded by his son and current president Bashar al-Assad in 2000. Deceased.

Ashraf, Hamid. Marxist leader.

Atabai, Kambiz. Remains the official spokesman for Empress Farah Pahlavi.

Atherton, Alfred. Foreign service officer and diplomat, he served as United States ambassador to Egypt in 1978–1979. Deceased.

Atrianfar, Mohammad. Iranian journalist and reformist politician, currently the head of the "Policymaking Council" of the daily newspaper Shargh. He is a member of the Executives of Construction Party and a senior political advisor to Akbar Hashemi Rafsanjani.

Axelrod, David. Top advisor to President Barack Obama, first in Obama's 2004 campaign for the U.S. Senate in Illinois and later as chief strategist for Obama's 2008 presidential campaign. Following the 2008 election he was appointed senior advisor to President Obama.

Azarbarzin, General Abdollah. The Iranian air force deputy commander.

Azhari, General Gholam-Reza. Military leader and prime minister of Iran. Deceased.

Azzam, Abdullah. Highly influential Palestinian Sunni Islamic scholar and theologian, he is also famous as a teacher and mentor of Osama bin Laden, He persuaded bin Laden to go to Afghanistan and help the jihad. He was assassinated by a bomb blast on November 24, 1989.

B

Badi'ie, General Amir-Hussein. Iranian air force commander.

Badrei, General Abdul-Ali. Commander of the Shah's elite guard.

Baker, Howard. Former senate majority leader, republican U.S. senator from Tennessee, White House chief of staff, and a former United States ambassador to Japan.

Bakhtiar, Shapour. Iranian politician and the last prime minister of Iran under Shah Mohammad Reza Pahlavi. After the Iranian Revolution he migrated to Paris, France, where he was assassinated in 1991 by suspected Hezbollah sympathizers with links to the Islamic Republic.

Ball, George. Undersecretary of state for economic and agricultural affairs in the administrations of John F. Kennedy and Lyndon B. Johnson, Ball also served as U.S. ambassador to the United Nations from June 26 to September 25, 1968. During the Nixon administration, George Ball helped draft American policy proposals in the Persian Gulf. Deceased

Bazargan, Mehdi. Prominent Iranian scholar, academic, long-time pro-democracy activist, and head of Iran's interim government, making him Iran's first prime minister after the Iranian Revolution of 1979. On February 5, 1979, after the revolution forced the Shah to leave Iran, Bazargan was appointed prime minister of Iran by the Ayatollah Khomeini. Bazargan resigned along with his cabinet on November 4, following the U.S. Embassy takeover and hostage-taking.

Beckwith, Charles Col. Known as "Chargin' Charlie," a career U.S. army soldier and Vietnam veteran, credited with the creation of Delta Force, a branch of the U.S. army. The general public knows him best due to the ill-fated 1980 Operation Eagle Claw in Iran.

Begin, Menachem. Sixth prime minister of the state of Israel. Before the independence, he was the leader of the Irgun, a revisionist breakaway from the larger mainstream Jewish paramilitary organization Haganah. Deceased.

Behesti, Mohammad. Iranian cleric, the secretary-general of the Islamic Republic Party, and the head of the Islamic Republic's judicial system. He was assassinated with more than seventy members of the Islamic Republic Party on June 28, 1981.

Bell, Griffin. Served as U.S. 72nd attorney general during the Carter administration. President Kennedy appointed Bell, who had been the co-chairman of Kennedy's presidential campaign in Georgia, to the Court of Appeals for the Fifth Circuit in 1961. Deceased.

Ben-Gurion, David. First prime minister of Israel. Ben-Gurion's passion for Zionism, which began early in life, culminated in his instrumental role in the founding of the state of Israel. Deceased.

Ben-Porat, Mordechai. A founding member of the Rafi Party. He was deputy speaker of the Knesset in 1965; deputy secretary-general of the Labor Party from 1970 to 1972; and a member of Israel's United Nations mission in 1977.

Bernard, Dr. Jean A. French physician and hematologist, he was professor of hematology and director of the Institute for Leukemia at the University of Paris. In 1932 Bernard gave the first description of the use of high dosage radiotherapy in the treatment of Hodgkin's disease. Deceased.

Bianco, Jean-Louis. Member of the National Assembly of France. He is a member of the Socialist Party.

Biden, Joe. Forty-seventh and current vice president of the United States. He was a U.S. senator from Delaware from January 3, 1973, until his resignation on January 15, 2009, following his election to the vice presidency.

bin Laden, Osama. Member of the prominent Saudi bin Laden family and the founder of the terrorist organization Al-Qaeda, best known for the September 11 attacks on the United States. Bin Laden is on the American Federal Bureau of Investigation's list of FBI Ten Most Wanted Fugitives. Since 2001, Osama bin Laden and his organization have been major targets of the United States' War on Terrorism.

Blumenthal, Michael. U.S. secretary of the treasury under President Carter from 1977-1979. He served in the State Department from 1961 until 1967 as advisor on trade to Presidents Kennedy and Johnson. In 2008 he was elected as a delegate to the Democratic National Convention, pledged to back Barack Obama.

Bolton, John. Conservative political figure, who has been employed in several Republican presidential administrations. He worked as the interim permanent U.S. representative to the UN from August 2005 until December 2006. He is regarded as one of the prominent members of the neoconservative movement.

Bonair, M. Christian. French interior minister.

Boutros-Ghali, Boutros. Egyptian diplomat who was the sixth secretary-general of the United Nations from January 1992 to January 1997. He describes his role and that of former Egyptian President Anwar Sadat as bringing about the peace accord between Egypt and Israel in March of 1979.

Bowen, David. Former U.S. congressman from Mississippi.

Brezhnev, Leonid. General Secretary of the Communist Party of the Soviet Union (and thus political leader of the Soviet Union) from 1964 to 1982, serving in that position longer than anyone other than Joseph Stalin. Deceased.

Brown, Harold. American scientist, was U.S. secretary of defense from 1977 to 1981 in the cabinet of President Carter. He had previously served in the Johnson administration as U.S. deputy defense secretary and secretary of the air force. While secretary of defense, he insisted on laying the groundwork for the Camp David accords.

Brzezinski, Zbigniew. Polish-born American political scientist and statesman, who served as national security advisor to President Carter from 1977 to 1981. He is currently professor of American foreign policy at Johns Hopkins University's School of Advanced International Studies.

Buckley, William. Former U.S. Army Colonel, Buckley was employed by the Central Intelligence Agency from 1955 to 1957 and again from 1965 until his untimely death. He was taken hostage from his last assignment in Beirut, Lebanon, where he was the political officer/station chief at the U.S. Embassy. Colonel Buckley died of illness and torture after fifteen months in captivity.

Bush, George W. Forty-third president of the United States from 2001 to 2009. He was the 46th governor of Texas from 1995 to 2000 before being sworn in as president on January 20, 2001. Bush is the eldest son of the 41st U.S. President George H. W. Bush and Barbara Bush.

Bush, George H. W. Forty-first president of the United States from 1989 to 1993. He held a variety of political positions prior to his presidency, including vice president of the United States in the administration of President Reagan (1981–1989) and director of the CIA under President Ford.

Byrd, Robert C. Senior U.S. senator from West Virginia and a member and former senate leader of the Democratic Party. He has been a senator since January 3, 1959, and is the longest-serving member in the Senate's history. He is also the oldest current member of Congress and is the first politician in U.S. history to serve as a U.S. senator uninterrupted for half a century.

C

Callaghan, James. Prime minister of the United Kingdom from 1976 to 1979 and leader of the Labour Party from 1976 to 1980, he is the only person to have served in all four of the Great Offices of State: prime minister, chancellor of the exchequer, home secretary and foreign secretary. Deceased.

Cambyses II. Son of Cyrus the Great (r. 559-530 BC), founder of the Persian Empire and its first dynasty. Following Cyrus' conquests of the Near East and Central Asia, Cambyses further expanded the empire into Egypt during the Late Period.

Carter, Jimmy. Thirty-ninth president of the United States from 1977 to 1981 and the recipient of the 2002 Nobel Peace Prize. Prior to becoming president Carter served two terms in the Georgia Senate and was governor of Georgia from 1971 to 1975. The final year of his presidential tenure was marked by several major crises, including the 1979 takeover of the American embassy in Iran and holding of hostages by Iranian students.

Carter, Rosalynn. Wife of former President Carter, and in that capacity served as the First Lady from 1977 to 1981.

Castro, Fidel. One of the primary leaders of the Cuban Revolution, the prime minister of Cuba from February 1959 to December 1976, and then the president of the Council of State of Cuba until his resignation from the office in February 2008. He is currently the first secretary of the Communist Party of Cuba.

Cave, George. CIA expert and a member of the delegation secretly sent to Iran by the White House to break the arms-for-hostages deadlock. Deceased.

Ceausescu, Nicolae. Secretary general of the Romanian Workers' Party, later the Romanian Communist Party, from 1965 until 1989, president of the Council of State from 1967, and president of Romania from 1974 until 1989. His government was overthrown in December 1989, and he was shot following a televised, two-hour session by a military court.

Chaban-Delmas, Jacque. French Gaullist politician. He served as prime minister under Georges Pompidou from 1969 to 1972. Deceased.

Chamran, Mustafa Ali. Among the closest associates of Khomeini, named Iran's minister of defense. He had studied in California and Egypt before he founded a Red Shiite secret society. Oversaw the training of Iranians in PLO camps.

Chavez, Hugo. President of Venezuela. A career military officer, he founded the left-wing Fifth Republic Movement after orchestrating a failed 1992 coup d'état against former President Carlos Andrés Pérez. Chávez was elected president in 1998 in a campaign centering on promises of aiding Venezuela's poor majority and was reelected in 2000 and in 2006.

Cheney, Dick. Served as the 46th vice president of the United States from 2001 to 2009 in the administration of George W. Bush. He began his political career as an intern for Congressman William A. Steiger, eventually working his way into the White House during the Ford administration, where he served as White House chief of staff.

Chevallier, Eric. A medical doctor, who graduated in political science and public policy from the Institut d'Etudes Politiques de Paris. He is currently coordinating a team within the French administration that is working on interministerial monitoring of international crisis and conflicts.

Chiles, Laughton. U.S. senator from Florida. Deceased.

Christopher, Warren. Diplomat, lawyer, and public servant. During Clinton's first term as president, Christopher served as the 63rd secretary of state. He also served as deputy attorney general in the Johnson administration, and as deputy secretary of state in the Carter administration.

Churchill, Winston. British politician known chiefly for his leadership of the United Kingdom during World War II. He served as prime minister from 1940 to 1945 and again from 1951 to 1955. A noted statesman and orator, Churchill was also an officer in the British army, historian, writer, and artist. Deceased.

Clark, Ramsey. Former United States attorney general, he worked for the U.S. Department of Justice, which included service as the 66th United States attorney general under President Johnson.

Clifford, Clark. Influential lawyer who served Presidents Truman, Kennedy, Johnson and Carter, serving as U.S. secretary of defense for Johnson. He made waves by threatening the newly established regime of Ayatollah Khomeini of Iran with war for its intransigence in negotiating the release of the hostages seized from the U.S. Embassy in Tehran. Deceased.

Clinton, Hillary. Sixty-seventh United States secretary of state, serving in the administration of President Barack Obama. She was a U.S. senator from New York from 2001 to 2009. As the wife of Bill Clinton, she was the First Lady of the United States from 1993 to 2001. She was a leading candidate for the Democratic presidential nomination in the 2008 election.

Clinton, William (Bill). Forty-second president of the United States from 1993 to 2001. He was the third-youngest president; only Theodore Roosevelt and John F. Kennedy were younger when entering office.

Cloonan, Jack. Worked as a special agent for the FBI's Osama bin Laden unit from 1996 to 2002. During that time he and his colleagues questioned numerous operatives from Al-Qaeda.

Conyers Jr., John. Member of the U.S. House of Representatives representing Michigan's 14th congressional district. A Democrat, he has served since 1965. In January 2007 Conyers became chairman of the House Judiciary Committee in the 110th United States Congress; he had been the committee's ranking Democrat since 1997.

Cottam, Richard. Former CIA officer and one of the primary experts on the Middle East and Iranian politics. Later he was a political science professor at the University of Pittsburg. Deceased.

Cranston, Alan. Journalist and Democratic senator from California.

Croesus. King of Lydia from 560/561 BC until his defeat by the Persians in about 547 BC. In Greek and Persian cultures the name of Croesus became a synonym for a wealthy man.

Culver, John. Politician of the Democratic Party, who represented Iowa in both the U.S. House of Representatives and the U.S. Senate. He was elected to the House of Representatives from Iowa as a Democrat in 1964, and he served in the House from 1965 until 1975.

Cutler, Lloyd. Attorney who served as White House counsel during the Democratic administrations of Carter and Clinton. Deceased.

Cyrus the Great. About 558 BC Cyrus succeeded his father Cambyses I as king of the Persians. After several campaigns Cyrus conquered eastern Iran and incorporated it into his empire.

D

D'Estaing, Giscard. French centre-right politician who was president of the French Republic from 1974 until 1981.

Daoud, Abu. Palestinian politician and militia commander in Fatah and the PLO. From 1971 he was a leader of Black September, a Fatah offshoot created to avenge the September 1970 expulsion of the fedayeen movement from Jordan and carry out international operations.

Darius I. A Zoroastrian Persian shahanshah (great king) of Persia. He reigned from September 522 to October 486 BC as the third Achaemenian King and is called by some arguably to be "the greatest of the Achaemenid kings."

Darius III. The last king of the Achaemenid Empire of Persia from 336 BC to 330 BC. It was under his rule that the Persian Empire was conquered during the wars of Alexander the Great.

Daugherty, William J. Now a political science professor, in 1979 he was assigned to the U.S. Embassy in Tehran and taken captive when Iranian militants, reacting to the news that the Shah had been admitted to the United States, overran the embassy. He and his colleagues then spent 444 days as hostages.

Dayan, General Moshe. Israeli military leader and politician. The fourth chief of staff of the Israel Defense Forces (1953–1958), he became a fighting symbol to the world of the new state of Israel. He went on to become defense minister and later foreign minister of Israel. Deceased.

Derian, Patricia. Served as assistant secretary of state for Human Rights and Humanitarian Affairs in the Carter administration.

Dinazade. Sister of Scheherazade, legendary teller of Tales of 1001 Nights.

Dubs, Adolph "Spike." U.S. ambassador to Afghanistan from May 13, 1978, until his death in 1979. He was killed in an exchange of fire after a kidnapping attempt.

Duncan, Charles. American entrepreneur, administrator, and statesman best known for serving as U.S. secretary of energy on the cabinet of President Carter from 1979 to 1981. He had previously served as Carter's United States deputy secretary of defense during the Iranian Revolution.

E

Eagleton, Thomas. U.S. Senator from 1968–1987. He is best remembered for briefly being a Democratic vice presidential nominee, sharing the ticket under George McGovern in 1972. Deceased.

Eban, Abba. Israeli diplomat and politician. In 1952 he was elected vice president of the UN General Assembly. Eban left the United States in 1959 and returned to Israel, where he was elected to the Knesset. From 1966 to 1974 he served as Israel's foreign minister. Deceased.

Eisenhower, Dwight. Thirty-fourth president of the United States from 1953 until 1961 and a five-star general in the United States army. During the Second World War, he served as supreme commander of the Allied Forces in Europe, with responsibility for planning and supervising the successful invasion of France and Germany in 1944–45. In 1951 he became the first supreme commander of NATO. Deceased.

Elghanian, Habib. Philanthropist who became the first Jew executed by Iran's radical regime after he was falsely charged and convicted of spying for Israel. His death was by firing squat, May 9, 1979.

Elizabeth II, Queen. British queen since 1952, ruling sixteen independent states and their overseas territories, she ascended the thrones of seven countries on the death of her father, King George VI.

Entazam, Amir. Spokesman and deputy prime minister in the interim cabinet of Mehdi Bazargan in 1979. In 1981 he was sentenced to life imprisonment on charges of spying for the U.S., a charge critics suggest was a cover for retaliation against his early opposition to theocratic government in Iran. He is now "the longest-held political prisoner in the Islamic Republic of Iran."

Entezam, Abdollah. Iranian minister of foreign affairs.

Eshkol, Levi. Third prime minister of Israel from 1963 until his death from a heart attack in 1969. He was the first Israeli prime minister to die in office.

Esther. Born Hadassah, she was a Jewish queen of the Persian Empire, the queen of Ahasuerus, and heroine of the biblical book of Esther, which is named after her. As a result of Esther's intervention and influence, Mizrahi Jews lived in the Persian Empire for 2400 years thereafter.

Ezra. Jewish priestly scribe who led approximately five thousand Israelite exiles living in Babylon to their home city of Jerusalem in 459 BC.

F

Farouk, King. Tenth ruler from the Muhammad Ali Dynasty and the penultimate king of Egypt and Sudan, succeeding his father, Fuad I, in 1936. He was overthrown in the Egyptian Revolution of 1952 and was forced to abdicate in favor of his infant son, Ahmed Fuad, who succeeded him as King Fuad II. He died in exile in Italy.

Ford, Charlotte. Socialite and great-granddaughter of Henry Ford.

Ford, Gerald. Thirty-eighth president of the United States, serving from 1974 to 1977, and the 40th vice president of the United States, serving from 1973 to 1974. As the first person appointed to the vice-presidency under the terms of the 25th Amendment, when he became president upon Nixon's resignation on August 9, 1974, he also became the only president that was not elected for either president or vice-president. Deceased.

Forouhar, Darisuh. Founder and leader of the Hezb-e Mellat-e Iran (Nation of Iran Party), a pan-Iranist opposition party in Iran, and served as minister of labor in the Provisional Revolutionary Government of Mehdi Bazargan in 1979. He later became a critic of the Islamic government, and in 1998 he and his wife were assassinated in one of the Chain murders of Iran, for which a deputy security official of the ministry of information was officially found culpable.

Frattini, Franco. Italian politician, currently Italy's foreign minister.

G

Gandhi. Mahatma. The pre-eminent political and spiritual leader of India during the Indian independence movement. He is officially honored in India as the father of the nation. Deceased.

Gast, General Philip C. Among his many postings from November 1977 to October 1979, he served as chief, Military Assistance Advisory Group, Iran. Retired.

Gates, Robert. Currently serving as the 22nd U.S. secretary of defense. Prior to this, Gates served for twenty-six years in the CIA and the National Security Council, and under President George H. W. Bush as director of the Central Intelligence Agency. Before he joined the CIA he served with the United States air force.

Gelb, Leslie. Assistant secretary of state in the Carter administration from 1977 to 1979, serving as director of the Bureau of Politico-Military Affairs and winning the Distinguished Honor Award, the highest award of the U.S. State Department.

Geraghty, Colonel Timothy. He commanded the 24th Marine Amphibious Unit in Beirut in 1983 as part of the multinational peacekeeping force. Upon his retirement from the Corps, he returned to the CIA to serve in the Counterterrorism Center.

Ghaffari, Hossein. Iranian Ayatollah allegedly tortured to death under the Shah's regime.

Gharabaghi, General Abbas. The last chief of staff under the Shah before he was toppled by the 1979 Islamic Revolution in Iran. He was named chief of staff on January 4, 1979, in the final days of the rule of the Shah, Mohammad Reza Pahlavi. He died in France in 2000 at the age of 82.

Ghotbzadeh, Sadegh. Close aide of Ayatollah Khomeini during his 1978 exile in France and Iranian foreign minister (November 30, 1979–August, 1980) during Iran hostage crisis following the Iranian Revolution. In 1982 he was executed for allegedly plotting the assassination of Ayatollah Khomeini and the overthrow of the Islamic Republic.

Gold, Dore. Former Israeli diplomat. He also served as president of the Jerusalem Center for Public Affairs as well as an advisor to former Israeli Prime Minister Ariel Sharon.

Goleniewski, Colonel Michael. Officer of Polish Military Intelligence and a spy for the Russian government during the 1950s. After his defection in 1961 he worked for the CIA. Deceased.

Gromyko, Andrei. Soviet politician and diplomat. He served as minister for foreign affairs for the Soviet Union (1957–1985) and chairman of the Presidium of the Supreme Soviet (1985–1988). Deceased.

Grimm, Paul. American employee of Texaco, ambushed and killed while on loan to the Oil Services Company of Iran. Mujahedeen, who supported Ayatollah Khomeini, claimed responsibility.

Guevara, Che. Argentine Marxist revolutionary, politician, author, physician, military theorist, mass executioner, and guerrilla leader. Since his death, his stylized image has become a global symbol of counterculture.

H

Habash, George. Palestinian nationalist. A Palestinian Christian, he founded the Popular Front for the Liberation of Palestine resistance organization and was the organization's secretary-general until 2000. Deceased.

Haig, Alexander. Retired U.S. army general who served as secretary of state under President Reagan and White House chief of staff under Presidents Nixon and Ford. In 1973 he served as vice chief of staff of the army, the number-two ranking officer in the army. Haig also served as the Supreme Allied Commander Europe, commanding all U.S. and NATO forces in Europe.

Halevy, Efraim. Former head of Mossad, the national intelligence agency of Israel. "Mossad" is the Hebrew word for institute or institution.

Haman. According to Old Testament tradition, he was a 5th-Century BC Persian noble and vizier of the empire under Persian King Ahasuerus. Haman is the antagonist in the book of Esther. In the story Haman and his wife Zeresh instigated a plot to kill all the Jews of ancient Persia. The plot was foiled by Queen Esther, the king's recent wife, who was herself a Jew.

Harel, Isser. Spymaster of the intelligence and the security services of Israel and the director of the Mossad (1952—1963). Deceased.

Harmelin, Yosef. Austrian-born Israeli politician, serving as an ambassador in Iran and South Africa and as director of Shabak from 1964 to 1974 and again from 1986-1988. He retired in 1988.

Hassan, Hani al. Leader of the Fatah organization in Germany and member of the Palestinian Authority Cabinet and the Palestinian National Council. He is the younger brother of Khaled al-Hassan, a Fatah founder.

Hassan II, King. King of Morocco from 1961 until his death in 1999.

Hatfield, Mark. Politician and educator from the state of Oregon. A Republican, he served for thirty years as a U.S. senator from Oregon, and also as chairman of the Senate Appropriations Committee.

Havel, Vaclav. Czech playwright, essayist, former dissident, and politician. He was the tenth and last president of Czechoslovakia (1989–92) and the first president of the Czech Republic (1993–2003).

Helms, Richard. Director of the Central Intelligence Agency (DCI) from 1966 to 1973. He was the only director to have been convicted of lying to Congress over CIA undercover activities. In 1977 he was sentenced to the maximum fine and received a suspended two-year prison sentence. He served from 1973 to 1976 as U.S. ambassador to Iran in Tehran. Deceased.

Herodotus. Greek historian who lived in the 5th century BC and is regarded as the "Father of History" in Western culture.

Herzog, Chaim. Served as the sixth president of Israel (1983–1993) following a distinguished career in both the British army and the Israel Defense Forces (IDF). Deceased.

Higgins, Robert. Army Lieutenant Colonel. Murdered, supposedly by agents of Hezbollah, in Lebanon.

Hitler, Adolph. Austrian-born German politician and the leader of the National Socialist German Workers Party, popularly known as the Nazi Party. He was the ruler of Germany from 1933 to 1945, serving as chancellor from 1933 to 1945 and as head of state (Führer und Reichskanzler) from 1934 to 1945. Committed suicide.

Holmes, Julius. Served as the executive officer for the U.S. Joint Chiefs of Staff, then in the Liaison section of Allied Forces Headquarters (AFHQ). In 1953 he was minister at the American Embassy in London, and In 1955 he served as ambassador to Iran, a position he reprised from 1961 to 1965. From 1956 to 1959 Holmes was the special assistant to the secretary of state for NATO Affairs. Deceased.

Homayoun, Dariush. Minister of Iranian Information under the Shah.

Hoveyda, Feredoun. Influential Iranian diplomat, writer, and thinker. He was the Iranian ambassador to the United Nations from 1971 until 1979. Hoveyda was nephew of Abdol Hossein Sardari, who is known for saving many Jews in Paris during World War II. Deceased.

Husayn (Hussein). Grandson of the Islamic prophet, Muhammad. He created a regime that would reinstate a "true" Islamic polity as opposed to what he considered the unjust rule of the Umayyads. As a consequence, Husayn was killed and beheaded in the Battle of Karbala in 680.

Hussein, bin Talal. King of Jordan from the abdication of his father, King Talal, in 1952, until his death. Hussein guided his country in the context of the Cold War and through four decades of Arab-Israeli conflict.

Hussein, Saddam. President of Iraq from July 16, 1979, until April 9, 2003. He was convicted of charges related to the executions of 148 Iraqi Shi'ites suspected of planning an assassination attempt against him and was sentenced to death by hanging. He was executed on December 30, 2006.

Huyser, General Robert "Dutch." Deputy commander in chief of the U.S. European Command, Stuttgart-Vaihingen, Germany, in September 1975, where he was one of the major users of Military Airlift Command airlift support. In January 1979, while still EUCOM deputy, President Carter sent Huyser to Iran. Sources disagree on the nature of his mission. According to Carter, Huyser, and American sources, he attempted to stabilize Iran during the turbulent early stages of the Islamic revolution.

I

Ismail, Shah. A Shah of Iran and the founder of the Safavid Persian Empire, which survived until 1736. He had re-unified all of Iran by 1509. He was a Shia Muslim and played a key role in the rise of the Twelver branch of Shia Islam.

Ivry, General David. Israeli ambassador to the U.S. from 2000 to 2002 and the ninth commander of the Israeli Air Force (IAF). In 1999, he was appointed first director of the Israeli National Security Council.

J

Jackson, Henry. U.S. congressman and senator for the state of Washington from 1941 until his death. Jackson was an unsuccessful candidate for the Democratic presidential nomination in 1972 and 1976.

Jam, General Feridoun. Senior Iranian army official and the son of former Iranian Prime Minister Mahmud Jam. He served as head of the Iranian Imperial Army Corps from 1969 to 1971. He left the army because of professional conflicts with Shah Mohammad Reza Pahlavi and retired in 1973. Deceased.

Javits, Jacob. Politician who served as U.S. senator from New York from 1957 to 1981. Deceased.

Jefferson, Thomas. The third president of the United States, the principal author of the Declaration of Independence, and one of the most influential Founding Fathers for his promotion of the ideals of republicanism of the United States. Major events during his presidency include the Louisiana Purchase and the Lewis and Clark Expedition.

Jennings, Peter. Canadian-American journalist and news anchor. He was the sole anchor of ABC's World News Tonight from 1983 until his death in 2005 of complications from lung cancer. A high-school dropout, he transformed himself into one of American television's most prominent journalists. Deceased.

Johnson, Lyndon. Often referred to as LBJ, served as the 36th president of the United States from 1963 to 1969 after his service as the vice president of the United States from 1961 to 1963. Johnson was selected by Kennedy to be his running mate for the 1960 presidential election. Deceased.

Jordan, Hamilton. Chief of staff to U.S. President Jimmy Carter. Deceased.

K

Kaddoumi, Farouk. Secretary-general of Fatah's central committee and PLO's political department in Tunisia. Upon Arafat's death Kaddoumi constitutionally succeeded him to the position of Fatah chairman. No new elections have been held since, and he still occupies that post.

Kalb, Marvin. American journalist, a senior fellow at the Joan Shorenstein Center on the Press, Politics and Public Policy and Faculty Chair for the John F. Kennedy School of Government's Washington programs. He spent thirty years as an award-winning reporter for CBS News and NBC News. He is a regular contributor to Fox News, National Public Radio, and America Abroad.

Kashani, Ahmed. Son of Grand Ayatollah Abol Qassem Kashani and a participant in the nationalization of the Iranian oil industry.

Keegan Jr., George J. Former major general and air force intelligence chief who often annoyed the Pentagon with warnings about Soviet military preparations. Deceased.

Kennedy, Edward (Ted). Senior U.S. senator from Massachusetts and a member of the Democratic Party. In office since November 1962, he died during his eighth full (and ninth overall) term in the Senate. The most prominent member of the Kennedy family, he was the youngest brother of President John F. Kennedy and Senator Robert F. Kennedy, both victims of assassinations, and the father of Congressman Patrick J. Kennedy. Deceased.

Kennedy, John F. The 35th president of the United States, serving from 1961 until his assassination in 1963.

Kerr, Malcolm. Political scientist and teacher who was an expert on Middle East politics. On January 18, 1984, Kerr was shot and killed near his office, probably by members of the terrorist group Islamic Jihad.

Khalatbari, Abbas Ali. Former Iranian foreign minister, he, along with several former members of the Majlis (parliament) and more than two dozen generals, including the last chief of the air force and two former heads of SAVAK, the secret police, was found guilty and shot.

Khalkali, Sadegh. Hardline Twelver Shi'a cleric of the Islamic Republic of Iran who is said to have "brought to his job as chief justice of the revolutionary courts a relish for summary execution" that earned him a reputation as Iran's "hanging judge." He is known for having ordered the execution of the Shah's family wherever found anywhere in the world. Deceased.

Khan, Prince Aga. The 49th and current Imam of the Ismaili Muslims, he has been in this position and has held the title of Aga Khan since July 11, 1957.

Khosrowdad, General Manuchehr. Staunch supporter of the Shah and said to be an excellent pilot. Among the IRAA pilots, he is considered to be the father of Iranian military aviation. Executed.

Khalid, King. King of Saudi Arabia from the assassination of King Faisal in 1975 until his own death in 1982.

Khamenei, Ali Hoseyni, Ayatollah, politician, and cleric. He has been Supreme leader of Iran since 1989 and was president of

Iran from 1981 to 1989. He has been described as one of only three people having "important influences" on the Islamic Republic of Iran, the other two being Ayatollah Ruhollah Khomeini, leader of the revolution, and Ayatollah Akbar Hashemi Rafsanjani, president of Iran for much of the 1990s.

Khan, Abdul Qadeer. Pakistani nuclear scientist and metallurgical engineer, widely regarded as the founder of Pakistan's nuclear program. He is seen as a national hero and is credited with helping Muslim countries to develop nuclear weapons.

Khan, Genghis. Founder, Khan (ruler), and Khagan (emperor) of the Mongol Empire, the largest contiguous empire in history. During his lifetime the Mongol Empire eventually occupied a substantial portion of Central Asia.

Khan, Hulagu. Mongol ruler who conquered much of Southwest Asia. He was a grandson of Genghis Khan and the brother of Arik Boke, Möngke Khan, and Kublai Khan.

Khan, Mahmoud. Captured Isfahan, ending the Safavid dynasty.

Kharrazi, Kamal. Iranian minister of foreign affairs appointed by President Mohammad Khatami, serving for eight years from August 20, 1997, to August 24, 2005. He was replaced by Manouchehr Mottaki, who was appointed by President Mahmoud Ahmadinejad. He has held a number of governmental, diplomatic, and academic posts and has led Iranian delegations at numerous international conferences.

Khatami, Ahmad. Iranian cleric, writer, political analyst, critic of Azeri literature, and member of Assembly of Experts. He has strong ties with the Mahmoud Ahmadinejad and Grand Ayatollah Ali Khamenei.

Khatami, Seyed Mohammad. Elected the fifth president of the Islamic Republic of Iran in May 1997 elections. He was involved in political activities and anti-Shah campaign.

Khayyam, Omar. Persian polymath, mathematician, philosopher, astronomer, and poet. He has also become established as one of the major mathematicians and astronomers of the medieval period. Recognized as the author of the most important treatise on algebra before modern times.

Khrushchev, Nikita. Leader of the Soviet Union, serving as general secretary of the Communist Party of the Soviet Union from 1953 to 1964, following the death of Joseph Stalin, and chairman of the Council of Ministers from 1958 to 1964. His party colleagues removed him from power in 1964, replacing him with Leonid Brezhnev. Deceased.

Khomeini, Ayatollah Ruhollah. Iranian religious leader and politician and leader of the 1979 Iranian Revolution which saw the overthrow of Mohammad Reza Pahlavi, the late Shah of Iran. He became the country's Supreme leader—a position created in the constitution as the highest-ranking political and religious authority of the nation—until his death.

Khomeini, Mustafa. Elder son of the founder of Islamic Republic of Iran Ayatollah Sayed Ruhollah Khomeini, Mustafa was a distinguished scholar of the theological center in Qom, He died on October 23, 1997. Cause of death was officially listed as bulimia with heart complications, but anti-government forces claimed he was martyred by SAVAK, the Shah's police force.

King Jr., Martin Luther. American clergyman, activist, and prominent leader in the African-American Civil Rights Movement. His main legacy was to secure progress on civil rights in the U.S. He is recognized as a martyr by two Christian churches. A Baptist minister, King became a civil rights activist early in his career. Martin Luther King Jr. Day was established as a U.S. national holiday in 1986. Assassinated.

Kissinger, Henry. German-born, American political scientist, diplomat, and winner of the Nobel Peace Prize. He served as national security advisor and later concurrently as secretary of state in the Nixon administration.

Koob, Kathryn. One of sixty-six Americans held hostage by Iranian students in Tehran for the 444 days between November 4, 1979, and January 20, 1981. Today she is on the faculty of Wartburg College in Waverly, Iowa, and continues to be in demand as a public speaker.

L

Lahidji, A. E. Lawyer and vice president of the Paris-based International Federation of Human Rights Leagues (FIDH).

Laingen, Bruce. Senior American official held

hostage during the Iran hostage crisis. He had been sent to Iran as the U.S. chargé d'affaires. After his ordeal, Laingen was awarded the State Department's Award for Valor along with several other recognitions.

Laird, Melvin. Politician and writer, he was a Republican congressman who also served as Nixon's' secretary of defense from 1969 to 1973.

Lake, Anthony. Diplomat, political figure, and academic, he has been a foreign policy advisor to many Democratic U.S. presidents and presidential candidates, and has served as national security advisor under President Clinton from 1993 to 1997.

Larijani, Ali. Iranian philosopher, politician, and the chairman/speaker of the Iranian parliament. He was the secretary of the Supreme National Security Council from August 15, 2005, to October 20, 2007, appointed to the position by President Mahmoud Ahmadinejad. In his post as secretary he effectively functioned as the top negotiator on issues of national security, including Iran's nuclear program.

Levey, Stuart. Undersecretary for Terrorism and Financial Intelligence, a role he has held since his Senate confirmation on July 21, 2004, he leads an office which marshals the Treasury Department's policy, enforcement, regulatory, and intelligence functions to sever the lines of financial support to international terrorists, WMD proliferators, narcotics traffickers, and other threats to our national security.

Lubrani, Uri. One of the world's leading experts on Iran. Ambassador Lubrani has had a long and distinguished career in the service of the state of Israel. His posts have included head of Mission to Iran, Government Coordinator for Lebanese Affairs, Coordinator of the Rescue of Ethiopian Jews, chief negotiator for the release of Israeli hostages, and ambassador to several countries, including Ethiopia and Uganda.

M

Majidi, Abdol. Minister of planning and budget for the Shah of Iran.

Maraghei, Muhammad Saed. Became Iran's prime minister after the fall of Ali Soheili's cabinet in 1943. Iran-Russia relations fell to low levels during his government as he sternly refused to entertain Soviet demand for an oil concession in Soviet-occupied Northern Iran. He resigned in November 1944. Deceased.

Maranches, Alexandre de. French military officer. Among other things, he is known to have predicted the Soviet invasion of Afghanistan to an American journalist who immediately reported his conversation to U.S. National Security Advisor Zbigniew Brzezinski. Deceased.

Marcos, Imelda (Mrs. Ferdinand). Widow of former dictator Ferdinand and an influential political figure in the Philippines.

Mashai. Esfandiar Rahim. Iran's first vice president under Ahmadinejad, who was quoted as saying that the Iranians are friends of all people in the world—even Israelis.

McCarthy, Joseph. Politician who served as a Republican U.S. senator from the state of Wisconsin from 1947 until his death in 1957. He was noted for making claims that there were large numbers of Communists and Soviet spies and sympathizers inside the United States federal government and elsewhere. Ultimately, McCarthy's tactics and his inability to substantiate his claims led him to be discredited and censured by the United States Senate.

McGovern, George. Former U.S. Representative, Senator, and Democratic presidential nominee. McGovern lost the 1972 presidential election in a landslide to Nixon. As a decorated World War II combat veteran, he was known for his opposition to the Vietnam War.

Meese, Edwin. Attorney, law professor, and author who served in official capacities within the Reagan gubernatorial administration (1967-1974), the Reagan presidential transition team (1980), and the Reagan White House (1981-1985), eventually rising to hold the position of the seventy-fifth attorney general of the U.S. (1985-1988).

Meir, Golda. Fourth prime minister of the state of Israel, she was elected prime minister of Israel on March 17, 1969, after serving as minister of labour and foreign minister. She was Israel's first and the world's third female to hold such an office. Deceased.

Meyer, Armin. Former U.S. ambassador to Lebanon, Iran, and Japan. Deceased.

Miliband, David. British politician, who is the current secretary of state for Foreign and Commonwealth Affairs and

Member of Parliament for the constituency of South Shields.

Miller, G. William. Sixty-fifth U.S. secretary of the treasury under President Carter from August 6, 1979, to January 20, 1981, Miller was the first and currently only Federal Reserve chairman to come from a corporate background rather than from economics or finance. He is also the only person to have served both as Federal Reserve chairman and as Treasury secretary. Deceased.

Miller, William. Chief of staff to the Senate Select Committee on Intelligence.

Mina, Dr. Parviz. Born in Iran. He received his B.Sc. and Ph.D. degrees in petroleum engineering from the University of Birmingham in England. He served in the Iranian Oil Industry for twenty-five years, and his last position before the 1979 revolution was as a member of the board of directors and managing director of international affairs of the National Iranian Oil Company.

Mofaz, Shaul. Israeli politician and former soldier, who currently serves as a member of the Knesset for Kadima. He formerly served as former minister of defense, minister of transportation, and as the 16th chief of the general staff of the Israel Defense Forces.

Moffet, Toby. Politician from the state of Connecticut. A Democrat, Moffett served in the U.S. House of Representatives as the member from Connecticut's 6th congressional district from 1974 to 1983.

Moghaddam, General Nasser. Fourth and last chief of SAVAK, he succeeded General Nematollah Nassiri, who was arrested by the Shah's order in 1978. He was executed under Ayatollah Khomeini's order after the Iranian Revolution.

Mohammad, ibn Abdullah. Founder of the religion of Islam, he is contrarily regarded by Muslims as a messenger and prophet of God, the last and the greatest law-bearer in a series of Islamic prophets, as taught by the Qur'an. He was also active as a diplomat, merchant, philosopher, orator, legislator, reformer, military general, and, according to Muslim belief, an agent of divine action. Muhammad fell ill and suffered for several days with head pain and weakness and died in 632 in Medina. He is buried where he died, which was in his wife Aisha's house, and is now housed within the Mosque of the Prophet in Medina.

Next to Muhammad's tomb there is another empty tomb that Muslims believe awaits Jesus.

Mondale, Walter. Politician and member of the Democratic-Farmer-Labor Party. He was the 42nd vice president of the United States (1977–1981) under President Carter, a two-term U.S. senator from Minnesota, and the Democratic Party nominee for president in 1984. Later, during the administration of Democratic President Clinton, he served as the United States ambassador to Japan from 1993-1996.

Mordecai. Son of Jair, of the tribe of Benjamin, one of the main personalities in the book of Esther in the Hebrew Bible.

Mossadegh, Mohammad. Prime minister of Iran from 1951 to 1953, when he was removed from power by a coup d'état. He was an author, administrator, lawyer, prominent parliamentarian, and politician, famous for his passionate opposition to foreign intervention in Iran. Deceased.

Mottaki, Manouchehr. Iranian minister of foreign affairs. While technically appointed by President Mahmoud Ahmadinejad, he is considered to be closer to more pragmatic conservative factions, and during the 2005 presidential election he was the campaign manager of Ali Larijani, the right-conservative candidate.

Mousavi (or Moussavi), Mir-Hossein. Iranian reformist politician, painter, and architect, who served as the fifth and last prime minister of the Islamic Republic of Iran from 1981 to 1989. Mousavi was a candidate for the 2009 presidential election. He was the last prime minister in Iran before the 1989 constitutional changes, which removed the post of prime minister.

Muawiyah I. A deeply controversial figure in Islam, initially he was one of the staunchest enemies of Mohammad and of Islam and the heir-apparent to the pagan throne of Mecca, which was occupied in effect by his father Abu Sofyan and mother Hinda. After the defeat of his family following the fall of Mecca, Muawiyah declared that he was now a Muslim and hence is regarded within Sunni Islam as a Sahabi (companion) of the Islamic prophet Muhammad. Shia Muslims refuse to recognize the sincerity of his conversion and cite as evidence his allegedly being cursed by Mohammad.

Murrow, Edward R. American broadcast journalist. He first came to prominence with a series of radio news broadcasts during World War II, which were followed by millions of listeners in the U.S. and Canada. He resigned from CBS to accept a position offered by President Kennedy as head of the United States Information Agency, parent of the Voice of America, in 1961. Deceased.

Muskie, Edmund. Democratic politician from Maine, he served as governor of Maine, as U.S. senator, and as U.S. secretary of state. He was the Democratic nominee for vice president in 1968 and was a candidate for the 1972 Democratic presidential nomination. Deceased.

N

Naas, Charles. U.S. diplomat. Deceased.

Nabonidus. Last king of the Neo-Babylonian Empire, reigning from 556-539 BCE.

Nahavandi, Houchang. Chief of shahbanu Farah's Secretariat (1976-78), minister of science and higher education (1978), arrested by the Bakhtiar government, escaped from prison, and took up residence in Paris (1979).

Nakash, Anis. Professional assassin, who was apprehended and imprisoned while in the employ of Iran and while making an attempt on the life of Shafur Baktiar in Paris.

Napoleon (Bonaparte). Later known as Emperor Napoleon I and previously Napoleone di Buonaparte, he was a military and political leader of France whose actions shaped European politics in the early 19th century. He emancipated Jews from laws that restricted them to ghettos and expanded their rights to property, worship, and careers.

Nasser, Gamal Abdul. Second president of Egypt from 1956 until his death in 1970. Along with Muhammad Naguib, he led the Egyptian Revolution of 1952, which removed King Farouk.

Nassiri, Nematollah. Director of SAVAK, the Iranian intelligence agency during the rule of Mohammad Reza Pahlavi. In late 1978 Nassiri was imprisoned with several other high-ranking officials. On February 16, 1979, he was executed by firing squad after a summary trial.

Nebuchadnezzar. Ruler of Babylon in the Chaldean Dynasty, he is mentioned in the book of Daniel and constructed the Hanging Gardens of Babylon. He conquered Judah and Jerusalem and sent the Jews into exile.

Nehemiah. Lived during the period when Judah (Israel) was a province of the Persian Empire. Helped oversee reconstruction of the Jewish Temple.

Netanyahu, Benjamin. Current prime minister of Israel, he previously held the position from June 1996 to July 1999 and is currently the chairman of the Likud Party. Netanyahu is the first (and, to date, only) Israeli prime minister born after the state of Israel's foundation. Netanyahu was foreign minister (2002-2003) and finance minister (2003-August 2005) in Ariel Sharon's governments.

Nimrodi, Yaacov. Israeli businessman, who played a central role in the early phase of the Iran arms affair.

Nissim, Moshe. Former Israeli politician, minister, and deputy prime minister. He was appointed minister without portfolio in Menachem Begin's government in January 1978. He became minister of justice in August 1980, a role he retained until April 1986, when he became minister of finance.

Nixon, Richard. Thirty-seventh president of the United States (1969–1974) and the only president to resign the office, he was also the 36th vice president of the United States (1953–1961) under President Eisenhower. Deceased.

O

Obama, Barack Hussein. The 44th president of the United States and the first African American to hold the office, Obama had previously been the junior U.S. senator from Illinois, serving from January 2005 until November 2008, when he resigned after his election to the presidency.

O'Hare, Madelyn Murray. The founder of American Atheists and, either openly or behind the scenes, was its president from 1963 to 1995. She is best known for the lawsuit that led to a landmark Supreme Court ruling that ended the practice of daily prayer in American public schools. She was murdered in 1995, along with her son and granddaughter.

Olahi, Admiral Kamilladin. Iranian naval commander under the Shah.

O'Neill, John. American anti-terrorism expert, who worked as a special agent and eventually assistant director in the Federal Bureau of Investigation until late 2001. In 1995 O'Neill began to intensely study the roots of the 1993 World Trade Center bombing. He subsequently learned of Al-Qaeda and Osama bin Laden and investigated the 1996 Khobar Towers bombing in Saudi Arabia and the 2000 USS Cole bombing in Yemen. O'Neill left the FBI to become the head of security at the World Trade Center, where he died at age forty-nine in the September 11, 2001, attacks.

Oveissi, General Gholam ali. Appointed military governor of Tehran to detain all suspects and enforce a dawn-to-dusk curfew. Shortly after these measures were enacted, a confrontation between SAVAK and Iranian citizens resulted in a considerable loss if lives (by some estimates, between 300 and 500). Oveissi was blamed for this and was assassinated in Paris in 1985 by Khomeini's agents.

P

Pacepa, General Ion. Highest-ranking intelligence official ever to have defected from the former Eastern Bloc, he is now a U.S. citizen, a writer, and a columnist.

Pahlavi, Ashraf. Twin sister of Mohammad Reza Pahlavi, the late Shah of Iran and the Pahlavi Dynasty.

Pahlavi, Farah. Widow of Mohammad Reza Pahlavi, the last Shah of Iran, and only empress of modern Iran. Though the titles and distinctions of the Iranian imperial family were abolished by the new government, she often is styled empress or shahbanu out of courtesy by foreign media as well as by supporters of the former monarchy.

Pahlavi, Mohammad Reza Shah. Monarch of Iran from September 16, 1941, until his overthrow by the Iranian Revolution on February 11, 1979, he was the second and last monarch of the House of Pahlavi of the Iranian monarchy. Deceased.

Pahlavi, Reza Cyrus. Eldest son of the late Emperor of Iran Shah Mohammad Reza Pahlavi and his shahbanou or Empress Consort Farah. He was the crown prince of Iran until the Iranian Revolution. He succeeded his father as head of the House of the Pahlavi dynasty.

Pahlavi, Reza Shah. An officer in Iran's Persian Cossack Brigade, he used his troops to support a successful coup against the government of the Qajar dynasty in 1921. In 1925 a specially convened assembly deposed Ahmad Shah Qajar, the last ruler of the Qajar dynasty, and named Reza Khan, who earlier had adopted the surname Pahlavi, as the new Shah. Handed the reigns of government over to his son, Mohammad Reza, in 1941.

Pakravan, Hassan. Well-known diplomat and minister in the Pahlavi pre-revolutionary government of Iran, he is not only notable for his political involvement with the Mohammad Reza Shah government and SAVAK but also his relationship with Ayatollah Ruhollah Khomeini. Deceased.

Parsons, Sir Anthony. British undersecretary for the Middle East and later United Kingdom permanent representative to the United Nations between 1979 and 1982. Deceased.

Percy, Charles (Chuck). Chairman of the Bell & Howell Corporation from 1949 to 1964 and United States senator from Illinois from 1967 to 1985.

Peres, Shimon. Ninth and current president of the state of Israel. He served twice as prime minister of Israel, once as interim prime minister, and has been a member of twelve cabinets in a political career spanning over sixty-six years.

Philip, Prince. Husband of Queen Elizabeth II since November 20, 1947, and her consort since February 6, 1952, Philip was originally a royal prince of Greece and Denmark.

Polo, Marco. Trader and explorer from the Venetian Republic, who gained fame for his worldwide travels as recorded in the book Il Milione ("The Million" or The Travels of Marco Polo). Marco, his father Niccolò, and his uncle Maffeo were some of the first Westerners to travel the Silk Road to China (which he referred to as Cathay) and visit Kublai Khan, the founder of the Yuan Dynasty.

Pompidou, Georges. Politician and prime minister of France from 1962 to 1968, he held this position for the longest tenure and later was president of the French Republic from 1969 until his death in 1974.

Poniatowski, Michel. Polish prince and French politician. He was a founder of the Independent Republicans and a part of the administration for President Valéry Giscard d'Estaing. He served as minister of health from 1973 to 1974 and minister of the interior in the d'Estaing government from 1974 to 1977. Deceased.

Precht, Henry. Political officer in the American Embassy in Tehran from 1972 to 1976 and chief of the Iran Desk in the U.S. State Department.

Pryce-Jones, David. Conservative British author and commentator, his most recent book accuses the French government of being anti-Semitic, pro-Arab, and of consistently siding against Israel in the hope of winning the favor of the Islamic world.

Q

Qaddafi, Muammar. The defacto leader of Libya since a 1969 coup, although he has held no public office or title since 1979. With the death of Omar Bongo of Gabon on June 8, 2009, he became the third-longest serving head of state.

Qutb, Sayyid. Egyptian author, educator, Islamist, poet, and the leading intellectual of the Egyptian Muslim Brotherhood in the 1950s and '60s; according to some he is "the man whose ideas would shape Al-Qaeda." Deceased.

R

Rabii, General Amirheossein. Iranian air force commander. Tried and executed by firing squad in the aftermath of the revolution.

Rabin, Yitzhak. Israeli politician and general, he was the fifth prime minister of Israel, serving two terms in office, 1974–1977 and 1992, until his assassination in 1995. In 1994 Rabin won the Nobel Peace Prize together with Shimon Peres and Yasser Arafat. He was assassinated by right-wing Israeli radical Yigal Amir, who was opposed to Rabin's signing of the Oslo Accords.

Rafsanjani Akbar Hashemi, Ayatollah, influential politician, writer, and former president, he currently holds the position of chairman of the Assembly of Experts. In 2005 he ran for a third term in office, losing to Mahmoud Ahmadinejad in the run-off round of the election.

Rajabi, Fatemeh. Journalist wife of Gholam Hossein Elham, a government spokesman and one of Ahmadinejad's most trusted confidants, Rajabi sometimes appears in the press more often than her husband. Furthermore, she has openly attacked Rafsanjani's allies for being corrupt and Ayatollah Khatami for being too liberal and friendly toward the West.

Rajavi, Maryam. Wife of Massoud Rajavi, a founder of the People's Mojahedin Organization of Iran (PMOI), she is the "president elect" of the National Council of Resistance of Iran.

Rajavi, Masoud. President of National Council of Resistance of Iran and the leader of People's Mujahedin of Iran (PMOI, also known as the MEK), a militant opposition organization active outside of Iran. After leaving Iran in 1981, he resided in France and Iraq. Since the 2003 invasion of Iraq he has not made any public appearances and is presumed to be either dead or in hiding.

Rainier, Prince. Ruled the Principality of Monaco for more than fifty years, making him one of the longest ruling monarchs of the 20th century. He was best known outside of Europe for having married American actress Grace Kelly. Deceased.

Raskin, Marcus. Prominent American social critic, political activist, author, and philosopher, working for progressive social change in the United States, he is the co-founder, with the late Richard Barnet, of the progressive think tank, the Institute for Policy Studies in Washington, D.C.

Rassam, Hormuzd. Assyriologist and traveler, who made a number of important and independent discoveries, including clay tablets that would later be deciphered as the world's oldest-known example of written literature.

Reagan, Ronald. Fortieth president of the United States and the 33rd governor of California, he began a career in radio. Later he went into filmmaking and then television, making fifty-two films and gaining enough success to make him a household name. Originally a member of the Democratic Party, he switched to the Republican Party in 1962. Deceased.

Ribicoff, Abraham. Democratic Party politician, who served in the U.S. Congress, was governor of Connecticut, and was President Kennedy's secretary of health, education, and welfare. Deceased.

Rice, Condoleezza. Professor, diplomat, author, and national security expert, she served as the 66th U.S. secretary of state.

Richardson, Elliott. Lawyer and politician, who was a member of the cabinet of presidents Nixon and Ford. As U.S. attorney general he was a prominent figure in the Watergate Scandal and resigned rather than refuse President Nixon's order to fire special prosecutor Archibald Cox. Deceased.

Rockefeller, David. Banker, statesman, globalist, and current patriarch of the Rockefeller family. He is the youngest and only surviving child of John D. Rockefeller Jr. and the only surviving grandchild of billionaire oil tycoon John D. Rockefeller, founder of Standard Oil.

Rockefeller, Nelson. Forty-first vice president of the United States, the 49th governor of New York, a philanthropist, and a businessman, he retired from politics when his term as vice president was over. Deceased.

Rogers, William P. Politician, who served as a cabinet officer in the administrations of both Eisenhower and Nixon. Deceased.

Romanoff, Tsar Nicholas. Last Emperor of Russia, Grand Duke of Finland, and claimed the title of King of Poland. Nicholas II ruled from 1894 until his abdication on March 15, 1917. On July 16, 1918, Bolshevik authorities, led by Yakov Yurovsky, shot Nicholas II, his immediate family, and four servant members in the cellar of a house in Yekaterinburg, Russia.

Roosevelt, Franklin Delano. Thirty-second President of the United States, he was a central figure of the 20th century during a time of worldwide economic crisis and world war. Elected to four terms in office, he served from 1933 to 1945 and is the only U.S. president to have served more than two terms. Deceased.

Roosevelt, Kermit (Kim). A son of U.S. President Theodore Roosevelt, Kermit was an explorer on two continents with his father, a graduate of Harvard University, served as a soldier in two world wars with both the British and U.S. armies, a businessman, and a writer. He fought a lifelong battle with depression and alcoholism and eventually committed suicide.

Rowhani, Hasan. Iranian politician and cleric and a member of the Supreme National Security Council, Rowhani's membership in the council is as one of the two representatives of the Ayatollah Khamenei, the Supreme leader of Iran. He was the chief negotiator with the European countries of UK, France, and Germany over Iran's nuclear program.

Roxana. Wife of Alexander the Great. She married Alexander at the age of eighteen. The marriage was an attempt to reconcile the Bactrian satrapies to Alexander's rule, although ancient sources describe Alexander's professed love for her. She bore him a posthumous son called Alexander IV Aegus, after Alexander's sudden death at Babylon in 323 BC. With the king's death, Roxana and her son became victims of the political intrigues of the collapse of the Alexandrian empire and were subsequently assassinated around 310 BC.

S

Sadat, Anwar el. Third president of Egypt, serving from October 15, 1970, until his assassination on October 6, 1981.

Sadat, Jehan. Widow of Anwar Sadat and, as such, first lady of Egypt from 1970 until Sadat's assassination in 1981. She is the recipient of several national and international awards for public service and humanitarian efforts for women and children.

Sadeghi, Gholam Hossein. Iranian minister of the interior under Mossadegh.

Sadiqi, Hossein. One of the leaders of Iran's National Font and the Shah's first choice as prime minister.

Sadr, Abullhassan Bani. First president of Iran following the 1979 Iranian Revolution and abolition of the monarchy. He soon fell out with Khomeini, who reclaimed the power of commander-in-chief on June 10, 1981.

Saeedi, Mohammad. Deputy head of Iran's Atomic Energy Organization.

Saleh, General Ataollah. Current commander-in-chief of the Iranian army since 2005, he has direct operational command authority over the commanders of the Iranian army's ground forces, air force, and navy.

Salinger, Pierre. White House press secretary to U.S. Presidents Kennedy and Johnson, he later became known for his work as an ABC News correspondent. He served briefly as a Democratic U.S. senator in 1964 and was campaign manager for the Robert F. Kennedy presidential campaign.

Sanjabi, Karim. An Iranian liberal political leader of the 20th century, he is notable as being one of the founders of the National Front (Iran). Deceased.

Sapir, Pinchas. Israeli politician during the first three decades following the country's founding, he held two important ministerial posts: minister of finance (1963-1968 and 1969-1974) and minister of trade and industry. Deceased.

Sarkozy, Nicolas. Twenty-third president of the French Republic, he assumed the office on May 16, 2007.

Saunders, Harold. Veteran high-ranking U.S. diplomat who participated in the 1978 Camp David Peace Accords involving U.S. President Jimmy Carter.

Scheherazade. Legendary Persian queen and the storyteller of One Thousand and One Nights.

Schlesinger, James R. Secretary of defense from 1973 to 1975 under presidents Nixon and Ford. He became America's first secretary of energy under Carter.

Schmidt, Helmut. German Social Democratic politician who served as chancellor of West Germany from 1974 to 1982. Prior to becoming chancellor, he had served as minister of defense and minister of finance.

Schwarzkopf Sr., Norman. Before retiring from the army in 1953 with the rank of major general, he was sent by the CIA as part of Operation Ajax to convince the exiled Shah of Iran, Mohammad Reza Pahlavi, to return and seize power. Schwarzkopf went so far as to organize the security forces he had trained to support the Shah. As such he helped to train what would later be known as SAVAK. He was the father of General H. Norman Schwarzkopf, the commander of all coalition forces for Operation Desert Shield/Storm.

Schwimmer, Adolph. Used his contacts and experience as a World War II flight engineer for the U.S. Air Transport Command to smuggle some thirty surplus war planes to the nascent Jewish state in 1948. In the eyes of federal law enforcers he had violated the U.S. Neutrality Act and faced charges when he returned to America in 1950. Convicted of violating the Neutrality Act to help Israel build an air force, he was later pardoned by President Clinton.

Segev, Samuel. Free Press Middle East correspondent.

Segev, General Yitzhak. Israeli military attaché in Tehran from 1977 to 1979.

Selassie, Haile. Ethiopia's regent from 1916 to 1930 and Emperor of Ethiopia from 1930 to 1974.

Shafigh, Shahryar. Son of Princess Ashraf Pahlavi, the twin sister of Mohammad Reza Shah Pahlavi, and Ahmad Shafiq of Egypt. After exile he joined his family in Paris, France, and began organizing a resistance movement inside Iran. He was assassinated in Paris on December 7, 1979, being shot twice in the head.

Shah, Nader (or Nadir). Ruled as Shah of Iran (1736–47) and was the founder of the Afsharid dynasty. Because of his military genius, some historians have described him as the Napoleon of Persia or the Second Alexander. His victories briefly made him the Middle East's most powerful sovereign, but his empire quickly disintegrated after he was assassinated in 1747.

shahryar. Ruled over a Persian Empire that extended to India, all the adjacent islands, and beyond the Ganges as far as China.

Shairatmadari, Ayatollah. At the time of the Iranian revolution in 1979 he was the leading Grand Ayatollah in Qom. He criticized Khomeini's system of government as not being compatible with Islam or representing the will of the Iranian people. He severely criticized the way that a referendum was conducted to establish Khomeini's system of government. This led Khomeini to put him under house arrest, imprison his family members, and torture his daughter-in-laws. Deceased.

Shaeffer, Francis. American evangelical Christian theologian, philosopher, and Presbyterian pastor. A number of scholars credit Schaeffer's ideas with helping spark the rise of the Christian Right in the United States. Deceased.

Shamir, Yitzhak. Prime minister of Israel from 1983 to 1984 and again from 1986 to 1992.

Shariati, Ali. Highly influential Iranian revolutionary and sociologist, who focused on the sociology of religion, he is known as one of the most original and influential Iranian social thinkers of the 20th century. Deceased.

Sharon, Ariel. Israeli general and statesman and former Israeli prime minister, he served as prime minister from March 2001 until April 2006, although he was unable to carry out his duties after suffering a stroke on January 4, 2006, when he fell into a coma and entered a persistent vegetative state.

Shariatmadari, Ayatollah. Among the most senior leading Twelver Shi'a clerics in Iran and Iraq, he is known for his forward-looking and liberal views. Deceased.

Sharif-Emami, Jafar. Prime minister of Iran, a cabinet minister, president of the Iranian senate, president of the Pahlavi Foundation, president of the Iran Chamber of Industries and Mines, and twice prime minister of Iran during the reign of Shah Mohammad Reza Pahlavi. Deceased.

Shafiq, Mohammad Musa. Afghan politician and poet, he became foreign minister in 1971 and prime minister in December 1972. He lost both positions when Mohammed Zahir Shah was overthrown on July 17, 1973. Executed.

Shawcross, Hartley Lord. British jurist and attorney general, he was leader of the British prosecution at the Nuremberg Trials after World War II. Deceased.

Shi, Qiao. Politician in the People's Republic of China. A recognized international studies expert within the Communist Party, Shi was at one time ranked third in the Communist Party leadership. Despite Western speculation in the 1990s, he never rose to paramount power and retired in 1998.

Shomron, Dan. Thirteenth chief of staff of the Israel Defense Forces from 1987 to 1991, during the Six-Day War he commanded a unit on the Egyptian front and was the first paratrooper to reach the Suez Canal. In 1974 he received the command over the Infantry and Paratroopers Branch of the Israeli army. In this function, he had command over Operation Entebbe in 1976. Deceased.

Shukeiri, Ahmed. First Chairman of the Palestine Liberation Organization from 1964–1967. Deceased.

Sick, Gary. American academic, author, and analyst of Middle East affairs, with special expertise on Iran, who served on the U.S. National Security Council under three presidents.

Soleimani, Ghasem. Director of Uranium Mining Operations at the Saghand Uranium Mine; listed in an annex to U.N. Security Council resolution 1803 of March 3, 2008, as a person linked to Iran's proliferation of sensitive nuclear activities or development of nuclear weapon delivery systems.

Spargapises. Son of Queen Tomyris, captured by the Persian king, Kyrus the Great, who, using him as a hostage, tried to force Queen Tomyris to surrender. He persuaded Kyrus to free him from his bonds and managed to escape. Afterward the Massagetae army defeated the Persians and killed Kyrus.

Stalin, Joseph. General secretary of the Communist Party of the Soviet Union's Central Committee from 1922 until his death in 1953, in the years following Lenin's death in 1924 he rose to become the leader of the Soviet Union.

Stassen, Harold. Twenty-fifth governor of Minnesota from 1939 to 1943. His name has become most identified with his fame as a perennial candidate for other offices, most notably and frequently president of the United States. Deceased.

Stempel, John. Served twenty-three years in the U.S. Foreign Service, including postings in Guinea, Burundi, Zambia, and Iran.

Sullivan, William. Career foreign service officer, he served as U.S. ambassador to Laos in 1964, the Philippines in 1973, and Iran from 1977 to 1979.

Swift (Cronin), Elizabeth Ann. Forty-year-old political officer at the United States Embassy in Tehran in 1979 when a mob of students commandeered the compound and took sixty-six Americans hostage. Upon her release from captivity, Cronin spent a year at Harvard's Center for International Affairs. She remained with the State Department and became a consular officer serving in Greece, Jamaica, and England. From 1989 to 1992 she served as the deputy assistant secretary of state for overseas citizens services, and she retired in 1995.

T

Taheri, Amir. Iranian-born conservative journalist and author based in Europe, his writings focus on the Middle East affairs and topics related to Islamist terrorism. He is also a former son-in-law of the late Shah of Iran.

Taleghani, Ayatollah Mahmoud. Iranian theologian, Muslim reformer, and a senior Shi'a cleric of Iran, Taleghani was a contemporary of the Iranian revolutionary leader Ayatollah Ruhollah Khomeini. He was instrumental in "shaping the groundswell movement" that led to the Iranian Revolution and brought Khomeini to power. Deceased.

Talib, Ali ibn Abi. Cousin and son-in-law of the Islamic prophet Muhammad, he ruled over the Islamic Caliphate from 656 to 661. Sunni Muslims consider Ali the fourth and final of the Rashidun (rightly guided Caliphs), while Shi'a Muslims regard Ali as the first Imam and consider him and his descendants the rightful successors to Muhammad. This disagreement split the Muslim community into the Sunni and Shi'a branches.

Tavakoli, Mohammed. Also known as Tavassoli, he was the principal mediator between Iran's revolutionary government and the U.S. embassy. He later was named governor of Tehran.

Tehrani, Dr. Ahmed. Ambassador under the Shah of Iran.

Thatcher, Margaret. British politician and prime minister of the United Kingdom from 1979 to 1990, she was the leader of the Conservative Party from 1975 to 1990. She is the only woman to have held either post.

Tito, Marshall. Yugoslav revolutionary and statesman, he was secretary-general and later president of the Communist Party (League of Communists), prime minister (1945–53), and later president of Yugoslavia. Deceased.

Tomseth, Victor. Worked for thirty years as a foreign service officer in Thailand, Iran, and Sri Lanka, and was U.S. ambassador to Laos from 1993 to 1996. He was among the fifty Americans held hostage for 444 days in Iran. He is a member of a group of over three hundred retired foreign service officers who supported Barack Obama's candidacy.

Tomyris. Queen who reigned over the Massagetae, an Iranic people of Central Asia east of the Caspian Sea, in approximately 530 B.C.

Torrijos, General Omar. Commander of the Panamanian National Guard and the de facto leader of Panama from 1968 to 1981, he never held elected office in Panama and was never president. Although he was considered a leftist dictator, he simultaneously had the support of the U.S. because he opposed communism. His politics were based on progressivism. He is best known for negotiating the 1977 treaties that eventually gave Panama full sovereignty over the Panama Canal.

Toufanian, General Hasan. Iranian vice minister of war and head of military procurement. Deceased.

Trudeau, Pierre. Fifteenth prime minister of Canada from April 20, 1968, to June 4, 1979, and from March 3, 1980, to June 30, 1984.

Turner, Stansfield. Retired admiral and former director of the Central Intelligence Agency, he is currently a senior research scholar at the University of Maryland.

Truman, Harry. Thirty-third president of the United States (1945–1953). As the 34th vice president, he succeeded Franklin D. Roosevelt, who died less than three months after he began his fourth term. Deceased.

U, V

Vance, Cyrus. U.S. secretary of state under President Carter from 1977 to 1980. In April 1980, Vance resigned in protest of Operation Eagle Claw, the secret mission to rescue American hostages in Iran. He was succeeded by Edmund Muskie. Deceased.

Vashti. Wife of king Ahasuerus who was replaced by Esther. She is part of the story behind the Jewish holiday of Purim, one of Judaism's festivals.

Villalon, Hector. Expatriate Argentine hired to negotiate an agreement that would free the U.S. hostages in Iran

W

Waldheim, Kurt. Austrian diplomat and politician, he was secretary-general of the UN from 1972 to 1981,and president of Austria from 1986 to 1992. Deceased.

Washington, George. Commander of the Continental army in the American Revolutionary War he served as the first president of the United States of America (1789–1797). For his central role in the formation of the United States, he is often referred to as the father of his country.

Weizman, Ezer. Seventh president of Israel, serving a seven-year term from 1993 to 2000, before the presidency he was commander of the Israeli air force and minister of defense. Deceased.

X

Xerxes I. The son of Darius the Great and descendent of Cyrus the Great, he succeeded his father in 486 BC with a smooth transition of power challenged by no subject nation of the huge Achaemenid empire.

Y

Yazdi, Ebrahim. Secretary-general of the Freedom Movement of Iran, which is considered an "illegal party" by some factions within the Iranian government. The stated goals of the Freedom Movement include guarding against abuses of the constitution, abuses of civil rights, and expanding opportunities.

Yazid, Caliph. Second caliph of the Umayyad Caliphate, he ruled for three years until his death in 683 CE. He is the object of strong animosity for a large faction of modern Muslims, most notably Shi'ites. His mother was a Christian Arab.

Young, Andrew. American politician, diplomat, and pastor from Georgia who has served as mayor of Atlanta, a congressman from the 5th District, and U.S. ambassador to the United Nations. He served as president of the National Council of Churches USA and was a supporter and friend of the Rev. Dr. Martin Luther King Jr.

Ysafrir, Eliezer. Senior Mossad (Israeli national intelligence agency) official.

Z

Zahedi, Ardeshir. Iranian diplomat during the 1960s and 1970s, serving as the country's foreign minister and its ambassador to the U.S. and the United Kingdom.

Zahedi, Fazlollah. Iranian general who named himself prime minister in 1953 after helping the U.S. and Britain overthrow Iran's elected government. Deceased.

Zand, Karim Khan. Ruler and de facto Shah of Iran from 1760 until 1779. He founded the Zand dynasty. He never styled himself as shah or king and instead used the title president. He was one of the generals of Nader Shah Afshar.

Zimmerman, Warren. Diplomat, humanitarian, and the last U.S. ambassador to Yugoslavia before its disintegration into civil war. He served in Moscow (1973-75 and 1981-84), Paris, Caracas, and Vienna, where he headed the US delegation at the Conference on Security and Cooperation in Europe. Deceased.

APPENDIX B:
BIBLIOGRAPHY

- -

Abrahamian, Ervand. Iran Between Two Revolutions. Princeton: Princeton University Press, 1982.

Alam, Asadollah. The Shah and I: The Confidential Diary of Iran's Royal Court 1969-1977. New York: St. Martin's Press, 1993.

Amuzegar, Jahangir. The Dynamics of the Iranian Revolution. Albany: State University of New York Press, 1991.

Arjomand, Said. The Turban for the Crown: The Islamic Revolution of Iran. New York: Oxford University Press, 1988.

Ball, George. The Past Has Another Pattern, Memoirs. New York: W. W. Norton & Co., 1982.

Bill, James A. George Ball: Behind the Scenes of U.S. Foreign Policy. New Haven: Yale University Press, 1997.

Bill, James A. The Eagle and the Lion: The Tragedy of American-Iranian Relations. New Haven: Yale University Press, 1988.

Brzezinski, Zbigniew. Power and Principle. Toronto, Canada: McGraw Hill, 1983.

Carter, Jimmy. Keeping Faith. Fayetteville: University of Arkansas Press, 1983.

Carter, Jimmy, and Don Richardson. Conversations with Carter. Boulder, CO: Lynne Rienner Publishers, 1998.

Chehabi, H. E. Iranian Politics and Religious Modernism: the Liberation Movement of Iran under the Shah and Khomeini. Ithaca: Cornell University Press, 1990.

Dayan, Moshe. Breakthrough. New York: Alfred Knopf, 1981.

Eisenhower, Dwight. Mandate for Change: 1953-1956: The White House Years. Garden City: Doubleday, 1963.

Evans, Michael D. The American Prophecies. New York: Warner Faith, 2004.

Evans, Michael, with Jerome Corsi. Showdown with Nuclear Iran. Nashville, TN: Thomas Nelson, 2006.

Evans, Mike. The Final Move Beyond Iraq. Lake Mary, FL: Strang, 2007.

Farber, D. Taken Hostage: The Iran Hostage Crisis and America's First Encounter with Radical Islam. Princeton, NJ: Princeton University Press, 2005.

Fardust, Hussein, and Ali Akbar Dareini. The Rise and Fall of the Pahlavi Dynasty: Memoirs of Former General Hussein. Bangalore, India: Motilal Banarsidass, 1999.

Farmanfarmaian, Manucher, and Roxane Farmanfarmaian. Blood and Oil. New York: Ransom House, 1997.

Ganji, Manoucher. Defying the Iranian Revolution: From a Minister to the Shah to a Leader of Resistance. Westport: Praeger, 2002.

Haig, Jr., Alexander M., with Charles McCarry. Inner Circles: How America Changed the World. New York: Warner Books, 1992.

Harris, David. The Crisis. New York: Little, Brown & Co., 2004.

Heikal, Mohamed. Iran: The Untold Story. New York: Pantheon, 1982.

Helms, Cynthia. An Ambassador's Wife in Iran. New York: Dodd, Mead 1981.

Huyser, Robert E. Mission to Tehran. New York: Harper & Row, 1986.

Kapuscinski, Ryszard. Shah of Shahs. New York: Random House, 1992.

Kessler, Ronald. Inside the White House. New York: Pocket Books, 1995.

Khomeini, Imam Ruhollah, and Hamid Algar trans. and annot. Islam and Revolution: Writings and Declarations. London: Routledge & Kegan Paul, 1981.

Kissinger Henry. White House Years. Boston: Little, Brown, 1979.

Kupelian, David. The Marketing of Evil. Nashville: Cumberland House, 2005.

Ledeen, Michael, and William Lewis. Debacle: the American Failure in Iran. New York: Alfred A. Knopf, 1981.

Leeden, Michael. The War Against the Terror Masters: Why it Happened, Where Are We Now, and How We'll Win. New York: MacMillan, 2003.

Lenczowski, George. American Presidents and the Middle East. Durham: Duke University Press, 1990.

Lilienthal, David. The Journals of David E. Lilianthal: The Harvest Years, 1959-1963. New York: Harper and Row, 1971.

Menashri, David. Post-Revolutionary Politics in Iran. London: Frank Cass, 2001.

Milani, Mohsen M. The Making of Iran's Islamic Revolution: From Monarchy to Islamic Republic. Boulder, CO Westview Press, 1994.

Mohammadi, Annabelle Sreberny and Ali. Small Media, Big Revolution: Communication, Culture and the Iranian. Minneapolis: University of Minnesota Press, 1994.

Moin, Baqer Khomeini. Life of the Ayatollah. New York: McMillan, 2000.

Montazam, Mir Ali Asghar. The Life and Times of Ayatollah Khomeini. London: Anglo-European Publishing, 1994.

Nahavandi, Houchang. The Last Shah of Iran. United Kingdom: Aquilion Ltd, 2005.

Netanyahu, Benjamin. Terrorism: How the West Can Win. New York: Farrar-Strauss-Giroux, 1986.

Pahlavi, Farah. An Enduring Love. New York: Hyperion, 1987.

Pahlavi, Mohammad Reza. Answer to History. New York: Stein & Day, 1980.

Parsa, Misagh. The Social Origins of the Iranian Revolution. Brunswick, N.J.: Rutgers University Press, 1989.

Parsi, Trita. Treacherous Alliance. New Haven: Yale University Press, 2007.

Roosevelt, Elliot. FDR: His Personal Letters. New York: Duell, Sloan and Pierce, 1947.

Rubin, Barry. Paved with Good Intentions. New York: Oxford Press, 1980.

Salinger, Pierre. America Held Hostage: the Secret Negotiations. Garden City: Doubleday, 1981.

Schaeffer. Francis A. The Great Evangelical Disaster. Westchester, IL: Crossway Books, 1984.

Segev, Samuel. The Iranian Triangle. New York: Free Press, 1988.

Seliktar, Ofira. Failing the Crystal Ball Test. Westport: Praeger, 2000.

Shawcross, William. The Shah's Last Ride. New York: Simon & Schuster, 1988.

Sick, Gary. All Fall Down. New York: Random House, 1986.

Sick, Gary. October Surprise. New York: Random House, 1992.

Simpson, John & Shubart, Tira. Lifting the Vail. Philadelphia: Coronet Books, 1995.

Silver, Eric. Begin: The Haunted Prophet. New York: Random House, 1984.

Smith, Tony. America's Mission: The United States and the Worldwide Struggle for Democracy in the Twentieth Century. Princeton, NJ: Princeton University Press, 1994.

Sobhani, Sohrab. The Pragmatic Entente: Israeli-Iranian Relations, 1948-1988. New York: Praeger, 1989.

Sullivan, William. Mission to Iran. New York: W.W. Norton, 1981.

Taheri, Ahmed. Holy Terror, The Inside Story of Islamic Terrorism. London: Sphere Books, Hutchinson Ltd, 1987.

Taheri, Amir. Nest of Spies. New York: Pantheon Books, 1988.

Taheri, Amir. The Spirit of Allah: Khomeini and the Islamic Revolution. Bethesda, MD: Adler & Adler, 1985.

Thornton, R.C. The Carter Years: Toward a New Global Order. New York: Paragon House, 2007.

Turner, Adm. Stansfield. Burn Before Reading. New York: Hyperion, 2005.

Vance, Cyrus. Hard Choices. New York: Simon & Schuster, 1983.

Viorst, Milton. In the Shadow of the Prophet: The Struggle for the Soul of Islam. Boulder, CO: Westview Press, 2001.

Walters, Barbara. Audition, a Memoir. New York: Random House, 2008.

Wells, David F. No Place for Truth: Or Whatever Happened to Evangelical Theology? Grand Rapids: Eerdmans, 1993.

Wilbur, Donald N. Reza Shah Pahlavi: The Resurrection and Reconstruction of Iran, 1878-1944. Hicksville: Exposition Press, 1975.

Zahedi, Ardeshir, and Pari Absalti, comp. and ed. Untold Secrets. Houshang Mirhashem Publisher of Rah-e-Zendegi Journal, February 2002.

Zahedi, Dariush. The Iranian Revolution Then and Now. Boulder: Westview Press, 2000.

Zonis, Marvin. Majestic Failure: The Fall of the Shah. Chicago: University of Chicago Press, 1991.

ENDNOTES

. . . .

[1] Louis Rene Beres and Tsiddon-Chatto, Col. (res.) Yoash, "Reconsidering Israel's Destruction of Iraq's Osiraq Nuclear Reactor," *Temple International and Comparative Law Journal 9 (2)*, 1995. Reprinted in *Israel's Strike Against the Iraqi Nuclear Reactor 7 June 1982*, Jerusalem: Menachem Begin Heritage Center, 2003, p.60.

[2] Rafael Eitan, "The Raid on the Reactor from the Point of View of the Chief of Staff," *Israel's Strike Against the Iraqi Nuclear Reactor 7 June, 1981*, Jerusalem: Menachem Begin Heritage Center: 2003, 31-33.

[3] Maj. Gen. (res.) David Ivry, "The Attack on the Osiraq Nuclear Reactor—Looking Back 21 Years Later," *Israel's Strike Against the Iraqi Nuclear Reactor 7 June, 1981*, Jerusalem: Menachem Begin Heritage Center, 2003, p. 35.

[4] Yitzhak Shamir, "The Failure of Diplomacy," *Israel's Strike Against the Iraqi Nuclear Reactor7 June, 1981*, Jerusalem, Menachem Begin Heritage Center: 2003, p. 16-17.

[5] On *GlobalSecurity.org*. This Internet site contains an extensive discussion of Iran's nuclear facilities, including a site-by-site description, reached by navigating through the following sequence: Iran > Facilities > Nuclear. The discussion of Iran's uranium mines is drawn from this site: http://www.globalsecurity.org/wmd/world/iran/mines.htm. (Accessed 2006)

[6] Saghand Mining Department, Atomic Energy Organization of Iran. http://www.aeoi.org.ir/NewWeb/Recenter.asp?id=26 See also: National Geoscience Database of Iran (NGDIR), "Mineral Resources of Iran."http://ngdir.ir/GeoportalInfo/SubjectInfoDetail.asp?PID=54&index=67. (Accessed 2005)

[7] "AP: Iran to Extract Uranium in Early 2006," News Max wires, at *NewsMax.com* September 6, 2004. http://www.newsmax.com/archives/articles/2004/9/5/115634.shtml. (Accessed 2005)

[8] "Esfahan/Isfahan. Nuclear Technology," *GlobalSecurity.org*, at: http://www.globalsecurity.org/wmd/world/iran/esfahan.htm. (Accessed 2006)

[9] "Revealed: Iran's Nuclear Factory," *The Sunday Times-World*, May 1, 2005, archived at *Timesonline.co.uk* at: http://www.timesonline.co.uk/article/0,,2089-1592578,00.html. (Accessed 2005)

[10] "Iran renews nuclear weapons development," *Daily Telegraph*, September 12, 2008; http://tehranwatch.blogspot.com/2008/09/iran-renews-nuclear-weapons-development.html. (Accessed July 2009)

[11]William J. Broad/David E. Sanger, "Iran said to have enough nuclear fuel for one weapon," *The New York Times*, November 20, 2008; www.nytimes.com/2008/11/20/world/middleeast/20nuke.html. (Accessed July 2009)

[12] Isabelle Lasserre, "L'Iran:un premiere bombe atomique d'ici a 2010?," *Le Figaro*, December 17, 2008. Translated from French; http://www.lefigaro.fr/international/2008/12/18/01003-20081218ARTFOG00008-l-iran-un-premiere-bombe-atomique-d-ici-a-.php. (Accessed July 2009)

[13] "Natanz," at *GlobalSecurity.org*. http://www.globalsecurity.org/wmd/world/iran/natanz.htm

[14] "EU powers to mull Iranian nuclear efforts," *Haaretz*, February 9, 2004. http://www.haaretz.com/hasen/pages/ShArt.jhtml?itemNo=472862&contrassID=1. (Accessed 2006)

[15] "Iran confirms uranium-to-gas conversion," a report published in the *China Daily*, May 10, 2005. http://www.chinadaily.com.cn/english/doc/2005-05/10/content_440631.htm

[16] Ibid.

[17] Tom Baldwin, "Iran faces sanctions after reactivating nuclear plant," *TimesOnLine.com*, August 9, 2005. http://www.timesonline.co.uk/article/0,,251-1727066,00.html See also: Seth Rosen, "Iran restarts its nuclear activities,"*The Washington Times,* August 9, 2005. http://www.washtimes.com/world/20050809-120112-3017r.htm. (Accessed 2006)

[18] "Iran Rejects U.N. Resolution," CBS News, September 25, 2005. http://www.cbsnews.com/stories/2005/09/25/world/main882946.shtml. (Accessed 2006)

[19] Remarks on UN reform, the Human Rights Council, and other Issues, Ambassador John R. Bolton, U.S. Permanent Representative to the United Nations, On-The-Record Briefing, January 25, 2006, Washington, D.C.; http://www1.umn.edu/humanrts/unreform-remarks.html. (Accessed July 2009)

[20] "Iran enriches uranium. Iran starts converting new uranium batch, diplomat says," *Reuters*, November 27, 2005. http://www.blog.ca/main/index.php/boris-newz/2005/11/17/iran_enriches_uranium~315692. (Accessed 2006)

[21] "Russia plan could end Iran talks impasse—ElBaradei," *Reuters,* December 6, 2005. http://today.reuters.co.uk/news/newsArticle.aspx?type=worldNews&storyID=2005-12-06T173520Z_01_DIT663295_RTRUKOC_0_UK-NUCLEAR-IRAN-ELBA-RADEI.xml. (Accessed 2006)

[22] Yehezkel Dror, "The New Ruler," Global Leadership for the 21st Century, Conference on the Future of the Jewish People, May 2008, Jerusalem Israel; The Jewish People Policy Planning Institute, http://www.jpppi.org.il/JPPPI/Templates/ShowPage.asp?DBID=1&LNGID=1&TMID=105&FID=452&PID=0&IID=510. p. 133. (Accessed August 2009)

[23] Information provided by the National Council of Resistance of Iran, U.S. Representative Office. "Information on Two Top Secret Nuclear Sites of the Iranian Regime (Natanz and Arak)," December 2002. The Report is available on the website *IranWatch.org* at the URL: http://www.iranwatch.org/privateviews/NCRI/perspex-ncri-natanzarak-1202.htm. (Accessed 2006)

[24] National Council for Resistance in Iran, "Disclosing a Major Secret Nuclear Site under the Ministry of Defense," Press Release, November 14, 2004. Archived on the website of *GlobalSecurity.org* at: http://www.globalsecurity.org/wmd/library/report/2004/new-nuke-info.htm. (Accessed 2006)

25 "Implementation of the NPT Safeguards Agreement in the Islamic Republic of Iran," Report by the Director General, International Atomic Energy Agency (IAEA) Board of Governors, GOV/2006/67, September 2, 2005. http://www.globalsecurity.org/wmd/library/report/2005/iran_iaea-gov_2005-67_2sep05.htm. (Accessed 2006)

26 "Questioning Iran's Pursuit of the Nuclear Fuel Cycle—Iran's Nuclear Fuel Cycle Facilities: A Pattern of Peaceful Intent?" U.S. Department of State, September 2005. http://www.globalsecurity.org/wmd/library/report/2005/iran-fuel-cycle-brief_dos_2005.pdf. (Accessed 2006)

27 Ibid.

28 Ibid.

29 Ibid.

30 Ibid.

31 Ibid.

32 "Abdul Qadeer Kahn 'Apologizes' for Transferring Nuclear Secrets Abroad." The statement is archived on the Federation of American Scientists website, www.fas.org, at the following URL: http://www.fas.org/nuke/guide/pakistan/nuke/aqkhan020404.html. (Accessed 2006)

33 Attachment A. Unclassified Report to Congress on the Acquisition of Technology Relating to Weapons of Mass Destruction and Advanced Conventional Munitions, 1 July Through 31 December 2003. The report can be found on the Internet on the website of the Central Intelligence Agency at the following URL: http://www.cia.gov/cia/reports/721_reports/july_dec2003.htm. (Accessed 2005)

34 Ibid.

35 "Iran Claims Solid Fuel for Missiles Achieved," *NewsMax.com*, July 27, 2005. http://www.newsmax.com/archives/articles/2005/7/27/104439.shtml, (Accessed 2006)

36 Anthony H. Cordesman, Arleigh A. Burke Chair, Center for Strategic and International Studies. *Iran's Developing Military Capabilities: Main Report Washington, D.C. Center for Strategic and International Studies.* Working Draft: December 14, 2004. The discussion of the shahab-3 missile is drawn from pages 25-27.

37 "Nuclear Weapons development—2006," *Global Security*.org, http://www.globalsecurity.org/wmd/world/iran/nuke2006.htm. (Accessed July 2009)

38 "Iran's nuclear program status," Congressional Research Service, November 20, 2008; p. CRS-10, http://www.fas.org/sgp/crs/nuke/RL34544.pdf. (Accessed July 2009)

39 HR282, Iran Freedom Support Act, U.S. House bill, April 27, 2006. http://www.theorator.com/bills109/hr282.html. (Accessed July 2009)

40 Dudi Cohen, "Israel will soon disappear," *Ynetnews*, October 10, 2006, http://www.ynetnews.com/articles/0,7340,L-3317417,00.html. (Accessed July 2009)

41 Michael Goldfarb, editor, "Ahmadinejad: World has lost its will," *Weekly Standard*, November 14, 2006; http://www.weeklystandard.com/weblogs/TWSFP/2006/11/ahmadinejad_world_has_lost_its_will_.html. (Accessed July 2009)

[42] "Iran determined to master nuclear fuel cycle," *Iran Daily*, November 15, 2006; http://iran-daily.com/1385/2708/html/index.htm. (Accessed July 2009)

[43] "Key judgments from a National Intelligence Estimate on Iran's nuclear activity," *The New York Times,* December 4, 2007; http://www.nytimes.com/2007/12/04/washington/04itext.html?pagewanted=2&_r=2. (Accessed July 2009)

[44] Ali Akbar Dareini, "Iran says it now runs more than 5000 centrifuges," *Associated Press*, November 26, 2008; http://www.google.com/hostednews/ap/article/ALeqM5jG7bnyWWJfgaYD-JwcqmImlpRujwD94MND800. (Accessed July 2008)

[45] David Albright and Jacqueline Shire, "IAEA Report on Iran," Institute for Science and International Security, 19 February 2009.

[46] "Responsible leadership for a sustainable future," 2009 G8 Summit, L'Aquila, Italy, July 8-10, 2009; http://www.g8italia2009.it/static/G8_Allegato/G8_Political_issues_FINAL_2240%5b3%5d.pdf. (Accessed July 2009)

[47] James Hider, "Middle East desire for nuclear power could trigger an arms race," *Times Online*, June 24, 2009, http://www.timesonline.co.uk/tol/news/world/middle_east/article6565549.ece#cid=OTC-RSS&attr=797093. (Accessed July 2009)

[48] Amira Hass, "Moussavi would shun nuclear weapons, says Iran scholar," *Haaretz*.com, June 28, 2009; http://www.haaretz.com/hasen/spages/1096071.html; "One of Ahmadinejad's close advisers is a redhead named Mohammad Ramin, who speaks fluent German. This mystery man grew up in Germany, maybe he's partly German. He's the one behind Ahmadinejad's statements about the Holocaust." (Accessed July 2009)

[49] Fouad Ajami, "Obama's Persian Tutorial," *Wall Street Journal*, June 23, 2009, p. 13.

[50] "Who is Mir Hossein Moussavi Khameneh?"; *The Weekly Standard,* Michael Goldfarb, June 11, 2009; http://www.weeklystandard.com/weblogs/TWSFP/2009/06/who_is_mir_hossein_moussavi_kha_1.asp. (Accessed June 2009)

[51] Ibid.

[52] Ibid.

[53] Ibid.

[54] *The New York Times*, April 6, 2009, http://www.time.com/time/world/article/0,8599,1904194,00.html?xid=rss-world-yahoo. (Accessed June 2009)

[55] Joe Klein, "Ten Day in Tehran," *Time*, June 29, 2009, p. 28

[56] "Iran Affirms Ahmadinejad's Victory after Official Recount"; *Haaretz*.com; June 29, 2009. C:\Documents and Settings\user\Local Settings\Temporary Internet Files\OLK75\Iran confirms Ahmadinejad victory after official recount—*Haaretz*—Israel News.htm. (Accessed June 2009)

[57] Herb Keinon, "FM calls for Security Council meeting on Iranian upheaval," *The Jerusalem Post*, June 23, 2009, p. 8

[58], Amira Hass, "Moussavi would shun nuclear weapons, says Iran scholar," *Haaretz*.com, June 28, 2009; http://www.haaretz.com/hasen/spages/1096071.html. (Accessed July 2009)

59 Thomas Friedman, "Could history repeat itself in Iran?" *Houston Chronicle*, July 22, 2009, Section B-9.

60 David Horowitz, "The second Islamic Revolution," *The Jerusalem Post*, June 26, 2009, p.24.

61 Roger Cohen, "The end of the beginning," *The New York Times Global Edition*, June 24, 2009, p. 7.

62 Christopher Dickey, "The Supreme Leader," *Newsweek*, June 29, 2009, p.36.

63 Reuel Marc Gerecht, "The Koran and the ballot box," *International Herald Tribune*, June 22, 2009, p. 6.

64 Muhammad Sahimi, "Rafsanjani's Sermon, Split in the Leadership," July 17, 2009; http://tehranbureau.com/rafsanjanis-sermon-split-leadership/. (Accessed July 2009)

65 Professor David Menashri, Director at The Center for Iranian Studies, Tel Aviv University, Tel Aviv, Israel, Phone conference with The Israel Project. (Accessed June 28, 2009)

66 Ibid.

67 Mya Guarnieri, "No honeymoon in Iran," *UPFRONT*, June 26, 2009, p. 20

68 Liora Hendelman-Baavur, "Iranian Women take the streets in anger and dismay," *The Jerusalem Post*, June 25, 2009, p. 9.

69 Martin Fletcher, "Iran clerics declare election invalid and condemn crackdown," *Times Online*; http://www.timesonline.co.uk/tol/news/world/middle_east/article6644817.ece. (Accessed July 2009)

70 Oliver Javanpour, "The global Muslim theocracy movement is worried," *The Jerusalem Post*, June 24, 2009; www.jpost.com/servlet/Satellite?cid=1245184920348&pagename-JPost%2FJPArticle%2FPrinter. (Accessed June 2009)

71 Mona El-Naggar, "Arab states see a possible silver lining in Iran," *International Herald Tribune*, June 25, 2009, p. 7.

72 Ibid.

73 "Hospitalized Iranians Seized," CNN.com/world; June 29, 2009; www.cnn.com/2009/WORLD/meast/06/27/iran.protessts. (Accessed June 2009)

74 Ibid.

75 Roger Cohen, "Iran's children of tomorrow," *International Herald Tribune*, June 23, 2009, p. 7

76 Samira Simone, "Feared Basij militia has deep history in Iranian conflict," June 22, 2009; http://www.cnn.com/2009/WORLD/meast/06/22/iran.basij.militia.profile/. (Accessed July 2009)

77 Sabina Amidi, "I married Iranian girls before execution," July 19, 2009; http://www.jpost.com/servlet/Satellite?cid=1246443842931&pagename=JPost%2FJPArticle%2FShowFull. (Accessed July 2009)

78 Ibid.

[79] Samira Simone, "Feared Basij militia has deep history in Iranian conflict," June 22, 2009; http://www.cnn.com/2009/WORLD/meast/06/22/iran.basij.militia.profile/. (Accessed July 2009)

[80] Robert F. Worth, *The New York Times* reprinted in the *Houston Chronicle*, July 29, 2009, pp, A1, A10.

[81] Borzou Daragahi, "Intent of show trial puzzles Iranians," *Houston Chronicle*, August 9, 2009; p. A29.

[82] Neil Macfarquhar, "Crackdown Across Iran shows power of new elite," *International Herald Tribune*, June 26, 2009, pp. 1,4.

[83] "Mahmoud Ahmadinejad," *The New York Times*, July 7, 2009; http://topics.nytimes.com/topics/reference/timestopics/people/a/mahmoud_ahmadine-jad/index.html. (Accessed July 2009)

[84] "Obama's Iran Abdication," *Wall Street Journal*, June 18, 2009, http://online.wsj.com/article/SB124520170103721579.html. (Accessed July 2009)

[85] Ibid, p. 163.

[86] Shmuley Boteach, "Spectator of the free world: Obama and Tehran, " *The Jerusalem Post*, June 23, 2009, p. 16.

[87] Ralph Peters, *New York Post*, June 16, 2009; http://www.nypost.com/seven/06162009/postopinion/opedcolumnists/the_obama_eff ect_174463.htm. (Accessed July 2009)

[88] "France Summons Iranian Ambassador over Vote Concern," *Reuters*, June 15, 2009; http://www.reuters.com/article/latestCrisis/idUSLF552369. (Accessed June 2009)

[89] Herb Keinon, "FM calls for Security Council meeting on Iranian upheaval," *The Jerusalem Post*, June 23, 2009, p. 8

[90] Najmeh Bozorgmehr, "Ahmadinejad turns on Obama," *Financial Times*, June 26, 2009, p. 2.

[91] "PM praises solidarity over Iran row," Guardian, July 9, 2009; http://www.guardian.co.uk/uk/feedarticle/8600167. (Accessed July 2009)

[92] Arnold Beichman, "Eight Years that Shook the World," Hoover Institution, *Hoover Digest*," http://www.hoover.org/publications/digest/4495741.html. (Accessed February 2008.)

[93] William Shakespeare, Macbeth Act 5, scene 1, 26–40.

[94]Laura Rosen, "With turmoil in Tehran, Obama's policy in flux," *Foreign Policy,* June 17, 2009; http://thecable.foreignpolicy.com/posts/2009/06/17/with_turmoil_in_tehran_obama_ s_policy_in_flux. (Accessed July 2009)

[95] Ali Akbar Dareini, "New Era for Iran, president declares," *Houston Chronicle*, July 8, 2009; p. A5.

[96] Croesus, after being reprieved by Cyrus. (Herodotus -The Histories, Bk 1,87) http://members.ozemail.com.au/~ancientpersia/quotes.html. (Accessed July 2009)

[97] The Circle of Ancient Iranian Studies; Cyrus, the Great, Father and Liberator; http://www.cais-soas.com/CAIS/History/hakhamaneshian/Cyrus-the-great/cyrus_the_great.htm. (Accessed June 2009)

98 Ezra 1:1-3 NIV

99 Isaiah 44:28 NIV

100 Ibid.

101 From Ancient Persia to Contemporary Iran—History of Iran Timeline; Ladjevardian, Reza, 2005; http://www.mage.com/TLgody.html. (Accessed June 2009)

102 Ibid.

103 Esther 3:8-9 NIV

104 Esther 4:14 NIV

105 Esther 4:16 NIV

106 Sun Myung Moon (born January 6, 1920) is the Korean founder and leader of the worldwide Unification Church. Moon has said that he is the Messiah and the Second Coming of Christ and is fulfilling Jesus' unfinished mission. http://en.wikipedia.org/wiki/Sun_Myung_Moon. (Accessed July 2009)

107 Islam 101; http://www.islam101.com/dawah/pillars.html. (Accessed June 2009)

108 From Ancient Persia to Contemporary Iran—History of Iran Timeline; http://www.mage.com/TLgody.html. (Accessed June 2009)

109 Historical Setting, *Pars Times*, http://www.parstimes.com/history/historicalsetting.html#Rezashah. (Accessed June 2009)

110 David Harris, *The Crisis* (New York: Little, Brown and Company, 2004), p. 47.

111 U.S. Department of State, Foreign Aid and Human Rights (1976); http://usinfo.state.gov/infousa/government/overview/54.html. (Accessed August 2008.)

112 Clair Apodaca, U.S. *Human Rights Policy and Foreign Assistance: a Short History*; Ritsumeikan International Affairs, Vol. 3, p. 64. (The paper was presented at the "Global Governance" project at a seminar held by the Institute of International Relations and Area Studies, Ritsumeikan University, March 8, 2004.)

113 Farah Pahlavi, *An Enduring Love* (New York: Hyperion, 1987), pp. 269-270.

114 Manucher Farmanfarmaian and Roxane Farmanfarmaian, *Blood & Oil: A Prince's Memoir of Iran, From the Shah to the Ayatollah* (New York: Random House, 2005), p. 292.

115 Asadollah Alam, *The Shah and I: The Confidential Diary of Iran's Royal Court 1969-1977* (New York: St. Martin's Press, 1993), p. 540.

116 "Amir Taheri's Interview with Ardeshir Zahedi," cited in *Untold Secrets* by Ardeshir Zahedi, a compilation of original materials. Compiled by: Pari Abasalti, Editor in Chief, and Houshang Mirhashem, Publisher of Rah-e-Zendegi Journal, February 2002, p. 15.

117 Manucher Farmanfarmaian and Roxane Farmanfarmaian, p. 266.

118 Dwight D. Eisenhower, *Mandate for Change, 1953-1956: The White House Years* (Garden City, NY: Doubleday, 1963), p. 165.

119 "Heroes and Killers in the 20th Century," Mohammad Mossadegh, Hero File, http://www.moreorless.au.com/heroes/mossadegh.html. (Accessed May 2008.)

[120] White House Transcript, "Remarks at Millennial Evening: the Perils of Indifference," April 12, 1999; http://www.historyplace.com/speeches/wiesel-transcript.htm. (Accessed July 2008.)

[121] Amir Tahiri, "Iran and the U.S.: Who Should Apologize and Why?" (Cited in *Untold Secrets* by Ardeshir Zahedi; a compilation of original materials. Compiled by: Pari Abasalti, Editor in Chief, and Houshang Mirhashem, Publisher of Rah-e-Zendegi Journal, February 2002, p. 43.)

[122] Personal Interview with Dr. Parviz Mina, Paris, France, April 18, 2008.

[123] Houchang Nahavandi, *The Last Shah of Iran*, translated from the French by Steve Reed (France: Editions Osmonde, 2004), p. 97.

[124] Barbara Walters, *Audition* (New York: Alfred A. Knopf, 2008), p. 201.

[125] Houchang Nahavandi, p. 30.

[126] Neil Farquhar, "Persepolis Journal; Shah's Tent City, Fit for Kings, May Lodge Tourists," *The New York Times,* September 7, 2001; http://query.nytimes.com/gst/fullpage.html?res=9C06E6DB1039F934A3575AC0A96 79C8B63. (Accessed July 2008.)

[127] U.S. Subcommittee Hearings 1973:507.

[128] Henry Kissinger, *White House Years* (Boston: Little, Brown, 1979), p. 1261.

[129] Ryszard Kapuscinski, *Shah of shahs* (New York: Vintage Books, a division of Random House, 1985), p. 137.

[130] Barbara Walters describes Ambassador Zahedi: "The ambassador was an imposing figure, tall and dark with a great head of hair, a prominent nose, a ready smile, and a glad hand for everyone. He was also smart, shrewd, and the Shah's most trusted adviser in the United States." She described the Iranian Embassy as "the Number one Embassy when it came to extravagance and just plain enjoyment...large parties with hundreds of guests, flowing champagne, mounds of fresh Iranian caviar, and a bulging buffet..." Barbara Walters, *Audition* (New York: Alfred A. Knopf, 2008) pp.248-249.

[131] Personal Interview with Ardeshir Zahedi, June 2008.

[132] Ardeshir Zahedi interview, June 2008.

[133] Asadollah Alam, p. 500. p. 477.

[134] National Security Archive, Memo from Henry Kissinger, July 25, 1972; http://www.gwu.edu/~nsarchiv/NSAEBB/NSAEBB21/03-01.htm. (Accessed April 2008.)

[135] Mike Evans, *Israel: America's Key to Survival* (Plainfield, NJ: Logos International), p. ix.

[136] Cited by Slater Bakhtavar, "Jimmy Carter's Human rights Disaster in Iran," *American Thinker.com,* August 26, 2007; http://www.americanthinker.com/2007/08/jimmy_carters_human_rights_dis.html. (Accessed June 2008.)

[137] Marvin Zonis, *Majestic Failure: The Fall of the Shah of Iran* (Chicago: University of Chicago Press, 1991), p. 60.

[138] *New York Times*, April 20, 1979, p. 12.

[139] Cited by Dariush Zahedi in *The Iranian Revolution Then and Now* (Boulder, CO: Westview Press, 2000), p. 155.

[140] Asadollah Alam, p. 500.

[141] Ibid, p. 484.

[142] Dariush Zahedi, pp. 39-40

[143] Personal Interview, Dr. Abdol Majid Majidi, Minister of Planning and Budget under the Shah, Paris, France, April 18, 2008.

[144] Clair Apodaca, p.79.

[145] Dr. Parviz Mina interview, April 19, 2008, Paris France.

[146] Comptroller General of the United States. "Iranian Oil Cutoff: Reduced Petroleum Supplies and Inadequate U.S. Government Response." Report to Congress, General Accounting Office, 1979.

[147] U.S. Senate Department briefing paper, May 15, 1977, Declassified. Document found in Archived in Chadwyck-Healy Volume, *Iran: The Making of U.S. Foreign Policy 1977-190*, Alexandria VA 1990.

[148] Asadollah Alam, The Shah and I: the Confidential Diary of Iran's Royal Court, 1968-1977 (London: I.B.Tauris, 2008), p.542.

[149] Ibid.

[150] CIA Report: Iran in the 1980s, pp. 1-3, Declassified. Archived in Chadwyck-Healy Volume, *Iran: The Making of U.S. Foreign Policy 1977-190*, Alexandria VA 1990.

[151] Manoucher Ganji, *Defying the Iranian Revolution: From a Minister to the Shah to a Leader of Resistance* (Westport: Praeger, 2002), p. 39.

[152] Annabelle Sreberny-Mohammadi and Ali Mohammadi, *Small Media, Big Revolution: Communication, Culture and the Iranian* (Minneapolis: University of Minnesota Press, 1994), p. 139.

[153] Confidential Document, U.S. Embassy to Secretary of State, "Opposition Views." January 1978. Declassified.

[154] Iran: Chronology of Revolution, 1978; http://ivl.8m.com/Chronology2.htm. (Accessed July 2008.)

[155] Eric Rouleau, *Le Monde*, "Khomeini's Iran," Fall 1980, http://www.foreignaffairs.org/19800901faessay8148/eric-rouleau/khomeini-s-iran.html. (Accessed February 2008.)

[156] U.S. State Department telegram Sullivan to Vance, April 25, 1978, Declassified. Archived in Chadwyck-Healey, *Iran: The Making of U.S. Policy 1977-1980*, Alexandria VA 1990.

[157] U.S. State Department Telegram Christopher to Sullivan, April 26, 1978, Declassified. Archived in Chadwyck-Healey, *Iran: The Making of U.S. Policy 1977-1980*, Alexandria VA 1990.

[158] Confidential Telegram, U.S. Embassy Tehran to Secretary of State, "Opposition lawyers capture Bar Association and plan closer scrutiny of political court cases," June 19, 1978. Declassified.

[159] Personal interview with Her Majesty Farah Pahlavi, March 28, 2008.

[160] William H. Sullivan, Dateline Iran: the Road not Taken; *Foreign Policy* No. 40, pp. 175-186.

[161] Zbigniew Brzezinski, *Power and Principle* (New York: Farrar, Straus, Giroux, 1983), p. 252.

[162] Mohammad Reza Shah Pahlavi, *Answer to History* (New York: Stein and Day, 1980), p. 165.

[163] Ardeshir Zahedi interview, June 2008.

[164] Michael Ledeen and William Lewis, *Debacle: the American Failure in Iran* (New York: Alfred A. Knopf, 1981), p.163.

[165] Cyrus Vance, *Hard Choices* (New York: Simon and Schuster, 1983), p. 316.

[166] Zbigniew Brzezinski, p.357.

[167] Baqer Moin, *Khomeini: Life of the Ayatollah* (New York: McMillan, 2000) p. 149.

*The organization appears to have small, tightly-knit groups in Tehran and in several European and American cities. Its headquarters in the U.S. is reportedly in Houston, TX (per a telegram from the American Embassy, Tehran, to the Department of State, February 1, 1978, declassified.)

[168] Ervand Abrahamian, *Iran Between Two Revolutions* (Princeton: Princeton University Press, 1982), pp. 466-467.

[169] Don A. Schance @ Tehran *Los Angeles Times* (Apr. 24, 1980) "New Soviet Links to Iran" p. 1: The Iranian government, in the words of Ayatollah Ruhollah Khomeini, has condemned both "Westoxification and Eastoxification."

[170] CIA intelligence memorandum, January 19, 1979, entitled "Iran: Khomeini's Prospects and Views."

[171] CIA intelligence memorandum, January 19, 1979, entitled "Iran" Khomeini's Prospects and Views."

[172] Samuel Segev, *The Iranian Triangle* (New York: The Free Press, 1988), p. 117.

[173] Kenneth R. Timmerman, Insight on the News, "The Truth About Mahmoud Abbas," July 8, 2003; http://findarticles.com/p/articles/mi_m1571/is_2003_July_8/ai_104842031. (Accessed July 2008.)

[174] "On October 29, hijackers of a German Lufthansa passenger jet demanded the release of the three surviving terrorists...being held for trial. [Two] were immediately released by ermany, receiving a tumultuous welcome when they touched down in Libya and giving their own firsthand account of their operation at a press conference broadcast worldwide. In both ESPN/ABC's documentary *The Tragedy of the Munich Games* and in Kevin Macdonald's Academy Award-winning documentary *One Day in September,* it is claimed that the whole Lufthansa hijacking episode was a sham, concocted by the West Germans and Black September so that the Germans could be rid of the three Munich perpetrators. The view is that the Germans were fearful that their mishandling of the rescue attempt would be exposed to the world if the three Fürstenfeldbruck survivors had ever stood trial." http://en.wikipedia.org/wiki/Munich_massacre. (Accessed July 2008.)

[175] Ion Mihai Pacepa, "Russian Footprints," *National Review Online*; http://article.nationalreview.com/print/?q=NjUzMGU4NTMyOTdkOTdmNTA1MW JlYjYyZDliODZkOGM=. (Accessed June 2008.)

176 "His Imperial Majesty Interview with Kayhan," *Kayhan International*, September 17, 1977.

177 Cyrus Vance, *Hard Choices* (New York: Simon and Schuster, 1983), p. 321.

178 President Jimmy Carter, Presidential Directive/NSC-13, May 13, 1977; Declassified May 29, 1990, Jimmy Carter Library; http://www.jimmycarterlibrary.org/documents/pd13.pdf. (Accessed April 2008.)

179 Asadollah Alam, *The Shah and I: The Confidential Diary of Iran's Royal Court 1969-1977* (New York: St. Martin's Press, 1993), p. 543.

180 Cited by Gary Sick in *All Fall Down: America's Tragic Encounter with Iran* (Lincoln, NE: iUnvierse.com, Inc., 2001), p.128.

181 Joseph Kraft, "Letter from Iran," *New Yorker*, December 18, 1978; http://www.newyorker.com/archive/1978/12/18/1978_12_18_138_TNY_CARDS_00 0324558?printable=true. (Accessed January 2008.)

182 U.S. State Department briefing paper for the President, November 8, 1977, p. 7, Declassified. Archived in Chadwyck-Healey, *Iran: The Making of U.S. Policy 1977-1980*, Alexandria VA 1990.

183 David R. Farber, *Taken Hostage: The Iran Hostage Crisis and America's First Encounter with Radical Islam* (Princeton, NJ: Princeton University Press, 2005), p. 81.

184 Ardeshir Zahedi interview, June 2008.

185 Author unattributed, *Time* magazine, "Greetings for The Shah," November 28, 1977; http://www.time.com/time/printout/0,8816,919138,00.html. (Accessed January 2008.)

186 *Time* editorial, "Greetings for the Shah," November 28, 1977; www.time.com/time/printout/0,8816,919138,00.html. (Accessed January 2008.)

187 *The New York Times*, November 16, 1977

188 *The New York Times*, November 17, 1977

189 *The Washington Post*, November 17, 1977, p. C6.

190 Ibid., p. C6.

191 Ibid, p. A22.

192 *The Washington Post*, November 29, 2977, p. C1.

193 "U.S. State Department briefing paper, W. Christopher to the President, December 12, 1977, Declassified. Archived in Chadwyck-Healey, *Iran: The Making of U.S. Policy 1977-1980*, Alexandria VA 1990.

194 Ardeshir Zahedi interview, June 2008.

195 Farah Pahlavi, *An Enduring Love* (New York: Simon and Schuster, 1987).,p. 270.

196 Farah Pahlavi interview, May 2008.

197 U.S. State Department briefing paper, December 132, 1977, Declassified. Archived in Chadwyck-Healey, *Iran: The Making of U.S. Policy 1977-1980*, Alexandria VA 1990.

198 Ibid.

[199] Ardeshir Zahedi interview, June 2008.)

[200] Jimmy Carter, *Keeping Faith: Memoirs of a President* (New York: Bantam books, 1982), p. 277.

[201] William Shawcross, *The Shah's Last Ride* (New York: Simon and Schuster, Inc., 1988), p. 131.

[202] Pierre Salinger, *America Held Hostage: The Secret Negotiations* (Garden City, NY: Doubleday, 1981), p.33.

[203] U.S. State Department document, Sullivan to Department, July 25, 1977, declassified. Archived in Chadwyck-Healey, *Iran: the Making of U.S. Policy* State 1977-1980, Alexandria VA 1990.

[204] Farah Pahlavi, p.279.

[205] Personal interview with Yitzhak Segev, May 28, 2008.

[206] Personal Interview with Dr. Ahmed Tehrani, Ambassador of Iran, June 12, 2008.

[207] Ardeshir Zahedi interview, July 2008.

[208] Ibid.

[209] Mohammad Reza Pahlavi, *Answer to History* (New York: Stein and Day, 1980), p. 155.

[210] Fouad Ajami, "A History Writ in Oil," *New York Times*, Thursday, June 5, 2008; http://query.nytimes.com/gst/fullpage.html?res=940DE5DB1638F93BA35756C0A96 E948260&sec=&spon=&pagewanted=3. (Accessed June 2008.)

[211] Dinesh D'Souza, "Giving Radical Islam its Start," January 29, 2007, *Townhall.com*; www.townhall.com/Common/Print.aspx. (Accessed December 2007.)

[212] Mustafa Alani, "Probable Attitudes of the GCC States Towards the Scenario of a Military Action Against Iran's Nuclear Facilities," Gulf Research Center, 2004, p. 11.

[213] Ion Mihai Pacepa, "Russian Footprints," *National Review* Online August 24, 2006; http://article.nationalreview.com/print/?q=NjUzMGU4NTMyOTdkOTdmNTA1MW JlYjYyZDliODZkOGM=. (Accessed June 2008.)

[214] Cited by William F. Jasper in "PLO: Protected Lethal Organization; Despite their terrorist track record, Yasser Arafat the PLO are not only protected from punishment, but are warmly welcomed at the UN," February 11, 2002; http://www.accessmylibrary.com/coms2/summary_0286-25029637_ITM. (Accessed June 2008.)

[215] Houchang Nahavandi, *The Last Shah of Iran*, translated from the French by Steeve Reed (France: Editions Osmonde, 2004), p. 77.

[216] James A. Bill, *The Eagle and the Lion: The Tragedy of American-Iranian Relations* (New Haven: Yale University Press, 1988), p.204.

[217] H. E. Chehabi, *Iranian Politics and Religious Modernism: the Liberation Movement of Iran under the Shah and Khomeini* (Ithica: Cornell University Press, 1990) p. 12.

[218] Confidential Memo, U.S. Embassy in Tehran, "Student Unrest," October 1, 1977. Declassified.

[219] M. Parsa, *The Social Origins of the Iranian Revolution* (Brunswick, N.J.: Rutgers University Press, 1989) p. 172; and

220 Central Intelligence Agency National Foreign Assessment Center, December 21, 1978, "Opposition Demonstrations in Iran: Leadership, Organization, and Tactics." Declassified.

221 Department of State Telegram, From the Embassy in Tehran to U.S. Embassies worldwide. Declassified.

222 Ibid

223 Dr. Parviz Mina interview, Paris, France, April 18, 2008.

224 Personal Interview with Uri Lubrani, May 2008.

225 Cited by Dariush Zahedi in *The Iranian Revolution Then and Now* (Boulder, Co: Westview Press, 2000), p. 136.

226 Ibid, p. 136.

227 Ryszard Kapuscinski, *Shah of shahs* (New York: Vintage Books, a division of Random House, 1985), p. 74.

228 Jahangir Amuzegar, *The Dynamics of the Iranian Revolution* (Albany: State University of New York Press, 1991), p. 259.

229 Chadwyck-Healey, *Iran: The making of U.S. Policy 1977-1980*, Alexandria VA 1990, Organizations Glossary, p. 151.

230 Misagh Parsa, *The Social Origins of the Iranian Revolution* (Brunswick, NJ: Rutgers University Press, 1989), p. 217

231 Cited by Ofira Seliktar in *Failing the Crystal Ball Test* (Westport, CT: Praeger Publishers, 2000), p. 133.

232 Mohammad Reza Pahlavi, The Shah of Iran, *Answer to History* (New York: Stein & Day, 1980), p.162.

233 Mr. Parviz Mina interview, April 18, 2008, Paris, France.

234 Michael A. Ledeen, *The War Against the Terror Masters: Why it Happened, Where we are now, and How We'll Win* (New York: McMillan, 2003), p. 12.

235 Ardeshir Zahedi interview, June 2008.

236 Department of State Telegram, From American Tehran, Declassified, Signed "Naas," August 17, 1978.

237 Iran: Chronology of a Revolution, 1978; http://ivl.8m.com/Chronology2.htm. (Accessed July 2008.)

238 Confidential telegram, From U.S. Embassy Tehran to Secretary of State, October 24, 1978. Drafted by GB Lambrakis. Declassified.

239 Ardeshir Zahedi interview, June 2008.

240 Houchang Nahavandi, pp. 194-195.

241 Ardeshir Zahedi interview, June 2008.

242 Charles Stuart Kennedy, "The Iranian Revolution: An Oral History with Henry Precht, Then-State Department Desk Officer," *Middle East Journal*, Volume 58, No. 1, Winter, p. 71.

243 Strobe Talbot, Dean Broils, Parviz Raein, *Time* magazine, "An Interview with the Shah," September 18, 1978, http://www.time.com/time/magazine/article/0,9171,916375,00.html. (Accessed March 2008.)

244 Amir Taheri, *The Spirit of Allah: Khomeini and the Islamic Revolution* (Bethesda, MD: Adler & Adler, 1985), pp. 176, 199-200.

245 Samuel Segev interview, May 2008.

246 Rovshan Ibrahimov, "Israeli Pipeline: Ashelon-Eilat-The Second Breath," April 9, 2007, http://www.turkishweekly.net/comments.php?id=2564. (Accessed March 2008.)

247 Fardust, Hussein and Ali Akbar Dareini. *The Rise and Fall of the Pahlavi Dynasty: Memoirs of Former General Hussein.* (Bangalore, India: Motilal Banarsidass, 1999), p. 217.

248 Benjamin Weiser, "Behind Israel-Iran Sales, 'Amber' Light from U.S.," *Washington Post*, August 16, 1987, pp. 1, A-26-A28.

249 R. K. Ramazani, *Iran's Foreign Policy 1941-1971* (Charlottesville: University Press of Virginia, 1975), p. 404.

250 Trita Parsi, *Treacherous Alliance: The Secret Dealings of Israel, Iran, and the U.S.* (New Haven: Yale University Press, 2007), p. 63.

251 The Old Testament books of Esther, Ezra, Nehemiah and Daniel outline the historic ties between the Persians and the Jews.

252 Cited by Benjamin Beit-Hallahmi in *The Israeli Connection: Whom Israel Arms and Why* (London: I.B. Tauris & Co. Ltd, 1988), p. 10.

253 R. K. Ramazani, "Iran and the Arab-Israeli Conflict," *Middle East Journal* 3 (1978); p. 414-415.

254 Gary Sick, p. 207

255 Samuel Segev interview, May 2008.

256 "The Islamic Republic of Iran," *Y-Net News*; August 1, 2006, http://www.ynetnews.com/Ext/Comp/ArticleLayout/CdaArticlePrintPreview/1,2506, L-3284215,00.html. (Accessed April 2008.)

257 Mohamed Heikal, *Khomeini and his Revolution*, Les Editions Jeune Afrique, 1983, pp. 164-167 (Translated from French.)

258 Trita Parsi, *Treacherous Alliance: The Secret Dealings of Israel, Iran, and the U.S.* (New Haven: Yale University Press, 2007), p. 44.

259 Benjamin beit-Hallahmi, *The Israeli Connection: Whom Israel Arms and Why* (London: I.B. Tauris & Co. Ltd, 1988), p. 12.

260 Yossi Melman, "Our Allies, the Iranian People," *Haaretz.com*, January 12, 2006, http://www.haaretz.com/hasen/spages/794384.html. (Accessed March 2008.)

261 Uri Lubrani interview, May 2008.

262 Ryszard Kapuscinski, *Shah of shahs* (New York: Vintage Books, a division of Random House, 1985), p. 78.

263 Samuel Segev, *The Iranian Triangle* translated by Haim Watzman (New York: the Free Press, 1988), p.107.

264 Personal Interview with David Ivry, May 20, 2008.

265 James A. Bill, Foreign Affairs: Winter 1978/79, "Iran and the Crisis of '78," http://www.foreignaffairs.org/19781201faessay9896/james-a-bill/iran-and-the-crisis-of-78.html. (Accessed March 2008.)

266 Arnaud de Borchgrave, "The Shah on War and Peace," *Newsweek,* November 14, 1977, p. 70.

267 Sohrab Sobhani, *The Pragmatic Entente: Israeli-Iranian Relations, 1948-1988* (New York: Praeger, 1989), p.101.

268 Samuel Segev interview, May 2008.

269 Elaine Sciolino, "Documents Detail Israeli Missile Deal with the Shah," *New York Times*, April 1, 1986.

270 Samuel Segev interview, May 2008.

271 NTI, Missile Overview, "Early Developments Under the Shah Pahlavi, 1977-1979," http://www.nti.org/e_research/profiles/Iran/Missile/index.html. (Accessed March 2008.)

272 Ibid.

273 Trita Parsi, p. 76.

274 Mr. Parviz Mina interview, April 18, 2008, Paris, France.

275 GeoCities.com, http://www.geocities.com/CapitolHill/7288/byeart.htm. (Accessed March 2008.)

276 Sohrab Sobhani, p. 129.

277 Trita Parsi, p. 32.

278 Moshe Dayan, *Breakthrough* (New York: Alfred Knopf, 1981), pp. 106-107.

279 Tehran Domestic Service, February 19, 1979, trans. in *Foreign Broadcast Information Service.*

280 Henry Kissinger, *White House Years* (Boston: Little, Brown, 1979), p. 1261.

281 Ardeshir Zahedi interview, June 2008.

282 Pierre Salinger, *America Held Hostage: the Secret Negotiations* (Garden City, NY: Doubleday, 1981), p. 59.

283 Donald N. Wilbur, *Reza Shah Pahlavi: the Resurrection and Reconstruction of Iran, 1878-1944* (Hicksville, NY: Exposition Press, 1975), p. 136.

284 Ibid, p. 141.

285 Cited by David Lilienthal in *The Journals of David E. Lilienthal: The Harvest Years, 1959-1963* (New York: Harper and Row, 1971), p. 234.

286 James A. Bill, *The Eagle and the Lion* (New Haven: Yale University Press, 1988), p. 137.

287 William Shawcross, *The Shah's Last Ride* (New York: Simon and Schuster, 1988), p. 85.

288 *U.S. News and World Report*, March 6, 1961.

289 David Lilienthal, pp. 257-258.

290 Personal Interview with Ahmad Tehrani, former Ambassador of Iran, June 12, 2008.

[291] W. Averill Harriman and Elie Abel, Special Envoy to Churchill and Stalin 1941-1946 (London: Hutchinson, 1975), p. 282.

[292] Elliot Roosevelt, ed., F.D.R.: His Personal Letters (New York: Duell, Sloan and Pierce, 1947), p.48.

[293] Cited by Marvin Zonis in Majestic Failure: The Fall of the Shah (Chicago: University of Chicago Press, 1991), p. 169.

[294] Defense Intelligence Agency Intelligence Appraisal, "Iran: Religious-inspired Opposition," march 29, 1978. Declassified.

[295] James A. Bill, George Ball: Behind the Scenes in U.S. Foreign Policy (Cumberland, RI: Yale University Press, 1998), p. 231.

[296] Gary Sick, All Fall Down: America's Tragic Encounter with Iran (New York: Penguin Books, 1986), p. 193.

[297] Amir Taheri, Nest of Spies (New York: Pantheon Books, 1988), p.90

[298] Gary Sick, p. 195.

[299] George Ball, The Past Has Another Pattern, Memoirs (New York: W. W. Norton & Co, 1982), pp. 456-457.

[300] T. D. Allman, "Reviewing Stand," Harper's Weekly, August 9, 1976, p. 20.

[301] David R. Farber, Taken Hostage: The Iran Hostage Crisis and America's First Encounter (New Haven: Yale University Press, 2004), p. 67.

[302] James A. Bill, George Ball: Behind the Scenes in U.S. Foreign Policy (New Haven: Yale University Press, 1997), p. 88.

[303] The World, BBC News, "The and Iran, Part II—The Shah and the Revolution," October 26, 2004; http://www.theworld.org/?q=node/3567. (Accessed May 2008.)

[304] Personal Interview with Marvin Kalb, May 2008.

[305] George Ball, The Past Has Another Pattern: Memoirs (New York: W.W. Norton, 1982), pp. 460-461.

[306] Zbigniew Brzezinski, Power and Principle: Memoirs of the National Security Adviser, 1977-1981 (New York: Farrar, Straus, Giroux, 1983), pp. 370-371

[307] Mohammad Reza Pahlavi, pp. 169-170.

[308] Uri Lubrani interview, May 2008.

[309] George W. Ball, "Issues and Implications of the Iranian Crisis," Declassified December 12, 1984; Princeton University Library, Seeley G. Mudd Manuscript Library, Princeton, NJ.

[310] George Ball, The Past Has Another Pattern: Memoirs (New York: W.W. Norton, 1982), pp. 458-459.

[311] James A. Bill, The Eagle and the Lion: The Tragedy of American-Iranian Relations (New Haven: Yale University Press, 1988), p. 168.

[312] George Ball, p. 435.

[313] Ardeshir Zahedi interview, July 2008.

314 State Department Memorandum to file, Precht, December 12, 1978, Declassified. Archived in Chadwyck-Healey, *Iran: The making of U.S. Policy 1977-1980*, Alexandria VA 1990.

315 Dinesh D'Souza, "Giving Radical Islam its Start"; Townhall.com, January 29, 2007; http://www.townhall.com/Common/Print.aspx. (Accessed December 2007.)

316 Farah Pahlavi interview, March 28, 2008.

317 Confidential Telegram, Secretary of State to American Embassy Paris, October 22, 1978, John Stempel. Declassified.

318 Ardeshir Zahedi interview, July 2008.

319 Memorandum of Conversation, Declassified, May 15, 1978, John D. Stempel, First Secretary.

320 Confidential letter, Charles W. Naas, Minister/Counselor, September 6, 1978. Declassified.

321 U.S. State Department Memorandum Stempel to State, May 25, 1978, Declassified. Archived in Chadwyck-Healey, *Iran: The Making of U.S. Policy 1977-1980*, Alexandria VA 1990.

322 State Department Telegram, Vance to Sullivan, November 30, 1978, Declassified. Archived in Chadwyck-Healey, *Iran: The Making of U.S. Policy 1977-1980*, Alexandria VA 1990.

323 State Department Telegram, Stempel to State Department, December 3, 1978, Declassified. Archived in Chadwyck-Healey, *Iran: The Making of U.S. Policy 1977-1980*, Alexandria VA 1990.

324 Ardeshir Zahedi interview, June 2008.

325 Personal Interview with Dr. Abdol Majid Majidi, former Minister of Planning and Budget under the Shah of Iran, Paris, France, April 18, 2008.

326 Central Intelligence Agency Intelligence Memorandum, 20 November 1978, declassified 28 October, 1985; obtained through Rice University, Houston, TX.

327 Admiral Stansfield Turner, *Burn Before Reading* (New York: Hyperion, 2005), p. 180.

328 Marvin Kalb interview, May 2008.

329 John Simpson & Tira Shubart, History of Iran, "Lifting the Veil; Life in Revolutionary Iran," 1995; p. 4, http://www.iranchamber.com/history/articles/lifting_veil_life_revolutionary_iran.php. (Accessed May 2008.)

330 Mir Ali Asghar Montazam, *The Life and Times of Ayatollah Khomeini* (London: Anglo-European Publishing Limited, 1994), p. 146

331 Uri Lubrani interview, May 2008.

332 William H. Sullivan, *Mission to Iran* (New York: W.W. Norton, 1981), p. 16.

333 Cyrus Vance, *Hard Choices: Critical Years in America's Foreign Policy* (New York: Simon and Schuster, 1983), p. 325.

334 Mohammad Reza Pahlavi, *Answer to History* (New York: Stein & Day, 1980), p. 161.

[335] State Department Memorandum, Vance to Sullivan, December 28, 1978, Declassified. Archived in Chadwyck-Healey, *Iran: The Making of U.S. Policy 1977-1980*, Alexandria VA 1990.

[336] William Shawcross, *The Shah's Last Ride* (New York: Simon and Schuster, 1988), p.30.

[337] State Department Memorandum, Stempel to State Department, Declassified. Archived in Chadwyck-Healey, *Iran: The Making of U.S. Policy 1977-1980*, Alexandria VA 1990.

[338] Human Rights in Iran, Hearing before the Subcommittee on International Organizations of the Committee on International Relations, House of Representatives, Ninety-Fifth Congress, First Session, October 26, 1977, p.14.

[339] Clive Irving, Sayings of the Ayatollah Khomeini (The astonishing beliefs of the man who has shaken the Western World); http://prophetofdoom.net/Prophet_of_Doom_Islams_Terrorist_Dogma_in_Muhamm ads_Own_Words.Islam. (Accessed July 2009)

[340] Ardeshir Zahedi interview, June 2008.

[341] The Museum of Broadcast Communications, http://www.museum.tv/archives/etv/V/htmlV/vietnamonte/vietnamonte.htm. (Accessed July 2008.)

[342] Houchang Nahavandi in *The Last Shah of Iran*, translated from the French by Steeve Reed (France: Editions Osmonde, 2004), p. 242

[343] http://www.indymedia.org.uk/en/2008/01/388699.html

[344] BBC Persian Service Archives, program for the 65th anniversary of the Service, produced by Shahryar Radpoor

[345] http://www.indymedia.org.uk/media/2008/01//388700.pdf

[346] Naraghi, Ehsan, Des Palais du Chah, Aux Prisons de la Revolution, *Editions Balland* 1991 Translated from the French by Nilou Mobasser

[347] http://www.indymedia.org.uk/media/2008/01//388700.pdf

[348] Azarbardin interview, June 2008.

[349] Robert E. Huyser, *Mission to Tehran* (New York: Harper and Row, 1986), pp. 31-32.

[350] Charles Mohr, "Vance, in Iran, Asserts Stability Depends on Rights," May 15, 1977, *The New York Times*, p. 3.

[351] *The New York Times*, May 15, 1977.

[352] Ibid.

[353] *The New York Times*, May 18, 1977.

[354] *The New York Times*, April 6, 1977, June 7, 1977, June 8, 1977, July 13, 1977.

[355] *The New York Times*, July 31, 1977

[356] *The New York Times*, June 20, 1977

[357] *The New York Times*, June 17, 1977

[358] *The New York Times*, November 6, 1977

[359] *The New York Times*, November 8, 1977

360 *The New York Times*, December 14, 1978

361 *The New York Times*, December 29, 1978

362 U.S. State Department Memorandum Stempel to State, September 25, 1978, Declassified. Archived in Chadwyck-Healey, *Iran: The Making of U.S. Policy 1977-1980*, Alexandria VA 1990.

363 Personal Interview, Valery Giscard d'Estaing, April 2008.

364 U.S. State Department Telegram Sullivan to State Department, October 1978. Archived in Chadwyck-Healey, *Iran: The Making of U.S. Policy 1977-1980*, Alexandria VA 1990.

365 Barry Rubin, *Paved with Good Intention* (New York and Oxford: Oxford University Press, 1980), p.220.

366 Mir Ali Asghar Montazam, *The Life and Times of Ayatollah Khomeini* (London: Anglo-European Publishing Limited, 1994), p. 169.

367 Ardeshir Zahedi interview, July 2008. (Zahedi revealed to me that his memoirs and a plethora of documents are housed in the vaults of a Swiss bank. He has left instructions that none be published before his death.)

368 *The Washington Post*, January 16, 1979, p. A18.

369 Farah Pahlavi interview, March 28, 2008.

370 David Pryce-Jones, The Middle East Forum, "Betrayal: France, the Arabs, and the Jews"; http://www.meforum.org/article/1636. (Accessed on January 2008.)

371 "How Iranian workers toppled a dictator"; June 30, 2006, http://www.workersliberty.org/node/6521. (Accessed January 2008.)

372 Dr. Parviz Mina interview, Paris, France, April 18, 2008.

373 Central Intelligence Agency National Foreign Assessment, January 12, 1979, "Iran: The radicals in the Opposition." Declassified.

374 Sick, pp. 51, 60-61.

375 CIA Letter to Sullivan, October 6, 1978, Declassified. Archived in Chadwyck-Healey, *Iran: The Making of U.S. Policy 1977-1980*, Alexandria VA 1990.

376 Declassified U.S. State Department document, 11 November 1978, obtained through Rice University, Houston, TX.

377 Cyrus Vance, *Hard Choices: Critical Years in America's Foreign Policy* (New York: Simon and Schuster, 1983), pp. 327-328.

378 William Shawcross, *The Shah's Last Ride* (New York: Simon and Schuster, 1988), p. 23.

379 Her Majesty Farah Pahlavi, *An Enduring Love* (New York: Hyperion, 1987), p. 262.

380 Ardeshir Zahedi Interview, June 2008.

381 Ibid.

382 Charles Nelson Brower and Jason D. Brueschke, *The Iran-United States Claims Tribunal*, (Boston:Brill/Martinus Nijhoff Publishers, 1998) p. 345

383 E. Lauterpacht, C. J. Greenwood, *International Law Reports* (Cambridge University Press: Cambridge, 1991), p. 402.

[384] Central Intelligence Agency National Foreign Assessment, January 12, 1979, "Iran: The radicals in the Opposition." Declassified.

[385] Ardeshir Zahedi interview, June 2008.

[386] John Simpson and Tira Shubart, *Lifting the Veil* (Philadelphia: Coronet Books, 1995), p. 4.

[387] Ardeshir Zahedi interview, June 2008.

[388] Ibid. p. 331.

[389] Mohsen M. Milani, *The Making of Iran's Islamic Revolution: From Monarchy to Islamic* (Boulder, CO: Westview Press, 1994), p. 116.

[390] Ardeshir Zahedi interview, June 2008.

[391] Farah Pahlavi interview, March 29, 2008.

[392] Ardeshir Zahedi interview, June 2008.

[393] Mohamed Heikal, *Khomeini and his Revolution*, Les Editions Jeune Afrique, 1983, (Translated from French), pp. 164-167.

[394] Interview with Shah of Iran, *Washington Post*, May 27, 1980, pp. 9-12, 1.

[395] William Sullivan, *Mission to Iran* (New York: W.W. Norton, 1981), p. 222.

[396] Jimmy Carter, Don Richardson, *Conversations with Carter* (Boulder, CO: Lynne Rienner Publishers, 1998), p. 158.

[397] Dante Alighieri Quotes, http://thinkexist.com/quotes/dante_alighieri/. (Accessed March 2008.)

[398] Michael Ledeen and Bernard Lewis, *Debacle: The American Failure in Iran* (New York: Alfred A. Knopf, 1981), p. 163.

[399] Jeane J. Kirkpatrick, "Dictators and Double Standards"; *Commentarymagazine*.com; November 1979; https://www.commentarymagazine.com/viewarticle.cfm/Dictatorships—Double-Standards-6189?page=all. (Accessed January 2008.)

[400] *The Washington Post*, October 31, 1978, p. A18.

[401] *The Washington Post*, November 8, 1978, p. A14.

[402] *The Washington Post*, January 8, 1979, P.A20.

[403] Dr. Abdol Majid Majidi interview, Paris, France, April 18, 2008.

[404] Alexander M. Haig Jr. with Charles McCarry, *Inner Circles: How America Changed the World* (New York: Warner Books, 1992), p. 538.

[405] Ibid., p. 538

[406] Muhammed Reza Pahlavi, *Answer to History* (New York: Stein & Day, 1980), pp. 172-173.

[407] Lt. General Shapur Azarbarzin interview, June 2008.

[408] Dr. Ahmed Tehrani interview, June 12, 2008.

[409] Lt. General Shapur Azarbarzin interview, June 2008.

[410] Farah Pahlavi interview, March 28, 2008.

[411] Alexander M. Haig Jr., p. 536.

[412] Robert E. Huyser, *Mission to Tehran* (New York: Harper and Row, 1986), p. 17.

[413] Michael Evans with Jerome Corsi, *Showdown with Nuclear Iran* (Nashville, TN: Nelson Current, 2006), p.3-4.

[414] Ardeshir Zahedi interview, June 2008.

[415] Mohammad Reza Pahlavi, p.173.

[416] Alexander M. Haig, Jr., p. 539

[417] Robert E. Huyser, pp. 146, 194, 205, 222.

[418] Jim Hoagland, "Carter Set to Tell European Allies He Fully Backs Shah," *The Washington Post*, January 5, 1979, p. A5.

[419] Ibid.

[420] Extract from *Le Pouvoir et le Vie*, Part 3, Chapter 6, V. Giscard d' Estaing, 2006; translated in Paris for Dr. Evans with permission from Mr. d'Estaing in May 2008; and personal interview with Giscard d'Estaing, May 2008.

[421] Zbigniew Brzezinski, , *Power and Principle: Memoirs of the National Security Adviser*, 1977-1981 (New York: Farrar, Straus, Giroux, 1983), p. 295

[422] M. Parsa, *The Social Origins of the Iranian Revolution* (Brunswick, N.J.: Rutgers University Press, 1989) p. 223

[423] Cyrus Vance, *Hard Choices* (New York: Simon and Schuster, 1983), pp. 336-337.

[424] Ibid. p. 380.

[425] Giscard d'Estaing interview, Paris, France, May 2008.

[426] Mir Ali Asghar Montazam, *The Life and Times of Ayatollah Khomeini* (London: Anglo-European Publishing Limited, 1994), pp. 144-145.

[427] Mohammad Reza Pahlavi, p. 171.

[428] Ibid., p. 172.

[429] Amir Taheri, *The Spirit of Allah: Khomeini and the Islamic Revolution* (Bethesda, MD: Adler & Adler, 1985) p.228.

[430] From the desk of Fjordman, "France and the Iranian Revolution," *The Brussels Journal*, January 24, 2007,

[431] Dr. Parviz Mina interview, Paris, France, April 18, 2008.

[432] Journal de 20 h, A2 October, 10, 1978 Video may be viewed online at http://www.ina.fr/archivespourtous/index.php?full=Khomeiny&genre=&chaine=&mode_document=&datedif_jour1=&datedif_mois1=&datedif_annee1=&action=ft&explorer_OK.x=4&explorer_OK.y=8&cs_page=0&cs_order=3

[433] Balta, Paul, http://www.clio.fr/BIBLIOTHEQUE/la_republique_islamique_diran.asp translated from the French by Dan Godzich

[434] *Le Monde*, February 1, 1979 translated from the French by Dan Godzich

[435] Balta, Paul, http://www.clio.fr/BIBLIOTHEQUE/la_republique_islamique_diran.asp translated from the French by Dan Godzich

[436] "Une Guerre," ("One War"), ñditions des Arénes, Paris, 1997.

[437] Mohamed Heikal, *Khomeini and his Revolution*, Les Editions Jeune Afrique, 1983, (Translated from French), pp. 155-159.

[438] Cited by Houchang Nahavandi in *The Last Shah of Iran*, translated from the French by Steeve Reed (France: Editions Osmonde, 2004), p. 241.

[439] Personal Interview with Charles Villeneuve, journalist, Paris, France, April 19, 2008.

[440] Giscard d'Estaing interview, April 2008.

[441] CIA Intelligence Memorandum: The Politics of Ayatollah Ruhollah Khomeini, November 20, 1978, Declassified. Chadwyck-Healey, *Iran: The Making of U.S. Policy 1977-1980*, Alexandria VA 1990.

[442] Mohamed Heikal, pp. 155-159.

[443] Lt. General Shapur Azarbarzin interview, June 2008.

[444] Samuel Segev interview, Jerusalem, Israel, May 15, 2008.

[445] Uri Lubrani interview, May 2008.

[446] Imam Khomeini, *Islam and Revolution: Writings and Declarations*, translated and annotated by Hamid Algar (London: Routledge & Kegan Paul, 1981), pp. 247-248.

[447] Jimmy Carter, *Keeping Faith* (Fayetteville, AR: The University of Arkansas Press, 1995), p.454.

[448] Discovery Channel, "Koppel on Iran," December 3, 1979, http://www.time.com/time/magazine/article/0,9171,948624,00.html. (Accessed January 2008.)

[449] Michael A. Ledeen, *The War Against the Terror Masters: Why it Happened, Where we are now, and How We'll Win* (New York: McMillan, 2003), pp. 14, 20.

[450] Personal Interview with Charles Villeneuve, journalist on Khomeini's flight to Tehran, Paris, France, April 19, 2008.

[451] Ardeshir Zahedi Interview, June 2008.

[452] William Shawcross, *The Shah's Last Ride* (New York: Simon and Schuster, 1988), p. 134

[453] Charles Villeneuve interview, April 2008.

[454] William Shawcross, *The Shah's Last Ride* (New York: Simon and Schuster, 1988), p. 26.

[455] Uri Lubrani interview, May 2008.

[456] Robert E. Huyser, pp. 293, 296.

[457] State Department Telegram, Vance to Sullivan, January 2, 1979, Declassified. Archived in Chadwyck-Healey, *Iran: The Making of U.S. Policy 1977-1980*, Alexandria VA 1990.

[458] *The New York Times*, December 29, 1978

[459] *The New York Times*, January 7, 1979

[460] Iran Politics Club, http://iranpoliticsclub.net/politics/hostage-story/index.htm. (Accessed May 2008.)

[461] *The New York Times*, January 14, 1979

462 "Tearful Shah Leaves Iran," *Gulfnews* Report, January 17, 1979, http://archive.gulfnews.com/indepth/onthisday/january/10182356.html; (Accessed March 2008.)

463 Mohamed Heikal, pp. 188-191.

464 William J. Daugherty, American Diplomacy.org; "Jimmy Carter and the 1979 Decision to Admit the Shah into the United States," http://www.unc.edu/depts/diplomat/archives_roll/2003_01-03/dauherty_shah/dauherty_shah.html. (Accessed March 2008.)

465 Ibid. p. 170.

466 Cyrus Vance, p. 336

467 Robert Huyser, pp. 274-275.

468 Mohamed Heikal, *Iran: The Untold Story* (New York: Pantheon, 1982), pp. 145-146.

469 Brainy Quotes, Alexander Haig, http://www.brainyquote.com/quotes/authors/a/alexander_haig.html; accessed March 2008.

470 Quoted in Fouad Ajami, *The Vanished Imam: Musa al Sadr and the Shia of Lebanon* (Ithaca: Cornell University Press, 1986), p. 25. (An old Shia saying attributed to the Imam Musa al-Jafar in 799; it was said by many that Khomeini matched this description.)

471 Dr. Ahmed Tehrani interview, June 12, 2008.

472 Houchang Nahavandi, *The Last Shah of Iran*, translated from the French by Steeve Reed (France: Editions Osmonde, 2004), p. 91.

473 Mohamed Heikal, *Khomeini and his Revolution*, Les Editions Jeune Afrique, 1983, (Translated from French), pp. 188-189.

474 Ardeshir Zahedi interview, June 2008.

475 Department of State Telegram, Charles W. Naas, Director, Officer of Iranian Affairs, Bureau of Near Eastern and South Asian Affairs, Department of State, August 17, 1977.

476 Lt. General Shapur Azarbarzin interview, June 2008.

477 Gary Sick, *All Fall Down: America's Tragic Encounter with Iran* (Lincoln, NE: iUniverse.com, 1986, 2001) p. 258.

478 Tony Smith, *America's Mission: the United States and the Worldwide Struggle for Democracy in the Twentieth Century* (Princeton, NJ: Princeton University Press, 1994), p. 259.

479 Mohamad Heikal, pp.191.

480 Jimmy Carter, *Keeping Faith* (Fayetteville, AR: University of Arkansas Press, 1995), p.455.

481 BBC World Service, "My Century...," Transcription, December 24, 1999, http://www.bbc.co.uk/worldservice/people/features/mycentury/transcript/wk51d5.shtml. (Accessed January 2008.)

482 Lt. General Shapur Azarbarzin interview, June 2008.

483 William R. Polk, "The United States and Iran: A Tragic Friendship," p. 6; http://www.williampolk.com/pdf/2007/The%20United%20States%20and%20Iran.pdf. (Accessed May 2008.)

484 BBC; On This Day: 1979, "Exiled Ayatollah Khomeini Returns to Iran." http://news.bbc.co.uk/onthisday/hi/dates/stories/february/1/newsid_2521000/2521003.stm. (Accessed January 2008.)

485 General David Ivry interview, May 20, 2008.

486 Newsweek, February 12, 1979, p.44.

487 Wikipedia, William H. Sullivan, http://en.wikipedia.org/wiki/William_H._Sullivan. (Accessed April 2008.)

488 Mohamed Heikal, pp. 188-191. (Translated from French.)

489 Samuel Segev, The Iranian Triangle (New York: Free Press, 1988), p. 109.

490 U.S. Congress, Committee to investigate the Iran-Contra Affair, 1987, p. 171.

491 Eric Schechter, C4ISR Journal, January 4, 2007, "Desert Duel"; http://www.c4isrjournal.com/story.php?F=2245036; accessed April 2008.

492 Samuel Segev, pp. 110-111.

493 Mohamed Heikal, Khomeini and his Revolution, Les Editions Jeune Afrique, 1983 (Translated from French), pp. 180-181.

494 Jimmy Carter, Keeping Faith: Memoirs of a President (New York: Bantam Books, 1982), p. 450

495 Lt. General Shapur Azarbarzin interview, June 2008.

496 Nadar Entessar, "Israel and Iran's National Security," Journal of South Asian and Middle Eastern Studies 4 (2004), p. 5.

497 Ibid, p. 4.

498 David Menashri, Post-Revolutionary Politics in Iran (London: Frank Cass, 2001), p. 266.

499 Samuel Segev, The Iranian Triangle (New York: Free Press, 1988), p. 4.

500 Gary Sick, October Surprise (Toronto: Random House, 1992), P.207.

501 General David Ivry interview, May 20, 2008

502 Don Hopkins, "The October Surprise: The Iranian Hostage Rescue Mission, and the 1980 Presidential Election," December 1998; http://www.donhopkins.com/drupal/node/104. (Accessed April 2008.)

503 Gary Sick, p. 200.

504 The Embassy capture will be chronicled in a later chapter in this book.

505 Milton Viorst, In the Shadow of the Prophet: The Struggle for the Soul of Islam (Boulder, CO: Westview Press, 2001), p. 195.

506 Ofira Seliktar, Failing the Crystal Ball Test (Praeger: Westport, CT, 2000), p. 128.

507 Personal Interview with General Yitzhak Segev, June 2008.

508 Extract from Le Pouvoir et le Vie, Part 3, Chapter 6, V. Giscard d' Estaing, 2006; translated in Paris for Dr. Evans with permission from Mr. d'Estaing in May 2008.

509 James A. Bill, *The Eagle and the Lion: The Tragedy of American-Iranian Relations* (New Haven: Yale University Press, 1988), pp.289-284.

510 Said Arjomand, *The Turban for the Crown: the Islamic Revolution in Iran* (New York: Oxford University Press, 1988), p. 190.

511 Jihad Watch, "D.C. Imam Glorifies Khomeini, Justifies Suicide Bombing, Preaches Islamic Supremacism," http://www.jihadwatch.org/archives/015242.php. (Accessed March 2008.)

512 Ned Temko, "PLO ponders Iran," *Christian Science Monitor,* February 28, 1979, p. 4.

513 Cyrus Kadivar, "Dialogue of Murder," January 11, 2003; http://www.payvand.com/news/03/jan/1058.html. (Accessed August 2008.)

514 Samuel Segev, "Hameshulah Hairani," *Ma'ariv* (Tel Aviv), 1981, p. 68.

515 Ahmed Taheri, *Holy Terror, The Inside Story of Islamic Terrorism* (London: Sphere Books, Hutchinson Ltd, 1987), pp. 95-100.

516 Nadar Entessar, p. 6.

517 Mohamed Heikal, p. 20-23.

518 Cyrus Vance, *Hard Choices* (New York: Simon and Schuster, 1983), p. 345.

519 Dr. Abdol Majid Majidi interview, April 2008.

520 520 Margaret Talbot, "The Agitator, Oriana Fallaci Directs her fury toward Islam" *The New Yorker*, June 5, 2006; http://www.newyorker.com/archive/2006/06/05/060605fa_fact. (Accessed July 2008.)

521 Ibid.

522 Cited by Philip Pilevsky in *I Accuse: Jimmy Carter and the Rise of Militant Islam* (Dallas: Durban house Publishing Company, Inc., 2007), p.126.

523 Amir Taheri, Benador Associates, "America Can't do a Thing"; http://www.benado-rassociates.com/article/8781. (Accessed January 2008.)

524 Charles Stuart Kennedy, The Iranian Revolution: An Oral History with Henry Precht, Then-State Department Desk Officer, *Middle East Journal*, Volume 58, No. 1, Winter 2004, pp. 64-65.

525 Ibid, p. 68.

526 Jamshid Amouzegar served as Minister of Health, Minister of Finance and prime minister (1977-1978.) He was chastised as prime minister for not establishing a coalition with the traditionalists who backed the Shah.

527 Ardeshir Zahedi interview, July 2008.

528 U.S. State Department Memorandum Stempel to Sullivan, August 22, 1978, Declassified. Archived in Chadwyck-Healey, *Iran: The Making of U.S. Policy 1977-1980*, Alexandria VA 1990. Archived in Chadwyck-Healey, *Iran: The Making of U.S. Policy 1977-1980*, Alexandria VA 1990.

529 U.S. State Department Memorandum Sullivan to Vance, August 29, 1978, Declassified.

530 R. C. Thornton, *The Carter Years: Toward a New Global Order* (New York: Paragon House, 2007), p. 273.

531 Chadwyck-Healey, *Iran: The Making of U.S. Policy 1977-1980*, Alexandria, VA 1990, U.S. State Department Memo, "A Comment on Terrorism in a Revolutionary Situation," February 28, 1979.

532 Ibid.

533 Walter Laqueur, "Why the Shah Fell," *Commentary*, March 1979; http://www.commentarymagazine.com/viewarticle.cfm/Why-the-Shah-Fell-6091. (Accessed January 2008.)

534 Walter Laqueur, "Trouble for the Shah," *The New Republic*, September 23, 1978, pp. 12-21.

535 William C. Rempel, *Los Angeles Times*, November 3, 1994, "Tale of Deadly Iranian Network Woven in Paris," http://www.shapourbakhtiar.com/article-tale-deadly-iranian.htm. (Accessed April 2008.)

536 William C. Rempel, *Los Angeles Times*, November 3, 1994, "Tale of Deadly Iranian Network Woven in Paris," http://www.shapourbakhtiar.com/article-tale-deadly-iranian.htm. (Accessed April 2008.)

537 Charles Villeneuve interview, April 2008.

538 Dr. Parviz Mina interview, April 2008.

539 Department of State Telegram, Declassified, October, 1978, From the American Embassy Paris to American Embassy Tehran., signed "Hartman."

540 Mohammad Reza Pahlavi, *The Shah of Iran, Answer to History* (Briarcliff Manor, NY: Stein and Day, 1980), p. 182.

541 Postscripts, "Iran: Imminent Threat or Paper Tiger?" November 1, 2007, http://notorc.blogspot.com/2007/11/iran-imminent-threat-or-paper-tiger.html. (Accessed April 2008.)

542 Confidential Memo, American Embassy in Tehran, L. Bruce Laingen, Charge d'Affaires, to State Department, October 15, 1979. Declassified.

543 Farah Pahlavi interview, March 2008.

544 Denis Leary, Think/Exist.com; http://thinkexist.com/quotation/i_think_we_should_take_iraq_and_iran_and_combine/203664.html.

545 Lawrence K. Altman, *New York Times*, "Dr. Jean A. Bernard, 98, dies; Found Cancer in Shah of Iran"; April 30, 2006. (Accessed June 2008.) http://www.nytimes.com/2006/04/30/world/europe/30bernard.html?ex=1304049600&en=9bb0bd1c47f2cffb&ei=5088&partner=rssnyt&emc=rss. (Accessed January 2008.)

546 Farah Pahlavi, *An Enduring Love* (New York: Hyperion, 1987), p. 242.

547 *Le Figero Magazine*, November 1979, Interview with Empress Farah Pahlavi, New York, NY.

548 Pierre Salinger. *America Held Hostage: the Secret Negotiations* (Garden City: Doubleday, 1981) p. 15.

549 Ibid, pp. 17-18.

550 *Magazine VSD*, November 11, 1979. (Translated from French.)

551 Ibid, p. 25.

552 Mohamed Heikal, *Khomeini and his Revolution*, Les Editions Jeune Afrique, 1983, pp. 155-159. (Translated from French.)

553 Uri Lubrani interview, May 2008.

554 Samuel Segev, *The Iranian Triangle* translated by Haim Watzman (New York: the Free Press, 1988), p. 119.

555 Find Articles, "Iran flexes its muscles: Iran has a grand plan to become one of the most influential countries in the region," *The Middle East*, May 2007; http://findarticles.com/p/articles/mi_m2742/is_378/ai_n25005917/print. (Accessed June 2008.)

556 Princess Ashraf Pahlavi, *Faces in a Mirror: Memoirs from Exile* (Englewood Cliffs, NF: Prentice-Hall, 1980), p. 9.

557 Cited by Mark Silverberg, featured writer, *The New Media Journal*.us; "The Strategy of Defeat"; December 27, 2007; http://www.therant.us/staff/silverberg/12272007.htm. (Accessed January 2008.)

558 Iran: Evaluation of U.S. Intelligence Performance prior to November 1978; Staff Report, Subcommittee on Evaluation, Permanent Select Committee on Intelligence, U.S. House of Representatives, January 1979.

559 Gary Sick, *All Fall Down: America's Tragic Encounter with Iran* (Lincoln: Penguin Books, 2001), p. 240.

560 Max Boot, "The End of Appeasement," *History News Network*, http://hnn.us/articles/1264.html. (Accessed June 2008.)

561 Cyrus Vance, *Hard Choices* (New York: Simon and Schuster, 1983), p. 374.

562 Mark Bowden, *The Atlantic.com*, "Among the Hostage-Takers"; December 2004, www.theatlantic.com/doc/200412/bowden. (Accessed January 2008.)

563 Stansfield Turner, *Burn Before Reading* (New York: Hyperion, 2005) p. 169

564 Ibid, p. 170

565 Farah Pahlavi, *An Enduring Love* (New York: Hyperion, 1987), p.340.

566 Farah Pahlavi interview, March 28, 2008.

567 Ardeshir Zahedi interview, June 2008.

568 Cynthia Helms, *An Ambassador's Wife in Iran* (New York: Dodd, Mead, 1981), p. 181.

569 Farah Pahlavi interview, March 28, 2008.

570 Ibid.

571 Ardeshir Zahedi interview, June 2008.

572 Excerpt from *Exile*, a book on President Richard Nixon by Robert Sam Anson, (Simon and Schuster: New York, 1984) New York. http://www.farahpahlavi.org/nixon.html. (Accessed July 2009)

573 George Lenczowski, *American Presidents and the Middle East* (Durham: Duke University Press, 1990) p. 200

574 *Time* editorial, "Anger and Frustration," April 14, 1980, www.time.com/time/printout/0,8816,923946,00.html. (Accessed January 2008.)

575 Sandra Mackey, *The Iranians* (New York: Plume, 1996) p.29.

[576] Lowell Ponte, "Carter's Appease Prize," *FrontPageMagazine*.com; http://front-pagemag.com/articles/Read.aspx?GUID=AED85BC7-49B9-41D6-9E60-CBB4EA2C73DB. (Accessed June 2008.)

[577] Jimmy Carter, *Keeping Faith: Memoirs of a President* (New York: Bantam Books, 1982) p. 458.

[578] Tehran Domestic Service, trans. in *FBIS*, November 8, 1979.

[579] Hizb-i-Wahdat, FAS.org,, http://www.fas.org/irp/world/para/hizbi_wahdat.htm. (Accessed March 2008.)

[580] Amir Taheri, *Holy Terror: The Inside Story of Islamic Terrorism* (London: Sphere Books, Hutchinson, Ltd., 1987), p. 206

[581] John Cooley, *Unholy wars: Afghanistan, America and International Terrorism* (London: Pluto Press, 2002), p. 18

[582] Ibid, pp. 202-203

[583] Perspectives of World History and Current Events, *Abdullah Azzam: The Godfather of Jihad*, http://ww.pwhce.org/azzam.html. (Accessed April 2008.)

[584] It seems ironic that the pilot who flew the Shah and his entourage from Tehran to Cairo later transported two Khomeini insiders, Abolhassan Bani Sadr and Masoud Rajavi, to Europe when they fell out of favor with the Ayatollah. The pilot later became a member of the *Mujahedeen*.

[585] Stansfield Turner, *Burn Before Reading* (New York: Hyperion, 2005), pp. 172-173.

[586] General Yitzhak Segev interview, June2008.

[587] Personal email correspondence with retired Marine Gunnery Sergeant John McClain, September 11, 2008.

[588] James A. Bill, *The Eagle and the Lion* (New Haven, 1988), p.254

[589] Guide to Cyrus R. Vance and Grace Sloane Vance Papers, Yale University Library, Compiled by Mark Bailey and Staff of Manuscripts and Archives; http://mssa.library.yale.edu/findaids/stream.php?xmlfile=mssa.ms.1664.xml; accessed April 2008.

[590] Andre Fontaine, "Foreign Affairs: Transatlantic Doubts and Dreams," http://www.foreignaffairs.org, According to the official version of history, CIA aid to the *Mujahedeen* began during 1980, that is to say, after the Soviet army invaded Afghanistan, 24 Dec 1979. But the reality, secretly guarded until now, is completely otherwise. Indeed it was July 3, 1979 that President Carter signed the first directive for secret aid to the opponents of the pro-Soviet regime in Kabul. And that very day, I wrote a note to the President in which I explained to him that in my opinion this aid was going to induce a Soviet military intervention." 19810201faessays8170/andre-fontaine/transatlantic-doubts-and-dreams.html. (Accessed February 2008)

[591] "Iran Hostage Crisis," http://www.infoplease.com/ce6/history/A0825448.html. (Accessed July 2009)

[592] Thomas A. Sancton, "The Hostage Drama," *Time*, November 3, 1980; http://www.time.com/time/magazine/article/0,9171,924494-2,00.html. (Accessed February 2008.)

[593] The American Presidency Project, Jimmy Carter, November 2, 1980, http://www.presidency.ucsb.edu/ws/index.php?pid=45443&st=&st1=. (Accessed April 2008.)

594 Gary Sick, *All Fall Down* (Lincoln, NE: iUnvierse.com, Inc., 2001), p. 377.

595 Ibid., 397–398.

596 James A. Leggette and Michael W. Funk, "Ronald Reagan and the Opening Salvos in the War on Terror,"*American Thinker*, June 7, 2005, http://www.americanthinker.com/2005/06/ronald_reagan_and_the_opening.html. (Accessed February 2008.)

597 Daniel Pipes, *New York Sun*, "Reagan's Early Victory in the War on Terror," June 15, 2004; http://www.danielpipes.org/article/1888. (Accessed January 2008.)

598 Ronald Reagan, *An American Life* (New York: Simon and Schuster, 1990), pp. 218-219.

599 Wikipedia; http://en.wikipedia.org/wiki/Blowback_(intelligence). (Accessed February 2008.)

600 Samuel Segev, *The Iranian Triangle* (New York: Free Press, 1988), p. 4.

601 Israel Shahak, "How Israel's Strategy Favors Iraq over Iran," *Middle East International*, March 19, 1993, p. 19.

602 Global Research.ca; "After the National Intelligence Estimate on Iran: Let the Debater Begin," January 3, 2008, http://www.globalresearch.ca/index.php?context=va&aid=7722. (Accessed April 2008.)

603 Samuel Segev, "Hameshulash Hairani," *Ma'ariv* (Tel Aviv), 1981, p. 98.

604 Samuel Segev, *The Iranian Triangle* (New York: Free Press, 1988), p. 232.

605 Council on Foreign Relations; State Sponsors: Iran; August 2007, http://www.cfr.org/publication/9362/#5. (Accessed February 2008.)

606 "Proxy Power: Understanding Iran's use of Terrorists"; Brookings Institution; http://brookings.edu/opinoins/2006/0726iran_byman.aspx. (Accessed February 2008.)

607 Iran Terror: List of Terror Attacks, July 19, 2005. (http://www.iranterror.com/content/view/38/56/. (Accessed February 2008.)

608 *The 9/11 Commission Report*, Chapter 7, Section 3 (Washington: U.S. Government Printing Office, 2004) p. 240.

609 Barry Rubin, "The Region: Just be our Friend," *Jerusalem Post Online*, October 5, 2008, http://www.jpost.com /servlet/Satellite?cid=1222017466148&pagename=JPost%2FJPArticle%2FShowFull. (Accessed October 2008.)

610"Iran: U.S. Accuses Iran of extending its support for Mideast terror groups," http://www.globalsecurity.org/wmd/library/news/iran/2005/iran-050311-rferl03.htm. (Accessed July 2009)

611 "Pandora's Box," Ancient Greek myth.

612 "Iran, Hezbollah, Hamas, and the Global Jihad: A New Conflict Paradigm for the West" 2007; Brig. Gen. (Ret.) Dr. Shimon Shapira and Daniel Diker, "Iran's Second Islamic Revolution: Strategic Implications for the West," Jerusalem Center for Public Affairs; p. 41; http://www.jcpa.org/. (Accessed January 2008.)

613 Mohammad Sahimi, "Iran's Nuclear Program: Part I, Its History," October 2, 2003, http://payvand.com/news/03/oct/1015.html. (Accessed March 2008.)

[614] James Earl Carter, Jr., State of the Union Address 1981; http://www.let.rug.nl/usa/P/jc39/speeches/su81jec.htm. (Accessed February 2008.)

[615] Bret Stephens, "How to Stop Iran without Firing a Shot"; May 15, 2006; http://www.opinionjournal.com/wsj/?id=110008382. (Accessed February, 2008.)

[616] Amir Taheri, "Reading Between the Lines," *Jerusalem Post*, May 13, 2006; http://www.benadorassociates.com/article/19490. (Accessed February 2008.)

[617] Michael Evans, *The Final Move Beyond Iraq: The Final Solution While the World Sleeps* (Lake Mary, FL: Front Line, 2007) p. 210.

[618] Cited by Mark Silverberg, featured writer, *The New Media Journal*.us; "The Strategy of Defeat"; December 27, 2007; http://www.therant.us/staff/silverberg/12272007.htm. (Accessed January 2008.)

[619] David Limbaugh, "Ashamed of America," *Townhall.com*, July 11, 2008, http://townhall.com/Columnists/DavidLimbaugh/2008/07/11/ashamed_of_america. (Accessed August 2008.)

[620]Nazila Fathi and Joel Brinkley, "U.S. Pursuing Reports that Link Iranian to Embassy Seizure in 1979," *New York Times*, July 1, 2005; http://www.nytimes.com/2005/07/01/international/middleeast/01tehran.html?_r=1& oref=slogin. (Accessed May 2008.)

[621] "Iran, Hizbullah, Hamas and the Global Jihad: A New Conflict Paradigm for the West" 2007; Gen. (Ret.) Moshe Yaalon, "The Second Lebanon War: From Territory to Ideology," Jerusalem Center for Public Affairs; p. 16. (Accessed January 2008.)

[622] Jonathan Steele, "Lost in Translation," *Guardian*, June 14, 2006, http://commentisfree.guardian.co.uk/jonathan_steele/2006/06/post_155.html. (Accessed March 2008.

[623] Jewish Virtual Library, Jews of Iran, http://www.jewishvirtuallibrary.org/jsource/anti-semitism/iranjews.html. (Accessed April 2008.)

[624] Marcos Aguinis, "Death Wish," *La Nacion*; cited in Citizens in Defense of Defense; http://defendingdefense.blogspot.com/2006/05/children-advanced-in-tight-knit.html. (Accessed February 2008.)

[625] Then Prime Minister of Israel, speaking before the U.S. House of Representatives Government Reform Committee on September 20th, 2001.

[626] "Ayatollah Ali Khamenei says Iran, Israel on 'collision course'," Ramin Mostaghim and Borzou Daragahi, *Los Angeles Times*, September 20, 2008; http://articles.latimes.com/2008/sep/20/world/fg-iran20. (Accessed July 2009)

[627]Patrick Devenny "Hezbollah's strategic threat to Israel," *Middle East Quarterly*, Winter 2006, pp. 31-38; http://www.meforum.org/806/hezbollahs-strategic-threat-to-israel. (Accessed July 2009)

[628] Foreign Broadcast Information Service—Daily Reports, July 20, 1994; Source—*Radio Iran*; Quoted in "The Islamic Republic of Iran and the Holocaust: Anti-Semitism and Anti-Zionism," Meir Litvak, *The Journal of Israeli History*, V. 25, No. 1, March 2006, PP. 267-284, 271.

[629] Comment by Mahmoud Ahmadinejad, March 1, 2007, Quoted in "Zionist regime offspring of Britain, nurtured by US—Ahmadinejad," *Islamic Republic News Agency* (IRNA), http://www2.irna.ir/en/news/view/line-20/0703015352005938.htm. (Accessed July 2009)

[630] Personal interview with Benjamin Netanyahu, 2007.

[631] Ibid.

[632] David Ignatius, "The Spy who wants Israel to talk," *Washington Post*, November 11, 2007; http://www.washingtonpost.com/wp-dyn/content/article/2007/11/09/AR2007110901941.html. (Accessed July 2009)

[633] Mahmoud Ahmadinejad, United Nations, September 17, 2005 speech; http://www.globalsecurity.org/wmd/library/news/iran/2005/iran-050918-irna02.htm. (Accessed July 2009)

[634] Golnaz Esfandiari, "Iran: President Says Light Surrounded Him During UN Speech," Radio Free Europe/ Radio Liberty, November 29, 2005. http://www.rferl.org/featuresarticle/2005/11/184CB9FB-887C-4696-8F54- 0799DF747A4A.html *RegimeChangeIran.blogspot.com* provides a link to a news broadcast where the videotape of Ahmadinejad's conversations with the mullahs over tea can be seen and heard: http://regimechangeiran.blogspot.com/2005/12/important-video-report-on-hidden-iman.html See also, Scott Peterson, "Waiting for the rapture in Iran,"*Christian Science Monitor*, 21 December 2005.

[635] "Iran: Part of the Axis of Evil," April 22, 2006; http://www.zionism-israel.com/log/archives/00000042.html. (Accessed July 2009)

[636] LookLex Encyclopedia, "Twelvers," http://i-cias.com/e.o/twelvers.htm. (Accessed July 2009)

[637] Financial Times Enforcement Network, USA Patriot Act, Section 311, http://www.fincen.gov/statutes_regs/patriot/section311.html. (Accessed August 2009)

[638] David Ignatius, "U.S. Sanctions with Teeth," *Washington Post,* February 29, 2007; http://washingtonpost.com/wp-dyn/content/article/2007/02/07/27/AR2007022701157_p. (Accessed July 2009)

[639] Stuart E. Eizenstat, "Mega-Trends in the Next Five Years Which Will Impact on World Jewry and Israel," Conference on the Future of the Jewish People, May 2008, Jerusalem Israel; The Jewish People Policy Planning Institute, http://www.jpppi.org.il/JPPPI/Templates/ShowPage.asp?DBID=1&LNGID=1&TMID=105&FID=452&PID=0&IID=510. pp. 67-68. (Accessed August 2009)

[640] Jamie Glazov, "The China-Russia-Iran Axis," *FrontPageMagazine*.com, January 22, 2008, http://www.frontpagemag.com/readArticle.aspx?ARTID=29604. (Accessed (August 2009)

[641] Trudy Rubin, "Hold Off Engaging Iran," *Miami Herald*, July 23, 2009; http://www.miamiherald.com/opinion/other-views/v-fullstory/story/1153627.html. (Accessed August 2009)

[642] "What is Globalization?" http://www.globalization101.org/What_is_Globalization.html?PHPSESSID=e54636b5a846c31e34b20315060d2a71. (Accessed August 2009)

[643] Benjamin Netanyahu, Translation, Prime Minister's Office, July 28, 2009; http://www.pmo.gov.il/PMOEng/Communication/PMSpeaks/speechmabal280709.htm. (Accessed August 2009)

[644] Jim Kingsdale's Energy Investment Strategies, "Iranian oil production verging on disaster," June 2008; http://www.energyinvestmentstrategies.com/2008/06/25/iranian-oil-production-verging-on-disaster/. (Accessed August 2009)

645 "Iran to end petrol import," Press TV, August 1, 2009; http://www.presstv.com/detail.aspx?id=102237&sectionid=351020102. (Accessed August 2009)

646 646 Benjamin Netanyahu, *Terrorism: How the West can Win*, (New York, NY: Garrar, Straus, Giroux, 1986), p. 181.

647 Jim Wolf, "Gates reassures Israel on U.S.-Iran strategy," *Reuters*, July 27, 2009; http://www.reuters.com/article/topNews/idUSTRE56Q0QK20090727. (Access August 2009)

648Ibid.

649 James Hider, Richard Beeston, Michael Evans, "Iran is ready to build an N-bomb—its just waiting for the Ayatollah's order," *The Times Online*, August 3, 2009; http://www.timesonline.co.uk/tol/news/world/middle_east/article6736785.ece#cid=O TC-RSS&attr=797093. (Accessed August 2009)

650 John Bolton, "It's crunch time for Israel on Iran," *Wall Street Journal*, July 28, 2009; http://online.wsj.com/article/SB10001424052970203609204574316093622744808. html. (Accessed August 2009)

651 Brainy Quotes, http://www.brainyquote.com/quotes/keywords/weapons_2.html. (Accessed August 2009)

652 Ibid.

653 Daily Inspirational Thoughts, Kindle Podcast.com; http://retirementwithapurpose.com/quotes/quotesprayer.html. (Accessed August 2009)

654 Benjamin Netanyahu, *Terrorism: How the West can Win*, (New York, NY: Garrar, Straus, Giroux, 1986), p. 14.

655 Ecclesiastes 3:1,8 (NKJV)

I N D E X

. . . .

A

Abortion, 311

Afghanistan, 83, 92, 101, 122, 140, 188, 196, 201, 315, 319, 321, 335, 353-5, 371, 384, 411, 416, 423,

Afkhami, Golam Reza, 128, 168, 409

Afshar, Amir-Khosrow, 123, 181, 183, 185, 409

Ahern, Thomas L., 341, 409

Ahmadinejad, Mahmoud, 40, 43, 45, 53-8, 60-1, 62-7, 69-76, 79, 82, 84-8,104. 233, 374-81, 387-92, 396, 398, 409

AIOC (Anglo Iranian Oil Company), 229

Air France, 270, 291-3, 371

al-Assad, Bashar, 409, 411

al-Assad, Hafez, 178, 411

Al-Qaeda, 335, 355, 370-1, 394, 410,

Alam, Asadollah, 113, 127-8, 317, 410

Albright, Madeleine, 115, 410

al-Deek, Khalil Said, 410

Alexander the Great, 96, 98, 410, 416, 418, 430, 438

Alexandria, 133, 448

Algiers Accords, 171, 197

Ali, 103-4, 410, 423, 431, 433, 438

Allies (ally), 103, 107-8, 111, 121, 124, 127, 138, 140, 149, 167, 200, 203, 207, 210-1, 235-6, 245, 255, 265-6, 280-1, 313-14, 352, 374-5, 387, 402

Allon, Yigal, 168, 410

al-Zawahiri, Ayman, 355, 410

American Embassy in Tehran, 339, 366, 384, 428

American Presidents, 80, 85, 125, 319, 438, 466

Americans, 115-16, 139, 145, 153, 165, 169, 203, 213, 228, 245, 247, 262, 270, 282, 285, 288-9, 309-10, 318, 330-1, 340, 342-3, 348, 352, 354, 359-60, 365-7, 369-70, 372-4, 383, 422, 433

Amini, (Dr.) Ali, 206, 250, 410-11

Anglo Iranian Oil Company (AIOC) 229

Ansary, Hushang, 171, 411

Arab countries, 58, 168, 354, 367, 388, 403

Arab neighbors, 55, 58, 201-2, 302, 304, 392, 405

Arafat, Yasser, 145-6, 170, 203, 307-9, 322, 335, 351-2, 355, 369, 411

Arak, 50, 53-4, 442

Ariani, Bahram, 198

Arms, 32-3, 53, 55, 58, 76, 87, 121-2, 125, 127, 137-8, 140, 146-9, 156-9, 171, 193, 197, 200-1, 205, 260, 273, 275, 290, 302-3, 315, 331, 334-5, 366, 370, 379, 391-5 403-4

Army, 64, 73, 76, 96, 99, 101, 103-4, 127, 135, 137-8, 164, 195, 205, 214, 249, 261, 275-7, 286, 291, 295-6, 332, 336

assassination, 134, 145, 247, 327, 346, 371, 418-19, 421, 428, 430

Atomic Energy Organization of Iran (AEOI), 39, 46, 53, 409, 441

Attabai, Kambiz, 342, 411

AWACS, 148, 157-8

Ayatollah, (See also Khomeini, Khamenei)

Azarbarzin, (Gen.) Shapur, 231, 258, 274, 289, 292, 301, 411

Azhari, Gholam Reza, 247, 274, 411

Azores, 331, 343

Azzam Abdullah, 355, 411

B

Ba'athist regime, 333

Babylon, 94-5, 410, 417, 426, 430

Babylonian Empire, 95, 425

Badi'ie, Amir-Hussein, 246, 411

Badrei, Abdul-Ali , 248, 411

Bakhtiar, Shapour, 162, 164, 174, 205, 240, 260-1, 264, 266, 275-6, 280, 283, 289-5, 301, 304, 315, 321-2, 412,

Ball, George, 135, 210-13, 215-16, 412, 437, 455-6

Balta, Paul, 229, 269-70, 460

Bani Sadr, Abolhassan, 229, 269, 272-3, 348-9, 356

Banks, 97, 170, 195, 352-3, 364-5, 393-4

Basij, 72-6, 83

Bazaars, 135, 144, 194-5, 207, 271

Bazargan, Mehdi, 218-20, 229, 299-301, 315, 317, 329, 338, 341, 347, 349, 356, 412

BBC (British Broadcasting Corporation), 228-31, 240, 462, 473

Begin, Menachem, 31-3, 35, 184, 188-9, 200-1, 303, 352, 369, 412,

Beirut, 322, 370-2, 413

Bill, James A., 176, 196, 205, 211, 306, 415, 437, 452, 454-6, 463, 467

Brzezinski, Zbigniew, 129, 135, 138-40, 162, 179, 184, 207, 211-2, 217-18, 223, 242, 246, 249-50, 262-4, 289, 315, 329-31, 353, 357, 366, 413

Bush, George W., 84, 146, 366, 376-7, 390, 399, 402, 413

Bushehr, 53, 56, 105

Byrd, Robert C., 306, 414

C

Cabinet, 32, 61, 274, 300, 353, 412-13, 416, 427, 429

Callaghan, James, 262-3, 414

Camp David Peace Accords, 184, 188, 203, 223, 244, 246, 256, 336, 352, 384, 413, 430

captives, 75, 84, 97, 303, 340-1, 347, 349, 353, 356-7, 360, 363, 416

Carter, Jimmy, 80, 83-5, 88, 108-12, 114, 121, 125, 127-9, 131, 133-5, 137, 140, 147-51, 155-64, 167, 171-2, 184, 186, 188-9, 197-200, 204-7, 209-13, 216-20, 222, 225, 228, 234-7, 242-3, 245-50, 254-7, 259-65, 272-3, 277, 280-1, 283-6, 288-91, 293-5, 301, 303, 309-10, 314-15, 319, 321, 325, 329-31, 338, 342-9, 351-3, 355, 360-1, 363-7, 376, 378-9, 384-5, 412-17

Centrifuges, 36-7, 40, 46, 51-3, 55-6, 61, 367, 402, 444

Chamran, Mustafa Ali, 147, 414

Chavez, Hugo Rafael,   45, 414

children, 72-3, 81, 89, 178, 196, 268, 292, 324-5, 335, 345, 380, 430

China, 100, 123, 334, 392, 394-6, 398-400, 405, 431

Churchill, Winston, 114, 206, 415

CIA, 47, 51, 114, 134, 144-5, 170, 187, 194, 209, 217, 220-5, 236, 238-40, 243, 245, 247, 256, 271-4, 285, 300, 316-17, 338, 341, 354-5, 357, 367, 409-10, 413-5, 417-19

Clark, Ramsey, 347, 415

Clinton, William Jefferson, 115-16, 415, 423-4, 431

Clinton, Hillary, 405, 415

Cottam, Richard, 225, 415

Council of Notables, 215, 250

Coup, 102, 112, 114-16, 121, 138, 203, 205, 245, 249, 257-8, 260, 264, 276, 314-5, 331, 367, 409, 411, 414, 427-8

Cyrus The Great, 88, 93-6, 98, 119, 187, 414-15, 434, 439, 446

D

Daoud, Abu, 146, 416

Darius, 96-8, 416, 434

Dayan, Moshe, 32, 175, 193-4, 202, 213, 416

Democratic Party, 128, 361, 377, 414-15, 421, 424, 429

Derian, Patricia, 136, 416

D'Estaing, Valery Giscard, 237-8, 262-8, 272, 277, 279-80, 291, 305, 416, 428

direct-dial telephone system, 274

Dobrynin, Anatoly, 355

Dubs, Adolph "Spike", 319, 416
Duncan, Charles, 256, 264, 416

E

Eban, Abba, 348
economy, 87, 127, 137, 224, 331, 397, 399, 400, 405, 409
Egypt, 58, 71, 92, 96-7, 103, 132, 140, 148, 167-8, 178, 187-8, 190, 199, 282-3, 288, 314, 328, 334-6, 343-5, 369-70, 384, 413-14, 430-1
Eilat-Ashkelon Pipeline, 133, 168, 187, 190, 200
Eisenhower, Dwight, 107, 112, 114-5, 204, 315, 416, 426
election, 56, 60-1, 74, 76-7, 80-1, 83-5, 87, 114, 128, 144, 199-200, 206, 236, 244, 263, 300, 316, 323, 363-4, 396, 411-12
  presidential, 63, 73, 356, 384, 409, 420, 423, 425
Eliot, Theodore L., Jr., 256, 264
Ellipse, 153-4, 156
Empress, 154, 158, 162, 216, 240, 245, 251, 275, 282, 328, 342-6, 427
Entezam, Abdollah, 250, 417
Entezam, Amir, 218. 300, 417
Eshkol, Levi, 187-8, 417
Esther, 88, 97-8, 409, 417-18, 425, 434
executions, 74, 83, 304-6, 324, 329, 333, 352, 358, 419, 421
exile, 103, 144, 147, 175, 213, 225, 228, 240, 269, 293, 345, 417-18, 426, 431

F

Falk, Richard, 210
Fallaci, Oriana, 310
Family Protection Act, 336
Fatah, 145-6, 203, 320, 411, 416, 419-20
Fatwa, 144, 384
Fedayeen, 146, 177, 319-20, 416
Ford, Gerald, 108, 112, 127, 167, 206, 212, 222, 288, 290, 413-14, 417-18, 429-30
Foreign Assistance Act, 109-10

France, 33, 38, 56, 58, 81, 102, 111, 143, 150, 175, 199, 214, 217, 228, 237-8, 240-1, 262, 267-70, 275, 277, 279-80, 284, 287, 291-3, 334, 370-1, 412, 416, 418, 425, 427-9, 431
  President of, 120, 305
Freedom Fighters, 89, 177, 404
Freedom of the Press, 162, 183
French, 32, 35-6, 81, 182, 214-15, 238-40, 264, 266-7, 277, 292, 374
fuel, 33-7, 45, 47-53, 358-60, 392, 400
  nuclear cycle, 48-50, 55

G

Generals, 96, 138, 182, 202, 257-8, 260-1, 285-6, 290, 304-5, 315, 421, 435
Geraghty, (Col.) Timothy,   372, 418
Germans, 103, 450
Gharagaghi, (Gen.) Abbas, 183, 216, 275, 418
Ghotbzadeh, Sadegh, 218, 273, 354, 418
Globalization, 392-3, 396-8
God, 54, 63, 83, 88, 94-5, 99, 158, 276, 287, 290, 296, 311, 345, 372, 387, 405
government, 108-9, 184, 214-17, 235-6, 244-5, 250, 254-5, 258-60, 291-2, 294, 335, 345-8, 366-7, 400-1, 426-7, 431
  coalition, 174, 255-6
  new, 183-4, 250, 275, 284, 306, 330, 427
  provisional, 289, 299, 301
  democratic, 318, 324, 406
Government of God, 334
Government of Iran, 69, 81, 124, 137, 172, 218, 376
Governor of Tehran, 219, 433
Great Britain, 29, 56, 58, 64, 102-3, 111-13, 120, 143, 157, 204, 228, 232, 262, 284
"Great Satan", 61, 64, 85, 301, 349-50, 361, 368
Guadeloupe Summit, 254, 261-5
Guardian Council, 63, 67-8
Gulf Region, 188, 334, 367-8, 392

H

Habash, George, 146, 418
Haig, Alexander, 32, 256-7, 259, 261, 418, 438, 462

Haman, 97-8, 418

Hamas, 71, 331, 355, 370, 372, 379, 386, 391, 393, 404, 468

Harel, Isser, 187, 384-6, 418

Harmelin, Yosef, 195, 296, 418

Hashemite Kingdom of Jordan, 32, 58, 92, 120, 145, 159-60, 167, 190, 198, 334, 404

Hassan, King of Morocco, 283-4

Havel, Vaclav, 170, 419

Heikal, Mohamed, 251, 453, 459-63, 465

helicopters, 33, 185, 195, 294, 331, 357-9

Helms, Richard, 220-22, 342, 419

Hezbollah, 71, 331, 333, 370, 372, 379, 386, 388, 391, 398, 404, 419, 468-9

hospitals, 72, 75, 100, 342, 404, 411

hostages, 7, 303, 330-1, 340-1, 344, 348-9, 351-4, 356-8, 360-1, 363-6, 384-5, 413-16, 422, 432-4, 437-8, 450-1

rescue, 87, 176, 348, 356-7, 359-60, 434, 450

Hoveyda, Fereydoun, 233-4, 305, 317, 419

human rights, 96, 109-11, 128, 134, 138, 140, 151, 155, 159, 162, 173, 207, 210, 226, 232-3, 235

Hussein, Saddam, 32-3, 51, 100, 123, 138, 171, 197, 227, 296, 303, 307, 331-6, 369, 375, 380-1, 384, 419

Huyser, Gen. Robert E. "Dutch", 10, 231, 256-61, 265, 280-1, 285-6, 289-90, 420

I

IAEA (International Atomic Energy Agency), 36, 38-9, 41-2, 46-9, 51-2, 56-7, 401, 442

ideology, 73, 239, 301-2, 304, 374, 377

Imam, (See also Khomeini, Ruhollah)

India, 92, 101, 159, 200, 417, 431, 437

International Herald Tribune, 224, 257

Iran, 38-43, 45-76, 81-8, 157-63, 167-75, 184-90, 193-207, 217-27, 238-50, 253-61, 329-39, 345-54, 374-80, 388-406, 419-25, 427-35

former president of, 67

left, 122, 147, 255, 275, 283

modernize, 125

policies, 112, 255, 290

post-Shah, 222

Refined Petroleum Sanctions Act, 399

threat, 202, 394

Iran-Iraq War, 41, 73, 303, 332, 351

Iranian Jews, 128, 193, 296, 379

Iranian military, 138, 229, 244, 248-9, 257, 260, 264, 276, 282, 290-1, 294-5, 331, 379

Iranian oil, 112, 187, 204, 229, 265, 302, 352, 398, 421

Iranian police, 178, 294

Iranian Revolution, 203, 229-30, 241, 308, 322, 412, 416, 418, 422, 424, 427, 430-1, 437-9, 448-9, 452-3, 460

Iranian students in Tehran, 153, 368, 414, 422

Iranian Studies, 68, 70, 445

Iranian television, 157, 241

Iranian Triangle, 189, 439, 450, 454, 462-3, 465, 467

Iranians

Army, 205, 249, 261, 276, 430

assets, 363-4

security forces, 159, 286

training of, 147, 414

troops, 73, 335

Iran's government, 376

Islamic Revolution, 249, 459

Proxies, 169, 370, 379, 386, 395, 404-5

Iraq, 31-4, 51-2, 61, 64, 123, 144-5, 170-2, 175, 196-7, 237-8, 335-6, 368-9, 379-80, 428, 473

Iraqis, 32, 202, 303, 333

Isfahan, 35-40, 42, 150-1, 242, 289, 441

Islam, radical, 149, 295, 311, 370, 386, 397

Islamic Conference Organization, 332

Islamic Republic of Iran, 66, 68, 85, 138, 241, 268, 270, 286, 322-3, 325, 349, 354, 409, 412, 417-18, 421-2

Islamic Revolution, 69, 125, 143, 177, 186, 217-19, 229, 245, 293, 304, 306, 308, 332-3, 360, 366, 438-9

Islamic Revolution in Iran, 132, 196, 307, 310, 332, 353, 418, 463

Israel, 31-4, 82, 187-91, 193-4, 198-203, 295-7, 301-3, 368-70, 385-9, 391-2, 401-5, 410-13, 416-19, 426-8

wipe off the map, 45, 52, 389
Israel-Iran relations, 168
Israeli Embassy in Tehran, 194, 203, 308
Israeli government, 133, 301, 369, 403
    Officials, 190
Israeli-Iranian Relations, 439, 454
Israeli withdrawal, 168, 201
Israel's Shah, 186
Italy, 33, 56-7, 82, 262, 410, 417, 444
Ivry, David, 195, 294, 303, 420

J

Jaleh Square Protest, 185-6, 241
Jam, Feridoun, 190, 260
Jennings, Peter, 292, 420
Jerusalem, 29, 94-5, 146, 241, 308-9, 336, 379, 387, 410, 417, 426
Jews, 31, 94-9, 146, 168, 181, 186-8, 226, 267, 302, 379-80, 385-9, 410, 416-19, 426
Jihad, 71, 227, 267, 269, 335, 355, 411
Jihad, Abu, 322
Johnson, Lyndon, 125, 190, 216, 301, 360, 413, 415, 420, 430
Jordan, (See also Hashemite Kingdom of)
Jordan, Hamilton,   330, 348, 364

K

Kaddoumi, Farouk, 275, 420
Kashani, Abol Qassem, 302
Kashani, Ahmed, 302, 421
Kennedy, John F., 80, 204-5, 207, 412, 415
Khalatbari, Abbas Ali, 194, 421
Khalkhali, Sadegh, 321
    ordered execution of Shah's family, 329
Khamenei, Ayatollah Ali, 43, 56, 61, 63-7, 69, 76, 83, 378, 387, 392, 398, 421
Khan, Aga, 110, 284, 421
Khan, Genghis, 100, 421
Khan, A. Q., 50-1, 102, 421
Khomeini, Ayatollah Ruhollah, 143-7, 175-9, 216-22, 228-31, 237-42, 263-77, 279-86, 289-96, 300-5, 307-11, 315-17, 321-5, 332-5, 349-54, 366-9, 373-81
    exile, 147, 238

followers, 220, 255
government, 286, 364
    insiders, 301, 356, 466
prevent, 275, 291
prompted, 292, 349
regime, 285, 301, 303, 305, 369
stop, 277, 290
Khrushchev, Nikita,   205, 422
Kissinger, Henry, 121, 124, 203, 212, 281, 422
Kurds, 171, 369
Kuwait, 190, 199, 203, 237, 242, 333, 336, 371, 381

L

Lahidji, A.E., 323-4, 422
Laingen, Bruce, 300, 323, 422
Larijani, Ali, 52, 423, 425
Lawyers, 137, 324, 415, 422, 425, 429
Leadership, 55, 66, 68, 80, 97, 99-100, 104, 133, 245, 270, 282, 335, 361, 415, 445, 452
Lebanon, 71, 83, 145, 147, 170, 194, 320, 370, 372, 374, 379, 391
Lenczowski, George, 347
Liberal Left, 84, 108, 111, 125, 377
Libya, 144-5, 196, 277, 320, 334, 406, 428
LMI (Liberation Movement of Iran), 218-20, 237, 437
Lorenz, Dominique, 270
Lubrani, Uri, 9, 128, 194-5, 213, 223, 257, 280, 290, 332, 423

M

Madaule, Jacques, 271
Mahdi, 57-8, 66, 87, 104, 176-7, 389-91, 410
Majidi, (Dr.) Abdol Majid, 128, 221, 256, 310, 423
Manescu, Corneliu, 123
Manzarieh Park, 307
Maraghei, Muhammad Sa'ed, 187, 423
Marenches, Comte Alexandre de, 266, 280, 283
Marines, 319, 331, 339
Meese, Edwin, 365, 424

Middle East, 58, 60, 70, 72, 86, 93, 105, 116, 136, 162, 169, 188, 196, 199-200, 203, 241, 251, 267, 302-3, 314, 333, 336, 352, 358, 369, 374, 379, 384-8, 392, 402, 406, 415, 421, 427, 431-3

Middle East Forum, 241

Milani, Mohsen, 249

Military, 36, 47, 65, 70-1, 76, 138, 184, 255-6, 259-63, 273, 282, 286, 290, 301, 331-2, 424-5

coup, 245, 249, 257, 276, 314-15, 331

military government, 164, 244-5, 247-8, 263

Miller, G. William, 217, 347, 352, 424

Mina, Parviz, 9, 116, 174, 242, 267, 322,

Minachi, Nasser, 218

missiles, 52, 199, 334, 388

Moghadam, (Gen.) Nasser, 181

Mohr, Charles, 232-3

Monaco, 120, 284, 428

Monarch, 116, 127, 136, 145, 147, 158, 168, 170, 172, 194, 202, 215-16, 219-20, 225, 234, 236

money, 71, 84, 137, 144, 171, 174, 176, 182, 217, 233, 258, 271, 275, 317, 322, 331

Montazam, Mir Ali Asghar, 265

Mordecai, 88, 98, 425

Morocco, 120, 159, 283-4, 288, 315, 328, 419

Mossad, 9-10, 187, 201, 290, 296, 384, 389, 418

Mossadegh, Mohammad, 112-14, 129, 250, 425, 430, 447

Moussavi, Mir Hossein, 61-2, 67, 70, 72, 77, 82, 425, 444

Muhammad, Prophet, 100, 377, 419, 425, 433

Mujahedeen, 121, 144-6, 177, 247, 320, 356, 418

Mujahedeen-e-Khalq (People's Strugglers), 82, 144, 177,

Mujahedin of Iran, 47, 147

mullahs, 47, 60, 67, 70, 79, 104, 115, 151, 175-6, 178, 224, 244, 296, 301, 304, 315

Munich Olympics, 145-6, 450 (174)

Muslim Brotherhood, 335-6

Muslims, 135, 279, 296, 302, 307, 309, 333, 336, 374, 377, 380, 388, 391, 424-5

N

Nahavandi, Houchang, 185, 287, 425

Nasser, Gamal Abdul, 188-9, 335, 424

Nassiri, Nematollah, 274, 426

Natanz, 36-8, 41, 45, 49, 403, 442

National Front, 121, 143, 162, 172, 174, 176, 206, 322, 430

National Iranian Oil Company, 9, 116, 132, 399, 411, 424

Nebuchadnezzar, 94, 426

Netanyahu, Benjamin, 405, 469-70

New York Times, 36, 72, 75, 120, 155, 228, 231-2, 234-7, 281, 340

Nichols, Jim, 206

Nimrodi, Ya'acov, 198, 426

9/11 Commission, 371

Nixon, Richard, 107-8, 112, 121-2, 125, 127, 418, 429

North Korea, 50-1, 307, 334, 393-4

NTI (Nuclear Threat Institute), 200

nuclear

activities, 37, 47-8, 442-3

facilities, 34, 37-8, 45-6, 48-9, 52, 392

Iran, 260, 403, 437

program, 33, 36, 41, 47, 50-1, 56-7, 61, 79, 375, 377, 389, 391, 395, 398-9, 403-4

proliferation, 56, 69, 87, 347, 400-1

weapons, 33, 38, 41, 43, 45, 48, 50, 53, 55, 82, 108, 392, 397, 401

O

Obama, Barack Hussein, 59, 62, 79-81, 83-6, 88, 378, 396, 402-3, 405, 411, 426, 446

October Surprise, 303

oil, 116-17, 125, 131-2, 168, 190, 194, 200, 302, 331, 368, 385, 395, 398

flow of, 133, 168

Oil Services Company of Iran, 247, 418

Olahi, Kamilladin Habib, 245, 426

OPEC (Organization of Petroleum Exporting Countries), 6, 116-17, 131-2, 167, 331

"Operation Ajax", 112-13, 431

"Operation Opera", 32

opposition, 6, 69, 75, 87, 131, 134, 145, 158, 161, 173-4, 226-7, 236, 243-4, 249-50, 252-3, 458

leaders, 70, 218-19, 224

Osirak, 31-33, 303, 336

Ottoman Empire, 101

Oveissi, Gholam Ali, 181, 185, 242, 248, 250, 260, 274-5, 426

P

Pacepa, General Ion, 169-70, 427

Pahlavi, (Crown Prince) Reza, 164, 181, 214, 245, 344-5, 427

Pahlavi, Farah Diba, 63, 111, 245, 282, 343, 447, 451, 456, 458-9, 465-6

Pahlavi, Mohammad Reza, (See also Shah of Iran), 111-14, 119-28, 121-2, 124-8, 132-40, 147-63, 157, 161-5, 167-91, 86-90, 193-9, 201-7, 205-7, 209-39, 216, 243-51, 253-66, 269-77, 279-89, 327-32, 341-6, 367, 418, 422, 426-7, 431

Pahlavi, Mohammad Reza Shah, 103, 167, 255, 287, 327, 431

Pakistan, 34, 50, 92, 122-3, 140, 197, 200, 232, 274, 355, 410, 421

palace, 184, 230, 251, 258-9, 274

Palestine Liberation Organization (See also PLO)

Palestinian Islamic Jihad, 370, 379

Palestinians, 169, 194, 201, 295, 308-9, 320, 322, 355, 403-4

Panama, 343-4, 433

Paris, 10, 218, 227, 237, 240-1, 256-7, 269-70, 275-6, 281-2, 291-2, 328-9, 425-6, 431, 447-8, 452, 458-61

People's Mojahedin Organization of Iran (PMOI), 47, 428

Persepolis, 98, 119-20

Persia, 91-3, 95, 97-101, 105, 409, 416, 431

Persian Empire, 92-3, 96, 98, 105, 414, 416-17, 426, 431

Persian Gulf, 88, 105, 107, 122-5, 149, 169, 189-90, 193, 211, 248, 255, 266, 314, 333, 368, 373-4

Persians, 31, 88, 92-3, 96-7, 99-101, 105, 228, 380, 390, 415, 432, 453

pilots, 32, 132, 138, 193, 251, 356

planes, 19, 28, 174, 197, 234, 258, 260, 282, 292-3, 295, 297, 343, 369, 371, 386

PLO (Palestine Liberation Organization), 144-6, 169-70, 177-8, 196, 199, 203, 308-9, 320-1, 334, 351-2, 355, 370, 386, 411, 416

Plutonium, 13-17, 19, 26, 53

PMOI (People's Mojahedin Organization of Iran), 47, 428

policy, 10, 19, 109, 123-4, 133, 163, 167, 222, 237, 318, 330, 386-7, 449-52, 456-8, 461, 464

Precht, Henry, 128-9, 211-12, 216-17, 316-17, 330, 428, 453, 456, 464

Princess Ashraf, 161, 184, 328-9, 336

production, 53, 55, 58, 198-9, 400, 402

"Project Flower", 200

protesters, 63, 69, 71, 74-5, 80-3, 154, 158

protests, 62-4, 72, 83-4, 153, 202, 224, 241-2, 274, 337, 360, 434

Q

Qaddafi, Muammar, 51, 275, 428

Qajar Dynasty, 101-2

Qom, 57, 69, 135-6, 179, 270, 289, 299309, 329, 339, 422, 431

Queen, 91, 96-7, 164, 182, 245, 416-17

Qutb, Sayyid, 335, 428

R

Rabii, (Gen.) Amir Hussein, 294-6, 428

Rabin, Yitzhak, 168, 189, 196, 428

Radcliffe, Donny, 156

radical Islam, 61, 149, 178, 295, 306, 311, 370, 386, 397, 405

Rafsanjani, Ali Akbar, 67-8, 374, 411, 421, 428

Rahman, Sheikh Omar Abdul, 384

Rainier III, Prince, 120, 428

Rajavi, Maryam, 82-3, 428

Rajavi, Masoud, 356, 428

Ramadan, 178

Reagan, Ronald, 32, 80, 303, 364-5, 467

refineries, 49, 200, 242, 398-400

regime, 31, 40, 54, 60, 64-6, 70, 75, 82, 85, 109, 127, 138, 226, 305-6, 315, 418-19
revolution, 6-7, 63-5, 70, 72-3, 131, 133-4, 162-3, 195, 205, 238-40, 273, 289, 294-5, 299-301, 304-5
Revolutionary Guards, 62-3, 65, 73, 75-6, 83, 195, 295, 304, 339, 356, 370, 374, 398
Ribicoff, Abraham, 158, 306, 429
Richardson, Elliot, 123, 429
Rockefeller, David, 284, 429
Rockefeller, Nelson, 124, 165, 429
Roman Empire, 98
Roosevelt, Franklin D., 206, 429
Roosevelt, Kermit "Kim", 112-14, 429
Roosevelt, Theodore, 112, 429
Rouleau, Eric, 136
Royal Guard, 190, 282, 284
Rubin, Barry, 238
Russia, 34, 42, 53, 57-8, 101-2, 124, 140, 271, 321, 392, 394-6, 398-400, 405, 429

S

Sadat, Jehan, 343, 346
Sadat, Anwar, 132, 159, 168, 184, 188-9, 196, 283, 288, 335-6, 343-6, 352, 384, 430
Sadiqi, Gholam Hossein, 174, 430
Saleh, (Maj. Gen.) Ataollah, 374, 430
Salehi, Ali Akbar, 39
sanctions, 42, 52-3, 55, 233, 352, 356, 363, 375, 392-4, 397, 399-400, 405, 469
Sanjabi, Karim, 162, 430
Sapir, Pinhas, 187, 430
Saunders, Harold, 200, 430
SAVAK, 140, 146, 150, 178-80, 187, 274, 321, 422, 424, 426-7, 431
Scheherazade, 91-2, 416, 430
Schlesinger, James R., 132, 264, 430
Schmidt, Helmut, 262-3, 430
Schwarzkopf, (Gen.) H. Norman, Sr., 112, 430
Schwimmer, Adolf, 198, 431
SCUD missiles, 32
Secretary of State, 121, 123, 224, 232
Security Council, 41-2, 353-4, 375, 392

Segev, Samuel, 189, 198-9, 205, 275, 296, 357, 369, 431
Segev, Yitzhak, 162, 295-6, 304, 357, 431
Selassie, Haile, 120, 369, 431
Shah of Iran (See also Pahlavi, Mohammad Reza)
Shah's
   death, 345
   departure, 137, 237, 281, 315, 368
   government, 175,184-5, 244, 275, 295
   military, 163, 273, 286
   regime, 147, 238, 266, 285, 304, 306, 313
Shahab-3, 51-2
Shari'ati, Ali, 143
Shariatmadari, Ayatollah, 183, 288-9, 432
Sharif-Emami, Jafar, 182-3, 279, 432
Sharon, Ariel, 368-9, 418, 426, 432
Shatt el Arab Waterway, 171
Shawcross, William, 225
Shia, 57, 66, 1101, 103, 105, 143-4, 149, 218, 221, 347, 349, 354, 391-2, 420, 425
Shomron, (Gen.) Dan, 357, 432
Shubart, Tira, 248
Sick, Gary, 188, 209, 213, 243, 303, 339, 432
Sickmann, Rodney, 340
Six-Day War, 122, 168, 190, 193, 432
Sober, Sidney, 220
Solana, Javier, 376
South Korea, 110
Soviet Union, 83, 103, 114, 121-2, 124, 132, 139-40, 159, 168-70, 201-2, 204-5, 314-15, 353-4, 413, 422, 432
Special Coordinating Committee, 284
Stalin, Joseph, 114, 124, 206, 235, 413, 422, 432
Stephens, Bret, 376
Sullivan, William, 135-9, 163-4, 172, 185, 217-25, 231, 238, 246-9, 253-6, 274, 289-90, 294-5, 317-20, 449, 456-7, 461-2
Supreme Leader, 60, 62, 66, 68, 70, 76, 80-1, 104, 324, 347, 387, 402, 422, 429
Switzerland, 122, 284
Syria, 92, 145, 168, 190, 202, 320, 334, 379, 386, 391, 406, 409, 411

T

Taheri, Amir, 113, 186, 210, 266, 315, 354, 376, 433

Taliban, 315, 331

Tavakoli, Mohammed, 219-20, 433

Tavassoli, Mohammed, 219-20, 433

Tehran, 35-6, 45-6, 56-7, 61-2, 122-3, 136-8, 155-7, 172-4, 193-6, 257-9, 264-7, 272-5, 281-3, 289-92, 294-6, 316-18

Tehran University, (See also University of Tehran)

Tehrani, Ahmed, 9, 163, 206, 287, 451, 455, 459, 462

terror, 28, 82-4, 89, 199, 362, 372, 386-7

terrorism, 320, 372-3, 385, 397, 413, 423

terrorist groups, 146, 160, 395, 397, 401, 404

terrorists, 83-4, 89, 144, 146, 169-70, 179, 196, 307, 366, 371-3, 384-5, 404

Tomseth, Victor, 219, 433

Torrijos, (Gen.) Omar, 343, 433

Toufanian, (Gen.) Hasan, 198, 200, 260, 433

Truman, Harry S., 114, 206, 415, 434

Tsafrir, Eliezer, 296

Turkey, 92, 97, 144, 175, 190, 232, 347, 369-70

Turner, Stansfield, 222, 246, 341, 357, 343

Twelver, 57-8, 66, 104, 389, 391, 420-21, 432

two-week siege, 177

U

UN Security Council, 56, 334, 375, 391, 395

United Kingdom, 38, 224, 414-15, 427, 433-4, 438

United States Information Agency, 204, 425

United States of America, 40-2, 108-9, 111-12, 114-16, 124-7, 161-2, 178-82, 201-4, 290-1, 329-30, 362-5, 375-7, 394-6, 409-17, 420-1, 426-9

Unity Party, 354

University of Tehran, 149, 178, 396

Uranium, 26, 34-6, 38-9, 41-2, 48, 50, 54, 56, 376, 391

U.S. Embassy, 174, 206, 218-20, 223, 237, 243, 281, 288, 300, 304, 319-20, 330-1, 339-41, 346-7, 415-16,

U.S. State Department, 48-50, 81, 125, 134, 148, 160, 169, 174, 217-18, 222-3, 244, 254-5, 313-14, 316-18, 323-4

V

Vance, Cyrus, 135-6, 138, 184, 217, 219, 243-4, 318, 329

Velayat-e-faqih, 64, 323-4, 337

Villalon, Hector, 348, 434

Villeneuve, Charles, 9, 272, 321

W

Waldheim, Kurt   , 162, 356, 434

Walid, Abu, 351

Washington, D.C., 46, 123, 125, 139-40, 148, 151, 156-8, 179, 184-5, 210, 224, 331, 375-6

Weinberger, Casper, 32, 413, 415, 417, 423, 430

West, 45, 116, 136, 144, 169, 173, 264, 295, 310, 367-8, 385-6, 392, 396, 405

White House, 107-9, 111, 128, 153-8, 184, 212-13, 222, 246, 256, 303, 313, 329, 403, 414-15

women, 59-60, 68-9, 73-4, 79, 83-4, 136, 149, 167, 178, 196, 233-4, 269-70, 324, 339-40

Woodward and Bernstein, 232

Woolsey, James, 10

Writer's Guild, 162

Y

Ya'alon, Moshe, 10

Yazdi, Ebrahim, 216, 282, 291, 316, 347, 434

Yom Kippur War, 132-3

Young, Andrew , 217, 317, 434

Z

Zahedi, Ardeshir, 113, 122-3, 139-40, 160, 179, 181-2, 184-5, 220, 227, 246-51, 261, 345, 434, 439

Zahedi, Fazlollah,   113, 434

Zimmerman, Warren, 281-2, 435

Zonis, Marvin, 126

"Mike Evans is a fighter for freedom in a world of darkening and narrowing horizons. In his devotion to Israel, Mike has consistently demonstrated the moral clarity necessary to defend Israel against the lies and distortions of its enemies."

THE HONORABLE BENJAMIN NETANYAHU,
Prime Minister of Israel

"I have known Mike Evans for more than two decades. I consider him to be a great friend of Jerusalem and the State of Israel. He has always been there for us in our time of need, speaking out with courage and compassion. Mike Evans is a true Ambassador to Jerusalem representing millions of Americans."

THE HONORABLE EHUD OLMERT,
Former Prime Minister of Israel

"I am so grateful for your ceaseless, life-long committed devotion to spreading the Word! You both are a blessing from the Lord to all of us!"

DR. ROBERT H. SCHULLER,
Pastor, The Crystal Cathedral

"What an awesome result of the work you are rendering in the Kingdom. You are a great asset among the body of believers that work in the vineyard."

BISHOP T. D. JAKES,
T. D. Jakes Ministries

"To God be the glory for all He has accomplished through your dedicated lives!"

REV. DAVID WILKERSON,
Times Square Church

DR. MICHAEL D. EVANS is one of America's top experts on Israel and the Middle East. For over two decades he has been a personal confidant to many of Israel's top leaders.

Dr. Evans is an award-winning journalist and has been published in the *Wall Street Journal, Newsweek, USA Today, The Washington Times, The Jerusalem Post,* and newspapers throughout the world. He is a member of the National Press Club and has been covering events in the Middle East for decades.

Michael Evans is the author of thirty-eight books, including the #1 *New York Times* bestseller *The Final Move Beyond Iraq,* and *New York Times* bestsellers *Beyond Iraq: The Next Move* and *The American Prophecies.*

Millions around the world have seen his award-winning television documentaries on Israel based on his books. Dr. Evans is a top network analyst and is in constant demand. He has appeared on hundreds of network radio and television programs such as Fox, MSNBC, *Nightline, Good Morning America, Crossfire,* CNN World News, BBC, the Rush Limbaugh show, and others.

Dr. Evans, an ordained minister, is on the board of directors of Ariel University, Ariel, Israel. He is chairman of the board of the Corrie ten Boom Holocaust Center in Haarlem, Holland; president and founder of the Middle East Media Group, Jerusalem Prayer Team (**www.jerusalemprayerteam.org**), Jerusalem World News, (**www.jerusalemworldnews.com**) and the Evans Institute of Middle East Studies.

Michael D. Evans has spoken to over 4,000 audiences worldwide. In the past decade alone, he has addressed more than one million people per year at public events, from the Kremlin Palace in Moscow to the World Summit on Terrorism in Jerusalem.

DISCOVER RADICAL ISLAM'S MISSION
TO DESTROY ISRAEL
AND CRIPPLE THE UNITED STATE

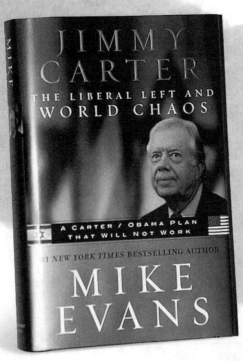

What if the plan to destroy Israel, including dividing Jerusalem, was embraced by our new president? What if that plan is seen as surrender and weakness, and emboldens radical Islam? If Jimmy Carter and his Liberal Left friends succeed by sacrificing America's strongest ally in the Middle East, Israel, to appease Arab rage, it will, in fact, make Jerusalem the center of gravity of the war on terror while unifying radical Islam. The results will be catastrophic for the United States, for Israel, and for the world. **$35.00**

Iranian President Mahmoud Ahmadinejad has said that Israel must be "wiped off the map." Such a radical statement might seem like bravado and bluster, but the Iranian connectio to the rocket attacks on Israel make it crystal clear that the Islamic Republic has every intention of following through with its threats of total destruction. Most troubling of all, Iran is pursuing nuclear weapons with reckless determination as part of its mission to annihilate Israel, which Ahmadinejad calls a "stain of disgrace." **$26.99**

TIME WORTHY BOOKS, P.O. BOX 30000 PHOENIX, AZ 85046

WWW.TIMEWORTHYBOOKS.COM